The 9/11 Investigations

The **9/11** Investigations

Staff Reports of the 9/11 Commission

———

Excerpts from the House-Senate
Joint Inquiry Report on 9/11

———

Testimony from fourteen key witnesses, including
Richard Clarke, George Tenet,
and Condoleezza Rice

EDITED BY

STEVEN STRASSER

WITH AN INTRODUCTION BY

Craig R. Whitney of *The New York Times*

PublicAffairs

NEW YORK

Published in the United States by PublicAffairs™, a member of the Perseus Books Group.

Book design and composition by Jenny Dossin. Text set in Adobe Janson Text.

ISBN 1-58648-279-3

First Edition
10 9 8 7 6 5 4 3 2 1

Contents

I
The 9/11 Commission
Staff Statements and Testimony

II

Excerpts from the House-Senate Joint Inquiry Report on 9/11

Appendixes

Introduction

CRAIG R. WHITNEY

On September 11, 2001, nineteen al Qaeda suicide hijackers—all of them with officially issued U.S. visas, fifteen of them citizens of Saudi Arabia, a strategic ally of the United States, four with Federal Aviation Administration pilot certificates—killed more than 3,000 innocent people in the most devastating attack ever on the American homeland. That crystal blue morning changed the world, shocking the United States into realizing that it had been drawn into a global war with brutal suddenness, just as it had been drawn into war sixty years earlier by the surprise Japanese attack on Pearl Harbor. Then as later, the attacks forced the United States government and the military establishment to mobilize resources and to reorganize, and made Americans see their place in the world in a new way.

Led by a president persuaded that the United States had no choice but to strike at the terrorist evil before it struck again, American soldiers went to Afghanistan, where the terrorists had their bases and the protection of the Islamic fundamentalist Taliban regime, and then to Iraq, where the administration believed terrorists had the backing of Saddam Hussein and possibly access to weapons of mass destruction.

The Taliban and Saddam Hussein were swept from power, but

no weapons of mass destruction were found, and Osama bin Laden, who founded al Qaeda and ordered the September 11 attacks, evaded capture. Islamic terrorism came to post-Saddam Iraq with a vengeance and took a daily toll of the lives of American soldiers and civilians there. Nearly three years after 9/11, the larger war and the terrorist threat to the American homeland continued unabated, and as they girded for a struggle that seemed destined to go on for decades, Americans were asking many questions.

Some questions had a powerful political charge: Did the Clinton administration do all it could to strengthen the nation's defenses against terrorist attack? Did the Bush administration take terrorism seriously enough as a threat to homeland security in the months leading up to 9/11? Why did the president and his advisers believe Iraq was behind the terrorists, though all their intelligence agencies said there was no evidence that it was? Did the administration pull away too soon from the fight against al Qaeda in Afghanistan to fight Saddam Hussein? Was it right in arguing that the success of democracy in Iraq would change the strategic balance in the Middle East and purge the poisoned mentality that has nurtured Islamic fundamentalist terrorism for so long?

Just as they did after Pearl Harbor, Americans had a right to demand an accounting from their government and their elected leaders after September 11. How could they have allowed this disaster to happen? Did the president and the civilian and military authorities charged with protecting the American homeland have no idea that terrorist attacks were coming? What did they do in light of the information they had, and could they have done more? Why did government fail in its fundamental duty to protect the lives and security of the American people? Most important of all, what lessons should be drawn for the future?

The National Commission on Terrorist Attacks Upon the United States, a bipartisan panel headed by Thomas H. Kean, the Republican former governor of New Jersey, was created by the president and Congress in November of 2002 to seek answers to these questions. It has come to be known as the 9/11 commission.

Independent inquiry into the causes of great tragedy by a legislatively-sanctioned body like the 9/11 commission is a tradition of American democracy. Ultimately, its success will be measured by how well it accomplishes the healing mission of helping the nation learn from its mistakes. But to have a chance of achieving success, it first had to probe hard and deeply into the pain.

The most difficult thing to get a bureaucracy or a political leader in any system to do after something goes terribly wrong is to acknowledge responsibility for failure. The natural bureaucratic response is to be defensive. Officials hide behind the veil of secrecy or national security, or executive privilege. They fear embarrassment, personal or institutional. Elected officials fear retribution from the electorate. Yet demanding accountability from the elected and appointed officials of government, and insisting on revealing and correcting their shortcomings, are the most basic rights and duties of citizens in a democracy.

The constitutional balance of powers gives Americans one way of getting answers from their government, with congressional oversight committees and, at times of crisis, special investigating bodies, balanced between the parties in the hope of establishing truth just as the adversarial system is designed to do in a criminal trial—imperfect as the procedure often is.

For its findings of responsibility to be credible, the 9/11 inquiry had to be perceived as fair and comprehensive. To accomplish that, the commission had to have all the facts—the right to demand and see all relevant evidence, not just to accept what government agencies saw fit to provide. It had to transcend the partisanship that flared in the heat of its hearings, just as criminal justice must transcend the interests of adversaries, to draw conclusions of lasting value for the future.

Past inquiries comparable in scope and nature to the 9/11 commission show how difficult it is to achieve such a result. A look at these investigations shows that they faced the same kinds of problems the 9/11 commission encountered in getting access to the information they needed. Failure or the perception of failure undermined the credibility and usefulness of the findings of two of these inquiries, which produced reports on Pearl Harbor and on the assassination of President John F. Kennedy. Yet they also exposed the same kinds of problems—missed clues, turf wars, lack of coordination between government agencies—that were revealed by the hearings of the 9/11 commission.

THE PEARL HARBOR INQUIRIES

The Japanese surprise attack on Pearl Harbor on December 7, 1941, damaged or destroyed 188 planes and eight battleships, the backbone of the Pacific Fleet except for the aircraft carriers that eventually helped win the war. Nearly 2,100 soldiers and sailors perished, the most casualties inflicted by any single attack on U.S. territory until September 11.

Nine separate investigations followed between 1941 and 1946. Most of them centered on questions that are also central to the 9/11 investigation: What did the government know, when did it know it, and what did it do with the knowledge it had?

The first inquiries were hampered by the need to preserve wartime military secrecy. The earliest full investigation was by a largely military presidential commission headed by Supreme Court Justice Owen Roberts. It found, in a report published in 1942 only forty-seven days after the attack, that Adm. Husband E. Kimmel, the Pacific Fleet commander, and Lt. Gen. Walter C. Short, the top Army officer in Hawaii, had made preparations for many things that Sunday morning, but not for something that had never been done before—a huge surprise bombing raid launched from aircraft carriers thousands of miles from their own shores.

Yet, the previous January, Admiral Kimmel had been warned by Adm. Harold R. Stark, the Chief of Naval Operations, of rumors of a Japanese plan to make a surprise air attack on Pearl Harbor. A month later, Kimmel had assured headquarters that he was taking the necessary precautions against "surprise attack (submarine, air, or combined) on Pearl Harbor." By the time negotiations with Japan to avert war reached the brink of failure in late November, though, he appears to have concluded that the Japanese would first attack in the Western Pacific, and that the biggest threat to Hawaii was enemy sabotage. A "war warning" from Washington on November 27 and three messages warning of the possibility of imminent war sent to Hawaii after December 3, the Roberts commission reported, "did not create in the minds of the responsible officers in the Hawaiian area apprehension as to probable imminence of air raids. On the contrary they only served to emphasize in their minds the danger from sabotage and surprise submarine attack."

When the Japanese raided Pearl Harbor, the entire U.S. Pacific Fleet was at anchor and the Army Air Force planes were not on alert but parked closely together on the runways, despite the war warnings. The Roberts commission accused both Kimmel and Short of dereliction of duty. But with the war on, the administration of President Franklin D. Roosevelt decided court-martial proceedings should be put off, and both officers were retired from active duty.

What the Roberts commission did not know, because of wartime secrecy, was that a top secret intelligence operation had broken the Japanese diplomatic code and decoded messages that gave hints pointing more specifically toward an attack on Pearl Harbor. Admiral Stark had access to these, known as "Magic" by the president and the few other officials who were briefed on them, but the Pacific Fleet commander did not. One of the messages revealed that on September 24, 1941, Tokyo had asked its consul-general in Honolulu to send regular reports, in painstaking detail, on the exact locations of the American ships in Pearl Harbor: which ships were tied up where, how many were at each dock and berth.

Was this message, as Kimmel put it after he learned about it long after the fact, "a bombing plan for Pearl Harbor"? Would this and other "Magic" intercepts, if passed on to Admiral Kimmel, have enabled him to prevent the success of the Japanese attack? Kimmel insisted on a naval court of inquiry to clear his name in light of the "Magic" intelligence, and in 1944, his fellow admirals exonerated him of all charges and censured Admiral Stark instead, for keeping his fleet commander in the dark.

Partisans of Kimmel and Short and conspiracy enthusiasts

have been arguing for sixty years that Roosevelt, Secretary of State George C. Marshall, and other top officials plotted to bring on war with Japan so that the United States could join the fight against the Axis, got it on December 7, and then hung their field commanders in Hawaii out to dry to conceal the plot.

After Roosevelt's death and the conclusion of hostilities, with the full cooperation of President Harry S. Truman, the Democratic-controlled Congress named a bipartisan "Joint Committee on the Investigation of the Pearl Harbor Attack" to try to arrive at the truth. Truman ordered the White House and all government agencies to cooperate fully with the committee and hold nothing back. Public hearings began in November 1945, and forty-three high-ranking government witnesses testified over seventy days. But the report the joint committee produced in 1946 did not put the issues to rest. One of its main shortcomings was that it was not unanimous.

For the majority, the conclusion was that there had been no conspiracy. "The record reflects that no one in Washington interpreted the harbor berthing plan of September 24 and related dispatches as indicative of an attack on the fleet at Pearl Harbor or was in any way conscious of the significance of the messages which it is now possible to read into them," the majority report said.

The "Magic" interception of messages from Tokyo to the Japanese negotiators after the impasse in the talks at the end of November had given clear warning of impending war, but no warning that it would start at Pearl Harbor, the majority concluded. "It is clear from the evidence that the salient questions in the minds of responsible officials in Washington in the few days before Pearl Harbor was not 'Would the Japanese attack?' but 'when' and 'where' would she attack?" the majority report said. "We do not believe that this intelligence, if taken together, would have predicted Pearl Harbor as a likely place of attack."

No such exoneration was given to Kimmel and Short, however. "The commanders in Hawaii were clearly and unmistakably warned of war with Japan. They were given orders and possessed information that the entire Pacific area was fraught with danger.

They failed to carry out these orders and to discharge their basic and ultimate responsibilities," the majority concluded.

Among the joint committee's findings was that the field commanders might have been better prepared if they had shared the intelligence reports they did have and exchanged notes about what they were doing to prepare for hostilities. In those prewar days of intense interservice rivalry, admirals and generals seldom talked. The war had taught them lessons about this, but in the postwar reorganization of national security that was coming, the joint committee recommended, figuring out how to make intelligence gathering a priority and how to share and coordinate intelligence from multiple sources and agencies should be an urgent priority.

For two Republican members of the joint committee, Senators Homer Ferguson of Michigan and Owen Brewster of Maine, blame for the disaster did not rest solely on officers in the field. The intercepted Japanese messages in the days before the attack, in their view, should have led the president and his subordinates to send more urgent warnings to Pearl Harbor. The fact that Washington kept the messages to itself made top officials there as responsible for the disaster as Kimmel and Short, they concluded in their minority report. Separately, Republican Senator Frank B. Keefe of Wisconsin, though endorsing the majority report, expressed a similar view.

So the Pearl Harbor committee investigation did not still the argument over whether the attack could have been foreseen or prevented. Conspiracy theorists continue to exchange rumors that Washington had radio intercepts from the Japanese fleet that showed it steaming eastward across the Pacific (though in fact it steamed in radio silence). And more than fifty years after Pearl Harbor, Congress reversed its own findings and declared in 2000 that Kimmel and Short should be posthumously rehabilitated.

THE KENNEDY ASSASSINATION

Like the Pearl Harbor inquiries, the President's Commission on the Assassination of President Kennedy, led by Supreme Court

Chief Justice Earl Warren, failed to satisfy the American people that it had resolved the fundamental issue it was set up to investigate: Did Lee Harvey Oswald alone kill John F. Kennedy in Dallas on November 22, 1963?

The question had potentially global implications at the height of the cold war, two years after Kennedy had tried to invade Cuba to overthrow Fidel Castro and a year after the Cuban Missile Crisis. Oswald had tried to defect to the Soviet Union, had lived there between 1959 and 1962, and had visited the Cuban embassy in Mexico City two months before the assassination. On November 24, Oswald was shot to death by a nightclub owner named Jack Ruby in the Dallas police headquarters basement. The tragedy created a national atmosphere of crisis, one that intensified through the 1960s because of the war in Vietnam and a gathering revolution in social and race relations at home.

Chief Justice Warren was himself a contentious figure because of his court's activist role in these larger questions. The commission he led was bipartisan, with two members of both House and Senate, plus the former director of the CIA, Allen W. Dulles, and a respected statesman, John J. McCloy. Set up only a week after the assassination, it had subpoena powers, but no investigative staff of its own. It relied on the FBI, the Secret Service, and the CIA to produce truthful answers to its questions, and it was under tremendous pressure to produce a report before the presidential election of 1964.

The Warren commission questioned 522 witnesses and presented its report on September 24. The essence of its twenty-six volumes came down to this: "The Commission has found no evidence that either Lee Harvey Oswald or Jack Ruby was part of any conspiracy, domestic or foreign, to assassinate President Kennedy," it said. "All of the evidence before the Commission established that there was nothing to support the speculation that Oswald was an agent, employee, or informant of the FBI, the CIA, or any other governmental agency. It has thoroughly investigated Oswald's relationships prior to the assassination with all agencies of the U.S. Government. All contacts with Oswald by any of these agencies were made in the regular exercise of their different responsibilities. No direct or indirect relationship between Lee Harvey Oswald and Jack Ruby has been discovered by the Commission, nor has it been able to find any credible evidence that either knew the other, although a thorough investigation was made of the many rumors and speculations of such a relationship."

"Because of the difficulty of proving negatives to a certainty the possibility of others being involved with either Oswald or Ruby cannot be established categorically, but if there is any such evidence it has been beyond the reach of all the investigative agencies and resources of the United States and has not come to the attention of this Commission," its report concluded.

The tentativeness of this conclusion allowed conspiracy theories to proliferate. But what gave them the most powerful nourishment was the widespread disillusionment with government that began with the Kennedy assassination, accelerated through the traumatic experience of Vietnam, and perhaps reached its climax with Watergate, a White House conspiracy to cover up a political dirty-tricks break-in led by President Richard M. Nixon himself. Facing impeachment, the president resigned in August 1975.

In this atmosphere of distrust, Congress tried to restore public confidence in institutions whose reputations had seemed unimpeachable at the time the Warren commission did its work. The most extensive effort was led by Senator Frank Church of Idaho, whose "Senate Select Committee to Study Government Operations with Respect to Intelligence Activities" from 1975 to 1976 led to important reforms in the operations of the FBI and the CIA.

The Church Committee questioned hundreds of people, some privately outside the hearings, and produced fourteen reports that, among other things, reveal some of the reasons for the weaknesses in the Warren commission's report and provide perspective on the difficulty today of getting clear institutional explanations for failure.

"In the days following the assassination of President Kennedy, nothing was more important to this country than to determine the facts of his death; no one single event has shaken the country more," the Church committee report on the assassination observed. Yet the FBI and the CIA both withheld information of possibly vital significance.

FBI Director J. Edgar Hoover had ordered an internal review of why the bureau had not kept closer track of Oswald's activities with both pro- and anti-Castro Cuban groups after his return from the Soviet Union, the Senate report found, and had taken disciplinary measures against officials for their failures, but Hoover never told the Warren commission about any of them because he thought it would simply use the information against him.

Shockingly, neither the FBI nor the CIA had told the commission that the CIA had plotted to assassinate Castro. With the knowledge of Kennedy's White House, the Church committee found, the CIA had established a unit that had met with Mafia figures who had Cuban connections to try to eliminate Castro, and it had held discussions with one disgruntled member of the Cuban leadership. Yet the CIA's top leaders had not revealed these facts to the Warren commission when it asked for information on the possibility of a foreign conspiracy to assassinate Kennedy, though they clearly might have been relevant.

"Why senior officials of the FBI and the CIA permitted the investigation to go forward, in light of these deficiencies, and why they permitted the Warren Commission to reach its conclusion without all relevant information is still unclear. Certainly, concern with public reputation, problems of coordination between agencies, possible bureaucratic failure and embarrassment, and the extreme compartmentation of knowledge of sensitive operations may have contributed to these shortcomings. But the possibility exists that senior officials in both agencies made conscious decisions not to disclose potentially important information," the Church committee reported after its operations ended in 1976. "Nevertheless, the Committee decided to make its findings public, because the people have a right to know how these special agencies of the Government fulfill their responsibilities."

The Church committee's work was continued in 1977 by a House Select Committee on Assassinations. "Virtually all former Warren Commission members and staff contacted by the committee said they regarded the CIA-Mafia plots against Fidel Castro to be the most important information withheld from the Commission," the new committee reported in 1979. "They all agreed that an awareness of the plots would have led to significant new areas of investigation and would have altered the general approach of the investigation."

Indeed, the House Select Committee arrived at a very different conclusion, after getting acoustics experts to listen to a dictabelt recording of the sounds from a motorcycle policeman's radio outside the Texas Schoolbook Depository in Dallas and finding a 95 percent possibility of a second gunman at the scene of the assassination:

> The committee concluded that it is probable that the President was assassinated as a result of a conspiracy. Nothing in the committee's investigation pointed to official involvement in that conspiracy. While the committee frankly acknowledged that its investigation was not able to identify the members of the conspiracy besides Oswald, or the extent of the conspiracy, the committee believed that it did not include the Secret Service, Federal Bureau of Investigation, or Central Intelligence Agency.

The conclusion seemed so weak as to be almost risible. Three members of the committee dissented from the conspiracy finding, and one of them also distanced himself from the committee's conclusion that the murder of the Rev. Dr. Martin Luther King Jr. was also possibly a conspiracy. "The questions will go on, perhaps in ratio to the intensity of public distrust in leaders and institutions," John Herbers wrote in the *New York Times* when the committee disbanded.

But the work of the Church committee and its successors had important consequences. Congressional oversight over both the CIA and the FBI was strengthened, and the culture of both agencies changed, just as the Pentagon and the military services had had to change in the aftermath of Vietnam. Intelligence gathering and law enforcement were more clearly separated. Ends no longer automatically justified means in the name of national security.

THE CHALLENGE OF TERRORISM

It was in this political-cultural context, created in part by the results of earlier national inquiries, that the governmental response to terrorism would be judged by the 9/11 commission.

Until the cold war unraveled after the collapse of the Berlin Wall in 1989, the administrations of presidents Ronald Reagan and George H. W. Bush paid comparatively little attention to terrorism, despite the Hezbollah attack that killed 241 marines in Lebanon in October of 1983 and the Libyan sabotage of Pan American Flight 103 that killed 270 people over Lockerbie, Scotland in 1988.

Before the first terrorist attack on the World Trade Center in New York City in 1993—and the later discovery of a related plot to blow up the city's river tunnels and the United Nations building—terrorism had been considered only a marginal threat to the United States itself. It took time for the implications to sink in.

Not until 1995 did President Bill Clinton establish a working level "Counterterrorism Security Group" inside the White House, chaired by Richard A. Clarke. It was not until 1996, Clarke wrote in a controversial book published on the eve of his public testimony before the 9/11 commission, that the government figured out that it was up against an Islamic terrorist network of global dimensions led by a renegade from a wealthy Saudi Arabian family, Osama bin Laden. And only after terrorist suicide truck bombers destroyed the American embassies in Tanzania and Kenya in August 1998, killing 257 (including twelve Americans) and wounding 5,000 people in Nairobi, did President Clinton order the first direct response against al Qaeda, a cruise missile attack on its training grounds in Afghanistan.

Spending on U.S. defensive actions against terrorism increased in 1999 and 2000, but President Clinton was distracted by the Monica Lewinsky affair. Even after suicide bombers used a boat full of explosives to blow up the U.S.S. *Cole* in Aden on October 12, 2000, killing seventeen sailors and injuring thirty-nine, the Clinton administration did not retaliate against al Qaeda, unsure that it had carried out the attack. Clarke and other officials were left to try to persuade the incoming administration of President George W. Bush that the threat of terrorist strikes on American soil posed an urgent danger. President Bush's first national security briefings, Clarke said, were not about terrorism but about two issues that seemed more important to the president then— Iraq, where his father's administration had left Saddam Hussein in power after Operation Desert Storm, and missile defense.

Then came September 11.

GENESIS OF THE 9/11 COMMISSION

This time, in contrast to Pearl Harbor or the Kennedy assassination, there was no rush to establish a wide-ranging independent inquiry into the terrorist attacks. President Bush, riding high in public opinion polls that showed most Americans had high regard for him as commander in chief in this new war against terrorism, had no interest in a congressional or independent inquiry that might damage his standing.

Less than a month after the attacks, House Republicans fought off attempts by the Democrats to call for an independent commission of inquiry with subpoena powers. In November 2001, with war on against al Qaeda and the Taliban in Afghanistan, Democrats and Republicans in both the House and Senate agreed to put off any inquiry, whether by Congress or by a blue-ribbon presidential panel. "It would be a distraction," said Warren B. Rudman, a former Republican senator.

But in December, with the Taliban out of the way, Senators Joseph I. Lieberman, Democrat of Connecticut, and John McCain, Republican of Arizona, introduced legislation for an independent bipartisan commission with subpoena power to make a full investigation of September 11.

The Democrats soon threw their support behind the measure, but the White House resisted, citing the decision in February 2002 by the House and Senate select committees on intelligence to conduct a joint investigation of their own. The key findings of that inquiry are included in this volume.

But the White House did not reckon with the families of the victims of the attacks on the World Trade Center, the Pentagon, and the four hijacked airplanes. The families were insistent that an even broader inquiry was needed, one with the power and prestige to explore all the reasons behind the attacks, and mounted an effective campaign to persuade individual lawmakers of their case.

Heeding their calls, enough Republican members of the House joined the Democrats to produce a majority vote on July 25, 2002 for an independent commission. The Senate and the White House still had to be convinced.

The writ of the House-Senate Joint Inquiry did not run beyond the intelligence community, and gave the two congressional committees only a year to complete the work. But their investigation was aggressive, and it had begun by this time to turn up embarrassing evidence of missed warning signals and coordination failures by government agencies that cried out for thorough examination. The White House, becoming aware from contacts with the victims' families how eager they were for a further bipartisan independent inquiry, stopped objecting that a wider investigation would only divert attention from the war against terrorism, and on September 20, seemed to give its backing to the idea. "The administration has met with some of the families of the 9/11 groups, who have talked about the need for a commission to look into a host of issues, and they have made compelling arguments," Ari Fleischer, the White House spokesman, explained.

But behind the scenes, the administration was insisting on conditions to cover the president's political flank. It wanted to ensure a bipartisan result and it wanted a commission to produce its findings within a year, not right in the middle of President Bush's re-election campaign, officials said. "They're not really negotiating in good faith," Stephen Push, whose wife, Lisa J. Raines, died in the plane that crashed into the Pentagon, told the *New York Times* in October.

Not until November 15 did the White House and Congress agree on a compromise to establish the commission with ten members, five from each party, and to give it eighteen months (later extended) to prepare its report, and allowing the president to choose the chairman—though, at the families' insistence, Senator McCain, one of the few Republicans who had insisted on a commission, got the right to appoint one of the five Republican commissioners.

President Bush's first choice to head the commission was Henry A. Kissinger, remembered by many people around the country as the Republican but Machiavellian foreign policy strategist of Richard M. Nixon's administration during the Vietnam War. The Democrats named George J. Mitchell, the former Senate majority leader, as vice chairman.

Both Kissinger and Mitchell abruptly withdrew within days of their nominations. Kissinger, whose appointment was widely criticized, did not want to divulge the names of all the clients of his worldwide consulting firm and said he would have had to delay the commission's work and dissolve it to avoid conflicts of interest. Mitchell said he did not want to sever ties with his law firm.

Kean and the longtime Democratic congressman from Indiana, Lee H. Hamilton, who replaced Kissinger and Mitchell, brought unquestioned reputations of respect and integrity to their jobs and vowed to do their best. "I lost a number of good friends on 9/11," Kean, president of Drew University in Madison, New Jersey, said. "So did a lot of people in this area. At this point, the country needs to come together. It will come together to help us in every way with our work."

THE HOUSE-SENATE JOINT INQUIRY REPORT

The 9/11 commission started its work on a firm foundation: the joint congressional inquiry report. Though heavily censored by the White House because of the secret evidence it contained, the congressional report was published in December 2002 after nine public hearings, thirteen closed sessions, and interviews of 300 people.

Though its charter was limited to examining the work of the

U.S. intelligence community, and the White House had not given it all the data it asked for, the congressional investigation produced a devastating portrayal of confusion, ineptitude, incompetence, and inadequacy in all the government agencies charged with monitoring the terrorist threat to the United States.

"The FBI had fewer than ten tactical analysts and only one strategic analyst assigned to al Qaeda before September 11," the congressional report said, and the Bureau's one strategic analyst was focused mainly on attacks against American installations overseas. At the CIA's counterterrorism center, there were only five analysts in the months leading up to the attack. The National Security Agency and the Defense Intelligence Agency had people looking at terrorist operations, but, the report found, "unfortunately, there was no mechanism in place to enable inter-agency collaboration," though "information that may seem unimportant to one agency may be critical to another."

The government, in short, had no way of knowing what it knew about the terrorist threat. Even the FBI, hampered by inability to get funding for up-to-date information technology, did not really know what it knew. When it did learn something from foreign intelligence, the FBI was hamstrung by its understanding of constitutional limitations on the use of such intelligence in criminal investigations.

As examples of the effects of these multiple failures, the congressional report told how two of the hijackers, Khalid al Mihdhar and Nawaf al Hazmi, had slipped past every possible barrier because of ineptitude. Al Mihdhar got into the United States because immigration officials had not been told that the CIA had discovered that he had been at an al Qaeda meeting in Malaysia. The CIA did not share what it knew with other agencies until late August 2001, asking then that both al Mihdhar and al Hazmi be "watchlisted" and denied entry. But by then, they were both already here. FBI headquarters would not allow a criminal investigation to be opened that might have poured more resources into tracking them, the congressional report said, because of its concern about the "wall" between foreign intelligence and domestic law enforcement. The same concern made the FBI bungle the investigation of Zacarias Moussaoui, who was trying to learn how to fly 747s at a flight school in Minneapolis when a suspicious Bureau agent detained him a month before the attacks; after September 11, the government charged him with planning a hijacking as well.

The congressional report detailed more frustrating failures. An FBI agent in the Phoenix field office had sent a message to the bureau in July outlining a theory that al Qaeda might be sending terrorists to civil aviation schools in the United States to get flight training for hijacking operations, the report said, but the message was not shared with any other government agency or even with the FBI's own analysts before 9/11.

"In short, for a variety of reasons, the Intelligence Community failed to capitalize on both the individual and collective significance of available information that appears relevant to the events of September 11," the joint congressional inquiry concluded. Its most important recommendation was the creation of a new cabinet-level position, Director of National Intelligence, to replace the director of the CIA in that function with the assignment of devising a coherent and effective strategy for combating terrorism at home and abroad involving all branches of government, including the newly established Department of Homeland Security.

The majority report did not point the finger of blame at individual officials. Nor did it sufficiently acknowledge that Congress itself bore most of the responsibility for the cuts in the intelligence community's budgets in the early to mid-1990s and flat funding subsequently that both the CIA and the FBI cited as explanations for the limitations on their capabilities.

A minority report by Republican Senator Richard C. Shelby of Alabama did name names, however. Six officials—CIA directors George J. Tenet and John Deutch, FBI Director Louis Freeh, National Security Agency Directors Michael Hayden and Kenneth Minnihan, and former NSA Deputy Director Barbara McNamara—"failed in significant ways to ensure that this country was as prepared as it could have been," Senator Shelby said.

9/11 COMMISSION HEARINGS
AND STAFF REPORTS

There matters lay, with no action on the domestic intelligence reform proposal, as the 9/11 commission began its work. Its mandate went beyond examining the performance of intelligence agencies. Continuously urged on by 9/11 families, it soon made clear that its inquiry would examine the government's performance right up to the top of the executive branch, the president and his aides.

Armed with a highly experienced investigative staff of more than eighty, the commission began hearings in the spring of 2003, but it had to fight every step of the way against bureaucratic resistance to full disclosure. "The administration underestimated the scale of the commission's work and the full breadth of support required," Kean and Hamilton said that July. "The task in front of us is monumental." Every government agency with any responsibility for preventing terrorist attacks came under the 9/11 commission's scrutiny, from the White House to the Immigration and Naturalization Service to the Federal Aviation Administration.

The White House promised full cooperation but resisted the commission's demands for files and documents, finally agreeing to provide only the excerpts that it judged relevant. But the commission staff worked diligently to develop evidence and, unusually in investigations of this kind, began making reports of its findings public in advance of the hearings, so that the public as well as the commissioners could be well informed when questioning of important government witnesses started. Staff reports, written in accessible and compelling style rather than bureaucratese, are included in this book.

Gradually, the picture of institutional dysfunction that had been sketched in news reports after September 11 and highlighted in the earlier joint congressional inquiry began to come into sharper focus. The approach of the 2004 election created even greater intensity.

One obvious failure, of course, was the airport security system, whose inadequacies had been recognized long before 9/11 with no action by either the FAA or the airlines that subcontracted the work to poorly trained and poorly paid security guards. FAA tests had found, Republican commissioner John F. Lehman said, that the U.S. airport security system was only about 10 percent effective in detecting real threats. Yet nothing had been done to improve it or to make cockpit doors invulnerable to break-ins in attempted hijackings. The rules even allowed passengers to bring aboard "pocket utility knives." Though the box cutters that the hijackers apparently used to subdue resistance on September 11 were banned, the rules provided no guidance on how to tell them apart from small knives.

"The last major terrorist attack on a U.S. flagged airliner had been with smuggled explosives, in 1988, in the case of Pan Am 103," a commission staff report said. "The Commission on Aviation Safety and Security created by President Clinton in 1996, named the Gore Commission for its chairman, the Vice President, had focused overwhelmingly on the danger of explosives on aircraft. Historically, explosives on aircraft had taken a heavy death toll, hijackings had not. So, despite continued foreign hijackings leading up to 9/11, the U.S. aviation security system worried most about explosives."

Airport security, made the responsibility of Federal authorities under the new Department of Homeland Security after 9/11, was a barn door closed after the horse had been stolen. Commission investigations reportedly also questioned why NORAD, the military's homeland air defense system, had been so slow to respond to alerts on September 11, when the first F–16 fighters were launched from Langley Air Force Base in Virginia forty-four minutes after Flight 11 struck the World Trade Center. This was barely seven minutes before Flight 77 hit the Pentagon—too late to intercept it even if the fighter pilot had been given authority to shoot it down first. Yet, bizarrely enough, a NORAD document revealed, the command had considered war-gaming a hypothetical suicide hijacking attack on the Pentagon only five months before it actually happened, raising more questions about the total lack of preparedness.

The commission staff reports were unsparingly critical of the FBI and of the CIA, a fact that Tenet had reason to note unhappily. As the intelligence community's chief, he had issued a directive on December 4, 1998, the commission staff reported, that stated: "We are at war. I want no resources or people spared in this effort, either inside CIA or the community." His declaration of war was faxed to other agencies, but nobody paid much attention to it or thought it applied to them, the commission staff found. In any case, the staff report said, Tenet and his predecessors "did not develop a management strategy for a war against terrorism before 9/11."

As for war, as Clarke had found in trying to develop a strategy for the Clinton White House, the U.S. military was reluctant to prepare for commando operations on the ground in Afghanistan. All the military's suggested plans for action involved huge, cumbersome forces that seemed more useful for taking over small countries than for dealing with terrorist organizations.

U.S. intelligence had begun detecting a "significant spike" in terrorist communications indicating plans for attacks in the spring of 2001, the commission staff found: "By late May there were reports of a hostage plot against Americans to force the release of prisoners, including Sheikh Omar Abd al Rahman, the 'Blind Sheikh,' who was serving a life sentence for his role in the 1993 plot to blow up sites in New York City. . . . The reporting noted that the operatives may opt to hijack an aircraft or storm a U.S. embassy." Yet the government issued only general warnings to the public because the intelligence was not specific about where an attack would occur.

The United States had intelligence reports of terrorist threats to use aircraft as weapons, another staff report said, but the CIA's Counterterrorist Center "did not analyze how a hijacked aircraft or other explosives-laden aircraft might be used as a weapon. If it had done so, it could have identified that a critical obstacle would be to find a suicide terrorist able to fly large jet aircraft." It could also have alerted the FBI to be on the lookout for terrorist suspects studying at American flight schools and ordered the FAA to order stronger security measures at airports and inside aircraft. A suicide hijacking by a terrorist group might be a possibility, the FAA's Office of Civil Aviation Security told air carriers and airports in 2000 and early 2001, according to the commission staff, but the FAA added that "fortunately, we have no indication that any group is currently thinking in that direction."

As the months wore on, the 9/11 commission piled up evidence of years of missed connections and mistaken assessments by administrations past and present. But September 11 happened on the watch of President Bush, and as the climactic hearings approached in the spring of 2004, the president was at serious risk of losing his reputation as the decisive wartime leader who had taken the fight to al Qaeda. The challenge came from Clarke, who testified dramatically at a hearing on March 24 that he had been unable, despite months of effort after Mr. Bush's inauguration, to get the president or Condoleezza Rice, his national security adviser, to focus on the threat from al Qaeda to the U.S. homeland. "My view is that this administration, while listening to me, either didn't believe me that there was an urgent problem or was unprepared to act as though there was an urgent problem," Clarke told a rapt audience at the hearing. The administration had largely ignored the threat and concentrated on Iraq instead, he charged. "The reason that I am strident in my criticism of the president of the United States is that by invading Iraq—something I was not asked by the commission—but by invading Iraq, the president of the United States has greatly undermined the war on terrorism."

His testimony, coming just after the publication of his book and its equally critical assertions of the president's preoccupation with Iraq, went off like a bombshell at a moment when American occupation forces in Iraq were dying at a rate that would soon rise even higher than it had been during the invasion a year before.

The White House went into overdrive to try to control the damage, sending Rice out to appear on talk shows and interviews to deny Clarke's assertions, but her efforts were undermined by the administration's refusal to let her testify publicly in commission hearings on the grounds of executive privilege. A storm of public pressure and warning signals from public opinion polls forced the White House to back down and let her appear in early April. The president and Vice President Dick Cheney also agreed to meet later with the commission, but behind closed doors and not under oath (as did President Clinton and Vice President Gore).

Condoleezza Rice's appearance on April 8, and that of CIA Director Tenet, FBI Director Robert S. Mueller III, Attorney General John Ashcroft, and their immediate predecessors a few days later, crackled with tension and confrontational exchanges between Republican witnesses and Democratic commission members. What the witnesses were describing as they testified was a government aware of a terrorist threat to American citizens and institutions overseas, but not structured to recognize the same threat here at home and act against it in time. Excerpts from those and other dramatic testimonies are included in this book.

The key question about the summer of 2001 was what President Bush himself had known and how he had acted on that knowledge. Testimony and staff reports at the hearings in April 2004 focused on the top secret Presidential Daily Brief the president had received at his ranch in Crawford, Texas, on August 6, 2001, a response to his request to the CIA for information on whether any of the new warnings about terrorism pointed to an attack on the United States. "Isn't it a fact, Dr. Rice, that the August 6th PDB warned against possible attacks in this country? And I ask you whether you recall the title of that PDB?" Democratic commissioner Richard Ben-Veniste asked. "I believe the title was 'Bin Laden Determined to Attack Inside the United States,'" Rice replied, but she insisted it did not call for any immediate action by the president. "It was historical information based on old reporting. There was no new threat information, and it did not, in fact, warn of any coming attacks inside the United States," she testified.

At the commission's insistence, the White House agreed to declassify the document, which was released on the following Saturday evening and is reproduced in this book.

"Clandestine, foreign government, and media reports indicate bin Ladin since 1997 has wanted to conduct terrorist attacks in the U.S.," the presidential brief said. "Bin Ladin implied in U.S. Television interviews in 1997 and 1998 that his followers would follow the example of World Trade Center Ramzi Yousef and 'bring the fighting to America.'" The brief added that two foreign intelligence services had picked up threats by bin Laden to "retaliate in Washington" and "mount a terrorist strike" and reminded President Bush that Ahmed Ressam, arrested in a car full of explosives at the Canadian border before the millennium celebrations in late 1999, had told the FBI his plan to attack the Los Angeles International Airport had been encouraged and facilitated by a top al Qaeda aide to bin Laden.

The FBI had seen "patterns of suspicious activity in this country consistent with preparations for hijackings or other types of attacks, including recent surveillance of federal buildings in New York," the brief told the president, and the bureau had "approximately 70 full field investigations throughout the U.S. that it considers bin Ladin-related. CIA and the FBI are investigating a call to our Embassy in the U.A.E. in May saying that a group of bin Ladin supporters was in the U.S. planning attacks with explosives."

After being told that bin Laden was bent on bringing devastation to the United States and that his operatives were already here, the president stayed on the ranch in Crawford, called no crisis meetings, and issued no orders, according to Rice's testimony, because he was assured that the responsible government authorities were already on the case. He also knew, presumably, that his senior national security officials were planning a White House meeting September 4 to approve a new counterterrorism strategy, a meeting Clarke had been urging ever since the inauguration in January. The August 6 briefing, Rice pointed out, "did not raise the possibility that terrorists might use airplanes as missiles."

But after it was published on Easter weekend of 2004, the document reverberated like a tocsin. And after an even more confrontational hearing on April 13, when Attorney General John Ashcroft blamed the FBI's inability to go after terrorist suspects more aggressively on restrictions that he said had been imposed by one of the Democratic commission members, Jamie S. Gorelick, when she was a member of the Clinton administration, President Bush called a rare formal news conference to explain his actions.

"I stepped back and I've asked myself a lot, Is there anything we could have done to stop the attacks?" he said. "Of course, I've asked that question as have many people of my government. Nobody wants this to happen to America. And the answer is that had I had any inkling whatsoever that the people were going to fly airplanes into buildings we would have moved heaven and earth to save the country."

CONCLUSIONS

The president's words echoed those of the commanders in Pearl Harbor who said they had no inkling whatsoever that an attack was coming there on December 7—only that war was expected to break out somewhere in the Pacific soon. Yet it is only the rare and fortunate commander, or commander in chief, who ever receives intelligence reports that are more specific.

The Bush administration did approve a new strategy to eliminate al Qaeda, on September 4, 2001. It was too late to prevent the attacks that came a week later, and, Rice said, "it would not have prevented Sept. 11th if it had been approved the day after we came to office." The question, for the 9/11 commission and for the country as the 2004 elections approached, was whether the reorganization of government that followed—with the establishment of a huge new Department of Homeland Security, the passage of the Patriot Act, tighter control of foreign immigration, and a new, Federally run airport security system—was sufficient remedy for the shortcomings that had left the country so vulnerable three years earlier.

Both the Joint House-Senate Inquiry and the 9/11 commission hearings and reports pointed toward a historic reorganization of domestic security structures on the scale of the post-World War II restructuring that established the Defense Department and the CIA.

Commissioner Kean described the commission staff reports as

an indictment of both the CIA and the FBI. "It failed and it failed and it failed and it failed," Kean said of the FBI. "This is an agency that does not work." John F. Lehman, another Republican member of the commission, said the report on the CIA was a "damning evaluation of a system that is broken, that doesn't function."

"We've got to seriously consider whether our whole counter intelligence apparatus has to be changed," Kean said in an interview published in the *New York Times* on April 6. A few days later, President Bush seemed to agree. "Now may be a time to revamp and reform our intelligence services," he said. Establishment of a new domestic intelligence office would be a centerpiece of such an effort to overcome past failure.

September 11 was a warning, but also an opportunity to set in place defenses against new and even more terrible terrorist attacks. With the Arab world in turmoil over the war in Iraq and the Bush administration's unconditional backing of Israel in its showdown with the Palestinian Authority, al Qaeda metastasized rapidly despite losing its sanctuary in Afghanistan. After attacks in Indonesia, Thailand, the Philippines, and then Madrid in the spring of 2004, the threat of terrorism to the United States and its Middle Eastern and European allies seemed even greater than it had been in 2001. The worst scenario would be an attack using nuclear, biological, or chemical weapons, and al Qaeda and its spawn were known to have tried to acquire them.

The reports and hearings of the 9/11 commission and the joint congressional inquiry show American democracy struggling to understand and find ways of dealing with an enemy it had never faced before. To explain past failures not only renders justice to the memory of the innocent victims of 9/11; it also helps build a national consensus on greater preparedness for the long battle to come. The effort is literally a matter of life or death.

A Note from the Editor

The excerpts in this book represent the highlights of more than two years of national hearings on the September 11 attacks. The Joint Inquiry by the House and Senate Intelligence Committees, charged with focusing on the performance of U.S. intelligence agencies, completed its work in December 2002. The National Commission on Terrorist Attacks Upon the United States, a bipartisan group created by congressional legislation in late 2002, was given a mandate to examine all aspects of the tragedy, from America's preparations to its immediate responses. The commission is scheduled to release its final report and recommendations in the summer of 2004.

Part One of this book contains commission staff reports. These are without exception well-written analyses of the tragedy, informed by the work of the Joint Inquiry as well as the substantial new evidence gathered by the National Commission. In this version, only the salutations and formalities at the beginning of each report have been cut, along with minor irrelevancies in the text. Excerpts from the testimony of key policymakers follow the appropriate report.

Part Two of this book contains excerpts from the Joint Inquiry report. The Joint Inquiry produced a document rich in detail and perspective. The excerpts from the declassified report included here, taken mostly from the narrative section, are intended to highlight those details. Each section begins with a paragraph written by this book's editor that attempts to frame the material that follows. In addition, many of the section headings have been revised to make them stylistically consistent with those of the preceding 9/11 Commission reports. But the text of the Joint Inquiry document, like that of the Commission reports, remains untouched except for minor editing changes.

One other note, on spelling: in the original documents, the transliteration of Arab names is wildly inconsistent. The big terror organization, for example, is called al Qaeda, al-Qa'ida and al Qida, among other things. For the sake of editorial cohesiveness, the names in these pages have been transliterated consistently.

The 9/11 Investigations

I

The 9/11 Commission

STAFF STATEMENTS AND TESTIMONY

THE NATIONAL COMMISSION ON TERRORIST ATTACKS UPON THE UNITED STATES

Staff Statement No. 1

Entry of the 9/11 Hijackers into the United States

As we know from the sizable illegal traffic across our land borders, a terrorist could attempt to bypass legal procedures and enter the United States surreptitiously. None of the 9/11 attackers entered or tried to enter our country this way. So . . . we will focus on the hijackers' exploitation of legal entry systems. . . . To break down some of al Qaeda's travel problem, view it from their perspective. For most international travel, a terrorist has to have a passport. To visit some countries, terrorists of certain nationalities must obtain a document permitting them to visit—a visa. Finally the terrorist must actually enter the country and keep from getting detained or deported by immigration or other law enforcement officials.

PASSPORTS

Four of the hijackers' passports have survived in whole or in part. Two were recovered from the crash site of United Airlines Flight 93 in Pennsylvania. One belonged to a hijacker on American Airlines Flight 11. A passerby picked it up and gave it to an NYPD detective shortly before the World Trade Center towers collapsed. A fourth passport was recovered from luggage that did not make it from a Portland flight to Boston onto the connecting flight, which was American Airlines Flight 11. In addition to these four, some digital copies of the hijackers' passports were recovered in post–9/11 operations.

Two of the passports that have survived, those of *Satam al Suqami* and *Abdul Aziz al Omari*, were clearly doctored. To avoid getting into the classified details, we will just state that these were "manipulated in a fraudulent manner," in ways that have been associated with al Qaeda. Since the passports of 15 of the hijackers did not survive, we cannot make firm factual statements about their documents. But from what we know about al Qaeda passport practices and other information, we believe it is possible that six more of the hijackers presented passports that had some of these same clues to their association with al Qaeda.

Other kinds of passport markings can be highly suspicious. To avoid getting into the classified details, we will just call these "suspicious indicators." Two of the hijackers, *Khalid al Mihdhar* and *Salem al Hazmi*, presented passports that had such suspicious indicators. We know now that each of these two hijackers possessed at least two passports. All of their known passports had these suspicious indicators. We have evidence that three other hijackers, *Nawaf al Hazmi*, *Ahmed al Nami*, and *Ahmad al Haznawi*, may have presented passports containing these suspicious indicators. But their passports did not survive the attacks, so we cannot be sure.

Fifteen of the 19 hijackers were Saudi nationals. There were significant security weaknesses in the Saudi government's issuance of Saudi passports in the period when the visas to the hijackers were issued. Two of the Saudi 9/11 hijackers may have obtained their passports legitimately or illegitimately with the help of a family member who worked in the passport office.

We do not yet know the answer to the question whether the knowledge of these particular clues existed in the intelligence community before 9/11. From the mid-1970s, when terrorists began to launch attacks in the Middle East and Europe, intelligence and border authorities knew that terrorists used forged or altered travel documents. By the 1980s the U.S. government had developed a "Red Book" used to guide and train consular, immigration, and customs officers throughout the world on spotting terrorists. It included photographs of altered or stolen passports, and false travel stamps (also known as cachets) used by terrorists. The importance of training border officials on use of the Red Book is evident from a U.S. government film entitled *The Threat is Real.* . . .

The U.S. government ceased publication of the "Red Book" by 1992, in part because it had fallen into the hands of terrorist groups, although there continued to be a number of government efforts to provide information about generic forgery detection and document inspection techniques.

Before 9/11, the FBI and CIA did know of some of the practices employed by al Qaeda. They knew this from training manuals recovered in the mid–1990s and from tracking and interrogations of al Qaeda operatives. Some of this knowledge was revealed in individual criminal cases prosecuted in the United States in the 1990s. And yet, between 1992 and September 11, 2001, we have not found any signs that intelligence, law enforcement, or border inspection services sought to acquire, develop, or disseminate systematic information about al Qaeda's or other terrorist groups' travel and passport practices. Thus, such information was not available to consular, immigration, or customs officials who examined the hijackers' passports before 9/11.

VISAS

The State Department is principally responsible for administering U.S. immigration laws outside of the United States. Consular officers, a branch of our diplomatic corps, issue several kinds of visas for visitors and for permanent immigrants. In 2000, these diplomats processed about 10 million applications for visitors' visas at over 200 posts overseas. U.S. law allows nationals of certain countries to enter without visas on a reciprocal basis, under the visa waiver program. None of the 9/11 hijackers, however, were nationals of a visa waiver country.

Before 9/11, visa applicants provided their passport and a photograph. A State Department employee checked the passport for any apparent questionable features. A consular officer could call the applicant in for an interview. The applicant's essential information went into a State Department database. The information was then checked against a large "consular lookout" database called CLASS, which included a substantial watchlist of known and suspected terrorists, called TIPOFF.

Our immigration system before 9/11 focused primarily on keeping individuals intending to immigrate from improperly entering the United States. In the visa process, the most common form of fraud is to get a visa to visit the United States as a tourist and then stay to work and perhaps become a resident. Consular officers concentrated on interviewing visa applicants whom they suspected might leave and not return.

Saudi citizens rarely overstayed their visas or tried to work illegally in the United States. The same was true for citizens of the United Arab Emirates. So, while consular officials in both countries always screened applicants in CLASS, including TIPOFF, they would not interview them unless there was something about the applications that seemed problematic.

Visa applicants from these countries frequently had their applications submitted by third party facilitators, like travel agencies. In June 2001, the U.S. consular posts in Saudi Arabia instituted a third party processing program called Visa Express. It required applicants to apply through designated travel agencies instead of by mail or in person. The program was established in part to try to keep crowds of people from congregating outside the posts, which was a security risk to the posts and to the crowds themselves. We have found no evidence that the Visa Express program had any effect on the interview or approval rates for Saudi applicants, or that it reduced the scrutiny given to their applications. It actually lengthened the processing time.

With the exception of our consulates in Mexico, biometric information—like a fingerprint—was not routinely collected from visa applicants before 9/11. Terrorists therefore easily could exploit opportunities for fraud. *Khalid Sheikh Mohammed*, the chief tactical planner and coordinator of the 9/11 attacks, was indicted in 1996 by Federal authorities in the Southern District of New York for his role in earlier terrorist plots. Yet, KSM, as he is known, obtained a visa to visit the United States on July 23, 2001, about six weeks before the 9/11 attacks. Although he is not a Saudi citizen and we do not believe he was in Saudi Arabia at the time, he applied for a visa using a Saudi passport and an alias, *Abdulrahman al Ghamdi*. He had someone else submit his application and a photo through the Visa Express program. There is no evidence that he ever used this visa to enter the United States.

Beginning in 1997, the 19 hijackers submitted 24 applications and received 23 visas. The pilots acquired most of theirs in the year 2000. The other hijackers, with two exceptions, obtained theirs between the fall of 2000 and June 2001. Two of the visas were issued in Berlin, and two were issued in the United Arab Emirates. The rest were issued in Saudi Arabia. One of the pilots, *Hani Hanjour*, had an application denied in September 2000 for lack of adequate documentation. He then produced more evidence in support of his student visa application, and it was approved. Except for *Hanjour*, all the hijackers sought tourist visas.

Of these 24 visa applications, four were destroyed routinely along with other documents before their significance was known.

To our knowledge, State consular officers followed their standard operating procedures in every case. They performed a name check using their lookout database, including the TIPOFF watchlist. At the time these people applied for visas, none of them—or at least none of the identities given in their passports—were in the database. . . .

All 20 of these applications were incomplete in some way, with a data field left blank or not answered fully. Such omissions were common. The consular officials focused on getting the biographical data needed for name checks. They generally did not think the omitted items were material to a decision about whether to issue the visa.

Three of the 19 hijackers submitted applications that contained false statements that could have been proven to be false at the time they applied. The applications of *Hani Hanjour, Saeed al Ghamdi*, and *Khalid al Mihdhar* stated that they had not previously applied for a U.S. visa when, in fact, they had. In *Hanjour's* case the false statement was made in an earlier application for a visit, in 1997, not his final visa application in 2000. *Hanjour* and *al Mihdhar* also made false statements about whether they had previously traveled to the United States. Information about these prior applications was retrievable at the Jeddah post where each applied.

These false statements may have been intentional, to cover up the applicants' travel on old passports to suspect locations like Afghanistan for terrorist training. On the other hand, these statements may have been inadvertent. During this period, Saudi citizens often had their applications filled out and submitted by third parties. Most importantly, evidence of the prior visas or travel to the United States actually would have reduced concern that the applicants were intending to immigrate, so consular officers had no good reason to deny the visas or travel.

Al Mihdhar's case was uniquely problematical. He had not been entered into the TIPOFF watchlist at the time of his second visa application in June 2001. In January 2000 the American consulate in Jeddah had been asked about *al Mihdhar's* visa status in conjunction with an ongoing urgent terrorist intelligence investigation and confirmed that this al Qaeda operative had a U.S. visa. When *al Mihdhar* applied again in June 2001, the check against the worldwide TIPOFF watchlist took place, but no system then in place included a notation of the prior visa status check. Neither the investigating agency nor the post had made the appropriate lookout entry. Thus, in effect, the post could not "remember" relevant suspicions a year-and-a-half earlier about this same person, who was traveling again with the same biographical information.

At least two of the hijackers were actually interviewed in person in connection with their visa applications. *Hanjour* was interviewed twice. *Satam al Suqami* was apparently interviewed in Riyadh. Another hijacker, *Ahmed al Nami*, was apparently interviewed briefly, but just to clarify an entry on his application. The three consular officers involved have some memory of these interviews. All stated that the reason for their interviews had nothing to do with terrorism. They saw nothing suspicious.

At least four individuals implicated in the 9/11 plot tried to get visas and failed: *Ramzi Binalshibh, Zakariya Essabar, Ali Abdul Aziz Ali,* and *Saeed al Gamdi.* This *Saeed al Gamdi* is a different person from the *Saeed al Ghamdi* who actually became a hijacker.

Ramzi Binalshibh, a Yemeni, apparently intended to train as a pilot along with his Hamburg friends, *Mohammed Atta, Marwan al Shehhi,* and *Ziad Jarrah. Binalshibh* applied for a visa three times in Berlin and once in Yemen. He first applied in Berlin on the same day as Atta. He was interviewed twice and denied twice. Yemen is a much poorer country than Saudi Arabia. Both times, consular officers determined he did not have strong ties to Germany and he might be intending to immigrate unlawfully to the United States. *Binalshibh* tried again in Berlin, this time for a student visa to attend aviation school in Florida. He was denied again for lack of adequate documentation and failure to show sufficient ties to Germany.

Essabar, a Moroccan who may also have intended to be a pilot, tried to get a visa in Berlin at least once and failed because he failed to demonstrate sufficient ties to Germany, such as a job or family there. Third country visa applicants in Berlin were held to significantly higher standards—in terms of documentation and showing ties with their country of residence—than were Saudi and Emirati citizens applying from their own countries.

Ali Abdul Aziz Ali is the nephew of Khalid Sheikh Mohammed and was heavily involved in financial and logistical aspects of the 9/11 plot. He tried to get a U.S. visa in Dubai about two weeks before the attacks. His visa application states that he intended to enter the United States on September 4, 2001, for one week. As a Pakistani visa applicant in a third country, he would have received greater scrutiny from U.S. officials from the start. In any event, it was deemed possible that he intended to immigrate, and accordingly he was denied a visa.

Saeed al Gamdi, also known as "Jihad" al Gamdi, apparently intended to participate in the 9/11 attacks. He is a Saudi and applied for a tourist visa in Jeddah on November 12, 2000, the same date as 9/11 hijacker *Ahmad al Haznawi*. *Al Haznawi* was approved, but *al Gamdi* was denied after an interview with a consular officer, because the consular officer believed he was intending to immigrate.

ENTRY INTO AND EXIT FROM THE UNITED STATES

With a visa, an individual can travel to a United States port of entry. Upon arrival, the individual must seek admission into the United States from an inspector of what used to be called the INS [Immigration and Naturalization Service], an agency whose personnel now form part of the Department of Homeland Security. Property being brought into the United States is checked by inspectors of the U.S. Customs Service, whose personnel are now also part of DHS.

The 19 hijackers entered the United States a total of 33 times. They arrived through ten different airports, though more than half came in through Miami, JFK, or Newark. A visitor with a tourist visa was usually admitted for a stay of six months. All but two of the hijackers were admitted for such stays. *Hanjour* had a student visa and was admitted for a stay of two years, and *Suqami* sought and was admitted for a stay of 20 days.

The four pilots passed through INS and Customs inspections a total of 17 times before 9/11. *Hanjour* came to the United States to attend school in three stints during the 1990s. His final arrival was in December 2000, through the Cincinnati/Northern Kentucky airport. The other three pilots, *Atta*, *al Shehhi*, and *Jarrah*, initially came in May and June 2000. They arrived for the last time between May and August 2001. All made a number of trips abroad during their extended stays in the United States.

Of the other 15, only *al Mihdhar* entered the United States, left, and returned. *Nawaf al Hazmi* arrived in January 2000 with *al Mihdhar* and stayed. *Al Mihdhar* left in June 2000 and returned to the United States on July 4, 2001. Ten of the others came in pairs between April and June 2001. Three more arrived through Miami on May 28.

The INS inspector usually had about one to one and a half minutes to assess the traveler and make a decision on admissibility and length of stay. For all the entries, a primary INS inspector would work a lane of incoming travelers and check the people and their passports. The inspector would try to assess each individual's demeanor. No one noted any anomalies in these passports despite the fact, we now believe, that at least two and as many as eight showed evidence of fraudulent manipulation. The inspector would use the passport data, especially if it was machine readable, to check various INS and Customs databases. The databases would show the person's immigration history information, as well as terrorist watchlist and criminal history information.

Of the five hijackers who entered the United States more than once, three of them violated immigration law.

Ziad Jarrah entered in June 2000 on a tourist visa and then promptly enrolled in flight school for six months. He never filed an application to change his immigration status from tourist to student. Had the INS known he was out of status, they could have denied him entry on any of the three subsequent occasions he departed and returned while he was a student.

Marwan al Shehhi came in through Newark in late May 2000, followed a week later by *Mohammed Atta*. Both were admitted as tourists and soon entered flight school in Florida. In September they did file applications to change their status. Before 9/11, regulations allowed tourists to change their status at any time, so they were in compliance. But both overstayed their periods of admission and completed flight school to obtain commercial pilot licenses. *Atta* and *al Shehhi* then left within a few days of one another and returned within a few days of one another in January 2001, while their change in visa status from tourist to student was still pending.

Atta and *al Shehhi* did get some attention when both said they were coming back to finish flight school. Primary inspectors noticed with each that their story clashed with their attempt to reenter on tourist visas. The rules required them to get proper student visas while they had been overseas, since their earlier pending applications for a change of status were considered abandoned once they left the United States. *Atta* and *al Shehhi* were each referred by the primary inspectors to secondary inspection.

At secondary, more experienced inspectors could conduct longer interviews, check more databases, take fingerprints, examine personal property, and call on other agencies for help. The inspectors involved have stated they do not remember these encounters. The reports indicate that both men repeated their story about still going to flight school and their pending applications for a change of status. The secondary inspectors admitted *Atta* and *al Shehhi* as tourists.

Flight 93 hijacker *Saeed al Ghamdi* was referred to secondary immigration inspection when he arrived in late June 2001. He had no address on his I–94 form. He spoke little English. He had a one-way ticket and about $500. The inspector wondered whether he was possibly intending to immigrate. *Al Ghamdi* convinced the inspector that he was a tourist and had enough money.

Customs officers took a second look at two of the hijackers but then admitted them. On *Marwan al Shehhi's* first entry into the United States, a customs officer referred him to secondary inspection, completed the inspection, and released him. In May 2001, *Waleed al Shehri* and *Satam Suqami* departed Florida for the Bahamas but were refused admission. On their way back to the United States, a customs officer conducting a pre-clearance in the Bahamas referred *al Shehri* to a secondary inspection. Customs then released *al Shehri* to return to the United States with *Suqami*.

We do know of one success by immigration secondary inspection that affected the 9/11 plot. An al Qaeda operative, *Mohammed al Kahtani*, arrived at Orlando airport on August 4, 2001. Evidence strongly suggests that *Mohammed Atta* was waiting there to meet him. *Al Kahtani* encountered an experienced and dedicated inspector, Jose Melendez-Perez [who was alerted by *al Kahtani's* arrogant attitude and ultimately refused *al Kahtani* entry because of holes in the visitor's claim to be visiting the United States for a week-long tourist trip].

During their stays in the United States at least six of the 9/11 hijackers violated immigration laws. We have noted *Jarrah's* fail-

ure to adjust his status while he was in flight school and the violations by *Atta* and *al Shehhi*. *Hani Hanjour* came on a student visa
in December 2000 but then did not attend the English language
school for which his visa was issued. *Nawaf al Hazmi* overstayed
his term of admission by nine months. *Suqami* overstayed his
term of admission by four months. None of these violations were
detected or acted upon by INS inspectors or agents.

Two programs might have helped detect such violations. One
dealt with violations of student status. The other dealt with overstays.

National security concerns about foreign students are not
new. By the late 1980s the INS had established a Student/
School System to track students, but the system did not work.
After the 1993 World Trade Center bombing, when it was discovered that a participant in the plot had been a student who had
overstayed his visa, the Department of Justice asked INS to devise
a better way to track students. INS officials recommended a new
student tracking system and a student ID card that used biometric
identifiers.

In 1996, Congress mandated a new system to be installed by
1998, without appropriating program funds. The INS scraped
together $10 million and piloted a successful student tracking
program in the Atlanta area in June 1997, which included a flight
school. However, advocates of education interests argued that the
program would be burdensome and costly. Upon the order of
senior INS management, the project manager was replaced. In
1998, INS indefinitely deferred testing of the biometric student
ID card. The program stalled. Senators declared an interest in
repealing the 1996 law and sought to obstruct further INS funding for it. Thus, when *Atta* and *al Shehhi* lied when questioned
about their student status on their reentries in January 2001, and
when *Hanjour* failed to show up for the school for which he was
issued a visa in December 2000, a student tracking system was far
from available to immigration inspectors or agents.

Congress required the Attorney General to develop an entry-
exit system in 1996. The system's purpose was to improve INS's
ability to address illegal migration and overstays of all types of

foreign visitors. By 1998, Congress had appropriated about $40 million to develop the system. Advocates for border communities, however, were concerned that an entry-exit system would slow down trade. INS officials decided to forego the system at the land borders and only to automate the entry process. The automation process was not successful. The result was that when hijackers *Suqami* and *Nawaf al Hazmi* overstayed their visas, the system Congress envisaged did not exist. Moreover, when federal law enforcement authorities realized in late August 2001 that *al Mihdhar* had entered with *al Hazmi* in January 2000 at Los Angeles, they could not reliably determine whether or not *al Hazmi* was still in the United States, along with *al Mihdhar*.

CONCLUSION

The Director of the FBI testified that "[e]ach of the hijackers . . . came easily and lawfully from abroad." The Director of Central Intelligence described 17 of the 19 hijackers as "clean." We believe the information we have provided . . . gives the Commission the opportunity to reevaluate those statements. Based on our evaluation of the hijackers' travel documents, the visa process, the entries into the United States, and the compliance with immigration law while the attackers were here, we have a few observations. Considered collectively, the 9/11 hijackers:

- Included among them known al Qaeda operatives who could have been watchlisted;

- Presented passports "manipulated in a fraudulent manner";

- Presented passports with "suspicious indicators" of extremism;

- Made detectable false statements on their visa applications;

- Were pulled out of the travel stream and given greater scrutiny by border officials;

- Made false statements to border officials to gain entry to the United States; and

- Violated immigration laws while inside the United States.

These circumstances offered opportunities to intelligence and law enforcement officials. But our government did not fully exploit al Qaeda's travel vulnerabilities.

Why weren't they exploited? We do not have all the answers. Certainly neither the State Department's consular officers nor the INS's inspectors and agents were ever considered full partners in a national counterterrorism effort. This is exemplified by the Bureau of Consular Affairs' statement that before 9/11 they were not informed by anyone in the State Department or elsewhere that Saudi citizens could pose security risks. Nor were the Consular Affairs bureau or INS given the resources to perform an expanded mission. Between 1998 and 2001, visa applications rose by nearly a third, an increase of 2.5 million per year. Trained staff did not keep pace with the volume increase. In Jeddah and Riyadh, for example, each consular officer had responsibility for processing, on average, about 30,000 applications per year and routinely interviewed about 200 people per day.

The INS before 9/11 had about 2,000 agents for interior enforcement. As long as the top enforcement priorities were removal of criminal aliens and prosecution of employers who hired illegal aliens, a major counterterrorism effort would not have been possible. This is not to pass judgment on immigration policy generally. What we can do is highlight the way those policy choices affected counterterrorism efforts before 9/11, and potentially affect them today. For our front line border inspection services to have taken a substantially more proactive role in counterterrorism, their missions would have had to have been considered integral to our national security strategy and given commensurate resources.

Today, the level of systematic effort by the intelligence community focused on terrorist travel is much greater. But terrorist travel intelligence is still seen as a niche effort, interesting for specialists, but not central to counterterrorism. Nor have policymakers fully absorbed the information developed by terrorist mobility specialists. Much remains to be done, within the United States and internationally, on travel and identity document security, penalties and enforcement policy with respect to document fraud, and travel document screening efforts at the borders. If we have one conclusion from our work so far, it is that disrupting terrorist mobility globally is at least as important as disrupting terrorist finance as an integral part of counterterrorism.

Susan Ginsburg, Thomas Eldridge, and Janice Kephart-Roberts did most of the investigative work reflected in this statement. The Commission was able to build upon a large and strong body of work carried out by many talented public servants at the Department of State, the Central Intelligence Agency, the former Immigration and Naturalization Service, the Department of Homeland Security, and the Federal Bureau of Investigation.

Staff Statement No. 2

Three 9/11 Hijackers: Identification, Watchlisting and Tracking

The Congressional Joint Inquiry highlighted [the story of three individuals who helped carry out the 9/11 attacks, Nawaf al Hazmi, Salem al Hazmi and Khalid al Mihdhar] as one of failed opportunities to put these suspected terrorists on a watchlist to prevent them from entering the United States. Therefore the lesson learned, as Director of Central Intelligence George Tenet put it, was to do a better job of putting people on the watchlist, to correct what he called "a weakness in our internal training and an inconsistent understanding of watchlist thresholds."

We believe the portrayal of this story as a "watchlisting" failure may literally be true. But we think this label is profoundly misleading.

1. No one can know the might have beens. But we do not think it is likely that putting the three future hijackers on a watchlist would, by itself, have prevented the 9/11 attacks. As we pointed out earlier, al Qaeda adapted to the failure of some of its operatives to gain entry into the United States. None of these three individuals were pilots.

2. The watchlisting label reinforces the sense that watchlisting is a chore off to the side from core intelligence work. Of course everyone rightly acknowledges it is a necessary chore, something

that busy intelligence officials just have to remember to do. Yet they did not see it as an integral part of their own intelligence work. The opportunity to prevent the attacks would not have arisen just from preventing these people from entering the United States. It would have come from intelligence work that used watchlisting as a tool.

3. The watchlisting label also distorts the analysis of accountability. It tends to cast a harsh light on whether one or two people at Headquarters did their job. That focus may be unfair. It is certainly too narrow.

We suggest instead that the watchlisting failure was just one symptom of a larger intelligence failure. The failure raises questions for the Commission about the CIA's and the Intelligence Community's management of transnational intelligence operations.

We will do what we can to reconstruct this story, given the appropriate constraints on what can be said about such topics in public. It is detailed, but the details are essential.

THE INITIAL LEAD
AND THE HINDSIGHT ISSUE

The lead in this case came from the analysis of communications by the National Security Agency, or NSA. The NSA, and the intelligence community, obtains what it calls "signals intelligence," or SIGINT. Some sources relevant to this case are no longer operational. We are therefore able to say a little more about it now without disclosing any of the details about the methods used to collect such intelligence.

The Intelligence Community obtained additional sources after the Embassy bombings in East Africa. These particular sources were important. They offered insight into a larger al Qaeda network in the Middle East and were linked directly to the East Africa bombings.

In late 1999, NSA analyzed communications associated with a man named Khalid, a man named Nawaf, and a man named

Salem. NSA analysts at the time thought Salem was Nawaf's younger brother. They were right.

We now know Nawaf was in Karachi, Pakistan; Khalid was in Yemen; Nawaf planned to leave Karachi on January 2; and they were making plans to meet in Malaysia. Nawaf planned to leave Karachi on January 2. By early on December 31, Pakistani time, U.S. officials in Islamabad, Pakistan's capital, were following the situation.

At this point the relevant working-level officials in the Intelligence Community knew little more than this. But they correctly concluded that "Nawaf" and "Khalid" may be part of "an operational cadre" and that "something nefarious might be afoot."

We believe every available resource should have been devoted to learning who these people were, and trying to spot and track them.

- NSA did not think it was its job to initiate this research on its own. It saw itself as an agency to support consumers, such as CIA. It tried to respond energetically to any request made of them. But it tends to wait to be asked.

- If NSA had been asked to try to identify these people, NSA would have started by checking its own database of earlier information from these same sources. Some of this information had been reported and disseminated around the community. Some had not. But it was all readily accessible in NSA's database. NSA's analysts would promptly have discovered who Nawaf was, that his full name was Nawaf al Hazmi, and that he was an old friend of Khalid.

- NSA analysts also could then have readily inferred that Salem might be named Salem al Hazmi.

- But NSA was not asked to do this work, at least not until much, much later.

Some might say that such comments display 20/20 hindsight,

elevating the importance of these reports out of hundreds of items. This is a reasonable argument. But in this case we think our critique is fair, and not distorted by hindsight. Why?

- At the end of 1999 and in early 2000, the period of the Millennium Alert, the danger from al Qaeda was, by all accounts, the number one national security priority of the United States. It was a focus of practically daily meetings by the top officials of the government.

- These particular sources of information were especially important ones. Their links to al Qaeda were, in the words of one cable, "notorious." They had been linked directly with the East Africa Embassy attacks. The relevant analysts have told us that, at the time, these sources were among the very best on al Qaeda.

The Intelligence Community had reported that Nawaf and Khalid were deploying to meet in Kuala Lumpur.

KUALA LUMPUR

Following up on intelligence, U.S. officials were active in Yemen and in the United Arab Emirates, where Khalid would get his connecting flight. Other information reinforced the picture of an emerging operation of some kind, and Salem's plans to arrive in Yemen soon.

Nawaf, Khalid, and now Salem made further arrangements. Nawaf made plans to arrive in Malaysia on January 4. The Intelligence Community thought Nawaf was still in Pakistan and was not leaving there until the 4th. Other officials could have worked on logical flight itineraries and perhaps realized that Nawaf could—and probably did—keep to his original plan, leaving Pakistan for Southeast Asia on January 2. He then planned to—and did—leave his Asian stopover (probably Singapore) for Kuala Lumpur on January 4.

This detail matters because it meant that a possible opportunity to check and track Nawaf's departure from Pakistan had already been lost. Officials in Pakistan tried to do this on the 4th. They had already missed Nawaf.

On January 3 both CIA Headquarters and U.S. officials around the world began springing energetically into action. With the information about Khalid's travel itinerary, U.S. officials in Yemen, the United Arab Emirates, and Malaysia performed as well as could be hoped. Longstanding efforts to build relationships with friendly foreign services paid dividends.

Though they had missed Nawaf, officials had more success in tracking Khalid. He was identified as Khalid al Mihdhar. His Saudi passport was photocopied. It showed he had a visa to visit the United States. U.S. officials in Jeddah quickly confirmed that their post had issued this visa in April 1999.

Khalid al Mihdhar was tracked as he arrived at Kuala Lumpur on January 5. He and other Arabs, still unidentified, were surveilled as they congregated in the Malaysian capital. On January 5 CIA headquarters notified officials around the world that "we need to continue the effort to identify these travelers and their activities . . . to determine if there is any true threat posed. . . ." This same cable said the FBI had been notified. The cable also asserts that al Mihdhar's travel documents also were given to the FBI. The weight of available evidence does not support that latter assertion.

At this point the case was considered important enough to mention in the regular updates on al Qaeda being given to the top officials in the U.S. government. On January 3 and 5 the head of CIA's unit on al Qaeda apparently briefed his bosses on these developments as part of his regular daily updates. These updates, which included other ongoing operational developments, were usually reviewed every day by Director Tenet and by the [Clinton administration's] National Security Adviser, Sandy Berger. On January 5 and 6, the [at the time] Director of the FBI Louis Freeh, and other top FBI officials were briefed on the operation as one of their regular updates and were told, correctly, that CIA was in the lead and that CIA had promised to let FBI know if an FBI angle to the case developed.

On January 6 two of the Arabs being tracked in Malaysia left for new destinations, one in Thailand and another in Singapore. After the fact, efforts were made to track them. U.S. officials in Kuala Lumpur wondered if one of these Arabs was the still mysterious Nawaf. Both returned to Kuala Lumpur within the next 24 hours, though the authorities did not know it at the time. The two individuals apparently were Nawaf al Hazmi and an individual now known as Khallad bin Attash. We'll discuss Khallad again. . . .

On January 7, and then again on January 10, CIA headquarters notified the field that it had run searches on the names it had so far about this case and said these searches produced no "hits." Headquarters was trying to support the operations in the field. The field had given them information about people being tracked. Headquarters had checked CIA's own database and had found nothing.

These headquarters officials had not checked the databases at NSA or specifically asked NSA to do so. As mentioned earlier, if NSA had done this job its analysts would quickly have identified "Nawaf" as Nawaf al Hazmi. Someone then could have asked the State Department to check that name too. State would promptly have found its own record on Nawaf al Hazmi. That record would have shown that he too had been issued a visa to visit the United States. They would have learned that the visa had been issued at the same place—Jeddah—and on almost the same day as the one given to Khalid al Mihdhar. But none of this was known at the time.

On January 8, surveillance reported that three of the Arabs under surveillance suddenly left Kuala Lumpur on a short flight to Bangkok, traveling together. U.S. officials in Kuala Lumpur asked U.S. officials in Bangkok for help. The next day, Headquarters, noticing what was going on and working on a Sunday, backed up Kuala Lumpur's message with another message, marked NIACT Immediate. That meant the incoming cable would alert the duty officer and insure that it was read and acted upon regardless of the hour.

Kuala Lumpur was able to identify one of the travelers as

Khalid al Mihdhar. After the flight left they learned that one of his companions had the name Alhazmi. Remember that the officials did not have information that would have allowed them to put that last name together with the name they did know about—Nawaf.

About the third person all they had was part of a name. It was part of the name of the alias being used by Khallad bin Attash. "Khallad" is a nickname, the Arabic word for "silver," and refers to Khallad's artificial leg. Khallad was then traveling under an alias. One reason he may have been traveling around East Asia at this time is that he may have been helping to plan possible hijackings on aircraft, perhaps in connection with an early idea for what would become the 9/11 plot. Khallad also had completed his work in helping plan the destruction of a U.S. warship visiting Yemen, the U.S.S. *The Sullivans*. The attack had just failed—unnoticed. The boat filled with explosives had sunk. Only the terrorists knew what had gone wrong. Almost everything was salvaged and prepared for another day. Khallad would later be a principal planner in the next try, nine months later. That was the October 2000 attack on another U.S. ship visiting Yemen, the U.S.S. *Cole*, an attack which almost sank the warship and did kill 17 American sailors.

BANGKOK AND BEYOND

The information came to Bangkok too late to track these travelers as they came in. Had authorities in Bangkok already been alerted for Khalid al Mihdhar as part of a general regional or worldwide alert, they might have tracked him coming in. Had they been alerted to look for a possible companion named Nawaf, they might have noticed him too, and even tracked Khallad as well. Instead the authorities were alerted only after Kuala Lumpur sounded the alarm. By that time the travelers had already disappeared into the streets of Bangkok. We now know that two other al Qaeda operatives then flew to Bangkok to meet with Khallad in order to pass him money. Some of this money was reportedly given to al Hazmi and al Mihdhar for their upcoming work in the U.S. None of this was known at the time.

On January 12 the head of the CIA's al Qaeda unit updated his bosses that surveillance in Kuala Lumpur was continuing. He may not have known that in fact the Arabs had dispersed and the tracking was falling apart. U.S. officials in Bangkok regretfully reported the bad news on January 13. The names they had were put on a watchlist in Bangkok, so that Thai authorities might notice if they left the country.

U.S. intelligence did learn that one of the travelers was using the name that was Khallad's alias. Kuala Lumpur promptly asked for more information and agreement "to share that information for watch-listing purposes." There was no apparent response, and Kuala Lumpur did not follow through on its own watchlisting ideas.

On January 14 the head of the CIA's al Qaeda unit updated his bosses that officials were continuing to track the suspicious individuals who had now dispersed to various countries. Unfortunately, there is no evidence of any tracking efforts actually being undertaken by anyone after the Arabs disappeared into Bangkok.

CIA Headquarters asked NSA to put al Mihdhar on that agency's watchlist, which had limited effectiveness. But there was no other effort to consider the onward destinations of these Arabs and set up other opportunities to spot them in case the screen in Bangkok failed. Just from the evidence in al Mihdhar's passport, one of those possible destinations and interdiction points would logically have been the United States. Hence this watchlisting effort could have been seen as integral to reviving a faltering tracking effort, quite apart from the other interests involved.

Weeks passed. Meanwhile, NSA would occasionally pass new information, generally of a personal nature, associated with Khalid, Salem, Salem's brother (Nawaf), and perhaps Khallad as well. At this time, though the Intelligence Community did not know it, al Mihdhar was in San Diego, California.

None of these reports seem to have jogged renewed attention until another matter reminded Kuala Lumpur about the case.

That post prodded Bangkok a bit, in February, about what had happened with those missing Arabs.

A few weeks later, in early March 2000, Bangkok responded to Kuala Lumpur's question. It was reported that Nawaf al Hazmi, now identified for the first time with his full name, had departed on January 15, on a United Airlines flight to Los Angeles. We have found no evidence that this information was sent to the FBI.

It was further reported that a person under the name Khallad was using had departed Thailand for the last time on January 20. His destination was Karachi.

As for Khalid al Mihdhar, his arrival on January 8 had been noted, but there was no record of his departure. In fact al Mihdhar had been on the United flight to Los Angeles with al Hazmi on January 15.

We presume this departure information was obtained back in January, on the days that these individuals made their departures. Because these names were watchlisted with the Thai authorities, we cannot yet explain the delay in reporting this news. But, since nothing particular was done with this information even in March, we cannot attribute much significance to this failure alone.

By March 2000 al Mihdhar and al Hazmi had already established their residence in San Diego. No one knew this at the time, because no follow up was done with any of this information until much later.

In January 2001, while working on the *Cole* attack, the CIA received information that Khallad had attended the meeting in Kuala Lumpur. As Director Tenet testified publicly before the Joint Inquiry, the Kuala Lumpur meetings "took on greater significance" because this information placed the Arabs who were there with a known al Qaeda operative. This discovery, however, did not lead to any fresh effort to pick up the trail of al Mihdhar and al Hazmi. By that time al Mihdhar had left the United States and returned to Yemen. But if a retrospective of existing information had been conducted at this point, al Hazmi might have been tracked down in the United States. And there would still have been time to watchlist al Mihdhar before he obtained a new United States visa and reentered the U.S. to join in the 9/11 attacks.

Finally, in the summer of 2001, a thoughtful CIA official detailed to the FBI, working with an FBI employee detailed to the CIA, did some energetic detective work that at last unearthed and reexamined these old puzzle pieces. It became apparent that both al Mihdhar and al Hazmi were in the United States. They were watchlisted in late August 2001.

It was then too late to catch al Mihdhar before he got another visa and returned to the United States to rejoin the operation. The connection to Salem al Hazmi, Nawaf's younger brother, had never been made, so there was no effort to track his movements while in Yemen, watchlist him before he obtained his visa, or catch him as he entered the United States on a Swissair flight to New York in June 2001. The search in the United States for Nawaf al Hazmi and al Mihdhar began. It had gotten off to a stuttering, quarrelsome start by September 11.

THE WATCHLISTING ISSUE

The Department of State initiated and sponsored the U.S. government's only pre–9/11 watchlist solely dedicated to catching terrorists. This list, called TIPOFF, was created in 1987 by an unassuming and enterprising public servant named John Arriza, who still helps sustain the program, which is now considerably expanded. The program was meant to keep terrorists from getting visas, of course. But, as the name implies, it also was a system to tip off intelligence and law enforcement agencies that a suspected terrorist was attempting to come to the United States.

Any overseas post that obtained appropriate derogatory information about an individual had been told to enter it into TIPOFF by sending the appropriate cable. If the State Department's Bureau of Intelligence and Research saw the information, they could and often did take the initiative to add the individual into TIPOFF. In 2001 the State Department provided more source documents for TIPOFF than any other agency, more than 2,000.

In December 1999 CIA Headquarters had repeated this guidance to its posts overseas, which technically also included its al

Qaeda unit at Headquarters. In 2001 CIA provided more than 1,500 source documents to TIPOFF. It was CIA Headquarters that finally nominated al Hazmi and al Mihdhar for inclusion in TIPOFF.

Sharing of information with the FBI was vital from an intelligence perspective, if the individuals were coming into the United States. But FBI did not maintain the terrorist watchlist. That was the State Department's job. FBI could contribute names like everyone else. In 2001 the FBI provided about 60 source documents for TIPOFF, fewer than were obtained from the public media, and a number approximately equivalent to the contribution that year from the Australian intelligence service.

It is worth noting that the Federal Aviation Administration's own "no-fly" list was totally independent from TIPOFF. Few names were on this no-fly list. So, before 9/11, adding someone to TIPOFF would not have any particular effect on their ability to board a commercial flight inside the United States. So, to be specific, adding al Hazmi and al Mihdhar to TIPOFF did not put them on a no-fly list, and did not keep them from flying on September 11.

Therefore, in thinking about the question of accountability, that potential list tends to expand to everyone. In effect, though, this means no one. At the time of the Joint Inquiry report, the general assumption was that the responsibility rested with some working-level official at CIA Headquarters. Yet, as we can see, many of the recipients of those January 2000 cables could have done their part. Kuala Lumpur thought about it. And so on.

That is why we think this issue must be examined from a broader perspective, that of the overall management of transnational intelligence operations. After all, why would the watchlisting make a difference? One purpose would have been to turn al Hazmi and al Mihdhar back when they reached Los Angeles, in effect throwing them back into the sea. That would have served one purpose. But it might not have prevented any attacks.

We think it may be more interesting to consider the intelligence mission. Remember why "TIPOFF" had that name. The intelligence mission was why the suspects were tracked in

Malaysia rather than being detained and deported. If the FBI had been given the opportunity to monitor al Hazmi and al Mihdhar in California, and had been patient for months, or a year, then some larger results might have been possible, even after al Mihdhar left. The universe of possibilities expands after Hani Hanjour joined al Hazmi in December 2000, after which the two of them lived in Phoenix for several months before driving across the country and linking up with other future hijackers in northern Virginia. Up to this point all of these hijackers named so far were involved in the hijacking of American Airlines 77, which hit the Pentagon. But in northern Virginia they linked up with a hijacker who would join the team assigned to United 175, thus creating a possible opportunity to penetrate the other teams associated with the "Hamburg cell" as well.

These are difficult "what ifs." It is possible that the Intelligence Community might have judged that the risks of conducting such a prolonged intelligence operation were too high—the risk of losing track of potential terrorists, for example. It is possible that the pre–9/11 FBI would not have been judged capable of conducting such an operation. But surely the Intelligence Community would have preferred to have the chance to make these choices. That is why we see this as an intelligence story—and a challenge for Intelligence Community management.

MANAGEMENT OF A TRANSNATIONAL CASE

In trying to second-guess the management of intelligence operations, the staff feels humbled as we encounter the experience and hard work of so many of the officials we have interviewed. Although we have some very seasoned intelligence professionals on our staff, we have listened hard to what the serving officials have told us. As you can see, these people cared deeply about combating terrorism. They have poured much of their life energy into this cause. And we believe that many of them were working in a system that was not well designed to take full advantage of their accumulated talents.

From the detail of this case, one can see how hard it is for the Intelligence Community to assemble enough of the puzzle pieces gathered by different agencies to make some sense from them, and then coordinate needed action—to collect or to disrupt. It is especially hard to do all this in a transnational case. This was, and is, a challenge for management.

In this case, there appears to have been at least two strategic errors in management. First, the managers of the case failed to get an all source background analysis of the players, canvassing what all agencies might know so they could assemble the best possible picture for action. This omission is already evident by the end of December 1999.

The second strategic error was that the managers of the case did not systematically set up ways to track the hijackers as they moved in predictable directions. Even if they slipped through the net in Bangkok, it was foreseeable that a traveler with a U.S. visa in his passport might seek to visit the United States. No one had the clear job of insuring that all the likely routes were covered.

Who had the job of managing the case to make sure these things were done? One answer is that everyone had the job. That was the perspective the Commission heard in its interview of the CIA's Deputy Director for Operations, James Pavitt. Deputy Director Pavitt has been at or near the top of this Directorate for about six and a half years. He stressed that the responsibility resided with all involved. Above all he stressed the primacy of the field. The field had the lead in managing operations. The job of Headquarters, he stressed, was to support the field, and do so without delay. If the field asked for information or other support, the job of Headquarters was to get it—right away.

This is a traditional perspective on operations and, traditionally, it has great merit. It reminded us of the FBI's pre–9/11 emphasis on the primacy of their Field Offices. When asked about how this traditional structure would adapt to the challenge of managing a transnational case, one that hopped from place to place as this one did, the Deputy Director argued that all involved were responsible for making it work. He underscored the responsibility of the particular field location where the suspects were being tracked at any given time. On the other hand, he also said that the Counterterrorism Center was supposed to "manage all the moving parts," while what happened on the ground was the responsibility of managers in the field.

With this background, it is easier to understand why the way Headquarters handled this case may not have been so unusual. As pointed out [earlier], travel intelligence was not seen as a central concern. Headquarters tended to support and facilitate, trying to make sure everyone was in the loop. From time to time a particular post would push one way, or Headquarters would urge someone to do something, but Headquarters never really took responsibility for the successful management of this case. Hence the managers at Headquarters did not realize that the two strategic errors cited above had occurred, and they scarcely knew that the case had fallen apart.

The director of the Counterterrorism Center at the time, Cofer Black, recalled to us that this operation was one among many and that, at the time, "it was considered interesting, but not heavy water yet." He recalls the failure to get the word to Bangkok fast enough, but has no evident recollection of why the case then dissolved, unnoticed.

Going the next level down, the director of the al Qaeda unit in CIA at the time recalled to us that he did not think it was his job to direct what should or should not be done. He did not pay attention when the individuals dispersed and things fell apart. He would not have expected NSA to do the retrospective work in its own database. But he was uncertain of his own authority to order them to do it. There was no conscious decision to stop the operation after the trail was temporarily lost in Bangkok. But he acknowledged that perhaps there had been a letdown after the extreme tension and long hours in the period of the Millennium Alert.

We believe both Black and the former al Qaeda unit head are capable veterans of the Directorate of Operations, among the best the Agency has produced. Therefore we find these accounts more telling about the system than about the people. In this system no one was managing the effort to ensure seamless handoffs of information or develop an overall interagency strategy for the operation.

Such management of transnational operations, fully integrating all source analysis, might require more employees. Deputy Director Pavitt told us, as he has told Congress, that he does not think the availability of more money would have prevented the 9/11 attacks. We are not sure that is right. Certainly since 9/11 the application of vast new resources within older management models has achieved some significant gains.

But this story is not just about the past. We wonder whether the management of transnational intelligence operations has adapted enough to cope with the challenge of the war on terrorism. Today's focus on travel intelligence has spotlighted the transnational character of the problem. This particular story is especially tragic. But we do not believe this operating style is unique to this case. We are not sure that these problems have been addressed. We are not sure they are even adequately acknowledged as a problem.

In an environment driven by reactions to the latest threat report and preoccupied with immediate operations, clear, accountable, and strategic management is a challenge. The Intelligence Community must overcome it.

––––––––

Douglas MacEachin, Barbara Grewe, Susan Ginsburg, Lloyd Salvetti, Alexis Albion, Thomas Eldridge, Michael Hurley, and Lorry Fenner did most of the investigative work reflected in this statement. Our staff was fortunate. We could build upon a substantial body of work carried out by the Joint Inquiry organized in 2002 by the intelligence committees of the House and Senate. We also relied on some high quality work performed by the National Security Agency, along with cooperation from the Central Intelligence Agency and the Department of State.

Staff Statement No. 3

The Aviation Security System
and the 9/11 Attacks

Before September 11, 2001, the aviation security system had been enjoying a period of relative peace. No U.S. flagged aircraft had been bombed or hijacked in over a decade. Domestic hijacking in particular seemed like a thing of the past, something that could only happen to foreign airlines that were less well protected.

The public's own "threat assessment" before September 11 was sanguine about commercial aviation safety and security. In a Fox News/Opinion Dynamics survey conducted at the end of the 1990s, 78 percent cited poor maintenance as "a greater threat to airline safety" than terrorism.

Demand for air service was strong and was beginning to exceed the capacity of the system. Heeding constituent calls for improved air service and increased capacity, Congress focused its legislative and oversight attention on measures to address these problems, including a "passenger bill of rights" to assure a more efficient and convenient passenger experience.

The leadership of the Federal Aviation Administration (FAA) also focused on safety, customer service, capacity and economic issues. The agency's security agenda was focused on efforts to implement a three-year-old Congressional mandate to deploy explosives detection equipment at all major airports and complete a nearly five-year-old rulemaking effort to improve checkpoint screening.

This staff statement will not address certain security performance issues leading up to 9/11 at the airports from which the hijacked planes departed. Such work is still ongoing. It should be noted that the airports themselves did not have operational or enforcement jurisdiction over checkpoint screening operations. Passenger prescreening and checkpoint screening, based on regulations from the FAA, were the responsibility of the air carriers. Nevertheless, airport authorities do play a key role in the overall civil aviation security system.

CIVIL AVIATION SECURITY DEFENSES

Before September 11, federal law required the FAA to set and enforce aviation security policies and regulations that would "protect passengers and property on an aircraft operating in air transportation or intra-state air transportation against an act of criminal violence or aircraft piracy." The layered system, one that recognized that no single security measure was flawless or impenetrable, was designed to provide a greater number of opportunities to foil those intending to do such violence.

The Civil Aviation Security system in place on September 11 was composed of seven layers of defense including:

- intelligence;
- passenger prescreening;
- airport access control;
- passenger checkpoint screening;
- passenger checked baggage screening;
- cargo screening; and
- on-board security.

The civil aviation security system in place on September 11 no longer exists. We will document serious shortcomings in that system's design and implementation that made the 9/11 hijackings possible. We want to make clear that our findings of specific vulnerabilities and shortcomings do not necessarily apply to the current system.

Two of the layers of defense—checked baggage screening and cargo security—are not relevant to the 9/11 plot. They are not addressed in this statement. A third layer, airport access control, is still under investigation and also will not be addressed in detail. Compelling evidence, including videotape of hijackers entering through checkpoint screening stations, suggests that the hijackers gained access to the aircraft on September 11 through passenger checkpoints. What we do know is that the hijackers successfully evaded or defeated the remaining four layers of the security system.

THE ENEMY VIEW

We approach the question of how the aviation security system failed on September 11 by starting from the perspective of the enemy, asking, "What did al Qaeda have to do to complete its mission?"

Sometime during the late 1990s, the al Qaeda leadership made the decision to hijack large, commercial, multi-engine aircraft and use them as a devastating weapon as opposed to hijacking a commercial aircraft for use as a bargaining tool. To carry out that decision would require unique skill sets:

- terrorists trained as pilots with the specialized skill and confidence to successfully fly large, multi-engine aircraft, already airborne, into selected targets;

- tactics, techniques, and procedures to successfully conduct in-flight hijackings; and

- operatives willing to die.

To our knowledge, 9/11 was the first time in history that terrorists actually piloted a commercial jetliner in a terrorist operation. This was new. This could not happen overnight and would require long term planning and sequenced operational training.

The terrorists had to determine the tactics and techniques needed to succeed in hijacking an aircraft within the United States. The vulnerabilities of the U.S. domestic commercial aviation security system were well advertised through numerous unclassified reports from agencies like the General Accounting Office and the Department of Transportation's Inspector General. The news media had publicized those findings.

The al Qaeda leadership recognized the need for more specific information. Its agents observed the system first-hand and conducted surveillance flights both internationally and within the United States. Over time, this information allowed them to revise and refine the operational plan. By the spring of 2001, the September 11 operation had combined intent with capabilities to present a real and present threat to the civil aviation system. As long as operational security was maintained, the plan had a high probability of success in conducting multiple, near simultaneous attacks on New York City and Washington, DC.

Let us turn now to a more specific look at the security system in place on September 11 related to anti-hijacking.

INTELLIGENCE

The first layer of defense was intelligence. While the FAA was not a member of the U.S. Intelligence Community, the agency maintained a civil aviation intelligence division that operated 24 hours per day. The intelligence watch was the collection point for a flow of threat related information from federal agencies, particularly the FBI, CIA, and State Department. FAA intelligence personnel were assigned as liaisons to work within these three agencies to facilitate the flow of aviation related information to the FAA and to promote inter-departmental cooperation. The FAA did not assign liaisons to either the National Security Agency or the Defense Intelligence Agency but maintained intelligence requirements with those agencies.

Intelligence data received by the FAA went into preparing Intelligence Case Files. These files tracked and assessed the significance of aviation security incidents, threats and emerging issues. The FAA's analysis of this data informed its security policies, including issuance of FAA Information Circulars, Security Directives, and Emergency Amendments. Such Security Directives and Emergency Amendments are how the FAA ordered air carriers and/or airports to undertake certain extraordinary security measures that were needed immediately above the established baseline.

While the staff has not completed its review and analysis as to what the FAA knew about the threat posed by al Qaeda to civil aviation, including the potential use of aircraft as weapons, we can say:

First, no documentary evidence reviewed by the Commission or testimony we have received to this point has revealed that any level of the FAA possessed any credible and specific intelligence indicating that Osama bin Laden, al Qaeda, al Qaeda affiliates or any other group were actually plotting to hijack commercial planes in the United States and use them as weapons of mass destruction.

Second, the threat posed by Osama bin Laden, al Qaeda, and al Qaeda affiliates, including their interest in civil aviation, was well known to key civil aviation security officials. The potential threat of Middle Eastern terrorist groups to civil aviation security was acknowledged in many different official FAA documents. The FAA possessed information claiming that associates with Osama bin Laden in the 1990s were interested in hijackings and the use of an aircraft as a weapon.

Third, the potential for terrorist suicide hijacking in the United States was officially considered by the FAA's Office of Civil Aviation Security dating back to at least March 1998. However, in a presentation the agency made to air carriers and airports in 2000 and early 2001 the FAA discounted the threat because, "fortunately, we have no indication that any group is currently thinking in that direction."

It wasn't until well after the 9/11 attacks that the FAA learned of the "Phoenix EC"—an internal FBI memo written in July of 2001 by an FBI agent in the Phoenix field office suggesting steps that should be taken by the Bureau to look more closely at civil aviation education schools around the country and the use of such programs by individuals who may be affiliated with terrorist organizations.

Fourth, the FAA was aware prior to September 11, 2001, of the arrest of Zacarias Moussaoui in Minnesota, a man arrested by the INS in August of 2001 following reports of suspicious behavior in flight school and the determination that he had overstayed his visa waiver period. Several key issues remain regarding what the FAA knew about Moussaoui, when they knew it, and how they responded to the information supplied by the FBI, which we are continuing to pursue.

Fifth, the FAA did react to the heightened security threat identified by the Intelligence Community during the summer of 2001, including issuing alerts to air carriers about the potential for terrorist acts against civil aviation. In July 2001, the FAA alerted the aviation community to reports of possible near-term terrorist operations . . . particularly on the Arabian Peninsula and/or Israel. The FAA informed the airports and air carriers that it had no credible evidence of specific plans to attack U.S. civil aviation. The agency said that some of the currently active groups were known to plan and train for hijackings and had the capability to construct sophisticated improvised explosive devices concealed inside luggage and consumer products. The FAA encouraged all U.S. Carriers to exercise prudence and demonstrate a high degree of alertness.

Although several civil aviation security officials testified that the FAA felt blind when it came to assessing the domestic threat because of the lack of intelligence on what was going on in the American homeland as opposed to overseas, FAA security analysts did perceive an increasing terrorist threat to U.S. civil aviation at home. FAA documents, including agency accounts published in the Federal Register on July 17, 2001, expressed the FAA's understanding that terrorist groups were active in the United States and maintained an historic interest in targeting aviation, including hijacking. While the agency was engaged in an effort to pass important new regulations to improve checkpoint screener performance, implement anti-sabotage measures, and conduct ongoing assessments of the system, no major increases in anti-hijacking security measures were implemented in response to the heightened threat levels in the spring and summer of 2001, other than general warnings to the industry to be more vigilant and cautious.

Sixth, the civil aviation security system in the United States during the summer of 2001 stood, as it had for quite some time, at an intermediate aviation security alert level—tantamount to a permanent Code Yellow. This level, and its corresponding security measures, was required when:

> Information indicates that a terrorist group or other hostile entity with a known capability of attacking civil aviation is likely to carry out attacks against U.S. targets; or civil disturbances with a direct impact on civil aviation have begun or are imminent.

Without actionable intelligence information to uncover and interdict a terrorist plot in the planning stages or prior to the perpetrator gaining access to the aircraft in the lead-up to September 11, 2001, it was up to the other layers of aviation security to counter the threat.

We conclude this section with a final observation. The last major terrorist attack on a U.S. flagged airliner had been with smuggled explosives, in 1988, in the case of Pan Am 103. The famous Bojinka plot broken up in Manila in 1995 had principally been a plot to smuggle explosives on airliners. The Commission on Aviation Safety and Security created by President Clinton in 1996, named the Gore Commission for its chairman, the Vice President, had focused overwhelmingly on the danger of explosives on aircraft. Historically, explosives on aircraft had taken a heavy death toll, hijackings had not. So, despite continued foreign hijackings leading up to 9/11, the U.S. aviation security system worried most about explosives.

PRESCREENING

If intelligence fails to interdict the terrorist threat, passenger prescreening is the next layer of defense. Passenger prescreening encompasses measures applied prior to the passenger's arrival at the security checkpoint. Prescreening starts with the ticketing process, and generally concludes with passenger check-in at the airport ticket counter.

The hijackers purchased their tickets for the 9/11 flights in a short period of time at the end of August 2001, using credit cards, debit cards, or cash. The ticket record provides the FAA and the air carrier with passenger information for the prescreening process.

The first major prescreening element in place on 9/11 was the FAA listing of individuals known to pose a threat to commercial aviation. Based on information provided by the Intelligence Community, the FAA required air carriers to prohibit listed individuals from boarding aircraft or, in designated cases, to assure that the passenger received enhanced screening before boarding. None of the names of the 9/11 hijackers were identified by the FAA to the airlines in order to bar them from flying or subject them to extra security measures. In fact, the number of individuals subject to such special security instructions issued by the FAA was less than 20 compared to the tens of thousands of names identified in the State Department's TIPOFF watch list. . . .

The second component of prescreening was a program to identify those passengers on each flight who may pose a threat to aviation. In 1998, the FAA required air carriers to implement an FAA-approved computer-assisted passenger prescreening program (CAPPS) designed to identify the pool of passengers most likely in need of additional security scrutiny. The program employed customized, FAA-approved criteria derived from a limited set of information about each ticketed passenger in order to identify "selectees."

FAA rules required that the air carrier only screen each selectee's checked baggage for explosives using various approved methods. However, under the system in place on 9/11, selectees

—those who were regarded as a risk to the aircraft—were not required to undergo any additional screening of their person or carry-on baggage at the checkpoint.

The consequences of selection reflected FAA's view that non-suicide bombing was the most substantial risk to domestic aircraft. Since the system in place on 9/11 confined the consequences of selection to the screening of checked bags for explosives, the application of CAPPS did not provide any defense against the weapons and tactics employed by the 9/11 hijackers.

On American Airlines Flight 11, CAPPS chose three of the five hijackers as selectees. Since Waleed al Shehri checked no bags, his selection had no consequences. Wail al Shehri and Satam al Suqami had their checked bags scanned for explosives before they were loaded onto the plane.

None of the Flight 175 hijackers were selected by CAPPS.

All five of the American Airlines Flight 77 hijackers were selected for security scrutiny. Hani Hanjour, Khalid al Mihdhar, and Majed Moqed were chosen via the CAPPS criteria, while Nawaf al Hazmi and Salem al Hazmi were made selectees because they provided inadequate identification information. Their bags were held until it was confirmed that they had boarded the aircraft.

Thus, for hijacker selectees Hani Hanjour, Nawaf al Hazmi, and Khalid al Mihdhar, who checked no bags on September 11, there were no consequences for their selection by the CAPPS system. For Salem al Hazmi, who checked two bags, and Majed Moqed, who checked one bag, the sole consequence was that their baggage was held until after their boarding on Flight 77 was confirmed.

Ahmad al Haznawi was the sole CAPPS selectee among the Flight 93 hijackers. His checked bag was screened for explosives and then loaded on the plane.

CHECKPOINT SCREENING

With respect to checkpoint screening, Federal rules required air carriers "to conduct screening . . . to prevent or deter the carriage aboard airplanes of any explosive, incendiary, or a deadly or dangerous weapon on or about each individual's person or accessible property, and the carriage of any explosive or incendiary in check baggage." Passenger checkpoint screening is the most obvious element of aviation security.

At the checkpoint, metal detectors were calibrated to detect guns and large knives. Government-certified X-ray machines capable of imaging the shapes of items possessing a particular level of acuity were used to screen carry-on items. In most instances, these screening operations were conducted by security companies under contract with the responsible air carrier.

As of 2001 any confidence that checkpoint screening was operating effectively was belied by numerous publicized studies by the General Accounting Office and the Department of Transportation's Office of Inspector General. Over the previous twenty years they had documented repeatedly serious, chronic weaknesses in the systems deployed to screen passengers and baggage for weapons or bombs. Shortcomings with the screening process had also been identified internally by the FAA's assessment process.

Despite the documented shortcomings of the screening system, the fact that neither a hijacking nor a bombing had occurred domestically in over a decade was perceived by many within the system as confirmation that it was working. This explains, in part, the view of one transportation security official who testified to the Commission that the agency thought it had won the battle against hijacking. In fact, the Commission received testimony that one of the primary reasons to restrict the consequences of CAPPS "selection" was because officials thought that checkpoint screening was working.

The evolution of checkpoint screening illustrates many of the systemic problems that faced the civil aviation security system in place on 9/11. The executive and legislative branches of government, and the civil aviation industry were highly reactive on aviation security matters. Most of the aviation security system's features had developed in response to specific incidents, rather than in anticipation. Civil aviation security was primarily accomplished through a slow and cumbersome rulemaking process—a reflection of the agency's conflicting missions of both regulating and promoting the industry. A number of FAA witnesses said this process was the "bane" of civil aviation security. For example, the FAA attempted to set a requirement that it would certify screening contractors. The FAA Aviation Reauthorization Act of 1996 directed the FAA to take such action, which the 1997 Gore Commission endorsed. But the process of implementing this action had still not been completed by September 11, 2001.

Those are systemic observations. But, to analyze the 9/11 attack, we had to focus on which items were prohibited and which were allowed to be carried into the cabin of an aircraft. FAA guidelines were used to determine what objects should not be allowed into the cabin of an aircraft. Included in the listing were knives with blades 4 inches long or longer and/or knives considered illegal by local law; and tear gas, mace, and similar chemicals.

These guidelines were to be used by screeners to make a reasonable determination of what items in the possession of a person should be considered a deadly or dangerous weapon. The FAA told the air carriers that common sense should prevail.

Hence the standards of what constituted a deadly or dangerous weapon were somewhat vague. Other than for guns, large knives, explosives and incendiaries, determining what was prohibited and what was allowable was up to the common sense of the carriers and their screening contractors.

To write out what common sense meant to them, the air carriers developed, through their trade associations, a Checkpoint Operations Guide. This document was approved by the FAA. The edition of this guide in place on September 11, 2001, classified "box cutters," for example, as "Restricted" items that were not permitted in the passenger cabin of an aircraft. The checkpoint supervisor was required to be notified if an item in this category was encountered. Passengers would be given the option of having those items transported as checked baggage. "Mace," "pepper spray," as well as "tear gas" were categorized as hazardous materials and passengers could not take items in that category on an airplane without the express permission of the airline.

On the other hand, pocket utility knives (less than 4 inch blade) were allowed. The Checkpoint Operations Guide provided no further guidance on how to distinguish between "box cutters" and "pocket utility knives."

One of the checkpoint supervisors working at Logan International Airport on September 11, 2001, recalled that as of that day, while box cutters were not permitted to pass through the checkpoint without the removal of the blade, any knife with a blade of less than four inches was permitted to pass through security.

In practice, we believe the FAA's approach of admonishing air carriers to use common sense about what items should not be allowed on an aircraft, while also approving the air carrier's checkpoint operations guidelines that defined the industry's "common sense," in practice, created an environment where both parties could deny responsibility for making hard and most likely unpopular decisions.

What happened at the checkpoints? Of the checkpoints used to screen the passengers of Flights 11, 77, 93 and 175 on 9/11, only Washington Dulles International Airport had videotaping equipment in place. Therefore the most specific information that exists about the processing of the 9/11 hijackers is information about American Airlines Flight 77, which crashed into the Pentagon. The staff has also reviewed testing results for all the checkpoints in question, scores of interviews with checkpoint screeners and supervisors who might have processed the hijackers, and FAA and FBI evaluations of the available information. There is no reason to believe that the screening on 9/11 was fundamentally different at any of the relevant airports.

Return again to the perspective of the enemy. The plan required all of the hijackers to successfully board the assigned aircraft. If several of their number failed to board, the operational plan might fall apart or their operational security might be breached. To have this kind of confidence, they had to develop a plan they felt would work anywhere they were screened, regardless of the quality of the screener. We believe they developed such a plan and practiced it in the months before the attacks, including in test flights, to be sure their tactics would work. In other words, we believe they did not count on a sloppy screener. All 19 hijackers were able to pass successfully through checkpoint screening to board their flights. They were 19 for 19. They counted on beating a weak system.

Turning to the specifics of Flight 77 checkpoint screening, at 7:18 A.M. Eastern Daylight Time on the morning of September 11, 2001, Majed Moqed and Khalid al Mihdhar entered one of the security screening checkpoints at Dulles International Airport. They placed their carry-on bags on the X-ray machine belt and proceeded through the first magnetometer. Both set off the alarm and were subsequently directed to a second magnetometer. While al Mihdhar did not alarm the second magnetometer and was permitted through the checkpoint, Moqed failed once more and was then subjected to a personal screening with a metal detection hand wand. He passed this inspection and then was permitted to pass through the checkpoint.

At 7:35 A.M. Hani Hanjour placed two carry-on bags on the X-ray belt in the Main Terminal checkpoint, and proceeded, without alarm, through the magnetometer. He picked up his carry-on bags and passed through the checkpoint. One minute later, Nawaf and Salem al Hazmi entered the same checkpoint. Salem al Hazmi successfully cleared the magnetometer and was permitted through the checkpoint. Nawaf al Hazmi set off the alarms for both the first and second magnetometers and was then hand-wanded before being passed. In addition, his shoulder-strap carry-on bag was swiped by an explosive trace detector and then passed.

Our best working hypothesis is that a number of the hijackers were carrying permissible utility knives or pocket knives. One example of such a utility knife is [the] "Leatherman" item. . . . It is very sharp.

According to the guidelines on 9/11, if such a knife were discovered in the possession of an individual who alarmed either the walk-through metal detector or the hand wand, the item would be returned to the owner and permitted to be carried on the aircraft.

ONBOARD SECURITY

Once the hijackers were able to get through the checkpoints and board the plane, the last layer of defense was onboard security. That layer was comprised of two main components: the presence of law enforcement on the flights and the so-called "Common Strategy" for responding to in-flight security emergencies, including hijacking, devised by the Federal Aviation Administration in consultation with industry and law enforcement.

But on the day of September 11, 2001, after the hijackers boarded, they faced no significant security obstacles. The Federal Air Marshal Program was almost exclusively directed to international flights. Cockpit doors were not hardened. Gaining access to the cockpit was not a particularly difficult challenge.

Flight crews were trained not to attempt to thwart or fight the hijackers. The object was to get the plane to land safely. Crews were trained, in fact, to dissuade passengers from taking precipitous or "heroic" actions against hijackers. . . .

CONCLUSION

From all of the evidence staff has reviewed to date, we have come to the conclusion that on September 11, 2001, would-be hijackers of domestic flights of U.S. civil aviation faced these challenges:

- avoiding prior notice by the U.S. intelligence and law enforcement communities;

- carrying items that could be used as weapons that were either permissible or not detectable by the screening systems in place; and

- understanding and taking advantage of the in-flight hijacking protocol of the Common Strategy.

A review of publicly available literature and/or the use of "test runs" would likely have improved the odds of achieving those tasks.

The "no-fly" lists offered an opportunity to stop the hijackers, but the FAA had not been provided any of their names, even though two of them were already watchlisted in TIPOFF. The prescreening process was effectively irrelevant to them. The on-board security efforts, like the Federal Air Marshal program, had eroded to the vanishing point. So the hijackers really had to beat just one layer of security—the security checkpoint process.

Plotters who were determined, highly motivated individuals, who escaped notice on no-fly lists, who studied publicly available vulnerabilities of the aviation security system, who used items with a metal content less than a handgun and most likely permissible, and who knew to exploit training received by aircraft personnel to be non-confrontational were likely to be successful in hijacking a domestic U.S. aircraft.

This staff statement represents the collective effort of the Aviation and Transportation Security Team. Our staff was able to build upon investigative work that has been conducted by various agencies, including the Federal Bureau of Investigation. The Department of Homeland Security's Transportation Security Administration is fully cooperating with our investigators, as are the relevant airlines and the Federal Aviation Administration.

Staff Statement No. 4

———

The Four Flights

We [reported earlier] about how the hijackers defeated all of the pre-boarding defense layers the U.S. civil aviation security system mounted on September 11, 2001. We will return now to the last line of defense, the Common Strategy in response to hijackings, as implemented onboard the aircraft by the flight crew.

COMMON STRATEGY

The anti-hijacking training for civil aviation aircraft crews in place on 9/11 was based on previous experiences with domestic and international hijacking and other hostage situations. It was aimed at getting passengers, crew, and hijackers safely landed. It offered little guidance for confronting a suicide hijacking.

Air carrier responsibilities for security and anti-hijacking training for flight crews were set forth in the Air Carrier Standard Security Program. In addition to specifying several hours of security training, it provided an outline of inflight hijacking tactics for both the cockpit and cabin crews. Among other things, this outline advised air crews to refrain from trying to overpower or negotiate with hijackers, to land the aircraft as soon as possible, to communicate with authorities, and to try delaying tactics.

One of the FAA officials most involved with the Common Strategy in the period leading up to 9/11 described it as an approach dating back to the early 1980s, developed in consultation with the industry and the FBI, and based on the historical record of hijackings. The point of the strategy was to "optimize actions taken by a flight crew to resolve hijackings peacefully" through systematic delay and, if necessary, accommodation of the hijackers. The record had shown that the longer a hijacking persisted, the more likely it was to have a peaceful resolution. The strategy operated on the fundamental assumptions that hijackers issue negotiable demands, most often for asylum or the release of prisoners, and that "suicide wasn't in the game plan" of hijackers.

Thus, on September 11, 2001, the Common Strategy, the last line of defense, offered no defense against the tactics employed by the hijackers of Flights 11, 77, 93 and 175.

THE HIJACKINGS OF SEPTEMBER 11, 2001

The day of Tuesday, September 11, 2001, began for U.S. civil aviation as one marked by exceptionally fine weather across the country, and the absence of any significant overnight problems requiring attention as the workday shifts took over across the system. . . .

We first wish to pay tribute to the brave men and women who are the source for most of what we know about what transpired onboard American Airlines Flight 11, United Airlines Flight 175, American Airlines Flight 77 and United Airlines Flight 93. [The heroes include] Flight Attendant Betty Ong who perished on Flight 11. . . . American Airlines Reservations Manager Nydia Gonzalez . . . spoke with Ms. Ong on that tragic morning and made sure that her voice was heard then, and continues to be heard to this day. But there are many others we wish to recognize, both passengers and crew, who were able to reach out to let their companies, friends, or families know what had befallen them, and in so doing enable us to tell their story. . . . Among them are:

- Also from Flight 11, Betty Ong's fellow Flight Attendant Madeline "Amy" Sweeney

- From Flight 175, Flight Attendant Robert Fangman, and passengers Peter Burton Hanson and Brian David Sweeney

- From Flight 77, Flight Attendant Rene May and passenger Barbara Olson

- From Flight 93, Flight Attendants Ceecee Lyles and Sandy Bradshaw, and passengers Todd Beamer and Jeremiah Glick.

There is every indication that all members of the flight crews did their duty with dedication and professionalism.

HIJACKER TACTICS

What do we know about the tactics used in the takeover of the four flights?

The hijackers strategically planned the flights they chose—early morning departures from east coast airports of large Boeing 757 and 767 aircraft fueled for a transcontinental flight to maximize the destructive power of the impact on their selected targets.

There is no evidence to suggest that the 9/11 hijackers or their associates purchased unused tickets for the hijacked flights. . . . [T]he seats selected by each hijacker team appear to have been determined by aircraft type, the Boeing 757 for Flights 77 and 93, and the Boeing 767 for Flights 11 and 175. The seat selections clearly recognized the difference between the single aisle (Boeing 757) and double aisle (Boeing 767) configurations. Thus for Flights 77 and 93, in order to ensure the hijacker pilot had ready access to the cockpit, he was seated in the very front of the plane, with the others placed close behind in First Class. For the twin-aisled Flights 11 and 175, which offer more operational maneuverability, the hijacker pilot sat in Business Class with accomplices both in front in First Class and just behind, covering both aisles.

The question has been raised about whether one or more of the hijackers may have used pilot's credentials in order to sit in the cockpit with the pilots during the flight to facilitate the takeover. A review of the requisite paperwork and other procedures, which must be followed to permit such "jump seat" privileges, provides no evidence that such a tactic was used by the hijackers.

We do know that the seating arrangement chosen by the hijackers facilitated the isolation of the front of the aircraft and the terrorist pilot's entry into the cockpit. The exact method of entry is not known. The strength of the cockpit doors in use on 9/11 would not have precluded forced entry. Cockpit keys were widely available on that day. Also, the Common Strategy did authorize flight crews to allow entry into the cockpit under certain circumstances. There is no way to know whether the terrorists had access to a key, but if not, access to the cockpit could be readily gained by luring the flight deck crew out of the cockpit or forcing the door open.

From what we have learned so far, the hijackers successfully gained control of the forward section of the cabin after the aircraft's seatbelt sign was turned off, the Flight Attendants began cabin service, and passengers were allowed to begin to move around the cabin. This was followed by the hijackers gaining access to the cockpit. There is scattered and conflicting evidence about what happened to the cockpit crew during the takeover, but what we do know is that at some point, the pilots were displaced and no longer in command of the aircraft.

The evidence we have examined to date indicates that the terrorists' tactics and techniques initially resembled the traditional hijacking scenarios.

The hijackers took over the aircraft by force or threat of force. This was reported on all four flights.

The hijackers gained access to the cockpit and sealed off the front of the aircraft from the passengers and cabin crew. This was reported, with slight variation, on all four flights.

Some of these reports included the presence of mace and/or

pepper spray in the cabin, and indications that passengers had difficulty breathing. We believe this indicates that the terrorists created a "sterile" area around the cockpit by isolating the passengers and attempting to keep them away from the forward cabin, in part, by using mace or pepper spray. Pepper spray was found in Atta's checked luggage that was recovered at Logan Airport.

The hijackers used the threat of bombs. This was reported for all but Flight 77. They also used announcements (reported for Flights 11, 77, and 93) to control the passengers, as the aircraft supposedly flew to an airport destination.

These long standing tactics for terrorist hijackings were consistent with the paradigm of the Common Strategy developed for flight crew response to hijackings. There were no reasons for the flight crew to respond outside the training they had received at the time their respective flight was hijacked.

Even so, as the hijackings progressed, there is evidence of growing awareness onboard the aircraft that something extraordinary was unfolding. Callers from both Flights 11 and 175 noted early in the process very erratic flying patterns and talked about the possibility that the hijackers were piloting the aircraft. Reports from Flight 175 included one passenger predicting the hijackers intended to fly the aircraft into a building. Another said the passengers were considering storming the cockpit.

Later, on Flight 77, at least one passenger was explicitly informed about what had happened to Flights 11 and 175. And, as is widely known in the case of Flight 93, the growing awareness among the passengers of what had already occurred with the other flights spurred a heroic attempt to take over the plane from the hijackers. The nation owes an eternal debt of gratitude to those who took action to ensure that Flight 93 never reached its target.

PILOT TRAINING

To successfully complete the 9/11 plot aboard the aircraft, at least one member of the team had to be able to pilot the plane, navigate it to the desired location, and direct it into the intended target. These tasks required extensive training and preparation.

FAA records show that four of the 19 hijackers—one aboard each flight—possessed FAA certificates as qualified pilots. FAA certification required that a candidate complete a requisite amount of flight training and pass both a written exam and practical skills test. Each of the four pilots received flight training in the United States, which is recognized as having one of the world's most advanced pilot training education and certification systems, and trains many pilots from many nations.

Among the five hijackers of American Airlines Flight 11, only Mohammed Atta held a certificate from the FAA as a qualified private and commercial pilot, including proficiency rating in multi-engine aircraft operation. Atta received his commercial pilot certificate in December 2000. Records indicate that Atta received Boeing flight simulator training sessions.

According to experts questioned by Commission staff, simulator training was critical for the hijacker to familiarize himself with the cockpit controls and proper operation of the Boeing 757 and 767—the type hijacked on 9/11—and to gain the operational proficiency, "feel," and confidence necessary to fly the aircraft into an intended target.

Among the five hijackers aboard United Airlines flight 175, only Marwan al Shehhi is known to have completed flight training and possessed an FAA pilot certification. Al Shehhi received his commercial pilot certificate in December 2000, on the same day and at the same facility as Atta received his. He also had Boeing flight simulator training.

Among the five hijackers aboard American Airlines Flight 77, Hani Hanjour was the sole individual who FAA records show completed flight training and received FAA pilot certification. Hanjour received his commercial multi-engine pilot certificate from the FAA in March 1999. He received extensive flight training in the United States including flight simulator training, and was perhaps the most experienced and highly trained pilot among the 9/11 hijackers.

Among the four hijackers aboard United Airlines Flight 93,

Ziad Jarrah was the lone individual who is recorded as having received flight training and FAA pilot certification. Jarrah received his private pilot certificate from the FAA in November 2000, and was recorded as having received Boeing flight simulator training. Staff would note that Jarrah had logged only 100 flight hours, and did not possess a commercial pilot certificate or multi-engine rating.

The staff would note the existence of computer-based software programs that provide cockpit simulation available on the open market to the general public. According to experts at the FAA such computer-based training packages, including products that simulate cockpit controls of the Boeing 757 and 767, provided effective training opportunities. The terrorists were known to use computers, and there is no reason to believe they did not have the computer literacy necessary to take advantage of computer-based training aids.

FLYING THE AIRCRAFT

Although the investigation is still ongoing into what methods the hijackers employed to navigate and direct the aircraft toward their target, the following information is offered in regard to this analysis.

Boeing 757 and 767 aircraft are outfitted with highly capable flight management systems and auto pilot features. Knowledge of these systems could be gained through simulator training, readily available operational manuals, and, perhaps, PC-based simulator software. Information from the flight recorder recovered from Flight 77 indicated that the pilot had input auto-pilot instructions for a route to Reagan National Airport.

It should be noted that the Flight Management Computer could be programmed in such a manner that it would navigate the aircraft automatically to a location of the hijackers' choosing, not merely a commercial airport, at a speed and altitude they desired, provided the hijackers possessed the precise positioning data necessary. By using sequenced waypoints dialed into the computer, the hijackers could also approach the target from the direction they wanted.

Financial records indicate that one of the hijackers had purchased a global positioning system perhaps for the purpose of acquiring precise positioning data on al Qaeda's 9/11 targets. They had also purchased a Boeing flight deck video and flight simulator software program. Flight manuals were also found among their belongings.

The Commission continues to acquire and analyze data on pilot training, operational requirements, flight information, and other relevant evidence that will provide the most informed theory of what means the hijackers used to fly the aircraft to their targets.

Whether the hijackers flew the aircraft manually, engaged the flight management computer to take them to a programmed destination, or employed some combination of the two, experts consulted by the Commission believe it quite credible that, given the certificates held by the hijackers, the training and educational opportunities available to them through publicly available flight operations manuals and computer-based flight training software, the hijackers—particularly Atta, Hanjour, and al Shehhi—had the know-how to complete the mission.

WEAPONS

Records of purchases by the hijackers and other evidence indicate that knives with blades of less than four inches long were their primary weapons of choice.

With regard to reports from crew and passengers, knives were cited on all four flights. The threat of a bomb was reported on Flights 11, 175, and 93. Box cutters were specifically indicated only in one report, from Flight 77.

Staff specifically notes reports from callers aboard at least two of the hijacked aircraft (Flights 11 and 175) suggesting that the terrorists used mace or pepper spray aboard the flight. As mentioned previously, the evidence suggests that one of the tactics employed by the hijackers on all the flights was to move passengers to the back of the airplane away from the cockpit. Mace, pepper spray, or a similar substance would have aided the terrorists in that effort and assisted them in maintaining a controlled area around the flight deck.

Both mace and pepper spray were specifically prohibited items under the Air Carrier Standard Security Program. The question of how these items were carried onboard remains an issue under investigation.

One is left to consider the following. Had the consequences of being a "selectee" under the passenger prescreening program, as nine of the terrorists were, required a more intense screening of the selectee, as had been the case before the prescreening system was computerized in 1998, the system would have stood a better chance of detecting the prohibited item, possibly depriving the terrorists of an important weapon.

Staff notes this in order to highlight a major policy question arising from the Commission's investigation. Was it wise to ease the consequences of being a prescreening selectee at a time when the U.S. government perceived a rising terrorist threat, including domestically, and when the limits of detection technology and shortcomings of checkpoint screening efficacy were well known?

Moreover, we believe that in practice the FAA's approach of admonishing air carriers to use common sense about what items should not be allowed on an aircraft, while also approving the air carrier's checkpoint guidelines that defined the industry's "common sense," created an environment where both parties could deny responsibility for making hard and most likely unpopular decisions.

GUN ONBOARD?

We continue to investigate allegations that a gun was used aboard American Airlines Flight 11. This allegation arose from a notation in an executive summary produced on September 11, 2001, by FAA staff indicating that the FAA Headquarters had received a report of a shooting aboard the plane, reportedly from an American Airlines employee at the company's operations center. The individual alleged to have made the report to the FAA denies having done so.

While staff continues to investigate the origins and accuracy of the report, we note: Regardless of what reports were received in the chaotic environment of various operations centers at the FAA, the airports, and the airlines, the only authoritative information about whether a shooting occurred on Flight 11 had to have come from individuals on the aircraft who were reporting what was taking place to contacts on the ground.

Two flight attendants aboard American Airlines Flight 11 placed calls to ground contacts to report what was happening on the aircraft. . . . Staff notes that the flight attendants did their duty with remarkable courage. The evidence shows that the flight attendants remained in phone contact with authorities for an extended period of time, providing valuable information with extraordinary professionalism. Their actions were nothing short of heroic.

Neither the tape recordings of the call from flight attendant Betty Ong nor the accounts by at least seven separate witnesses to the calls placed by Ms. Ong or Ms. Madeline Sweeney reported the presence of a gun or the occurrence of a shooting. The witnesses' accounts of the phone calls are consistent and are quite specific about the kind of weapons that were reported present— knives, mace, and a bomb—as well as the nature of the assaults on board—the "stabbing" of two crew members and a passenger.

In order to accept the accuracy of the initial FAA executive summary with regard to a shooting (disregarding the evidence by eyewitnesses to the contrary), one would have to believe that the American Airlines System Operations Center (SOC) relayed to the FAA the account of a shooting that no witness recalls while neglecting to include the account of a stabbing that was widely reported, including to personnel in the SOC. This seems highly implausible.

Finally, staff notes that the alleged victim of the shooting was seated in 9(B). Both the seat and its occupant are described by several of the witness accounts from the aircraft as the place where the stabbing occurred.

At this point in the investigation it seems evident that the form of attack on the business class passenger—the only attack upon a passenger reported by eyewitnesses—became garbled as the account of the assault was relayed between airline and FAA authorities in the fog and confusion of the rapidly unfolding events of the day.

Other relevant evidence bears mentioning. While investigators have uncovered evidence of numerous knife purchases by the 19 hijackers leading up to September 11, 2001, no firearm purchases or possession are in evidence.

Further, the tactics of all four hijacking teams involved in the plot were similar. No evidence has been uncovered to suggest that the hijackers on any of the other flights used firearms, and none were found in evidence at any of the crash sites, notably the crash site of United Airlines Flight 93 where items from the aircraft were collected as evidence. To the contrary, the common tactic among the four teams of employing knives and mace, and the wielding of a bomb (either real or simulated), is indicated by all other evidence. It seems unlikely that one of the teams would depart from the tactical discipline of the plotters' mutual strategy.

Finally, though it appears erroneous at this point in the investigation, staff continues to develop information on how the gun story may have come to be reported. . . . Our investigation continues.

CONCLUSION

We started [this statement by recalling] the world before 9/11, and the factors and pressures that influenced the civil aviation security system prior to that day. We cannot and will not forget the events of 9/11. The lessons of that tragedy continue to inform our work, especially our effort to develop recommendations to make America safer and more secure.

Our staff was able to build upon investigative work that had been conducted by various agencies, including the Federal Bureau of Investigation. The Department of Homeland Security's Transportation Security Administration is fully cooperating with our investigators, as are the relevant airlines and the Federal Aviation Administration.

Staff Statement No. 5

Diplomacy

[The Commission] staff has developed initial findings . . . on the diplomatic efforts to deal with the danger posed by Islamic extremist terrorism before the September 11 attacks on the United States. We will specifically focus on the efforts to counter the danger posed by the al Qaeda organization and its allies.

COUNTERTERRORISM IN U.S. FOREIGN POLICY

Terrorism is a strategy. As a way to achieve their political goals, some organizations or individuals deliberately try to kill innocent people, non-combatants. The United States has long regarded such acts as criminal. For more than a generation, international terrorism has also been regarded as a threat to the nation's security. In the 1970s and 1980s terrorists frequently attacked American targets, often as an outgrowth of international conflicts like the Arab-Israeli dispute. The groups involved were frequently linked to states. After the destruction of Pan American flight 103 by Libyan agents in 1988 the wave of international terrorism that targeted Americans seemed to subside.

The 1993 attempt to blow up the World Trade Center called attention to a new kind of terrorist danger. A National Intelligence Estimate [NIE] issued in July 1995 concluded that the most likely threat would come from emerging, "transient" terrorist groupings that were more fluid and multinational than the older organizations and state-sponsored surrogates.

This "new terrorist phenomenon" was made up, according to the NIE, of loose affiliations of Islamist extremists violently angry at the United States. Lacking strong organization, they could still get weapons, money, and support from an assortment of governments, factions, and individual benefactors. Growing international support networks were enhancing their ability to operate in any region of the world.

Since the terrorists were understood as loosely affiliated sets of individuals, the basic approach for dealing with them was that of law enforcement. But President Clinton emphasized his concern about the problem as a national security issue in a Presidential Decision Directive, PDD–39, in June 1995 that stated the U.S. policy on counterterrorism. This directive superseded a directive signed by President Reagan in 1986. President Clinton's directive declared that the United States saw "terrorism as a potential threat to national security as well as a criminal act and will apply all appropriate means to combat it. In doing so, the U.S. shall pursue vigorously efforts to deter and preempt, apprehend and prosecute, or assist other governments to prosecute, individuals who perpetrate or plan to perpetrate such attacks."

The role of diplomacy was to gain the cooperation of other governments in bringing terrorists to justice. PDD–39 stated: "When terrorists wanted for violation of U.S. law are at large overseas, their return for prosecution shall be a matter of the highest priority and shall be a continuing central issue in bilateral relations with any state that harbors or assists them." If extradition procedures were unavailable or put aside, the United States could seek the local country's assistance in a rendition, secretly putting the fugitive in a plane back to America or some third country for trial.

COUNTERTERRORISM AND FOREIGN POLICY IN PRACTICE: FOUR EXAMPLES

Ramzi Yousef, 1995

The U.S. government believed that the World Trade Center attack of 1993 had been carried out by a "cell" led by Abdul Basit Mahmoud Abdul Karim, better known by his alias, Ramzi Yousef. Yousef had escaped and was a fugitive. By early 1995 he was also wanted for his participation in a plot to plant bombs on a dozen American airliners in the Far East. Yousef had fled to Pakistan. The United States learned where he was and, working effectively with Pakistani officials, carried out a rendition that sent him back to America for trial.

Khalid Sheikh Mohammed, 1996

In 1995 the United States also learned that Khalid Sheikh Mohammed, "KSM," was living in Doha, Qatar and was reportedly employed by a government agency there. The United States obtained other specific details that could locate KSM, who was then sought as a suspect in the Ramzi Yousef airlines plot. Working with the U.S. ambassador in Doha, the FBI and CIA worked on how to capture KSM. But they were reluctant to seek help from the Qatari government, fearing that KSM might be tipped off.

The U.S. government instead considered the option of capturing KSM without Qatari help. The available options were rejected as unwieldy and too risky. Therefore, after first waiting for a sealed indictment against KSM to be handed down by a New York grand jury, the U.S. government asked the Emir of Qatar for help in January 1996. Qatari authorities first reported that KSM was under surveillance. They then asked for development of an alternative plan that would conceal their aid to Americans. They then reported that KSM had disappeared.

KSM would later become a principal planner of the 9/11

attacks and was captured in 2003. We do not know whether KSM was tipped off in 1996. According to some unconfirmed information, KSM may have left Qatar in 1995 for an extended period after being warned by his nephew, Ramzi Yousef, that U.S. authorities were looking for him. According to this same information, he may have returned to Qatar later that year, but then became concerned again following the December 1995 capture of Wali Khan, another conspirator in the airliner bombing plot, and left Qatar for good in early 1996. The government of Qatar has not yet provided an account of this episode or its government's past relationship to KSM.

Osama bin Laden, 1996

The U.S. government was also interested in another individual with disturbing ties to terrorists, a Saudi named Osama bin Laden. Bin Laden was then based in Sudan. Under the influence of the radical Islamist Hassan al Turabi, Sudan had become a safe haven for violent Islamist extremists. By 1995, the U.S. government had connected bin Laden to terrorists as an important terrorist financier.

Since 1979 the Secretary of State has had the authority to name State Sponsors of Terrorism, subjecting such countries to significant economic sanctions. Sudan was so designated in 1993. In February 1996, for security reasons, U.S. diplomats left Khartoum. International pressure further increased as the regime failed to hand over three individuals involved in a 1995 attempt to assassinate Egyptian president Hosni Mubarak. The United Nations Security Council imposed sanctions on the regime.

Diplomacy had an effect. In exchanges beginning in February 1996, Sudanese officials began approaching U.S. officials, asking what they could do to ease the pressure. During the winter and spring of 1996, Sudan's defense minister visited Washington and had a series of meetings with representatives of the U.S. government. To test Sudan's willingness to cooperate on terrorism the United States presented eight demands to their Sudanese contact.

The one that concerned bin Laden was a request for intelligence information about bin Laden's contacts in Sudan.

These contacts with Sudan, which went on for years, have become a source of controversy. Former Sudanese officials claim that Sudan offered to expel bin Laden to the United States. Clinton administration officials deny ever receiving such an offer. We have not found any reliable evidence to support the Sudanese claim.

Sudan did offer to expel bin Laden to Saudi Arabia and asked the Saudis to pardon him. U.S. officials became aware of these secret discussions, certainly by March 1996. The evidence suggests that the Saudi government wanted bin Laden expelled from Sudan, but would not agree to pardon him. The Saudis did not want bin Laden back in their country at all.

U.S. officials also wanted bin Laden expelled from Sudan. They knew the Sudanese were considering it. The U.S. government did not ask Sudan to render him into U.S. custody.

According to Samuel Berger, who was then the deputy national security adviser, the interagency Counterterrorism and Security Group (CSG) chaired by Richard Clarke had a hypothetical discussion about bringing bin Laden to the United States. In that discussion a Justice Department representative reportedly said there was no basis for bringing him to the United States since there was no way to hold him here, absent an indictment. Berger adds that in 1996 he was not aware of any intelligence that said bin Laden was responsible for any act against an American citizen. No rendition plan targeting bin Laden, who was still perceived as a terrorist financier, was requested by or presented to senior policymakers during 1996.

Yet both Berger and Clarke also said the lack of an indictment made no difference. Instead they said the idea was not worth pursuing because there was no chance that Sudan would ever turn bin Laden over to a hostile country. If Sudan had been serious, Clarke said, the United States would have worked something out.

However, the U.S. government did approach other countries hostile to Sudan and bin Laden about whether they would take bin Laden. One was apparently interested. No handover took place.

Under pressure to leave, bin Laden worked with the Sudanese government to procure safe passage and possibly funding for his departure. In May 1996, bin Laden and his associates leased an Ariana Airlines jet and traveled to Afghanistan, stopping to refuel in the United Arab Emirates. Approximately two days after his departure, the Sudanese informed the U.S. government that bin Laden had left. It is unclear whether any U.S. officials considered whether or how to intercept bin Laden.

Khobar Towers, 1996

In June 1996 an enormous truck bomb was detonated in the Khobar Towers residential complex for Air Force personnel in Dhahran, Saudi Arabia. Nineteen Americans were killed and 372 were wounded. The operation was carried out principally if not exclusively by Saudi Hezbollah, an organization that had received support from the government of Iran. It is still unclear whether Osama bin Laden or his associates played any supporting role in this attack. This case and concern about terrorism from Hezbollah shadowed American counterterrorism policy for the next five years.

The Khobar bombing began as a law enforcement case. The director of the FBI, Louis Freeh, personally led a massive effort to gather evidence of responsibility. That investigation culminated in a June 2001 indictment of 13 members of Saudi Hezbollah and one unidentified member of Lebanese Hezbollah. Although the public indictment details some contacts of these groups with the Iranian government, no Iranian was named or charged in this indictment. In his interview with the Commission, Director Freeh described the responsibility of the Iranian government in very strong terms. He apparently provided a similar depiction to the White House in 1999.

The Khobar bombing also was an intelligence case. That aspect of the case developed significant information implicating key agencies and senior officials of the Iranian government. DCI [Director of Central Intelligence] [George] Tenet also characterized this case to us in strong terms. He could not recall when he arrived at this judgment or how he communicated it.

The Khobar case highlights a central policy problem in counterterrorism: the relationship between evidence and action. [The Clinton administration's] Secretary of State Madeleine Albright emphasized to us, for example, that even if some individual Iranian officials were involved, this was not the same as proving that the Iranian government as a whole should be held responsible for the bombing. National Security Adviser Berger held a similar view. He stressed the need for a definitive intelligence judgment. The evidence might be challenged by foreign governments. The evidence might form a basis for going to war. Therefore, he explained, the DCI and the Director of the FBI must make a definitive judgment based on the professional opinions of their experts.

In this and other episodes before 9/11 we found that the CIA and the FBI tended to be careful in discussing the attribution for terrorist acts. In the Khobar case and others, the circle of individuals working with the evidence was tightly compartmented in order to prevent leaks that might limit the President's options or his time for decision. Whatever analysts might say privately, their written work was conservatively phrased and caveated. Evidence was catalogued in neutral detail. In the Khobar case, as in some others, the time lag between terrorist act and any definitive attribution grew to months, then years, as the evidence was compiled.

THE AFGHANISTAN PROBLEM

From 1980 to 1991 the United States supplied billions of dollars worth of secret assistance to rebel groups in Afghanistan fighting against Soviet occupation and the Soviet-installed successor government. This assistance was funneled through Pakistan. The Pakistani Army's intelligence service, the ISID, helped train the rebels and distribute the arms.

The war against the Soviets became a "jihad" for many Muslims. It was a clear fight against a foreign, atheist regime. Saudi

Arabia contributed billions of dollars of its own, consulting with the Americans and Pakistanis. Arab volunteers flocked to Afghanistan. One, who became a fundraiser and celebrity for the cause, was Osama bin Laden.

These foreigners, who received little if any U.S. assistance, had a slight impact on the war. However, some established links to both Pakistan and Afghan leaders that would prove useful in the future. Most volunteers stayed only brief periods before returning home, where their governments often viewed them with intense suspicion and little support. Angry at their treatment, these alienated fighters began to turn their grievances toward other targets.

In 1989 the Soviet Union withdrew its last forces, leaving behind an unpopular Marxist government. Soviet departure removed the main impetus for foreign volunteers, many of whom began to search for a new focus. Some joined already returned compatriots in a series of increasingly violent, domestic extremist groups. Others were attracted to a transnational struggle against perceived enemies of Islam. In 1988 bin Laden and a small circle of other leaders created al Qaeda with the aim of its creating and coordinating such a global struggle, the elite "foundation" for this "Islamic Army." The U.S. government knew nothing about it.

By the time of the Soviet withdrawal, Pakistan was home to an enormous—and generally unwelcome—Afghan refugee population. The badly strained Pakistani education system had little ability or interest in extending secular education to the refugees or to many Pakistanis, where the government increasingly viewed privately funded religious schools as a cost-free alternative. Over time, these schools produced large numbers of half-educated young men with no marketable skills but deeply held fundamentalist views. These young men, a ready source of manpower for both continued fighting in Afghanistan and the Kashmir insurgency, provided the continuing core of what, by 1994, became the Taliban movement. Imposing a ruthless version of Islamic law, the Taliban seemed to be a potential force for order. The Pakistani government gave them significant assistance. In September 1996, the Taliban captured Kabul and controlled most of the country. They declared the creation of the "Islamic Emirate of Afghanistan."

After suffering some disruption from his relocation to Afghanistan, Osama bin Laden and his colleagues rebuilt. In August 1996 he issued a public declaration of jihad against American troops in Saudi Arabia. In February 1998 this was expanded into a public call for any Muslim to kill any American, military or civilian, anywhere in the world.

By early 1997 intelligence and law enforcement officials in the U.S. government had finally received reliable information disclosing the existence of al Qaeda as a worldwide terrorist organization. That information elaborated a command-and-control structure headed by bin Laden and various lieutenants, described a network of training camps to process recruits, discussed efforts to acquire weapons of mass destruction, and placed al Qaeda at the center among other groups affiliated with them in its "Islamic Army."

This information also dramatically modified the picture of inchoate "new terrorism" presented in the 1995 National Intelligence Estimate. But the new picture was not widely known. It took still more time before officials outside the circle of terrorism specialists, or in foreign governments, fully comprehended that the enemy was much larger than an individual criminal, more than just one man, "OBL," and "his associates."

For example, in 1996 Congress passed a law that authorized the Secretary of State to designate foreign terrorist organizations that threaten the national security of the United States—a designation that triggers economic, immigration, and criminal consequences. Al Qaeda was not designated by the Secretary of State until the fall of 1999.

While Afghanistan became a sanctuary for al Qaeda, the State Department's interest in Afghanistan remained limited. Initially after the Taliban's rise, some State diplomats were, as one official said to us, willing to "give the Taliban a chance" because it might be able to bring stability to Afghanistan. A secondary consideration was that stability would allow an oil pipeline to be built through the country, a project to be managed by the Union Oil Company of California, or UNOCAL.

During 1997 working-level State officials asked for permission to visit and investigate militant camps in Afghanistan. The Taliban stalled, then refused. In November 1997 Secretary Albright described Taliban human rights violations and treatment of women as "despicable." A Taliban delegation visited Washington in December. U.S. officials pressed them on the treatment of women, negotiating an end to the civil war, and narcotics trafficking. Bin Laden was barely mentioned.

UN Ambassador Bill Richardson led a delegation to South Asia—and Afghanistan—in April 1998. No U.S. official of this rank had been to Kabul in decades. Ambassador Richardson used the opening to support UN negotiations on the civil war. In light of bin Laden's new public fatwa against Americans in February, Ambassador Richardson asked the Taliban to turn bin Laden over to the United States. They answered that they did not control bin Laden and that, in any case, he was not a threat to the United States.

The Taliban won few friends. Only three countries recognized it as the government of Afghanistan: Pakistan, Saudi Arabia, and the United Arab Emirates.

THE SAUDI EFFORT AND ITS AFTERMATH

In May 1998 the Clinton administration issued a new presidential directive on terrorism, PDD–62. It described ten policy programs. Program number one was "Apprehension, Extradition, Rendition, and Prosecution." The lead agency was the Justice Department, supported by the Department of State.

As this directive was issued a plan was being developed to capture and bring bin Laden to justice. This plan would use Afghan agents of the CIA. Top policymakers, including the CIA leadership, did not think the plan would work. They welcomed a diplomatic alternative.

Saudi Arabia was a problematic ally in combating Islamic extremism. One of the world's most religiously conservative societies, the Kingdom's identity is closely bound to its religious links, especially as the guardian of Islam's two holiest sites. The obligation to donate to charity is a basic pillar of faith for all Muslims. Traditionally, throughout the Muslim world, there is no formal oversight mechanism for donations. Individuals select and aid the recipients directly. As Saudi wealth increased, the amounts that individuals, and the state, could and did contribute grew dramatically. Substantial sums went to finance Islamic charities of every kind.

Until 9/11, few Saudis would have considered government oversight of charitable donations necessary; many would have perceived it as interference in the performance of their faith. At the same time, the government's ability to finance most state expenditures with energy revenues has not created the need for a modern income tax system. As a result, there were strong religious, cultural, and administrative barriers to monitoring charitable spending.

Attitudes toward the United States were mixed. The United States was aligned with Israel in a conflict where Saudis ardently sympathized with the Palestinian cause. Yet for more than half a century the Saudi monarchy has had close relations with the United States, finding common cause in the commercial exploitation of its oil wealth and the anti-Communism of the cold war. In 1990 the Kingdom had chosen to host U.S. armed forces in the first war against Iraq. In 1998 it was still the base for ongoing military operations against Iraq.

The ruling monarchy also knew bin Laden was an enemy. Bin Laden had not set foot in Saudi Arabia since 1991, when he escaped a form of house arrest and made his way to Sudan. Bin Laden had fiercely denounced the rulers of Saudi Arabia publicly in his August 1996 fatwa. But the Saudis were content to leave him in Afghanistan, so long as they were assured he was not making any trouble for them there.

Events soon drew Saudi attention back to bin Laden. In the spring of 1998 the Saudi government successfully disrupted a major bin Laden-organized effort to launch attacks on U.S. forces in the Kingdom using a variety of man-portable missiles. Scores of individuals were arrested. The Saudi government did not publicize what had happened, but U.S. officials learned of it. Seizing this opportunity, DCI Tenet urged the Saudis to help deal with bin Laden. President Clinton, in May, designated Tenet as his representative to work with the Saudis on terrorism. Director Tenet visited Riyadh a few days later, then returned to Saudi Arabia in early June.

Crown Prince Abdullah agreed to make an all-out secret effort to persuade the Taliban to expel bin Laden for eventual delivery to the United States or another country. Riyadh's emissary would be the Saudi intelligence chief, Prince Turki bin Faisal. Director Tenet said it was imperative now to get an indictment against bin Laden. A sealed indictment against bin Laden was issued by a New York grand jury a few days later, the product of a lengthy investigation. Director Tenet also recommended that no action be taken on other U.S. options, such as a covert action plan. Vice President Gore thanked the Saudis for their efforts.

Prince Turki followed up in meetings during the summer with Mullah Omar and other Taliban leaders. Employing a mixture of possible bribes and threats, he received a commitment that bin Laden would be handed over. After the Embassy bombings in August, Vice President Gore called Riyadh again to underscore the urgency of bringing the Saudi ultimatum to a final conclusion.

In September 1998 Prince Turki, joined by Pakistan's intelligence chief, had a climactic meeting with Mullah Omar in Kandahar. Omar reneged on his promise to expel bin Laden. When Turki angrily confronted him, Omar lost his temper and denounced the Saudi government. The Saudis and Pakistanis walked out. The Saudi government then cut off any further official assistance to the Taliban regime, recalled its diplomats from Kandahar, and expelled Taliban representatives from the Kingdom. The Saudis suspended relations without a final break.

The Pakistanis did not suspend relations with the Taliban. Both governments judged that Iran was already on the verge of going to war against the Taliban. The Saudis and Pakistanis feared that a further break might encourage Iran to attack. They also wanted to leave open room for rebuilding ties if more moderate voices among the Taliban gained control.

Crown Prince Abdullah visited Washington later in September. In meetings with the President and Vice President he briefed them on these developments. The United States had information that corroborated his account. Officials thanked the Prince for his efforts, wondering what else could be done.

The United States acted too. In every available channel U.S. officials, led by State's aggressive counterterrorism coordinator, Michael Sheehan, warned the Taliban of dire consequences if bin Laden was not expelled. Moreover, if there was any further attack, he and others warned, the Taliban would be held directly accountable, including the possibility of a military assault by the United States.

These diplomatic efforts may have made an impact. The U.S. government received substantial intelligence of internal arguments over whether bin Laden could stay in Afghanistan. The reported doubts extended from the Taliban, to their Pakistani supporters, and even to bin Laden himself. For a time, bin Laden was reportedly considering relocating and may have authorized discussion of this possibility with representatives of other governments. . . . In any event, bin Laden stayed in Afghanistan.

This period may have been the high-water mark for diplomatic pressure on the Taliban. The outside pressure continued. But the Taliban appeared to adjust and learn to live with it, employing a familiar mix of stalling tactics again and again. Urged on by the United States, the Saudis continued a more limited mix of the same tactics they had already employed. Prince Turki returned to Kandahar in June 1999, to no effect.

From 1999 through early 2001, the United States also pressed the United Arab Emirates, one of the Taliban's only travel and financial outlets to the outside world, to break off its ties and enforce sanctions, especially those relating to flights to and from Afghanistan. Unfortunately, these efforts to persuade the UAE achieved little before 9/11. As time passed, the United States also obtained information that the Taliban was trying to extort cash from Saudi Arabia and the UAE with various threats and that these blackmail efforts may have paid off.

After months of heated internal debate about whether the step would burn remaining bridges to the Taliban, President Clinton issued an executive order in July 1999 effectively declaring that the regime was a state sponsor of terrorism. UN economic and travel sanctions were added in October 1999 in UN Security Council Resolution 1267.

None of this had any visible effect on Mullah Omar, an illiterate leader who was unconcerned about commerce with the outside world. Omar had no diplomatic contact with the West, since he refused to meet with non-Muslims. The United States also learned that at the end of 1999 the Taliban Council of Ministers had unanimously reaffirmed that they would stick by bin Laden. Relations between bin Laden and the Taliban leadership were sometimes tense, but the foundation was solid. Omar executed some subordinates who clashed with his pro-bin Laden line.

By the end of 2000 the United States, working with Russia, won UN support for still broader sanctions in UN Security Council Resolution 1333, including an embargo on arms sales to the Taliban. Again these had no visible effect. This may have been because the sanctions did not stop the flow of Pakistani military assistance to the Taliban. In April 2001 State Department officials in the Bush administration concluded that the Pakistani government was just not concerned about complying with sanctions against the Taliban.

Reflecting on the lack of progress with the Taliban, Secretary Albright told us that "we had to do something." "In the end," she said, "it didn't work. But we did in fact try to use all the tools we had."

Other diplomatic efforts with the Saudi government centered on letting U.S. agents interrogate prisoners in Saudi custody in cases like Khobar. Several officials have complained to us that the United States could not get direct access to an important al Qaeda financial official, Madani al Tayyib, who had been detained by the Saudi government in 1997. American officials raised the issue. The Saudis provided some information. In September 1998 Vice President Gore thanked the Saudis for their responsiveness on this matter, though he renewed the request for direct U.S. access. The United States never obtained this access.

The United States also pressed Saudi Arabia and the UAE for more cooperation in controlling money flows to terrorists or organizations linked to them. After months of arguments in Washington over the proper role of the FBI, an initial U.S. delegation on terrorist finance visited these countries to start working with their counterparts in July 1999. U.S. officials reported to the White House that they thought the new initiatives to work together had begun successfully. Another delegation followed up with Saudi Arabia and other Gulf states in January 2000. In Saudi Arabia the team concentrated on tracing bin Laden's assets and access to his family's money, exchanges that led to further, fruitful work. Progress on other topics was limited, however. The issue was not a consistent U.S. priority. Moreover, the Saudis were reluctant or unable to provide much help. Available intelligence was also so non-specific that it was difficult to confront the Saudis with evidence or cues to action.

The Bush administration did not develop any diplomatic initiatives on al Qaeda with the Saudi government before the 9/11 attack. Vice President Cheney apparently called Crown Prince Abdullah on July 4, 2001, only to seek Saudi help in preventing threatened attacks on American facilities in the Kingdom.

PRESSURING PAKISTAN

Although Pakistan exists because of its Islamic identity, political Islam played a relatively minor role in its national politics until the 1970s. Following a 1977 coup, however, military leaders turned to Islamist groups for support. Fundamentalist groups became more prominent. South Asia has given birth to some of the most influential schools of Islamic fundamentalist thought, whose views shaped Taliban thinking. In addition, since the 1970s the influence of the Wahhabi school of Islam has grown as a result of Saudi-funded institutions and contact with Wahhabi ideas in Afghanistan.

For its entire existence Pakistani politics has also been preoccupied with its conflict with India. Three wars had been fought by 1971; another could easily happen—especially over the disputed territory of Kashmir. The Pakistani army is the country's strongest and most respected institution. The army sees hostile or unstable neighbors in every direction. It has adjusted by spinning webs of secret relationships. Secret Pakistani aid for the Taliban seemed for a time to make sense to the army as part of an effort to gain what some officers called "strategic depth" in a possible conflict with India. Their tolerance of bin Laden made sense to them too, at least for a time, in part because bin Laden's terrorist training camps were also training fighters for Pakistani-sponsored operations in Kashmir. The U.S. government believed Pakistani intelligence officers had direct links to bin Laden, perhaps concealed from the civilian leaders.

U.S. relations with Pakistan have been troubled since the Soviet withdrawal from Afghanistan. Cold war cooperation turned to arguments about military coups, nuclear proliferation, and the growing power of Islamic extremism in Pakistani life. Friendship during the Afghan jihad was replaced by concerns about corruption and regional stability. Secretary Albright hoped to promote a more robust approach to South Asia when she took office. But the administration had a full agenda of concerns including a possible nuclear weapons program, illicit sales of missile technology, terrorism, an arms race and danger of war with India, and a succession of weak democratic governments. The American ambassador to Islamabad in most of the immediate pre–9/11 period, William Milam, told us that U.S. policy "had too many moving parts" and could never determine what items had the highest priority.

A principal envoy to South Asia for the administration, Deputy Secretary of State Strobe Talbott, explained the emphasis on nuclear weapons both because of the danger of nuclear war and because nuclear proliferation might increase the risk that terrorists could access such technology. In May 1998 both Pakistan and India had tested nuclear weapons. These tests marked a setback to nonproliferation policy and reinforced U.S. sanctions on both countries. But the tests also spurred more engagement in order to reduce the threat of war.

Bin Laden and terrorist activity in Afghanistan were not significant issues in high-level contacts with Pakistan until after the Embassy bombings of August 1998. After the U.S. missile strikes on Afghanistan, bin Laden's network and their relationship with the Pakistani-supported Taliban did become a major issue in high-level diplomacy.

After the strikes President Clinton called Pakistani leader Nawaz Sharif, and he was sympathetic to America's losses. But the Pakistani side thought the strikes were overkill, the wrong way to handle the problem.

The United States asked the Saudis to put pressure on Pakistan to help. A senior State Department official concluded that Crown Prince Abdullah put "a tremendous amount of heat" on Sharif during his October 1998 visit to Pakistan.

Sharif was invited to Washington and met with President Clinton on December 2, 1998. Tension with India and nuclear weapons topped the agenda, but the leaders also discussed bin Laden. Pakistani officials defended Mullah Omar, and thought the Taliban would not object to a joint effort by others to get bin Laden.

In mid-December President Clinton called Sharif, worried both about immediate threats and the longer-term problem of bin Laden. The Pakistani leadership promised to raise the issue directly with the Taliban, in Afghanistan. But the United States received word in early 1999 that the Pakistani army remained reluctant to confront the Taliban, in part because of concerns about the effect on Pakistani politics.

In early 1999 the State Department counterterrorism office proposed a comprehensive diplomatic strategy for all the states involved in the Afghanistan problem, including Pakistan. It specified both carrots and sticks, including the threat of certifying Pakistan as not cooperating on terrorism. A version of this diplomatic strategy was eventually adopted by the State Department. Its author, Ambassador Sheehan, told us that it had been watered down to the point that nothing was then done with it.

By the summer of 1999 the counterterrorism agenda had to compete with cross-border fighting in Kashmir that threatened to explode into war. Nevertheless, President Clinton contacted Sharif in June, urging him strongly to get the Taliban to expel bin Laden. Clinton suggested Pakistan use its control over oil supplies to the Taliban and its access to imports through Karachi. The Pakistani leadership offered instead that Pakistani intelligence services might try to capture bin Laden themselves.

President Clinton met with Prime Minister Sharif in Washington on July 4. The prime subject was resolution of the crisis in Kashmir. The President also complained to the Prime Minister about Pakistan's failure to take effective action with respect to the Taliban and bin Laden. Later the United States agreed to assist in training a Pakistani special forces team for the bin Laden operation. Particularly since the Pakistani intelligence service was so deeply involved with the Taliban and possibly bin Laden, U.S. counterterrorism officials had doubts about every aspect of this new joint plan. Yet while few thought it would do much good, fewer thought it would do any actual harm. Officials were implementing it when Prime Minister Sharif was deposed by General Pervez Musharraf in October 1999. General Musharraf was scornful about the unit and the idea.

At first the Clinton administration hoped that Musharraf's takeover might create an opening for action on bin Laden. National Security Adviser Berger wondered about a trade of getting bin Laden in exchange for softer treatment of a relatively benign military regime. But the idea was never developed into a policy proposal. Meanwhile the President and his advisers were anxious about a series of new terrorist threats associated with the Millennium and were getting information linking these threats to al Qaeda associates in Pakistan, particularly Abu Zubaydah. President Clinton sent a message asking for immediate help on Abu Zubaydah and another push on bin Laden, renewing the idea of using Pakistani forces to get him. Musharraf told Ambassador Milam that he would do what he could. But he preferred a diplomatic solution on bin Laden. Though he thought terrorists should be brought to justice, he did not find the military ideas appealing.

Administration officials debated whether to keep working with the Musharraf government or confront the General with a blunter choice, to either adopt a new policy or "Washington will draw the appropriate conclusions." One such threat would be to cancel a possible presidential visit in March. U.S. envoys were given instructions that were firm, but not as confrontational as some U.S. officials had advocated. Musharraf was preoccupied with his domestic agenda but replied that he would do what he could, perhaps meeting with the Taliban himself.

Despite serious security threats, President Clinton made a one-day stopover in Islamabad on March 25, 2000, the first presidential visit since 1969. The main subjects were India-Pakistan tensions and proliferation, but President Clinton did raise the bin Laden problem. The Pakistani position was that their government had to support the Taliban and that the only way forward was to engage them and try to moderate their behavior. They asked for evidence that bin Laden had really ordered the Embassy bombings a year and a half earlier. In a follow-up meeting the next day with Under Secretary of State Thomas Pickering, President Musharraf argued that Pakistan had only limited influence over the Taliban.

Musharraf did meet with Mullah Omar and did urge him to get rid of bin Laden. In early June the Pakistani interior minister even joined with Pickering to deliver a joint message to Taliban officials. But the Taliban seemed immune to such pleas, especially from Pakistani civilians like the interior minister. Pakistan did not threaten to cut off its help to the Taliban regime. By September the United States was again criticizing the Pakistani government for supporting a Taliban military offensive to complete the conquest of Afghanistan.

CONSIDERING NEW POLICIES
TOWARD AFGHANISTAN AND PAKISTAN

The civil war in Afghanistan posed the Taliban on one side, drawn from Afghanistan's largest ethnic community, the Pashtuns, against the Northern Alliance. Pashtuns opposing the Taliban, like the Karzai clan, were not organized into a political and military force. The main foe of the Taliban was the Northern Alliance led by Ahmed Shah Massoud, a hero of the Afghan jihad and a leader of ethnic Tajiks. The Taliban were backed by Pakistan. The Northern Alliance received some support from Iran, Russia, and India.

During 1999 the U.S. government began thinking harder about whether or how to replace the Taliban regime. Thinking in Washington divided along two main paths. The first path, led by the South Asia bureau at the State Department, headed by Assistant Secretary of State Karl Inderfurth, and his counterpart on the NSC [National Security Council] staff, was for a major diplomatic effort to end the civil war and install a national unity government.

The second path, proposed by counterterrorism officials in the NSC staff and the CIA, was for the United States to take sides in the Afghan civil war and begin funneling secret military aid to the Taliban's foe, the Northern Alliance. These officials argued that the diplomatic approach had little chance of success and would not do anything, at least in the short term, to stop al Qaeda. Critics of this idea replied that the Northern Alliance was tainted by associations with narcotics traffickers, that its military capabilities were modest, and that an American association with this group would link the United States to an unpopular faction that Afghans blamed for much of the misrule and war earlier in the 1990s.

The debate continued inconclusively throughout the last year and a half of the Clinton administration. The CIA established limited ties to the Northern Alliance for intelligence purposes. Lethal aid was not provided.

The Afghan and Pakistani dilemmas were handed over to the Bush administration as it took office in 2001. The NSC counterterrorism staff, still led by Clarke, pushed urgently for a quick decision in favor of providing secret military assistance to the Northern Alliance to stave off its defeat. The initial proposed amounts were quite small, with the hope of keeping the Northern Alliance in the field, tying down Taliban and al Qaeda fighters.

National Security Adviser Condoleezza Rice discussed the

issue with DCI Tenet. In early March 2001, Clarke presented the issue of aid to the Northern Alliance to Rice for action. Deputy National Security Adviser Stephen Hadley suggested dealing with this as part of the overall review they were conducting of their strategy against al Qaeda. In the meantime, lawyers could work on developing the appropriate authorities. Rice agreed, noting that the review would need to be done very soon but that the issue had to be connected to an examination of policy toward Afghanistan. Rice, Hadley, and the NSC staff member for Afghanistan, Zalmay Khalilzad, told us that they opposed aid to the Northern Alliance alone, contending that the program needed to include Pashtun opponents of the regime and be conducted on a larger scale. Clarke supported a larger program, but he warned that delay risked the Alliance's defeat.

The issue was then made part of the reviews of U.S. policy toward Afghanistan and Pakistan. The government developed formal policy papers that were discussed by subcabinet officials, the "Deputies," on April 30, June 27 and 29, July 16, and September 10. During this same time period the administration was developing a formal strategy on al Qaeda, to be codified in a National Security Presidential Directive (NSPD). The al Qaeda elements of this directive had been completed by Deputies in July. On September 4, the principals apparently approved the submission of this directive to the President.

The Afghanistan options debated in 2001 ranged from seeking a deal with the Taliban to overthrowing the regime. By the end of the Deputies meeting on September 10, the officials had formally agreed upon a three-phase strategy. It called first for dispatching an envoy to give the Taliban an opportunity to expel bin Laden and his organization from Afghanistan, even as the U.S. government tried to build greater capacity to pressure them. If this failed, pressure would be applied on the Taliban both through diplomacy and by encouraging anti-Taliban Afghans to attack al Qaeda bases, part of a planned covert action program including significant additional funding and more support for Pashtun opponents of the regime.

If the Taliban's policy failed to change after these two phases, the

Deputies agreed that the United States would seek to overthrow the Taliban regime through more direct action. The Deputies also agreed to revise the draft NSPD on al Qaeda and add the new strategy on Afghanistan to the directive. According to Hadley, the timeframe for this strategy was about three years. Deputy Secretary of State Richard Armitage said that the Department initially continued the previous administration's policy on Afghanistan but that, after seven or eight months, State was moving clearly in the direction of a policy aimed at overthrowing the Taliban. If the United States was going to arm the Northern Alliance, he said, it was doing it to initiate regime change and should give Massoud and others the strength to achieve total victory.

On Pakistan the policy review concluded that the United States should attempt to improve relations with Pakistan. Assistant Secretary of State Christina Rocca called this moving from "half engagement" to "limited engagement." The United States should be willing to lift, or seek congressional support in lifting, some of the existing sanctions toward Pakistan. The administration recognized how difficult this would be.

On June 19 and 20 Pakistani foreign minister Sattar visited Washington to meet officials from the new administration. National Security Adviser Rice told him that Afghanistan was the big problem and could leave the relationship dead in the water. Sattar, Rice recalled to us, seemed to have heard it all before. But she told him that, at some point, Pakistan will be judged by the company it keeps.

A week later, Clarke followed up, urging that the United States think about what it would do after the next attack, and then take that position with Pakistan now, before the attack. Deputy National Security Adviser Hadley suggested that Clarke prepare an option for the Deputies to consider. Yet, when President Bush sent a letter on the terrorism danger to President Musharraf on August 4, the tone was similar to past requests.

Deputy Secretary Armitage acknowledged to us that, before 9/11, the new strategy toward Pakistan had not yet been implemented. After 9/11 Pakistan was confronted with a direct choice: You are either with us or against us. Musharraf made his choice.

CONCLUSION

- From the spring of 1997 to September 2001 the U.S. government tried to persuade the Taliban to expel bin Laden to a country where he could face justice and stop being a sanctuary for his organization. The efforts employed inducements, warnings, and sanctions. All these efforts failed.

- The U.S. government also pressed two successive Pakistani governments to demand that the Taliban cease providing a sanctuary for bin Laden and his organization and, failing that, to cut off their support for the Taliban. Before 9/11 the United States could not find a mix of incentives or pressure that would persuade Pakistan to reconsider its fundamental relationship with the Taliban.

- From 1999 through early 2001, the United States pressed the UAE, one of the Taliban's only travel and financial outlets to the outside world, to break off ties and enforce sanctions, especially related to air travel to Afghanistan. These efforts achieved little before 9/11.

- The government of Saudi Arabia worked closely with top U.S. officials in major initiatives to solve the bin Laden problem with diplomacy. On the other hand, before 9/11 the Saudi and U.S. governments did not achieve full sharing of important intelligence information or develop an adequate joint effort to track and disrupt the finances of the al Qaeda organization.

Scott Allan, Michael Hurley, Warren Bass, Dan Byman, Thomas Dowling, and Len Hawley did much of the investigative work reflected in this statement. We are grateful to the Department of State for its excellent cooperation in providing the Commission with needed documents and in helping to arrange needed interviews both in the United States and in nine foreign countries. We are also grateful to the foreign governments who have extended their cooperation in making many of their officials available to us as well. The Executive Office of the President and the Central Intelligence Agency have made a wealth of material available to us that sheds light on the conduct of American diplomacy in this period.

Excerpts of testimony from
Madeleine Albright
and Colin Powell

EXCERPTS OF TESTIMONY FROM
MADELEINE ALBRIGHT,
FORMER U.S. SECRETARY OF STATE

"The problem is not combating al Qaeda's inherent appeal, for it has none. The problem is changing the fact that major components of American foreign policy are either opposed or misunderstood by much of the world."

We certainly recognized the threat posed by the terrorist groups. Although terror was not new, we realized we faced a novel variation. Instead of being directed by a hostile country, the new breed of terrorist was independent, multinational and well-versed in modern information technology. During our time in office, the transnational threat was a dominant theme in public statements, private deliberations and foreign relations. This was reflected in the administration's decision to expand the CIA's counterterrorism center, intensify security cooperation with other countries, enlarge counterterrorism training assistance, double overall counterterrorism expenditures, increase anti-terrorist rewards, freeze terrorist assets, train first responders here at home, plan for the protection of infrastructure against cyber attacks and reorganize the National Security Council with a mandate to prepare the government to shield our people from unconventional dangers. . . .

Before Y2K, we undertook the largest counterterrorism operation in U.S. history to that time. Cabinet members or their representatives met virtually every day for the sole purpose of detecting and preventing terrorist attacks. I fully embraced an aggressive policy before and especially after August 7, 1998, when terrorist explosions struck our embassies in Kenya and Tanzania. This was my worst day as secretary of state. Within a week, we had clear evidence that Osama bin Laden was responsible. The question for us was whether to rely on law enforcement or take military action. We decided to do both. We prosecuted the conspirators we had captured, but we also launched cruise missiles at al Qaeda training camps in Afghanistan. The timing of the strikes was prompted by credible, predictive intelligence that terrorist leaders, possibly including bin Laden, would be gathering at one of the camps.

The day after the strike, the White House convened a meeting to study further military options. Our primary target, bin Laden, had not been hit so we were determined to try again. In subsequent weeks, the president specifically authorized the use of force and there should have been no confusion that our personnel were authorized to kill bin Laden. We did not, after all, launch cruise missiles for the purpose of serving legal papers. To use force effectively, we placed war ships equipped with cruise missiles on call in the Arabian Sea. We also studied the possibility of sending a U.S. special forces team into Afghanistan to try and snatch bin Laden.

But success in either case depended on whether we knew where bin Laden would be at a particular time. Although we consumed all the intelligence we had, we did not get this information, and instead we occasionally learned where bin Laden had been or where he might be going or where someone who appeared to resemble him might be. It was truly maddening. I compared it to one of those arcade games where you manipulate a lever hooked to a claw-like hand that you think once you put your quarter in will actually scoop up a prize, but every time you try to pull the basket out the prize falls away.

The Africa embassy bombings intensified our efforts to neutralize bin Laden and also to protect our own people. Every morning that I was in Washington, I personally reviewed the latest information about threats to our diplomatic posts. I was struck by the number of danger signals we received and also by the difficulty of making a clear judgment about whether a threat was credible enough to warrant closing an embassy.

Even as we took protective measures and looked for ways to use force effectively, we pressed ahead diplomatically. Shortly after our cruise missile strikes, the Taliban called the State Department to complain. This led to a prolonged dialogue during which we repeatedly pushed for custody of bin Laden. The Taliban replied by offering a menu of excuses. They said that surrendering bin Laden would violate their cultural tradition of hospitality and that they would be overthrown by their own people if they yielded bin Laden in response to U.S. pressure. Perhaps, they said, bin Laden will leave voluntarily. At one point they told us he had already gone. In any case, we were assured that bin Laden was under house arrest. That was a lie, since he continued to show up in the media threatening Americans. In 1999, we developed a new strategy aimed at pulling all the diplomatic levers we had simultaneously. We went to each of the countries we thought had influence with the Taliban and asked them to use that influence to help us get bin Laden.

One such country was Pakistan, whose leaders were reluctant to apply real pressure to the Taliban because it would alienate radicals within their own borders. There was a limit to the incentives we could offer to overcome this reluctance. Pakistan's nuclear tests in 1998 had triggered one set of sanctions; a military coup in 1999 triggered more. Nevertheless, in our discussions with Pakistani leaders we were blunt. We told them that bin Laden is a murderer who plans to kill again. We need your help in bringing him to justice. Our ambassador delivered this message, so did Tom Pickering. So did I. So did the president of the United States. In return, we received promises but no decisive action. We couldn't offer enough to persuade Pakistani leaders, such as General Musharraf, to run the risks that would have been necessary. It was not until September 11th that Musharraf had the motivation in his own mind to provide real cooperation. And even that has not yet resulted in bin Laden's capture, though it apparently has led to several attempts on Musharraf's life.

The other two countries we went to were Saudi Arabia and the United Arab Emirates, and both agreed to deliver the right message. The Saudis sent one of their princes to confront the Taliban directly. And he came back and told us the Taliban were idiots and liars. The Saudis then downgraded diplomatic ties with the Taliban, cut off official assistance and denied visas to Afghans traveling for non-religious reasons. And the UAE did the same. Our diplomats, including Ambassador Pickering, also met directly with Taliban leaders. We told them that if we did not get bin Laden, we would impose sanctions both bilaterally and through the UN, which we did. We also warned them clearly and repeatedly that they would be held accountable for any future attacks traceable to al Qaeda. In retrospect, we know that the Taliban and bin Laden had a symbiotic relationship. The Taliban needed the money and muscle al Qaeda provided; bin Laden needed space for his operatives to live and train. And there was never a real chance the Taliban would turn bin Laden over to us or to anybody else. . . .

We were not attacked on September 11th by a noun, terrorism. We were attacked by individuals affiliated with al Qaeda. They are the enemies who killed our fellow citizens and foreigners, and defeating them should be the focus of our policy. If we pursue goals that are unnecessarily broad, such as the elimination not only of threats but also of potential threats, we will stretch ourselves to the breaking point and become more vulnerable— not less—to those truly in a position to harm us. We also need to remember that al Qaeda is not a criminal gang that can simply be rounded up and put behind bars. It is the center of an ideological virus that has wholly perverted the minds of thousands and distorted the thinking of millions more. Until the right medicine is found, the virus will continue to spread, and that remedy begins with competence. Bin Laden and his cohorts have absolutely nothing to offer their followers except destruction, death and the illusion of glory. Puncturing this illusion is the key to winning the battle of ideas.

The problem is not combating al Qaeda's inherent appeal, for it has none. The problem is changing the fact that major components of American foreign policy are either opposed or misunderstood by much of the world. According to the State Department's advisory group on public diplomacy, published recently, the bottom has indeed fallen out of support for the United States. This unpopularity has handed bin Laden a gift that he has eagerly exploited. He is viewed by many as a leader of all those who harbor anti-American sentiments, and this has given him a following that is wholly undeserved. If we are to succeed, we must be sure that bin Laden goes down in history not as a defender of the faith or champion of the dispossessed, but rather as what he is: a murderer, a traitor to Islam and a loser.

The tarnishing of America's global prestige will require considerable time and effort to undo, and that's why we need long-range counterterrorism plans that [take] advantage of the full array of our national security tools. This plan must include the comprehensive reform of our intelligence structures; a vastly expanded commitment to public diplomacy and outreach, especially within the Arab and Muslim worlds; a far bolder strategy for stabilizing Afghanistan; revised policies toward the key countries of Pakistan and Saudi Arabia; expansion of the Nunn-Lugar program to secure weapons of mass destruction materials on a global basis; a new approach to handling and sharing of information concerning terrorist suspects; and a change in the tone of American national security policy to emphasize the value of diplomatic cooperation. . . .

We should all expect and prepare ourselves for the likelihood that further strikes will take place on our own soil, and we must be united in making sure that if and when that happens it will do absolutely nothing to advance the terrorists' goals. It will not cause divisions within and among the American people; on the contrary, it must bring us closer together and make us even more determined to fulfill our responsibilities. For more than two centuries, our countrymen have fought and died so that liberty might live, and since September 11th we have been summoned, each in our own way, to a new round in that struggle. We cannot underestimate the risks or anticipate the final victories will come easily or soon, but we can draw strength from the knowledge of what terror can and cannot do. Terror can turn life to death and laughter to tears and shared hopes to sorrowful memories. It can crash a plane and bring down towers that scrape the sky. But it cannot alter the essential goodness of the American people or diminish our loyalty to one another or cause our nation to turn its back on the world.

QUESTIONS FROM COMMISSIONERS

JOHN F. LEHMAN: [A]lmost as soon as the Clinton administration came in there was an [Iraqi] attempt to assassinate President Bush. There was a very minor strike launched against the intelligence service of Saddam—intelligence headquarters, and with the assurance that no one would be there so it would be in the middle of the night. After the Khobar bombing there were many in the administration who wanted to retaliate, but in fact nothing was done. After the '93 WTC [World Trade Center] attack there essentially was nothing done, pending the five-year trial. After the embassy bombing, there was, again, an attempt to make cruise missile attacks against the training camps and then against the pharmaceutical plant in Sudan. As you recall, there were criticisms at the time that this was a wag-the-dog scenario, that it was during the various stages of the president's problems, and that there was no real evidence there; that it was an innocent pharmaceutical plant. You were part of the inner sanctum at the time. In your view, was there real evidence that this was part of a bin Laden network?

ALBRIGHT: You've said a lot of different things. Let me just say that I do believe that when we had evidence, we used force. And the response on the '93—on the attempted assassination of President Bush—we reacted I think, very strongly. That's certainly what the Iraqis thought. And I was the one that had the rather peculiar moment of delivering the message to the Iraqi ambassador at the United Nations, while sitting in his residence under a portrait of Saddam Hussein, that we were bombing Baghdad and then went to the Security Council with the proof of it. So I think that we acted very well on that, and should be a sign that we were prepared to use military force when it was appropriate and we had intelligence in order to make it effective.

I think on the issue of '98, we were prepared to use force, and did use it immediately after the bombings of the embassies, as I said earlier. On actionable intelligence, I believed, and continue to believe, that the plant in Sudan was connected to this network that Osama bin Laden had had in Sudan and that it was an appropriate strike. And as you point out—and I think this is the very hard part for all of us, Mr. Secretary—is that we have to put ourselves into the pre–9/11 mode, and it's hard, because we've been in our post–9/11 prism, where we should be, and yet things were very different before 9/11. And as you point out, we were mostly accused of overreacting, not underreacting. And I believe we reacted appropriately, and as I said earlier, we would have acted more had we had actionable intelligence. And so, I think we dealt very appropriately with the issue and I think our record stands well.

. . .

SLADE GORTON: [P]re–9/11, the only military response to any al Qaeda attack, whether successful or one of the many that you said was frustrated during your period of time—the only military response was the response in the immediate aftermath of the embassy bombing. And while many other potential covert or cruise missile kinds of responses were considered, all ran up against an objection that the intelligence wasn't actionable, that you didn't know—there was no appropriate target, or that there would be collateral damage. So every such suggestion was frustrated and came to naught before 9/11; is that not correct?

ALBRIGHT: Well, I have no way of judging what happened inside the Bush administration from January to September.

GORTON: Well, you do know that nothing happened.

ALBRIGHT: Well, I do know that, but I also do know that many of the policy issues that we had developed were not followed up. And I have to say, with great sadness, to watch an incoming administration, kind of, take apart a lot of the policies that we did have, whether it had to do with North Korea or the Balkans, was difficult. So I think you have to ask people that were in the Bush administration as to how they saw things on this particular issue. But I do think, in all fairness, that 9/11 was a cataclysmic event that changed things and that they must have had similar reactions. But clearly there are many issues and many questions now about how they were responding to the terrorist threat and how seriously they took it.

GORTON: So at least during probably the year 2000, if not earlier, and 2001, up to 9/11, a rational al Qaeda could determine that terrorism was essentially cost-free, or only at a cost so modest that it was well worthwhile?

ALBRIGHT: I don't believe that actually. I think that if you look at what we were doing, we were on an upward trajectory of ramping up our dealing with terrorist activities, whether it was putting the infrastructure into place that the Bush administration is using on tracking finances, on trying to get more money into the CIA, of developing counterterrorism centers and activities. So I think, no. I mean, it's hard for me to get inside the head of al Qaeda, but no, I do not think they must have thought it was cost-free. . . .

.   .   .

JAMES R. THOMPSON: [N]one of the years of the Clinton effort, as vigorous as it was, either stopped the spread of al Qaeda, brought us Osama bin Laden or prevented September 11th. And it's really hard for me to see how criticism can be leveled against the Bush administration, which was brand new and had only seven months to try and look at, and in many cases, continue the policy of the Clinton administration toward al Qaeda and Osama bin Laden.

This was not one of those things they blew up like the Balkans or North Korea. Is that a fair conclusion?

ALBRIGHT: I think that fighting terrorism is a very difficult job, and it is clear from our experience of eight years, I think it's very hard to find Osama bin Laden. We had a hard time. I regret that they have not been able to find him. It is very difficult. We are dealing with a brand-new threat in a way that spreads through these variety of groups where people are given sanctuary and where, in fact, I think there is a question in the long term how we deal with it in terms of educational issues, in terms of trying to get the moderate Muslims to help us. . . .

And it is the threat of our time. And the devil's marriage between these shady groups and the spread of weapons of mass destruction is unfortunately the problem that we are all dealing with, that we cannot deed to our children and grandchildren. So I am very glad that this commission is looking into this because it's the lessons learned, not so much the blame placing.

.   .   .

EXCERPTS OF TESTIMONY FROM COLIN POWELL, U.S. SECRETARY OF STATE

"Anybody who thinks that Osama bin Laden might just be laying around somewhere and you can go pick him up, well, maybe. Good luck. But that's a wish, not a strategy or not a military action."

We wanted to move beyond the roll-back policy of containment, criminal prosecution and limited retaliation for specific terrorist attacks. We wanted to destroy al Qaeda. We understood that Pakistan was critical to the success of our long-term strategy. To get at al Qaeda, we had to end Pakistan's support for the Taliban so we had to recast our relations with that country. But nuclear sanctions caused by Pakistan's nuclear weapons test, and the nature of the new regime, the way President Musharraf took office, made it difficult for us to work with Pakistan. We knew, however, that achieving sustainable relations with Pakistan meant moving more aggressively to strengthen and shape our relations with India as well.

So we began this rather more complex diplomatic approach very quickly upon assuming office, even as we were putting the strategy on paper, and deciding its other more complicated elements. For example, in February of 2001, Presidents Bush and Musharraf exchanged letters. Let me quote a few lines from President Bush's February 16th letter to President Musharraf of Pakistan. This is just a few weeks after coming into office. Quote, the president said to President Musharraf, Pakistan is an important member of the community of nations and one with which I hope to build better relations, particularly as you move ahead to return to civilian constitutional government. We have concerns of which you are aware, but I am hopeful that we can work together on our differences in the years ahead. We should work together, the president continued, to address Afghanistan's many problems. The most pressing of these is terrorism, and it inhibits progress in all other issues. The continued presence of Osama bin Laden and his al Qaeda organization is a direct threat to the United States and its interests that must be addressed. I believe al Qaeda also threatens Pakistan's long-term interests. We join the United Nations in passing additional sanctions against the Taliban, to bring bin Laden to justice, and to close the network of terrorist camps and their territory. The president concluded, I urge you to use your influence with the Taliban to bring this about.

President Bush was very concerned about al Qaeda and about the safe haven given them by the Taliban, but he knew that implementing the diplomatic road map we envisioned would be difficult. The deputies went to work, reviewing all of these complex regional issues. Early on, we realized that a serious effort to remove al Qaeda's safe haven in Afghanistan might well require introducing military force, especially ground forces. This, without the cooperation of Pakistan, would be out of the question. Pakistan had vital interests in Afghanistan and was deeply suspicious of India's intentions. Pakistan's and India's mutual fears and

suspicion threatened to boil over into nuclear confl
administration got into the early months of its existence
mildly, the situation was delicate and dangerous. Any error to
effect change had to be calibrated very carefully to avoid misper-
ception and miscalculation. . . .

From early 2001 onward, we pressed the Taliban directly and
sought the assistance of the government of Pakistan and other
neighboring states to put additional pressure on the Taliban to
expel bin Laden from Afghanistan and shut down al Qaeda. On
February 8th, 2001, less than three weeks into the administration,
we closed the Taliban office in New York, implementing the U.N.
resolutions passed the previous month—I must say with the
strong support and the dedicated efforts of Secretary Albright
and Undersecretary Pickering.

In March, we repeated the warning to the Taliban that they
would be held responsible for any al Qaeda attack against our
interests. In April 2001, senior departmental officials traveled to
Uzbekistan, Kazakhstan, the Kyrgyz Republic, Tajikistan, to lay
out our key concerns, including about terrorism and Afghanistan.
We asked these Central Asian nations to coordinate their efforts
with the various Afghan players who were opposed to the Taliban.
We also used what we call the Bonn Group of concerned countries, to bring together Germany, Russia, Iran, Pakistan, the
United States to build a common approach to Afghanistan. At the
same time, we encouraged and supported the Rome group of
expatriate Afghans to explore alternatives to the Taliban.

In May, Deputy Secretary Armitage met with First Deputy
Foreign Minister Trubnikov of the Russian Federation to renew
the work of the U.S.-Russia working group in Afghanistan. These
discussions had previously been conducted at a lower level. We
focused specifically on what we could do together about Afghanistan and about the Taliban. This, incidentally, laid the groundwork for obtaining Russian cooperation on liberating Afghanistan
immediately after 9/11. . . .

And then, as we all know, 9/11 hit and we had to accelerate all
of our efforts and go onto a different kind of footing altogether. I
just might point out that, with respect to Pakistan, consistent

with the decisions that we had made in early September, after 9/11, within two days, Mr. Armitage had contacted the Pakistani intelligence chiefs who happened to be in the United States and laid out what we now needed from Pakistan. The time for diplomacy and discussions were over; we needed immediate action. And Mr. Armitage laid out seven specific steps for Pakistan to take to join us in this effort. We gave them 24, 48 hours to consider it and then I called President Musharraf and said, We need your answer now. We need you as part of this campaign, this crusade. And President Musharraf made a historic and strategic decision that evening when I spoke to him and changed his policy and became a partner in this effort as opposed to a hindrance to the effort.

QUESTIONS FROM COMMISSIONERS

RICHARD BEN-VENISTE: You and I met with other members of the commission on the 21st of January of [2004]. On that occasion, you advised us of a full-day meeting on Saturday, September 15th, in which the question of striking Iraq was discussed. You advised us that the deputy secretary of defense advanced the argument that Iraq was the source of the problem and that the United States should launch an attack on Iraq forthwith. You advised us that [Deputy Defense Secretary Paul] Wolfowitz was unable to justify that position. Have I accurately described your recollection of what occurred?

POWELL: There was a meeting of the National Security Council that Mr. Wolfowitz also attended on that day at Camp David, as you describe. There was a full day of discussions on the situation that we found ourselves in, who was responsible for it. And as part of that full day of discussion, Iraq was discussed. And Secretary Wolfowitz raised the issue of whether or not Iraq should be considered for action during this time. And after fully discussing all sides of the issue, as I think it is appropriate for such a group to do, the president made a tentative decision that afternoon—I would call it a tentative decision—that we ought to focus on Afghanistan because it was clear to us at that point that al Qaeda was responsible, the Taliban was harboring al Qaeda and that that should be the objective of any action we were to take.

He did not dismiss Iraq as a problem. But he said: First things first, we will examine all of the sources of terrorism directed against the United States and the civilized world, but we'll start with Afghanistan. Now, he confirmed that over the next couple of days in meetings we had with him. And when he came back down from Camp David and we met on Monday, he made it a firm decision and gave us all instructions as to how to proceed. And then he announced that to the nation later in the week. And so he heard arguments, as he should, from all members of his administration on the different alternatives. I think this is what a president would expect us to do, and he decided on Afghanistan.

. . .

BOB KERREY: The bottom line for me is it just pains me to have to say that on the 11th of September that 19 men and less than a half a million dollars defeated every single defensive mechanism we had in place—utterly. It wasn't even a close call. They defeated everything we had in place on 11 September, with hardly, it seems to me, any doubt about their chance of success. And I'll just stop there and give you a chance to tell me what you think went wrong.

POWELL: Let me speak to our administration, and I'll speak more generally to get to the heart of the question. I think, in our deliberations and our meetings . . . the Pentagon was starting to develop plans. It was looking at contingencies that it might have to deal with. And you can pursue this with [Defense] Secretary [Donald] Rumsfeld this afternoon. But in this whole period, to say that using military force to get al Qaeda when it wasn't going to be a surgical strike—anybody who thinks that Osama bin Laden might just be laying around somewhere and you can go pick him up, well, maybe. Good luck. But that's a wish, not a strategy or not a military action.

So you would have had, really, to go after al Qaeda by going after the Taliban, and that meant invading another country. And it meant invading another country without the support of any of the surrounding countries where you would need some access to get there. And so I don't know that in this period from '93 through the summer of 2001 you had a sufficient political base and sufficient political understanding, both here and in the international community, that would have given you a basis for saying that we know enough about al Qaeda, we know enough about the Taliban, that we are going in to invade this country and remove this threat.

KERREY: . . . I was there in '91 when you and former President Bush and Secretary Cheney went to the world and persuaded the world that we needed to drive Iraq out of Kuwait. Public opinion wasn't on your side either when you began. Public opinion wasn't on the side of President Clinton when he suggested that we needed to intervene in Bosnia. It wasn't on the side of the administration when they decided to intervene in Kosovo. [H]istory's replete of examples where political leaders made a decision in spite of public opinion being on the other side, and saying, I've got to persuade people because I see it being an urgent necessity.

POWELL: I don't think that, in the case of al Qaeda and Afghanistan during this period, it rose to that level of urgent necessity, that the people thought that we've got to go do this now, even if it includes major invasion of a country without the support of any of the surrounding countries. Do we have a sufficient cause and justification to undertake such action? And the previous administration can speak for itself. They've spoken for themselves, they said they didn't see it. And frankly in our first 7 months in office, as we looked at this we realized that it might come to that. That's the realization that we come to. And you come to these kinds of realizations after a great deal of study and debate. . . . A lot of people came in, and we put together a more comprehensive policy and we reached the conclusion in early September that it might come to that and we have to understand that we might have to go in and take this kind of large-scale military action if that was the only way to eliminate this threat.

. . .

TIMOTHY J. ROEMER: Richard Clarke in his new book, on page 228, says, Colin Powell took the unusual steps, during the transition, of asking to meet with the CSG, the Counterterrorism Security Group, took notes, and was surprised at the unanimity of the recommendations and the threat of al Qaeda. He paid careful attention and asked Mr. Armitage to follow up on it. Very blunt, very praiseworthy, very complimentary of your understanding the problem. In that PowerPoint presentation that he made to you, he in fact said, they're here. One of the slides said that al Qaeda was in the United States. Doesn't that in fact say two things: one, that nine months is too long to act. You have to take some immediate steps. And two, if you're going to go from a rollback strategy to an elimination strategy, if you're going to go from swatting flies to exterminating the flies, you've got to have something to exterminate them with, whether it's Predator, Northern Alliance, aid to Uzbekistan, covert operations—you have to be taking some of these actions. The U.S.S. *Cole*—why didn't we take at least some of those actions in the meantime as this nine-month bottom-up review took place?

POWELL: . . . At the time that [Clarke] gave me the briefing, I was not the secretary of state. This administration was not in office. And if, according to this slide, Mr. Clarke and the members of the previous administration who were briefing me that day—this was the 20th of December, a month before inauguration—if they were aware that al Qaeda representatives were already in the country running around and knew that, and knew that these 19— if that's the reference in that passage—they were running around inside the country, the obligation frankly is on them, not why didn't we do something beginning a month later. Why hadn't they done something while they were preparing the PowerPoint presentation?

Staff Statement No. 6

The Military

Beginning in the 1970s, the U.S. government asked the armed forces to develop a capability for combating terrorism. Though this was initially conceived narrowly for hostage rescue, the failure of the 1980 Iran hostage rescue mission demonstrated the need to build more robust forces. By the mid-1980s the U.S. government also began considering capabilities for offensive counterterrorism missions that would use military forces to attack terrorist organizations on their home ground. These were the years in which the organization now known as the Joint Special Operations Command was created. As the international terrorism danger subsided at the end of the 1980s, little additional effort seemed needed for an offensive counterterrorism capability. In George H. W. Bush's presidency and the early years of the Clinton administration, the [Pentagon] was a secondary player in counterterrorism efforts which focused on the apprehension and rendition of wanted suspects.

After the 1996 attack on an Air Force residential complex in Saudi Arabia, Khobar Towers, the Department of Defense (DOD) and the military gave particular attention to defending against attack. In their lexicon, "anti-terrorism" means defensive force protection. "Counter-terrorism" refers to offensive operations. After Khobar Towers, anti-terrorism had the priority claim on attention and resources.

Under the directive on counterterrorism policy issued by President Clinton in May 1998, Presidential Decision Directive 62, there were ten program areas. The only one that highlighted a DOD role was the tenth, on the protection of Americans overseas. The directive stated that the Defense Department, through the unified regional commanders, was responsible for the protection of U.S. forces stationed abroad. The Joint Chiefs of Staff also established a special office dedicated to what DOD officials describe as a decades-old, high-priority mission to protect U.S. troops from unconventional attack.

At home, the military's role was specialized support to state and local authorities for dealing with the consequences of terrorist attack, and security support for special events, such as the Olympics. [Clinton's] Defense Secretary William Cohen and [Cohen's] deputy, John Hamre, gave significant attention to the danger of an attack with unconventional weapons and took some initial, innovative steps to develop a domestic military capability to assist civil authorities in the event of such an attack.

Abroad, the role of the military was to provide support for law enforcement, such as military transport for terrorist renditions, or support for other agencies as they responded to a terrorist attack. The undersecretary of defense for policy at the time, Walter Slocombe, told us that it would have been extraordinary to assign the military a leading role in counterterrorism efforts abroad since military force was not the primary counterterrorism instrument.

OPERATION INFINITE REACH

After the U.S. embassies in Nairobi and Dar es Salaam were attacked on August 7, 1998, President Clinton directed his advisers to consider military options. The difficult relationship between evidence and action, mentioned earlier today, was soon clarified with extraordinary intelligence that fixed responsibility quickly and authoritatively on Osama bin Laden personally, as well as his organization.

Focused by intelligence suggesting that terrorist leaders, including bin Laden, would be meeting at a terrorist camp in Afghanistan, President Clinton organized a tightly compartmented planning effort to prepare a set of strikes, code-named "Operation Infinite Reach." He and his advisers agreed on a set of targets in Afghanistan. His advisers recommended that the U.S. government should strike whether or not there was firm evidence that the terrorist commanders were at these facilities. Secretary Cohen told us it was also important to send a signal that the United States was coming and was not going to tolerate terrorist activity against America.

More difficult was the question of whether to strike other al Qaeda targets in Sudan. Two possible targets were identified in Sudan, including a pharmaceutical plant at which, the President was told by his aides, they believed VX nerve gas was manufactured with Osama bin Laden's financial support. Indeed, even before the embassy bombings, NSC counterterrorism staff had been warning about this plant. Yet on August 11, the NSC staff's senior director for intelligence advised National Security Adviser [Samuel] Berger that the "bottom line" was that "we will need much better intelligence on this facility before we seriously consider any options." By the early morning hours of August 20, when the President made his decision, his policy advisers concluded that enough evidence had been gathered to justify the strike. The President approved their recommendation on that target, while choosing not to proceed with the strike on the other target in Sudan—a business believed to be owned by bin Laden. [Director of Central Intelligence George] Tenet and National Security Adviser Berger told us that, based on what they know today, they still believe they made the right recommendation and that the President made the right decision. We have encountered no dissenters among his top advisers.

This strike was launched on August 20. The missiles hit their intended targets, but neither bin Laden nor any other terrorist leaders were killed. The decision to destroy the plant in Sudan became controversial. Some at the time argued that the decisions were influenced by domestic political considerations, given the controversies raging at that time. The staff has found no evidence that domestic political considerations entered into the discussion or the decision-making process. All evidence we have found points to national security considerations as the sole basis for President Clinton's decision.

The impact of the criticism lingered, however, as policymakers looked at proposals for new strikes. The controversy over the Sudan attack, in particular, shadowed future discussions about the quality of intelligence that would be needed about other targets.

OPERATION INFINITE RESOLVE
AND PLAN DELENDA

Senior officials agree that a principal objective of Operation Infinite Reach was to kill Osama bin Laden, and that this objective obviously had not been attained. The initial strikes went beyond targeting bin Laden to damage other camps thought to be supporting his organization. These strikes were not envisioned as the end of the story. On August 20, the chairman of the Joint Chiefs of Staff (JCS), General Hugh Shelton, issued a planning order for the preparation of follow-on strikes. This plan was later code-named Operation Infinite Resolve. The day after the strikes the President and his principal advisers apparently began considering follow-on military planning. A few days later the NSC staff's national coordinator for counterterrorism, Richard Clarke, informed other senior officials that President Clinton was inclined to launch further strikes sooner rather than later.

On August 27 Undersecretary Slocombe advised Secretary Cohen that the available targets were not promising. There was, he said, also an issue of strategy, the need to think of the effort as a long-term campaign. The experience of last week, he wrote, "has only confirmed the importance of defining a clearly articulated rationale for military action" that was effective as well as justified.

Active consideration of follow-on strikes continued into September. In this context Clarke prepared a paper for a political-military plan he called "Delenda," from the Latin "to destroy." Its military component envisioned an ongoing campaign of regular, small strikes, occurring from time to time whenever target information was ripe, in order to underscore the message of a concerted, systematic, and determined effort to dismantle the infrastructure of the bin Laden terrorist network. Clarke recognized that individual targets might not have much value. But, he wrote to Berger, we will never again be able to target a leadership conference of terrorists, and that should not be the standard.

Principals repeatedly considered Clarke's proposed strategy, but none of them agreed with it. Secretary Cohen told us that the camps were primitive, easily constructed facilities with "rope ladders." The question was whether it was worth using very expensive missiles to take out what General Shelton called "jungle gym" training camps. That would not have been seen as very effective. National Security Adviser Berger and others told us that more strikes, if they failed to kill bin Laden, could actually be counterproductive—increasing bin Laden's stature.

These issues need to be viewed, they said, in a wider context. The United States launched air attacks against Iraq at the end of 1998 and against Serbia in 1999, all to widespread criticism around the world. About a later proposal for strikes on targets in Afghanistan, Deputy National Security Adviser James Steinberg noted that it offered "little benefit, lots of blowback against [a] bomb-happy U.S."

In September 1998, while the follow-on strikes were still being debated among a small group of top advisers, the counterterrorism officials in the Office of the Secretary of Defense were also considering a strategy. Unaware of Clarke's plan, they developed an elaborate proposal for a "more aggressive counterterrorism posture." The paper urged Defense to "champion a national effort to take up the gauntlet that international terrorists have thrown at our feet." Although the terrorist threat had grown, the authors warned that "we have not fundamentally altered our philosophy or our approach." If there were new "horrific attacks," they wrote that then "we will have no choice nor, unfortunately, will we have a plan." They outlined an eight-part strategy "to be more proactive and aggressive." The Assistant Secretary of Defense for Special Operations and Low Intensity Conflict, Allen Holmes, brought the paper to Undersecretary Slocombe's chief deputy, Jan Lodal. The paper did not go further. Its lead author recalls being told by Holmes that Lodal thought it was too aggressive. Holmes cannot recall what was said, and Lodal cannot remember the episode or the paper at all.

The President and his advisers remained ready to use military action against the terrorist threat. But the urgent interest in launching follow-on strikes had apparently passed by October. The focus shifted to an effort to find strikes that would clearly be effective, to find and target bin Laden himself.

MILITARY PLANNING CONTINUES

Though plans were not executed, the military continued to assess and update target lists regularly in case the military was asked to strike. Plans largely centered on cruise missile and manned aircraft strike options, and were updated and refined continuously through March 2001.

Several senior Clinton administration officials, including National Security Adviser Berger and the NSC staff's Clarke, told us that President Clinton was interested in additional military options, including the possible use of ground forces. As part of Operation Infinite Resolve, the military produced them.

In December 1998 General Shelton ordered planning for the use of Special Operations Forces to capture OBL [Osama bin Laden] network leaders and transport them away from Kandahar. A second order issued on the following day examined the possible interception of aircraft. Plans refined throughout 1999 added successive options within the Infinite Resolve plan, including the possible use of strike aircraft, as well as Special Operations Forces. The targets included not only terrorist training camps, but also many other targets associated with bin Laden and the known infrastructure of his organization.

The relationship of the White House and the Pentagon was complex. As Lieutenant General Gregory Newbold, director of operations for the Joint Staff, put it, the military was often frustrated by civilian policymakers whose requests for military options were too simplistic. For their part, White House officials were often frustrated by what they saw as military unwillingness to tackle the counterterrorism problem.

General Shelton told us that he was aware of criticism that the Pentagon was too reluctant to engage the military against al Qaeda and OBL before 9/11. He said that, when he provided military advice to policymakers, he wanted to ensure they understood that military force is not "magic." He remarked that while the U.S. military is a great force, risks associated with using that force must be explained, though such cautions may be frustrating to those eager to conduct a military operation.

General Shelton said that "given sufficient actionable intelligence, the military can do the operation." But he explained that a tactical operation, if it did not go well, could turn out to be an international embarrassment for the United States. Shelton and many other military and civilian DOD officials we interviewed recalled their memories of episodes such as the failed hostage rescue in Iran in 1980, and the "Black Hawk Down" events in Somalia in 1993. General Shelton made clear, however, that upon direction from policymakers the military would proceed with an operation and carry out the order.

Secretary Cohen said the Pentagon was always ready to capture bin Laden if it could and to kill him if necessary. Cohen says he told other policymakers, "We can do this. It's high risk, but if you've got the information to tell us where he is, we will be prepared to recommend that we use force."

Another set of concerns came from the commander-in-chief of the U.S. Central Command (CENTCOM), General Anthony Zinni. Before 9/11 any military action in Afghanistan would be carried out by CENTCOM. The Special Operations Command did not have the lead; it provided forces that could be used in a CENTCOM-led operation. The views of the key field commander carried great weight. General Zinni told us he did not believe that some of the options his command was ordered to develop would be effective, particularly missile strikes. Zinni thought a better approach would have been a broad strategy to build up local counter-terrorism capabilities in neighboring countries, using military assistance to help countries like Uzbekistan. This strategy, he told us, was impeded by a lack of funds and limited interest in countries, like Uzbekistan, that had dictatorial governments.

As for the strike options, Zinni thought they would have little military effect and might threaten regional stability. Zinni told us that he advised the JCS chairman, General Shelton, about his reservations. Planning updates were generally not briefed to the policymakers. When they were briefed, the military carefully laid out the pros and cons of each option.

Military officers explained to us that sending Special Operations Forces into Afghanistan would have been complicated and risky. Such efforts would have required bases in the region; however, the basing options in the region were unappealing. Pro-Taliban elements of Pakistan's military might warn bin Laden or his associates of pending operations. The U.S. government had information that the former Pakistan Interservices Intelligence Directorate (ISID) head Hamid Gul, as a private citizen, contacted Taliban leaders in July 1999 and advised them that the United States was not planning to attack Afghanistan. He assured them that, as he had "last time," he would provide three or four hours of warning should there be another missile launch.

With nearby basing options limited, an alternative was to fly from ships in the Arabian Sea or from land bases in the Persian Gulf, as was later done after 9/11. Such operations would then have to be supported from long distances, overflying the airspace of nations that might not be supportive or aware of the U.S. efforts.

Finally, military leaders again raised the problem of "actionable intelligence," warning that they did not have information about where bin Laden would be by the time forces would be able to strike him. If they were in the region for a long period, perhaps clandestinely, the military might attempt to gather intelligence and wait for an opportunity. One special operations commander said his view of actionable intelligence was that if "you give us the action, we'll give you the intelligence." But this course would be risky, both in light of the difficulties already mentioned and the danger that U.S. operations might fail disastrously—as in the 1980 Iran rescue failure.

CRUISE MISSILES AS THE DEFAULT OPTION

Cruise missiles became the "default option" because it was the only option left on the table after the rejection of others. The Tomahawk's long range, lethality, and extreme accuracy made it the missile of choice. However, as a means to attack al Qaeda and OBL-linked targets pre–9/11, cruise missiles were problematic.

Tomahawk cruise missiles had to be launched after the vessels carrying them moved into position. Once these vessels were in position, there was still an interval as decisionmakers authorized the strike, the missiles were prepared for firing, and they flew to their targets. Officials worried that bin Laden might move during these hours from the place of his last sighting, even if that information had been current.

Moreover, General Zinni told Commission staff that he had been deeply concerned that cruise missile strikes inside Afghanistan would kill numerous civilians. Zinni pointed out that most of the places where bin Laden was likely to be found were populated areas, and a percentage of the missiles would also simply go awry. Zinni estimated that a cruise missile strike might kill up to 2,000 innocent Afghans. In discussing the potential repercussions of missile strikes in his region of military responsibility, he warned, "It was easy to take the shot from Washington and walk away from it. We had to live there."

NO ACTIONABLE INTELLIGENCE

The paramount limitation cited by senior officials on every proposed use of military force was the lack of "actionable intelligence." By this, they meant precise intelligence on where bin Laden would be, and how long he would be there.

National Security Adviser Berger said that there was never a circumstance where the policymakers thought they had good intelligence but declined to launch a missile at OBL-linked targets for fear of possible collateral damage. He told us the deciding factor was whether there was actionable intelligence. If the shot missed bin Laden, the United States would look weak, and bin Laden would look strong.

There were frequent reports about bin Laden's whereabouts and activities. The daily reports regularly described where he was, what he was doing, and where he might be going. But usually, by the time these descriptions were landing on the desks of DCI [Director of Central Intelligence] Tenet or National Security Adviser Berger, bin Laden had already moved. Nevertheless, on occasion, intelligence was deemed credible enough to warrant planning for possible strikes to kill Osama bin Laden.

Kandahar, December 1998

The first instance was in December 1998, in Kandahar. There was intelligence that bin Laden was staying at a particular location. Strikes were readied against this and plausible alternative locations. The principal advisers to the President agreed not to recommend a strike. Returning from one of their meetings, DCI Tenet told staff that the military, supported by everyone else in the room, had not wanted to launch a strike because no one had seen bin Laden in a couple of hours. DCI Tenet told us that there were concerns about the veracity of the source and about the risk of collateral damage to a nearby mosque. A few weeks later, Clarke described the calculus as one that had weighed 50 percent confidence in the intelligence against collateral damage estimated at, perhaps, 300 casualties.

After this episode Pentagon planners intensified efforts to find a more precise alternative to cruise missiles, such as using precision strike aircraft. This option would greatly reduce the collateral damage. Not only would it have to operate at long ranges from home bases and overcome significant logistical obstacles, but the aircraft might be shot down by the Taliban. At the time, Clarke complained that General Zinni was opposed to the forward deployment of these aircraft. General Zinni does not recall blocking such an option. The aircraft apparently were not deployed for this purpose.

The Desert Camp, February 1999

During the winter of 1998–99, intelligence reported that bin Laden frequently visited a camp in the desert adjacent to a larger hunting camp in the Helmand province of Afghanistan, used by visitors from a Gulf state. Public sources have stated that these visitors were from the United Arab Emirates [UAE]. At the beginning of February, bin Laden was reportedly located there, and apparently remained for more than a week. This was not in an urban area, so the risk of collateral damage was minimal. Intelligence provided a detailed description of the camps. National technical intelligence confirmed the description of the larger camp and showed the nearby presence of an official aircraft of the UAE. The CIA received reports that bin Laden regularly went from his adjacent camp to the larger camp where he visited with Emiratis. The location of this larger camp was confirmed by February 9, but the location of bin Laden's quarters could not be pinned down so precisely. Preparations were made for a possible strike at least against the larger camp, perhaps to target bin Laden during one of his visits. No strike was launched.

According to CIA officials, policymakers were concerned about the danger that a strike might kill an Emirati prince or other senior officials who might be with bin Laden or close by. The lead CIA official in the field felt the intelligence reporting in this case was very reliable; the OBL unit chief at the time agrees. The field official believes today that this was a lost opportunity to kill bin Laden before 9/11.

Clarke told us the strike was called off because the intelligence was dubious, and it seemed to him as if the CIA was presenting an option to attack America's best counterterrorism ally in the Gulf. Documentary evidence at the time shows that on February 10 Clarke detailed to Deputy National Security Adviser Donald Kerrick the intelligence placing OBL in the camp, informed him that DOD might be in position to fire the next morning, and added that General Shelton was looking at other options that might be ready the following week.

Clarke had just returned from a visit to the UAE, working on counterterrorism cooperation and following up on a May 1998 UAE agreement to buy F–16 aircraft from the United States. On February 10, Clarke reported that a top UAE official had vehemently denied that high-level UAE officials were in Afghanistan. Evidence subsequently confirmed that high-level UAE officials had been hunting there.

By February 12 bin Laden had apparently moved on and the immediate strike plans became moot. In March the entire camp complex was hurriedly disassembled. We are still examining several aspects of this episode.

Kandahar, May 1999

In this case sources reported on the whereabouts of bin Laden over the course of five nights. The reporting was very detailed. At the time CIA working-level officials were told that strikes were not ordered because the military was concerned about the precision of the source's reporting and the risk of collateral damage. Replying to a frustrated colleague in the field, the OBL unit chief wrote that "having a chance to get OBL three times in 36 hours and foregoing the chance each time has made me a bit angry. . . . the DCI finds himself alone at the table, with the other princip[als] basically saying 'we'll go along with your decision Mr. Director,' and implicitly saying that the Agency will hang alone if the attack doesn't get bin Laden." These are working-level perspectives.

According to DCI Tenet the same circumstances prevented a

strike in each of the cases described above: The intelligence was based on a single uncorroborated source, and there was a risk of collateral damage. In the first and third cases, the cruise missile option was rejected outright, and in the case of the second, never came to a clear decision point. According to National Security Adviser Berger, the cases were "really DCI Tenet's call." In his view, in none of the cases did policymakers have the reliable intelligence that was needed. In Berger's opinion, this did not reflect risk aversion or a lack of desire to act on DCI Tenet's part. The DCI was just as stoked up as he was, said Berger. Each of these times, Berger told us, "George would call and say, 'We just don't have it.'" There was a fourth episode involving a location in Ghazni, Afghanistan, in July 1999. We are still investigating the circumstances.

There were no occasions after July 1999 when cruise missiles were actively readied for a possible strike against bin Laden. The challenge of providing actionable intelligence could not be overcome before 9/11.

MILLENNIUM PLOTS

In late 1999, the military engaged in substantial preparations in anticipation of possible terrorist attacks around the Millennium. The Joint Chiefs of Staff developed a plan to react as rapidly as possible to an al Qaeda strike anywhere in the world. The Pentagon was also prepared to provide assistance within the United States to other federal agencies in response to an act or threatened act of terrorism.

In the summer of 2000, the Joint Chiefs of Staff refined its list of strikes and special operations possibilities to a set of thirteen options within the Operation Infinite Resolve plan. Planning by the Joint Chiefs of Staff and CENTCOM also focused primarily on the development of the Predator unmanned aerial vehicle for the purposes of intelligence collection and targeting of bin Laden and al Qaeda leaders. . . .

THE ATTACK ON THE U.S.S. *COLE*

On October 12, 2000, suicide bombers in an explosives-laden skiff rammed into a Navy destroyer, the U.S.S. *Cole*, in the port of Aden, Yemen, killing 17 U.S. sailors and almost sinking the vessel. In January 2000, jihadists had also tried to bomb the U.S.S. *The Sullivans* using identical tactics, but the plot failed when the skiff carrying the explosives sank under their weight—something unknown to the U.S. government until after the attack on the *Cole*. The FBI, the CIA, and the Yemeni government all launched investigations to determine who had attacked the *Cole*. DOD's role was primarily the provision of aircraft for the interagency emergency response team kept on standby for such occasions.

After the attack on the U.S.S. *Cole*, National Security Adviser Berger asked General Shelton for military plans to act quickly against bin Laden. General Shelton tasked General Tommy Franks, the new commander of CENTCOM, to look again at the options. According to Director for Operations Newbold, Shelton wanted to demonstrate that the military was imaginative and knowledgeable enough to move on an array of options, and to show the complexity of the operations. Shelton briefed Berger on the thirteen options. CENTCOM also developed a "Phased Campaign Concept" for wider-ranging strikes, including against the Taliban, and without a fixed endpoint. The new concept did not include contingency plans for an invasion of Afghanistan. The concept was briefed to Deputy National Security Adviser Kerrick and other officials in December 2000.

Neither the Clinton administration nor the Bush administration launched a military response for the *Cole* attack. Berger and other senior policymakers said that, while most counterterrorism officials quickly pointed the finger at al Qaeda, they never received the sort of definitive judgment from the CIA or the FBI that al Qaeda was responsible that they would need before launching military operations. Documents show that, in late 2000, the President's advisers received a cautious presentation of the evidence showing that individuals linked to al Qaeda had carried out or supported the attack, but that the evidence could not establish that bin Laden himself had ordered the attack. DOD prepared plans to strike al Qaeda camps and Taliban targets with cruise missiles in case policymakers decided to respond.

Essentially the same analysis of al Qaeda's responsibility for the attack on the U.S.S. *Cole* was delivered to the highest officials of the new administration five days after it took office. The same day, Clarke advised National Security Adviser [Condoleezza] Rice that the government "should take advantage of the policy that 'we will respond at a time, place and manner of our own choosing' and not be forced into knee-jerk responses." Deputy National Security Adviser Stephen Hadley told us that "tit-for-tat" military options were so inadequate that they might have emboldened al Qaeda. He said the Bush administration's response to the *Cole* would be a new, more aggressive strategy against al Qaeda.

Pentagon officials, including Vice Admiral Scott Fry and Undersecretary Slocombe, told us they cautioned that the military response options were limited. Bin Laden continued to be elusive. They were still skeptical that hitting inexpensive and rudimentary training camps with costly missiles would do much good. The new team at the Pentagon did not push for a response for the *Cole*, according to Secretary of Defense [Donald] Rumsfeld and Paul Wolfowitz, his deputy. Wolfowitz told us that by the time the new administration was in place, the *Cole* incident was "stale." The 1998 cruise missiles strikes showed OBL and al Qaeda that they had nothing to fear from a U.S. response, Wolfowitz said. For his part, Rumsfeld also thought too much time had passed. He worked on the force protection recommendations developed in the aftermath of the U.S.S. *Cole* attack, not response options.

THE EARLY MONTHS OF
THE BUSH ADMINISTRATION

The confirmation of the Pentagon's new leadership was a lengthy process. Deputy Secretary of Defense Wolfowitz was not confirmed until March 2001, and Undersecretary of Defense for

Policy Douglas Feith did not take office until July 2001. Secretary Cohen said he briefed Secretary-designate Rumsfeld on about 50 items during the transition, including bin Laden and programs related to domestic preparedness against terrorist attacks using weapons of mass destruction. Rumsfeld told us he did not recall what was said about bin Laden at that briefing. On February 8, General Shelton briefed Secretary Rumsfeld on the Operation Infinite Resolve plan, including the range of options and CENT-COM's new phased campaign plan. These plans were periodically updated during the ensuing months.

Brian Sheridan—the outgoing Assistant Secretary of Defense for Special Operations and Low Intensity Conflict (SOLIC), the key counterterrorism policy office in DOD—never briefed Rumsfeld. Lower-level SOLIC officials in the Office of the Secretary of Defense told us that they thought the new team was focused on other issues and was not especially interested in their counterterrorism agenda. Undersecretary Feith told the Commission that when he arrived at the Pentagon in July 2001, Rumsfeld asked him to focus his attention on working with the Russians on agreements to dissolve the Anti-Ballistic Missile (ABM) Treaty and preparing a new nuclear arms control pact. Traditionally, the primary DOD official responsible for counter-terrorism policy had been the assistant secretary of defense for SOLIC. The outgoing assistant secretary left on January 20, 2001, and had not been replaced when the Pentagon was hit on September 11.

Secretary Rumsfeld said that transformation was a focus of the administration. He said he was interested in terrorism, arranging to meet regularly with DCI Tenet. But his time was consumed with getting new officials in place, preparing the Quadrennial Defense Review, the Defense Planning Guidance, and reviewing existing contingency plans. He did not recall any particular counterterrorism issue that engaged his attention before 9/11, other than the development of the Predator unmanned aircraft system for possible use against bin Laden. He said that DOD, before 9/11, was not organized or trained adequately to deal with asymmetric threats.

As recounted in the previous staff statement, the Bush administration's NSC staff was drafting a new counterterrorism strategy in the spring and summer of 2001. National Security Adviser Rice and Deputy National Security Adviser Hadley told us that they wanted more muscular options. In June 2001 Hadley circulated a draft presidential directive on policy toward al Qaeda. The draft came to include a section that called for development of a new set of contingency military plans against both al Qaeda and the Taliban regime. Hadley told us that he contacted Deputy Secretary Wolfowitz to advise him that the Pentagon would soon need to start preparing fresh plans in response to this forthcoming presidential directive.

The directive was approved at the Deputies level in July and apparently approved by top officials on September 4 for submission to the President. With this directive still awaiting the president's signature, Secretary Rumsfeld did not order the preparation of any new military plans against either al Qaeda or the Taliban before 9/11. Rumsfeld told us that immediately after 9/11, he did not see a contingency plan he wanted to implement. Deputy National Security Adviser Hadley and Deputy Secretary Wolfowitz also told us the military plans presented to the Bush administration immediately after 9/11 were unsatisfactory.

ROADS NOT TAKEN

Officials we interviewed flatly said that neither Congress nor the American public would have supported large-scale military operations in Afghanistan before the shock of 9/11—despite repeated attacks and plots, including the embassy bombings, the Millennium plots, concerns about al Qaeda acquiring WMD [weapons of mass destruction], the U.S.S. *Cole*, and the summer 2001 threat spike. Deputy Secretary Wolfowitz warned that it would have been impossible to get Congress to support sending 10,000 U.S. troops into Afghanistan to do what the Soviet Union failed to do in the 1980s. Vice Admiral Scott Fry, the former operations director for the JCS, noted that "a two-or-four division plan would require a footprint [troop level] and force that was larger than the political leadership was willing to accept."

Special Operations Forces always saw counterterrorism as part of their mission and trained for counterterrorist operations. "The opportunities were missed because of an unwillingness to take risks and a lack of vision and understanding of the benefits when preparing the battle space ahead of time," said Lieutenant General William Boykin, the current deputy undersecretary of defense for intelligence and a former founding member of Delta Force. Before 9/11, the U.S. Special Operations Command was a "supporting command," not a "supported command." That meant it supported General Zinni and CENTCOM, and did not independently prepare plans itself. General Pete Schoomaker, the chief of staff of the U.S. Army and former Commander of the U.S. Special Operations Command, said that if the Special Operations Command had been a supported command before 9/11, he would have had the al Qaeda mission rather than deferring to CENTCOM's lead. Schoomaker said he spoke to Secretary Cohen and General Shelton about this proposal. It was not adopted.

There were also activists in the most senior levels of the uniformed military, the Joint Chiefs of Staff. Noting the frustration of others in DOD and elsewhere grappling with the al Qaeda problem, General Newbold, the JCS operations director, prepared a comprehensive plan designed to incorporate military, economic and political activities to influence and pressure the Taliban to expel OBL, and follow with massive strikes if necessary. Newbold said he briefed this plan at the end of 2000 to General Shelton and NSC counterterrorism coordinator Clarke. Much of it was beyond the scope of the Defense Department to implement. Like other options produced by the military before 9/11, this plan too was eventually given back to the Joint Chiefs with no direction for further action. The military continued to develop and refine this plan.

CONCLUSIONS

In summary, our key findings to date include the following:

- In response to the request of policymakers, the military prepared a wide array of options for striking bin Laden and his organization from May 1998 onward;

- When they briefed policymakers, the military presented both the pros and cons of those strike options, and briefed policymakers on the risks associated with them;

- Following the August 20, 1998 missile strikes, both senior military officials and policymakers placed great emphasis on actionable intelligence as the key factor in recommending or deciding to launch military action against bin Laden and his organization;

- Policymakers and military officials expressed frustration with the lack of actionable intelligence;

- Some officials inside the Pentagon, including those in the Special Forces and the counterterrorism policy office, expressed frustration with the lack of military action;

- The new Administration began to develop new policies toward al Qaeda in 2001, but there is no evidence of new work on military capabilities or plans against this enemy before September 11; and

- Both civilian and military officials of the Defense Department state flatly that neither Congress nor the American public would have supported large-scale military operations in Afghanistan before the shock of 9/11.

Bonnie Jenkins, Michael Hurley, Alexis Albion, Ernest May, and Steve Dunne did much of the investigative work reflected in this statement. The Department of Defense and Central Intelligence Agency have cooperated fully in making available both the documents and interviews that we have needed for our work on this topic.

Excerpts of testimony from
William Cohen
and Donald Rumsfeld

EXCERPTS OF TESTIMONY FROM
WILLIAM COHEN,
FORMER U.S. SECRETARY OF DEFENSE

"I remain concerned that the controversy over not finding Iraq's weapons of mass destruction will lead to the erroneous assumption that all this talk about the dangers of WMD is just another exercise in the cynical exploitation of fear. . . . I think this is a dangerous delusion. The enemy is not only coming, he has been here. He will continue to try to examine our weaknesses and exploit the crevices in our security and destroy our way of living as well as our lives."

In my written statement, I outlined some of the major initiatives that I had the department undertake between January of '97 and 2001. They included enhancing force protection; support for covert and special operations activity; designating and organizing a National Guard to serve as the first responders in the wake of attacks against our cities; organizing a joint task force for civil support to assist the cities and states against terrorist attacks that might take place; helping to train 100 major cities in consequence management against terrorist attacks; engaging in personal diplomacy and public appearances to alert the American people to the threat posed by anthrax, ricin, VX and radiological materials, the danger of them falling into the hands of terrorist groups.

These initiatives were undertaken as the department was engaged in waging war in Kosovo; we attacked Saddam Hussein in Operation Desert Fox; as we destroyed a suspected WMD site in Sudan; as we coped with the dangers of cyber attacks against our critical infrastructure, including the unknown consequences of a critical massive cyber failure that was then known as Y2K. I believe that we devoted some $3 billion to $4 billion in defense spending at that time to cope with that for fear that the terrorists would try to exploit that millennium turnover. We launched an attack upon al Qaeda's training camp in Afghanistan as has been discussed earlier today. We continued efforts to capture or kill Osama bin Laden after discovering his role in the bombing of the embassies in Africa and then later with the U.S.S. *Cole*. And we developed new intelligence-gathering capabilities that could be directed against Osama bin Laden and others as, again, you have discussed here earlier this morning. In addition, the department also worked closely with the CIA, the FBI and other agencies, and as a result, I believe we were able to thwart a number of terrorist activities directed here against Americans and abroad. . . .

Even now, after September 11th, I think it's far from clear that our society truly understands the gravity of a threat that we face or is yet willing to do what I believe is going to be necessary to counter it. Even after September 11th, after the anthrax and the ricin attacks in the United States, I remain concerned that the controversy over not finding Iraq's weapons of mass destruction will lead to the erroneous assumption that all this talk about the dangers of WMD is just another exercise in the cynical exploitation of fear. After all, it's commonly noted—it was noted here again this morning—there were no attacks since September 11th. I think this is a dangerous delusion. The enemy is not only coming, he has been here. He will continue to try to examine our weaknesses and exploit the crevices in our security and destroy our way of living as well as our lives.

QUESTIONS FROM COMMISSIONERS

FRED F. FIELDING: After [the cruise-missile attack on al Qaeda camps on] August 20th of '98, there were at least three opportunities to which we have been privy to use force against bin Laden. However, in each case, it was determined that there wasn't actionable intelligence. I guess the first question I'd like to say is whose call is that?

COHEN: . . . Frankly, it was following the bombing of the embassies in East Africa that the antennae were really up. We were collecting at a level that I saw—it was unprecedented in terms of the amount of information coming in pointing to bin Laden and then getting the information that there would be a gathering of terrorists in Afghanistan. After reviewing all that information, the determination was made: This was a target certainly that we should attack—that plus the so-called pharmaceutical plant in Sudan. But it was that kind of a process whereby—what do we have? Do we have to be certain? The answer is no. Do you have to be pretty sure? I think that the answer is yes if you're going to be killing a lot of people. We're prepared to engage in collateral damage if the target that we're after is certainly important. But all those factor into a decision. But having, quote, actionable intelligence means reliable and the basis of that reliability. . . .

FIELDING: [W]hat directions did you give the military for development of military plans against bin Laden after August 20th for our guidance?

COHEN: Our plans were to try to, quote, capture and/or kill—or kill, I should say in this particular case—capture or kill bin Laden. That was the directive that went out, the memorandum of notification. The president had signed several of those, refining them on each and every occasion. Taking that directive, we had our people in a position, should there be, quote, actionable intelligence—again, the key word. And we can—we should discuss that and debate that issue of what constitutes it. . . .

Were there plans to use Special Forces to supplement the Northern Alliance so that they were able to apprehend and hold on to bin Laden? The answer was yes. There were packages that were developed with our Special Forces at Fort Bragg. There were a number of proposals quote, on the table or on a shelf, prepared to be utilized in the event that we were certain—and not certain to 100 percent degree—but reasonably certain that he was going to be at a given area.

I know a question has been raised, Well, why wouldn't you put a unit in there with the anticipation that they could help gather intelligence and track him down? And I've tried to address this in my written statement. But consider the notion, we have 13,500 troops in Afghanistan right now, not to mention the Pakistanis, and we can't find bin Laden to date. So the notion that you're going to put a small unit, however good, on the ground, or a large unit, and put them into Afghanistan and track down bin Laden, I think is folly. But if we had people on the ground, if we had the Northern Alliance, if they were reliable, did we have people prepared to go? The answer was yes. General Shelton, I think, will tell you, it's very difficult to kill an individual with a missile. We all know that. You're talking about six hours from the time you, quote, spun-up, you've got the coordinates, GPS signals—target that individual. You're six hours away. To put troops on the ground is probably double that time. By the time you take a package and fly them from Fort Bragg or compose some elements that were already in the Gulf, you're talking more than six hours.

. . .

JOHN F. LEHMAN: [B]efore the war in Afghanistan, there was a lot—he was much more accessible. So there were options. But somehow the Special Operations Command . . . did not come up with discrete options. Why was that?

COHEN: Where does fault lie? If you think that we were irresponsible in not putting a small unit into Afghanistan when you had virtually no support activities. For example, I mentioned this operation in Kosovo. They had incredible intelligence support just tens of miles away. Now you're going to put a small unit of Special Forces into Afghanistan, where there is no intelligence support miles away, but thousands of miles away. What do you do in terms of search and rescue? This is something I know you were concerned about certainly as secretary of the Navy. . . . If we lose one of our pilots, or lose one of our people, you got to send in search and rescue. Well, how about refuelers for the C–130 gunships, et cetera? All of those factors were involved on the part of military planning. Do you just put special forces in and say, we know how good you are, go do the job and good luck? The answer is no. You try to make sure you protect them as much as you can and measure the probability of success against the risk that they are put at.

· · ·

EXCERPTS OF TESTIMONY FROM DONALD RUMSFELD, U.S. SECRETARY OF DEFENSE

"You can go from overhead and attack Afghanistan, and in a very short order, you run out of targets that are lucrative. You can pound the rubble in al Qaeda training camps 15 times and not do much damage. They can put tents right back up."

First I must say, I knew of no intelligence during the six-plus months leading up to September 11th that indicated terrorists would hijack commercial airliners, use them as missiles to fly into the Pentagon or the World Trade Center towers. The president set about forming what is today a 90-nation coalition to wage the global war on terrorist networks. He promptly set U.S. and coalition forces—air, sea and ground—to attack Afghanistan, to overthrow the Taliban regime and destroy that al Qaeda stronghold. In short order, the Taliban regime was driven from power. Al Qaeda's sanctuary in Afghanistan was removed. Nearly two-thirds of their known leaders have been captured or killed. A transitional government is in power and a clear message was sent: Terrorists who harbor terrorists will pay a price.

Those were bold steps. And today, in light of September 11th, no one questions those actions. Today I suspect most would support a preemptive action to deal with such a threat. Interestingly, the remarkable military successes in Afghanistan are taken largely for granted, as is the achievement of bringing together a 90-nation coalition. But imagine that we were back before September 11th and that a U.S. president had looked at the information then available, gone before the Congress and the world and said we need to invade Afghanistan and overthrow the Taliban and destroy the al Qaeda terrorist network based on what little was known was known before September 11th. How many countries would have joined? Many? Any? Not likely. We would have heard objections to preemption similar to those voiced before the coalition launched Operation Iraqi Freedom. We would have been asked, How could you attack Afghanistan when it was al Qaeda that attacked us, not the Taliban? How can you go to war when countries in the region don't support you? Won't launching such an invasion actually provoke terrorist attacks against the United States? I agree with those who have testified here today—Mrs. Albright, Secretary Cohen and others—that unfortunately history shows that it can take a tragedy like September 11th to waken the world to new threats and to the need for action. . . .

Indeed, because we were doing [a major review of counterterrorism policy] in the department as well as in the National Security Council policy review, we were better prepared to respond when the 9/11 attack came. The day of September 11th, the morning, I was hosting a meeting for some members of Congress. And I remember stressing how important it was for our country to be prepared for the unexpected. Shortly thereafter, someone handed me a note saying a plane had hit one of the World Trade Center towers. Shortly thereafter, I was in my office with a CIA briefer and I was told that a second plane had hit the other tower. Shortly thereafter, at 9:38, the Pentagon shook with an explosion of then unknown origin. I went outside to determine what had happened. I was not there long because I was back in the Pentagon with a crisis action team shortly before or after 10:00 A.M. On my return from the crash site and before going to the executive support center, I had one or more calls in my office, one of which was with the president.

I went to the National Military Command Center where General [Richard] Myers, who was the vice chairman of the chiefs at that time, had just returned from Capitol Hill. We discussed, and I recommended, raising the defense condition level from five to three and the force protection level. I joined the air threat telephone conference call that was already in progress. And one of the first exchanges was with the vice president. He informed me of the president's authorization to shoot down hostile aircraft coming to Washington D.C. My thoughts went to the pilots of the military aircraft who might be called upon to execute such an order. It was clear that they needed rules of engagement telling them what they could and could not do. They needed clarity. There were standing rules of engagement, but not rules of engagement that were appropriate for this first-time situation where civilian aircraft were seized and being used as missiles to attack inside the United States. . . .

A number of questions have been raised. Some have asked: When the administration came into office, was there consideration of how to deal with the U.S.S. *Cole*? It's a fair question. One concern was that launching another cruise missile strike, months after the fact, might have sent a signal of weakness. Instead, we implemented the recommendations of the *Cole* commission and began developing a more comprehensive approach to deal with al Qaeda, resulting in NSPD[National Security Presidential Directive]–9.

Some have asked: Why wasn't bin Laden taken out? And if he had been hit, could it have prevented September 11th? I know of no actionable intelligence since January 20th that would have allowed the U.S. to capture or kill bin Laden. It took 10 months to capture Saddam Hussein in Iraq, and coalition forces had passed by the hole he was hiding in many, many times during those months. They were able to find him only after someone with specific knowledge told us precisely where he was. What that suggests, it seems to me, is that it's exceedingly difficult to find a single individual who is determined not be found.

Second, even if bin Laden had been captured or killed in the weeks before September 11th, no one I know believes that it would necessarily have prevented September 11th. Killing bin Laden would not have removed al Qaeda's sanctuary in Afghanistan. Moreover, the sleeper cells that flew the aircraft into the World Trade Towers and the Pentagon were already in the United States months before the attack. Indeed, if actionable intelligence had appeared—which it did not—9/11 would likely still have happened. And ironically, much of the world would likely have called the September 11th attack an al Qaeda retaliation for the U.S. provocation of capturing or killing bin Laden. . . .

How can we wage war not just on terrorist networks, but also on the ideology of hate that they spread? The global war on terror will, in fact, be long. And I am convinced that victory in the war on terror will require a positive effort as well as an aggressive battle. We need to find creative ways to stop the next generation of terrorists from being recruited, trained and deployed to kill innocent people. For every terrorist that coalition forces capture or kill, still others are being recruited and trained. To win the war on terror, we have to win the war of ideas: the battle for the minds of those who are being recruited and financed by terrorist networks across the globe. . . .

What can be done? Not long ago, we marked the 20th anniversary of a terrorist attack in Beirut, Lebanon, when the suicide bomb truck attacked the Marine barracks. And that blast killed more than 240 Americans. Soon after that attack, President Reagan and Secretary of State [George] Shultz asked me to serve as the Middle East envoy for a period. That experience taught me lessons about the nature of terrorism that are relevant today as we prosecute the global war on terror.

After the attack, one seemingly logical response was to put a cement barricade around the buildings to prevent more truck bombings—a very logical thing to do. And it had the effect of preventing more truck bombings. But the terrorists very quickly figured out how to get around those barricades, and they began lobbing rocket-propelled grenades over the cement barricades. And the reaction then was to hunker down even more, and they started seeing buildings along the corniche that runs along the sea in Beirut draped with metal wire mesh coming down from several stories high so that when rocket-propelled grenades hit the mesh, they would bounce off, doing little damage. It worked, again, but only briefly. And the terrorists again adapted. They watched the comings and goings of embassy personnel and began hitting soft targets. They killed people on their way to and from work. So for every defense, first barricades then wire mesh, the terrorists moved to another avenue of attack.

One has to note that the terrorists had learned important lessons: that terrorism is a great equalizer, it's a force multiplier, it's cheap, it's deniable, it yields substantial results, it's low risk and it's often without penalty. They had learned that a single attack by influencing public opinion and morale can alter the behavior of great nations. Moreover, I said that free people had learned lessons as well: that terrorism is a form of warfare that must be treated as such. Simply standing in a defensive position, absorbing blows is not enough. It has to be attacked, and it has to be deterred.

QUESTIONS FROM COMMISSIONERS

BOB KERREY: Dr. Rice also said that she wasn't satisfied with the off-the-shelf military response options that were available after the *Cole*, the so-called tit-for-tat options that I think she was referring to—20 August 1998 against the camps in Afghanistan. Did she ask for military options? Or were there military options requested during your term, because our investigation shows that there were no new military plans developed against al Qaeda or bin Laden prior to September 11th.

RUMSFELD: I think it's accurate to say . . . that there were military options. And I characterize it as options and not a comprehensive plan to deal with al Qaeda and countries that harbor al Qaeda, but options to react—response options, military response options to deal with specific terrorist events. And I was briefed on them, as I indicated in my testimony. And I suspect that Dr. Rice was briefed on them. I can just say that I don't remember ever seeing, in the first instance, I don't remember anyone being briefed on military proposals to react to something where they were fully satisfied. Nor do I ever remember military people being fully satisfied with the intelligence available. That's the nature of the world we live in. . . .

KERREY: Why do we need a . . . full-blown plan like we're building a house or something here?

RUMSFELD: . . . Afghanistan was harboring the al Qaeda. Afghanistan was something like 8,000 miles from the United States. It was surrounded by countries that were not particularly friendly to the United States of America. Afghanistan, as I said publicly on one occasion, didn't have a lot of targets. I mean, you can go from overhead and attack Afghanistan, and in a very short order, you run out of targets that are lucrative. You can pound the rubble in al Qaeda training camps 15 times and not do much damage. They can put tents right back up.

        .   .   .

SLADE GORTON: That program [to destroy al Qaeda], as we understand it, had three parts. First, there would be one more diplomatic attempt with the Taliban to see if they would give up Osama bin Laden. Second, we would begin to arm the Northern Alliance and various tribes in Afghanistan to stir up trouble there and hope that perhaps they could capture Osama bin Laden. And third, if those didn't work, there would be a military response that would be substantial, much more than, you know, lobbing cruise missiles into the desert. But as we understand it, this was seen as a three-year program, if we had to go to the third stage. My question is, given World Trade Center, given the embassy bombings, given the millennium plot, given the *Cole*, given the declaration of war by Osama bin Laden, what made you think that we had the luxury of that much time?—even seven months, much less three years, before we could cure this particular problem?

RUMSFELD: Well, let me answer two ways. Number one, I didn't come up with the three years. I tend to scrupulously avoid predicting that I am smart enough to know how long something's going to take because I know I don't know. Where that number came from, I don't know. In fact, dealing with the terrorism threat is going to take a lot longer than three years. And in fact, dealing with the Afghanistan piece of it took a lot less, as you point out. It's interesting that you cite that because in fact, the president and Secretary [of State Colin] Powell made an attempt early on, one last try, to separate the Taliban from the al Qaeda, and it failed. Not surprisingly, they'd been rather stiff. But it failed flat.

GORTON: It even failed after 9/11, didn't it?

RUMSFELD: That's my point. After 9/11 it failed flat. . . . [W]e decided, I decided, the president decided, everyone decided quite early that we had to put U.S. forces in that country. And that was not a part of that plan. That was something that came along after September 11th.

Staff Statement No. 7

Intelligence Policy

[This statement] will focus on the role of the Central Intelligence Agency as an instrument of national policy. The issues related to the collection of intelligence, analysis and warning, and the management of the intelligence community will be taken up [in a separate report].

FRAMING THE ISSUE

The CIA plays a dual role in counterterrorism. Like other members of the Intelligence Community, the CIA is an intelligence producer: It collects and analyzes foreign intelligence and provides this information to policymakers. When directed by the president, the CIA is also responsible for executing policy through the conduct of covert action. U.S. law defines a covert action as a U.S. government activity to influence conditions in another country, "where it is intended that the role of the United States Government will not be apparent or acknowledged publicly." The law requires a formal presidential finding to authorize a covert action, which is also briefed to congressional leaders. Significant actions under a finding are often authorized in a separate Memorandum of Notification informing congressional leaders.

The Director of Central Intelligence (DCI) . . . also has dual responsibilities. He is the president's senior intelligence adviser. He is also the head of an agency, the CIA, that executes policy. In speaking with the Commission, DCI [George] Tenet was blunt: "I am not a policymaker." He presents intelligence and offers operational judgments, but he says it is ultimately up to policymakers to decide how best to use that intelligence. "It is their job to figure out where I fit into their puzzle," Tenet said.

Both the DCI and the Deputy Director for Operations, James Pavitt, invoked lessons learned from the Iran-Contra scandal: The CIA should stay well behind the line separating policymaker from policy implementer. The CIA does not initiate operations unless it is to support a policy directive, said Tenet. For Pavitt, the lesson of Iran-Contra was, "we don't do policy from out here . . . and you don't want us to."

Yet, as a member of the National Security Council, the DCI is one of a handful of senior officials who advise the president on national security. The DCI's operational judgments can, and did, influence key decisions in the U.S. government's policy toward al Qaeda. As we reported [earlier], the DCI may be designated as the President's envoy for conducting relevant diplomacy with foreign governments, as in the case of Saudi Arabia. In confronting terrorism before 9/11 and today, the DCI was, and is, both the principal analyst of the terrorist enemy and the commander for many operations in the field. Day-to-day conduct of the current war on terrorism is managed principally at CIA headquarters. In the case of al Qaeda, the line between policymaker and policy implementer is hard to discern.

RENDITIONS

Under the presidential directives in the Clinton administration, PDD [Presidential Decision Directive]–39 and PDD–62, the CIA had two main operational responsibilities for combating terrorism—rendition and disruption. PDD–62 remained in effect during the first months of the Bush administration and was still in force on 9/11. These operations are managed out of an Intelligence Community center, the Counterterrorist Center (CTC). Though it includes analysts, the CTC has always given primacy to operations. The director of the CTC effectively reports to the DCI through the CIA's deputy director for operations.

We will first discuss the CIA's support with renditions. In other words, if a terrorist suspect is outside of the United States, the CIA helps to catch and send him to the United States or a third country.

In ordinary criminal cases, the foreign government makes an arrest. The Justice Department and the FBI seek to extradite the suspect. The State Department facilitates the process.

The world of counterterrorism rarely follows these usual procedures. Overseas officials of CIA, the FBI, and the State Department may locate the person, perhaps using their own sources. If possible, they seek help from a foreign government. Though the FBI is often part of the process, the CIA is usually the major player, building and defining the relationships with the foreign government intelligence agencies and internal security services.

The CIA often plays an active role, sometimes calling upon the support of other agencies for logistical or transportation assistance. Director Tenet has publicly testified that 70 terrorists were rendered and brought to justice before 9/11.

These activities could only achieve so much. In countries where the CIA did not have cooperative relationships with local security services, the rendition strategy often failed. In at least two such cases when the CIA decided to seek the assistance of the host country, the target may have been tipped off and escaped. In the case of bin Laden, the United States had no diplomatic or intelligence officers living and working in Afghanistan. Nor was the Taliban regime inclined to cooperate. The CIA would have to look for other ways to bring bin Laden to justice.

DISRUPTIONS

Under the relevant directive of the Clinton administration, foreign terrorists who posed a credible threat to the United States were subject to "preemption and disruption" abroad, consistent with U.S. laws. The CIA had the lead. Where terrorists could not be brought to justice in the United States or a third country, the CIA could try to disrupt their operations, attacking the cells of al Qaeda operatives or affiliated groups. In 1996, the CTC devised an innovative strategy combining intelligence and law enforcement tools to disrupt terrorist activity around the world. That strategy encouraged foreign intelligence services to make creative use of laws already in place to investigate, detain, and otherwise harass known or suspected terrorists.

Disruptions of suspected terrorist cells thwarted numerous plots against American interests abroad, particularly during high threat periods. After the Embassy bombings of 1998 the U.S. government disrupted planned attacks against at least one American embassy, in Albania. In late 1999 preceding the Millennium celebrations, the activities of 21 individuals were disrupted in eight countries. In two subsequent phases of intensive threat reporting—the Ramadan period in late 2000, and the summer prior to 9/11—the CIA again went into what the DCI described as "Millennium threat mode," engaging with foreign liaisons and disrupting operations around the world. At least one planned terrorist attack in Europe may have been successfully disrupted during the summer of 2001. Renditions and disruptions continued as an important component of U.S. counterterrorism policy throughout the period leading up to 9/11. They are still widely used today.

USING COVERT ACTION IN AFGHANISTAN

To disrupt Osama bin Laden himself or his base in Afghanistan, a very different strategy of disruption would have to be developed. In 1996, as an organizational experiment undertaken with seed money, the CTC created a special "Issue Station" devoted exclusively to bin Laden. Bin Laden was then still in Sudan and was considered by the CIA to be a terrorist financier. The original name of the station was "TFL," for terrorist financial links. The bin Laden (OBL) Station was not a response to new intelligence, but reflected interest in and concern about bin Laden's connections.

The CIA believed that bin Laden's move to Afghanistan in May 1996 might be a fortunate development. The CIA knew the ground in Afghanistan, as its officers had worked with indigenous tribal forces during the war against the Soviet Union. The CIA definitely had a lucky break when a former associate of bin Laden walked into a U.S. embassy abroad and provided an abundance of information about the organization. These revelations were corroborated by other intelligence. By early 1997, the OBL Station knew that bin Laden was not just a financier but an organizer of terrorist activity. It knew that al Qaeda had a military committee planning operations against U.S. interests worldwide and was actively trying to obtain nuclear material. Although this information was disseminated in many reports, the unit's sense of alarm about bin Laden was not widely shared or understood within the intelligence and policy communities. Employees in the unit told us they felt their zeal attracted ridicule from their peers.

In 1997 CIA headquarters authorized U.S. officials to begin developing a network of agents to gather intelligence inside Afghanistan about bin Laden and his organization and prepare a plan to capture him. By 1998 DCI Tenet was giving considerable personal attention to the OBL threat.

Since its inception, the OBL Station had been working on a covert action plan to capture bin Laden and bring him to justice. The plan had been elaborately developed by the spring of 1998. Its final variant in this period used Afghan tribal fighters recruited by the CIA to assault a terrorist compound where bin Laden might be found, capture him if possible, and take him to a location where he could be picked up and transported to the United States. Though the plan had dedicated proponents in the OBL unit and was discussed for months among top policymakers, all of CIA's leadership, and a key official in the field, agreed that the odds of failure were too high. They did not recommend it for approval by the White House.

After the East Africa bombings, President Clinton signed successive authorizations for the CIA to undertake offensive operations in Afghanistan against bin Laden. Each new document responded to an opportunity to use local forces from various countries against bin Laden himself, and later his principal lieutenants. These were authorizations for the conduct of operations in which people on both sides could be killed. Policymakers devoted careful attention to crafting these sensitive and closely held documents.

In accordance with these authorities, the CIA developed successive covert action programs using particular indigenous groups, or proxies, who might be able to operate in different parts of Afghanistan. These proxies would also try to provide intelligence on bin Laden and his organization, with an eye to finding bin Laden and then ambushing him if the opportunity arose.

The CIA's Afghan assets reported on about half a dozen occasions before 9/11 that they had considered attacking bin Laden, usually as he traveled in his convoy along the rough Afghan roads. Each time, the operation was reportedly aborted. Several times the Afghans said that bin Laden had taken a different route than expected. On one occasion security was said to be too tight to capture him. Another time they heard women and children's voices from inside the convoy and abandoned the assault for fear of killing innocents, in accordance with CIA guidelines.

The Plan

As time passed, morale in the OBL unit sagged. The former deputy chief told the Joint Inquiry that they felt like they were "buying time," trying to stop OBL and "disrupting al Qaeda members until military force could be used." In June 1999 National Security Adviser [Samuel] Berger reported to President Clinton that covert action efforts against bin Laden had not been fruitful. In the summer of 1999 new leaders arrived at the CTC and the OBL unit. The new director of CTC was Cofer Black. He and his aides worked on a new operational strategy for going after al Qaeda. The focus was on getting better intelligence. They proposed a shift from reliance on the Afghan proxies alone to an effort to create the CIA's own sources. They called the new strategy simply, "The Plan." CTC devised a program for hiring and training better officers with counterterrorism skills, recruiting more assets, and trying to penetrate al Qaeda directly. The Plan also aimed to close up gaps in intelligence collection within Afghanistan, by enhancing technical collection and recruiting forces capable of tracking and capturing bin Laden wherever he might travel. The Plan also proposed increasing contacts between the CIA and the Northern Alliance rebels fighting the Taliban.

The Predator

The Plan resulted in increased reporting on al Qaeda. Still, going into the year 2000, the CIA had never laid American eyes on bin Laden in Afghanistan. President Clinton prodded his advisers to do better. NSC [National Security Council] Counterterrorism Coordinator Richard Clarke helped Assistant DCI for Collection Charles Allen and Vice Admiral Scott Fry of the Joint Staff work together on the military's ongoing efforts to develop new collection capabilities inside Afghanistan. With the NSC staff's backing, the CTC and the military came up with a proposal to fly an unmanned drone called the Predator over Afghanistan to survey the territory below and relay video footage. That information, the White House hoped, could either boost U.S. knowledge of al Qaeda or be used to kill bin Laden with a cruise missile. The Predator had performed well in the recent Kosovo conflict, where it spotted Serb troop concentrations. The aircraft is slow and small, but it is hard to see and intercept.

Assistant DCI Allen said that the CIA's senior management was originally reluctant to go ahead with the Predator program, adding that "it was a bloody struggle." But the NSC staff was firm, and the CIA agreed to fly the Predator as a trial concept. Drones were flown successfully over Afghanistan 16 times in fall 2000. At least twice the Predator saw a security detail around a tall man in a white robe whom some analysts determined was probably bin Laden. The Predator was spotted by Taliban forces. They were unable to intercept it, but the Afghan press service publicized the discovery of a strange aircraft that it speculated might be looking for bin Laden. When winter weather prevented the Predator from flying during the remainder of 2000, the CTC looked forward to resuming flights in 2001.

U.S.S. *Cole*

When the American destroyer, the U.S.S. *Cole*, was bombed in Yemen in October 2000, al Qaeda was immediately suspected of having struck again. The CTC developed an offensive initiative for Afghanistan, regardless of policy or financial constraints. It was called the "Blue Sky memo." In December 2000, the CIA sent this to the NSC staff. The memo recommended increased support to anti-Taliban groups and to proxies who might ambush bin Laden. The CTC also proposed a major effort to back Northern Alliance forces in order to stave off the Taliban army and tie down al Qaeda fighters, thereby hindering terrorist activities elsewhere. No action was taken on these ideas in the few remaining weeks of the Clinton administration. The "Blue Sky" memo itself was not apparently discussed with the incoming top Bush administration officials during the transition. The CTC began pressing these proposals after the new team took office.

THE BUSH ADMINISTRATION

The CIA briefed President-elect George W. Bush and incoming national security officials on covert action programs in Afghanistan. Deputy DCI [John] McLaughlin said that he walked through the elements of the al Qaeda problem with National Security Adviser Condoleezza Rice, including an explanation of the special authorities signed by President Clinton. DCI Tenet and Deputy Director for Operations Pavitt gave an intelligence briefing to President-elect Bush, Vice President-elect Cheney, and Dr. Rice, which included the topic of al Qaeda. Pavitt recalled conveying that bin Laden was one of the gravest threats to the country. President-elect Bush asked whether killing bin Laden would end the problem. Pavitt said he and the DCI answered that killing bin Laden would have an impact but not stop the threat. CIA later provided more formal assessments to the White House reiterating that conclusion. It added that the only long-term way to deal with the threat was to end al Qaeda's ability to use Afghanistan as a sanctuary for its operations.

Arming Predator

During fall 2000, Clarke and other counterterrorism officials learned of a promising and energetic Air Force effort that was already trying to arm the Predator with missiles. Clarke and Assistant DCI Allen urged flying the reconnaissance version of the Predator in the spring, as soon as the weather improved, and using the armed Predator against bin Laden as soon as possible.

DCI Tenet, supported by military officers in the Joint Staff, balked at this plan. They did not want to go ahead with reconnaissance flights alone and argued for waiting until the armed version was ready before flying Predator again at all. Given the experience in the fall of 2000, they worried that flying the reconnaissance version would forfeit the element of surprise for the armed Predator. They also feared one of these scarce aircraft might be shot down, since Taliban radar had previously tracked it, forcing it into a more vulnerable flight path. They also contended that there were not enough Predators to be able to conduct reconnaissance flights over Afghanistan and still have aircraft left over for the testing then underway in the United States to develop the armed version.

Clarke believed that these arguments were stalling tactics by CIA's risk-averse Directorate of Operations. He wanted the reconnaissance flights to begin on their own both for collection and to allow for possible strikes with other military forces. He thought the reconnaissance flights could be conducted with fewer aircraft than had been used in 2000, so that testing on the armed version might continue.

DCI Tenet's position prevailed. The reconnaissance flights were deferred while work continued on the armed version.

The armed Predator was being readied at an accelerated pace during 2001. The Air Force officials who managed the program told us that the policy arguments, including quarrels about who would pay for the aircraft, had no effect on their timetable for operations. The timetable was instead driven by a variety of technical issues. A program that would ordinarily have taken years was, they said, finished in months; they were "throwing out the books on the normal acquisition process just to press on and get it done." In July, Deputy National Security Adviser Stephen Hadley ordered that the armed Predator be ready by September 1. CIA officials supported these accelerated efforts. The Air Force program manager told us that they were still resolving technical issues as of 9/11, and "we just took what we had and deployed it."

Meanwhile policymakers were arguing about the unprecedented step of creating a missile system for use by an agency outside of the Department of Defense. DCI Tenet was concerned.

At a meeting of NSC principals on September 4, National Security Adviser Rice summarized a consensus that the armed Predator was not ready, but that the capability was needed. The group left open issues related to command and control. In the meantime, the Principals Committee agreed the CIA should consider going ahead with flying reconnaissance missions with the Predator. Shortly after the meeting, DCI Tenet agreed to proceed with such flights.

Developing a New Strategy

In March 2001, National Security Adviser Rice tasked DCI Tenet to draw up a new document on covert action authorities for Afghanistan that would consolidate existing authorities and add new, broader ones. DCI Tenet presented these draft documents to Deputy National Security Adviser Hadley later that month, but observed that ordinarily policy should be developed first and then the authorities should be devised to implement the policy, rather than doing it the other way around. Hadley agreed and, with Rice's evident approval, the draft authorities were put aside until the new administration had finished determining what its new policies would be for al Qaeda, Afghanistan, and Pakistan.

This policy review apparently began in March and continued throughout the spring and summer of 2001. At the end of May, National Security Adviser Rice met with DCI Tenet and their counterterrorism experts. She asked about "taking the offensive" against al Qaeda, and asked Clark and the CTC chief Cofer Black to develop a full range of options. A plan for a larger covert action effort was a major component of the new al Qaeda strategy, codified in a draft presidential directive that was first circulated in early June. The emerging covert action plan built upon ideas the CIA and Clarke had been working on since December 2000. A notable change was that Rice and Hadley wanted to place less emphasis on the Northern Alliance, and more on anti-Taliban Pashtuns. Clarke was impatient to get at least some money to the Northern Alliance right away in order to keep them in the fight.

Meanwhile, the Intelligence Community began to receive its greatest volume of threat reporting since the Millennium plot. By late July, there were indications of multiple, possibly catastrophic, terrorist attacks being planned against American interests overseas. The CTC identified 30 possible overseas targets and launched disruption operations around the world.

Some CIA officials expressed frustration about the pace of policymaking during the stressful summer of 2001. Although Tenet said he thought the policy machinery was working in what he called a rather orderly fashion, Deputy DCI McLaughlin told us he felt a great tension—especially in June and July 2001—between the new administration's need to understand these issues and his sense that this was a matter of great urgency. Officials, including McLaughlin, were also frustrated when some policymakers, who had not lived through such threat surges before, questioned the validity of the intelligence or wondered if it was disinformation, though they were persuaded once they probed it.

Two veteran CTC officers who were deeply involved in OBL issues were so worried about an impending disaster that one of them told us that they considered resigning and going public with their concerns. DCI Tenet, who was briefing the President and his top advisers daily, told us that his sense was that officials at the White House had grasped the sense of urgency he was communicating to them.

By early August, DCI Tenet said that intelligence suggested that whatever terrorist activity might have been originally planned had been delayed. At the same time, the Deputies Committee reached a consensus on a new Afghan policy, paving the way for Northern Alliance aid. NSC principals apparently endorsed the new presidential directive on al Qaeda at their meeting on September 4.

On September 10, Deputy National Security Adviser Hadley formally tasked DCI Tenet to draw up new draft authorities for the broad covert action program envisioned in that directive, including significant additional funding and involving Pashtun elements as well as the Northern Alliance. Hadley also asked Tenet to include a separate section in these new authorities authorizing a further range of covert action activities to disrupt command-and-control elements of al Qaeda.

Events would, of course, overtake this tasking. Within days of the September 11 attacks, a new counterterrorism policy was in place.

KEY ISSUE AREAS

The story of CIA activities before 9/11 brings up a number of key issues for considering how policymakers made use of covert capabilities for attacking bin Laden. These issues include the CIA's authorities and capabilities for going after bin Laden in Afghanistan.

Capture or Kill?

Many CIA officers, including Deputy Director for Operations Pavitt, have criticized policymakers for not giving the CIA authorities to conduct effective operations against bin Laden. This issue manifests itself in a debate about the scope of the covert actions in Afghanistan authorized by President Clinton. NSC staff and CIA officials differ starkly here.

Senior NSC staff members told us they believed the president's intent was clear: He wanted bin Laden dead. On successive occasions, President Clinton issued authorities instructing the CIA to use its proxies to capture or assault bin Laden and his lieutenants in operations in which they might be killed. The instructions, except in one defined contingency, were to capture bin Laden if possible.

Senior legal advisers in the Clinton administration agreed that, under the law of armed conflict, killing a person who posed an imminent threat to the United States was an act of self-defense, not an assassination. As former National Security Adviser Berger explained, if we wanted to kill bin Laden with cruise missiles, why would we not want to kill him with covert action? Clarke's recollection is the same.

But if the policymakers believed their intent was clear, every CIA official interviewed on this topic by the Commission, from DCI Tenet to the official who actually briefed the agents in the field, told us they heard a different message. What the United States would let the military do is quite different, Tenet said, from the rules that govern covert action by the CIA. CIA senior managers, operators, and lawyers uniformly said that they read the relevant authorities signed by President Clinton as instructing them to try to capture bin Laden, except in the defined contingency. They believed that the only acceptable context for killing bin Laden was a credible capture operation.

"We always talked about how much easier it would have been to kill him," a former chief of the OBL Station said. Working-level CIA officers said they were frustrated by what they saw as the policy restraints of having to instruct their assets to mount a capture operation. When Northern Alliance leader [Ahmed Shah] Massoud was briefed on the carefully worded instructions for him, the briefer recalls that Massoud laughed and said, "You Americans are crazy. You guys never change."

To further cloud the picture, two senior CIA officers told us they would have been morally and practically opposed to getting CIA into what might look like an assassination. One of them, a former CTC chief, said he would have refused an order to directly kill bin Laden.

Where NSC staff and CIA officials agree is that no one at CIA, including Tenet and Pavitt, ever complained to the White House that the authorities were restrictive or unclear. Berger told us: "If there was ever any confusion, it was never conveyed to me or the President by the DCI or anybody else."

The Trouble with Proxies

Senior CIA officials were cautious about engaging U.S. personnel within Afghanistan. CIA officers faced enormous dangers in Afghanistan, a large, desolate country in the midst of a civil war, where there were no reliable means for either inserting or extracting personnel. They did, however, take on significant risk. CIA teams penetrated deep into Afghanistan on numerous occasions before 9/11—for example, to evaluate airfields suitable for capture operations. These were hazardous missions: Officers flew through mountainous terrain on rickety helicopters exposed to missile attack from the ground. CIA personnel continued these missions over the course of the next year, and on each occasion risked their lives.

But reluctance to authorize direct action by CIA personnel against bin Laden inside the Afghanistan sanctuary led policymakers to rely on local forces, or proxies. These groups provided intelligence on bin Laden's location and on al Qaeda forces and training camps; they also were asked to conduct operations to capture bin Laden.

For covert action programs, proxies meant problems. First,

proxies tend to tell those who pay them what they want to hear. The CIA employs many means to test and verify the truth of the intelligence its agents provide, but these tests are not foolproof. Second, a strategy emphasizing proxies takes significant time to produce the desired results. Proxy forces invariably need training and instruction to carry out operations.

Both these factors bedeviled the CIA's use of proxy forces in Afghanistan before 9/11. The most widely used forces were tribal fighters with whom CIA officers had established relations dating back over a decade to the jihad against Soviet occupation. CIA officers dealing with these tribal fighters had some confidence in their ability to target bin Laden.

These agents collected valuable intelligence at great personal risk. Yet when it came to their ability to conduct paramilitary operations, senior CIA officials had their doubts. As was mentioned earlier, senior CIA officials did not go forward with a spring 1998 plan to use Afghan forces to capture bin Laden. This was in part because they were not convinced that the Afghans could carry out the mission successfully. There is little evidence that the CIA leadership ever developed greater faith in the operational skills of these proxy forces for paramilitary action. Deputy Director for Operations Pavitt said he does not know if the attempted ambushes against bin Laden that the tribal fighters reported ever actually occurred.

The CIA employed proxy forces other than the Afghan tribal groups against bin Laden, but with no more confidence in their abilities. DCI Tenet thought the most able proxies were the hardened warriors of Massoud's Northern Alliance who had been at war with the Taliban for years. Though there was continuing disagreement within the Agency about relying on the Northern Alliance, CIA leaders put more and more weight behind this option through 2000 and 2001. They were always aware that the primary objective of Massoud's forces was to defeat the Taliban, not to find bin Laden or attack al Qaeda.

By deciding to use proxies to carry out covert actions in Afghanistan before 9/11, both administrations placed the achievement of policy objectives in the hands of others.

CONCLUSION

Before 9/11 no agency did more to attack al Qaeda, working day and night, than did the CIA. But there were limits to what the CIA was able to achieve by disrupting terrorist activities abroad and using proxies to try to capture bin Laden and his lieutenants in Afghanistan. CIA officers were aware of these limitations. One officer recognized as early as mid-1997 that the CIA alone was not going to solve the bin Laden problem. In a memo to his supervisor he wrote, "All we're doing is holding the ring until the cavalry gets here." Deputy Director for Operations Pavitt told Commission staff that "doing stuff on the margins" was not the way to get this job done. If the U.S. government was serious about eliminating the al Qaeda threat, it required robust, offensive engagement across the entire U.S. government.

DCI Tenet also understood the CIA's limitations. He told staff that the CIA's odds of success in Afghanistan before 9/11 were between 10 and 20 percent. This was not because the CIA lacked the capabilities to attack the target, he said, but because the mission was extremely challenging. Covert action was not "a silver bullet," but it was important to engage proxies and to build various capabilities so that if an opportunity presented itself, the CIA could act on it. "You could get really lucky on any given day," Tenet said.

Indeed, serendipity had led to some of the CIA's past successes against al Qaeda. But absent a more dependable government strategy, CIA senior management relied on proxy forces to "get lucky" for over three years, through both the late Clinton and early Bush administrations. There was growing frustration within the CTC and in the NSC staff with this lack of results. The development of the Predator and the push to aid the Northern Alliance were certainly products of this frustration.

The Commission has heard numerous accounts of the tireless activity of officers within the CTC and the OBL Station trying to tackle al Qaeda before 9/11. DCI Tenet was also clearly committed to fighting the terrorist threat. But if officers at all levels questioned the effectiveness of the most active strategy the policymakers were employing to defeat the terrorist enemy, the Commission needs to ask why that strategy remained largely unchanged throughout the period leading up to 9/11.

Alexis Albion, Michael Hurley, Dan Marcus, Lloyd Salvetti, and Steve Dunne did much of the investigative work reflected in this statement. For this area of our work we were fortunate in being able to build upon a great deal of excellent work already done by the Congressional Joint Inquiry. The Central Intelligence Agency has cooperated fully in making available both the documents and interviews that we have needed so far on this topic.

Excerpts of testimony from George J. Tenet, Director, Central Intelligence Agency

"In about the mid-'90s . . ., we started to rebuild a clandestine human operations capability. . . . There must be a relentless focus on ensuring that the intelligence capability this country has is allowed to grow in the critical areas that allow us to have capability inside sanctuaries where people are going to go hide."

In 1998, bin Laden issued a fatwa telling all Muslims it was their duty to kill Americans and their allies, civilian and military, wherever they may be. We recognized, through our collection analysis and disruption efforts of the '90s, that we had to change to meet this evolving threat. We had captured and rendered terrorists for years, but we knew we needed to go further to penetrate the sanctuary bin Laden found in Afghanistan. We knew that because our technical coverage was slipping, al Qaeda's operational security was high. We were taking terrorists off the street, but the threat level persisted.

And finally, we had to operate against a target that was buried deep in territory controlled by the Taliban, an area where we needed to expand our on-the-ground presence. Stand-off operations required predictive intelligence: knowing precisely where a target would be many hours in advance. That we did not have.

We needed close-in access to understand the target and maximize our chances for success. And while we were collecting, we continued to build a coalition of friendly services around the world that would expand our regional access.

So we did change. We developed a new baseline strategy in 1999. Simply we called it The Plan. We worked on The Plan through the summer. We told our customers and counterparts in Washington all about it. Under this plan, we developed a broad array of both human and technical sources. Our efforts were designed to disrupt the terrorists and their plots, collect information, recruit terrorist spies, all to support new operational initiatives.

To penetrate bin Laden's sanctuary, we also worked with Central Asian intelligence services and with the Northern Alliance and its leader, Ahmed Shah Massoud, on everything from technical collection to building an intelligence capability to potential renditions. And we developed a network of agents inside Afghanistan who were directed to track bin Laden. We worked with friendly tribal partners for years to undertake operations against him.

Our human intelligence rose markedly from 1999 through 2001. By September 11th, a map of Afghanistan would show that these collection programs, human networks, were in place in numbers to nearly cover the country. The array meant that when the military campaign to topple and destroy the Taliban began in October of 2001, we were able to support it with an enormous body of information and a large stable of assets. These networks gave us the platform from which to launch the rapid take-down of the Taliban. . . .

As a country, you must be relentless on offense, but you must have a defense that links visa measures, border security, infrastructure protection and domestic warnings in a way that increases security, closes gaps and serves a society that demands high levels of both safety and freedom. We collectively did not close those gaps rapidly or fully enough before September 11th. We have learned and are doing better in an integrated environment that allows us to respond faster and more comprehensively than three years ago. And much more work needs to be done.

QUESTIONS FROM COMMISSIONERS

JAMIE S. GORELICK: [O]ur nation was not simply responding via law enforcement, if you will, to the threat that was faced. You were out there very active and, in many cases, successful. Is that correct?

TENET: Commissioner Gorelick, we used all the tools at our disposal. I've testified there were over 70 renditions, but renditions in and of themselves don't stop this. Active penetrations, disruptions of the kind you talked about were also being aggressively pursued through intelligence channels. . . . The predominant focus and threat of the reporting took us overseas, but we could not discount the possibility of an attack on the homeland, although the data just didn't exist with any specificity to take you there. I mean, that was what was maddening about this.

You see in my long testimony, all the disruption efforts were things where people were actually getting wrapped up about to do things. We did not have this same kind of granularity inside the country, nor did the reporting take us—in the tactical sense— to give us the kind of specificity we needed to give us opportunities to do things that would have led us to conclude that the plot was inside the United States now.

GORELICK: [M]y view of the reporting is that it talked about threats to American interests and while the specifics that you had were abroad, by no means did you say, "Don't worry about the domestic United States." Is that correct?

TENET: . . .What is one of the most important systemic lessons for all of us? I'll tell you what I think it is, OK? For a period of how many years, go back to the mid-'90s, all the way through 2001, what did we do relentlessly? We raced from threat to threat to threat. We resolved the threat; it either happened or it didn't happen. And from the homeland perspective, what was the galvanizing mechanism that forced real defensive preparation and measures to be put in place?

So, you know, the question systemically is, if you go through the '90s and you're aware of hijackings, airline commissions—and I'm not picking on a sector here, but my point is this: The country was not systemically protected because even in racing through all these threats, sometimes exhaustively—we exhausted ourselves—there was not a system in place to say, "You got to go back and do this and this and this and this." It's not criticizing anybody, but the moral of the story is, if you'd taken those measures systemically over the course of time and closed seams, you might have had a better chance of succeeding, stopping, deterring or disrupting.

So it's easy to go talk about what I didn't get them to do on day one, day two or day three, and almost is the wrong way to talk about this, from a historical perspective, with a lot of experience, with a lot of mistakes we made and everybody else made. No perfection in this deal. We didn't stop this attack.

And so, the question is looking forward: How do you enhance your prospects of success? With respect to everybody going to more meetings isn't necessarily going to help—OK—and different policymakers are going to basically communicate in different ways. So one size doesn't fit all. You have to judge. I can only give you personal perspective from where I sat.

. . .

THOMAS H. KEAN: Looking back at that period—when we probably did have some opportunities to get him and didn't—in hindsight, what did you need and what could you—what could the government have given you—what authorities what resources, what change—what could have been done to change that history?

TENET: Governor, let me give you a big systemic answer that I feel pretty passionately about. You know, in about the mid-'90s at the time we were trying to take this all on, we started to rebuild a clandestine human operations capability that went away in this country. We were trying to recapitalize NSA [National Security Agency]. We were trying to get ourselves better imagery capability. And on the human side, I'm still five years away from being able to look at you in the eye and say—because it's terribly—you got to recruit the right people, have the right training infrastructure. We've built all those things.

There has to be—you know, just like people talk about other instruments of power, there must be a relentless focus on ensuring that the intelligence capability this country has is allowed to grow in the critical areas that allow us to have capability inside sanctuaries where people are going to go hide. The investment strategy is laid out; the strategic game plan is there. People have to sort of take a look at this from the perspective of: How do we ensure—on just the capabilities side—we ensure that the country gets the intelligence it deserves, no matter what it costs?

Now, from the perspective of integration, the sharing of data, the relationship on the domestic side—I mean, one of the things that obviously needs to be built here is seamless flows of data from your law enforcement community to your intelligence community. . . . And [FBI Director] Bob Mueller is building a digital communications system that allows you to connect the dots of his empire in the United States so all the data comes forward in a way that we can see it and feel it and touch it the same way and understand its integrity.

And all of that data that we collect, sir, ultimately we have to treat the state and local governments and their police forces as if they're part of this fight in a way, because they are not really interested in how you did the operation. They need the data. Thousands of people who walk around our streets that can collect data need to be educated.

Now, to be sure, we'll get into longer-term intelligence, systemic issues [later], I suspect.

And to be sure, we have to ask ourselves some pretty tough questions about, are we organized the right way? Is this the structure you want for the next 50 years? It's been here for 57 years. What kinds of issues do we have to put on the table? All with the notion of fusing and integrating operations and data in a manner that's seamless so that there's never the assertion that I didn't see this piece of information that could have saved lives.

KEAN: Do you believe you're getting the support from the administration and the Congress to do that?

TENET: Yes. But we need to ensure that there's continuity in the approach over a long period of time. And this commission has to establish benchmarks and report cards and do-outs that the country has to have people come back and talk about every year. Because as this thing fades, my fear is people are going to say, it's five years away, it's six. It's not. It's coming. They are still going to try and do it, and we need to sort of—men and women here who have lost their families have to know that we've got to do a hell of a lot better.

Staff Statement No. 8

National Policy Coordination

The National Security Act of 1947 created the National Security Council so that advice to the president from the State Department could mesh with advice from the military establishment. Since then, presidents have progressively redefined the Council's functions, broadened participation, and greatly elevated the status of its staff. Throughout, the NSC staff operated under the authority of the president with the duty to ensure that the president's policies are adequately developed, articulated, understood, and implemented purposefully by the government as a whole.

Counterterrorism issues had not been a high priority during the administration of George H.W. Bush. When the Clinton administration took office in 1993, terrorism issues were handled in a small directorate of the NSC staff for "International Programs," commonly referred to as "drugs and thugs." Terrorist attacks early in the new administration, particularly the 1993 attempt to blow up the World Trade Center, quickly changed this perspective.

The first World Trade Center attack also spotlighted the problem of how or whether the NSC could bridge the divide between foreign policy and traditionally domestic issues such as criminal justice. That attack, handled by the FBI as a matter for domestic law enforcement, had been carried out by a mixture of American citizens, resident aliens, and foreign nationals with ties overseas.

President Clinton concluded that the National Security Act of 1947 allowed the NSC to consider issues of domestic security arising from a foreign threat. The President later issued a formal directive on counterterrorism policy. This was Presidential Decision Directive 39, signed in June 1995 after at least a year of interagency consultation and coordination. That directive characterized terrorism as a national security concern as well as a matter for law enforcement. It also articulated a "lead agency" approach to counterterrorism policy. It had four main program areas: reducing vulnerabilities, deterring terrorism, responding to terrorism, and preventing terrorists from acquiring weapons of mass destruction. In each area responsibilities were assigned to the departments and agencies of the government.

These efforts were to be coordinated by a subordinate NSC committee called the CSG. During the Clinton administration these initials stood for "Counterterrorism and Security Group." This committee was chaired by an NSC staff member, Richard Clarke. The CSG was the place where domestic security agencies, such as the FBI, regularly met alongside representatives from the traditional national security agencies.

Since 1989 each administration has organized its top NSC advisory bodies in three layers. At the top is the National Security Council, the formal statutory body whose meetings are chaired by the president. Beneath it is the Principals Committee, with cabinet-level representatives from agencies. The Principals Committee is usually chaired by the national security adviser. Next is the Deputies Committee, where the deputy agency heads meet under the chairmanship of the deputy national security adviser. Lower-ranking officials meet in many other working groups or coordinating committees, reporting to the deputies and, through them, to the principals. The CSG was one of these committees.

This ordinary committee system is often adjusted in a crisis. Because of the sensitivity of the intelligence and the military options being considered, President Clinton created a "Small Group" in which a select set of principals would frequently meet without aides to discuss Khobar Towers or Osama bin Laden. The participants would usually be National Security Adviser

Samuel Berger, DCI [Director of Central Intelligence] George Tenet, Secretary of State Madeleine Albright, Defense Secretary William Cohen, Joint Chiefs of Staff Chairman Hugh Shelton, Deputy National Security Adviser James Steinberg, White House Chief of Staff John Podesta, Richard Clarke, and Vice President Gore's national security adviser, Leon Fuerth. Attorney General Janet Reno and FBI Director Louis Freeh would sometimes participate.

National Security Adviser Berger told us that he designed the Small Group process to keep the highly-sensitive information closely held. There were few paper records. One tradeoff in such a system was that other senior officials in agencies around the government sometimes had little knowledge about what was being decided in this group, other than what they could obtain from the principals or Clarke. This sometimes led to misunderstandings and friction.

PRESIDENTIAL DECISION DIRECTIVE 62 AND THE NATIONAL COORDINATOR

In early 1998, the Clinton administration prepared a new presidential directive on counterterrorism. Its goals were to strengthen the "lead agency" approach in ten program areas, reemphasize the importance President Clinton attached to unconventional threats at home and abroad, and strengthen interagency coordination. The draft directive would strengthen Clarke's role by creating the position of a national coordinator for counterterrorism who would be a full member of the Principals Committee or Deputies Committee for meetings on these topics.

The duties of the national coordinator were debated in the preparation of this directive. Prior episodes, including Iran-Contra in the 1980s, had underscored the problems of operations run by White House or NSC staff whose legal authorities are derived solely from the president and are therefore outside of the usual process of congressional confirmation, budgeting, or oversight. Responding to such concerns, the May 1998 directive,

Presidential Decision Directive 62, provided that the coordinate would not direct operations, that the CSG would ordinarily report to the Deputies Committee, and that the new structure would not change the established budget process.

Nevertheless, as it evolved during the Clinton administration, the CSG effectively reported directly to principals, and with the principals often meeting only in the restricted Small Group. This process could be very effective in overseeing fast-developing but sensitive operations, moving issues quickly to the highest levels, and keeping secrets. However, since the Deputies and other sub-cabinet officials were not members of the CSG, this process created a challenge for integrating counterterrorism issues into the broader agenda of these agencies and the U.S. government.

Clarke was a controversial figure. A career civil servant, he drew wide praise as someone who called early and consistent attention to the seriousness of the terrorism danger. A skilled operator of the levers of government, he energetically worked the system to address vulnerabilities and combat terrorists. Some colleagues have described his working style as abrasive. Some officials told us that Clarke had sometimes misled them about presidential decisions or interfered in their chain of command. National Security Adviser Berger told us that several of his colleagues had wanted Clarke fired. But Berger's net assessment was that Clarke fulfilled an important role in pushing the interagency process to fight bin Laden. As Berger put it, "I wanted a pile driver."

Clarke often set the agenda and laid out the options, but he did not help run any of the executive departments of the government. Final decisionmaking responsibility resided with others.

CHANGING STRATEGY AGAINST BIN LADEN AND HIS NETWORK

President Clinton often discussed terrorism publicly as the dark side of globalization. He was particularly and vocally concerned about the danger of terrorists acquiring weapons of mass destruction, especially biological weapons. He tended to receive his intelligence in written briefings rather than personally from the DCI, and he frequently would pass back questions to follow up on items related to bin Laden or other terrorist threats. National Security Adviser Berger and others told us that the East Africa embassy bombings of August 1998 were a watershed event in the level of attention given to the bin Laden threat. Before August 1998, several officials told us their attention on terrorism was focused more on Iranian-sponsored groups, such as Hizbollah.

After the August 1998 military strikes against Afghanistan and Sudan, Clarke turned his attention to a government-wide strategy for destroying the bin Laden threat. His proposed strategy was Political-Military Plan Delenda, circulated among CSG and Small Group participants in late August and September 1998. As mentioned [previously], the term "Delenda" is from the Latin "to destroy," evoking the famous Roman vow to erase rival Carthage. The plan's goal was to immediately eliminate any significant threat to Americans from the "Osama bin Laden network," to prevent further attacks, and prevent the group from acquiring weapons of mass destruction. The strategy sought to combine four main approaches:

- Diplomacy to eliminate the sanctuary in Afghanistan and bring terrorists to justice;

- Covert action to disrupt terrorist cells and prevent attacks. The highest priority was to target the enemy in Afghanistan;

- Financial measures, beginning with the just-adopted executive order to freeze the funds of bin Laden-related businesses; and

- Military action to attack targets as they were developed. This would be an ongoing campaign, not a series of responses or retaliations to particular provocations.

This strategy was not formally adopted, and Cabinet-level participants in the Small Group have little or no recollection of it, at

least as a formal policy document. The principals decid
the rolling military campaign described in the plan.
Clarke continued to use the other components of the Delenda
plan to guide his efforts.

The momentum from the August 1998 attacks and the initial
policy responses to it carried forward into 1999. We have described
those responses in our other staff statements.

In June 1999, National Security Adviser Berger and Clarke
summarized for President Clinton what had been accomplished
against bin Laden. An active program to disrupt al Qaeda cells
around the world was underway and recording some successes.
The efforts to track bin Laden's finances with help from Saudi
Arabia and the United Arab Emirates had not yet been successful.
The U.S. government was pressing Pakistan and the Emirates to
cut off support for the Taliban. Covert action efforts in Afghanistan had not borne fruit. Proposals to intervene against the Taliban by helping the Northern Alliance had been deferred. The
intelligence needed for missile attacks to kill bin Laden was too
thin, and this situation was not likely to change.

Berger and Clarke said it was a "virtual certainty" that there
would be more attacks on American facilities. They were also
worried about bin Laden's possible acquisition of weapons of
mass destruction, a subject on which they had recently received
some fragmentary but disturbing intelligence. The quality of that
intelligence was unlikely to improve, his advisers reported.

Given this overall picture, they returned to the idea they had
discussed in the fall of 1998, of a preemptive strike on terrorist
camps such as the one reportedly involved in WMD [weapons of
mass destruction] work. Alternatively, they wrote, the government could retaliate after the next attack, but the camps might
then be emptied. The Small Group met to consider some of these
ideas on June 24, 1999. From some notes, it appears the Group
discussed military strikes against al Qaeda infrastructure, but
rejected this approach for reasons including the relatively slight
impact of strikes balanced against the potentially counterproductive results.

The NSC staff kept looking for new options or ideas. Later in

1999, for example, the new leadership team at the CIA's Counterterrorist Center produced a plan for increased intelligence collection and relationships with other potential partners for clandestine or covert action against bin Laden. Berger and Clarke made sure that these efforts received both attention and authorizations to proceed.

THE MILLENNIUM ALERTS

As 1999 drew to a close, Jordanian intelligence discovered an al Qaeda-connected plot to attack tourists gathering in Jordan for Millennium events. Intelligence revealed links to suspected terrorists who might be in the United States. Meanwhile a Customs agent caught Ahmed Ressam, an Algerian jihadist, trying to cross with explosives from Canada into the United States.

Both staff and principals were seized with this threat. The CSG met constantly, frequently getting the assistance of principals to spur particular actions. These actions included pressuring Pakistan to turn over particular suspects and issuing an extraordinary number of domestic surveillance warrants for investigations in the United States. National Security Adviser Berger said that principals convened on a nearly daily basis in the White House Situation Room for almost a month. The principals communicated their own sense of urgency throughout their agencies.

By all accounts, the Millennium period was also a high point in the troubled relationship with the FBI. Before 9/11, the FBI did not ordinarily produce intelligence reports. Records of the FBI's intelligence work usually consisted of only the reports of interviews with witnesses or memoranda requesting the initiation or expansion of an investigation. The senior FBI headquarters official for counterterrorism, Dale Watson, was a member of the CSG, and Clarke had good personal relations with him and FBI agents handling al Qaeda-related investigations. But the NSC staff told us that the FBI rarely shared information about its domestic investigations. The Millennium alert period was an exception. After the Millennium surge subsided, National Security Adviser Berger and his deputy, James Steinberg, complained that, despite regular meetings with Attorney General Reno and FBI Director Freeh, the FBI withheld terrorism data on the grounds that it was inappropriate to share information related to pending investigations being presented to a grand jury.

In a January 2000 note to Berger, Clarke reported that the CSG drew two main conclusions from the Millennium crisis. First, it had concluded that U.S.-led disruption efforts "have not put too much of a dent" into bin Laden's network abroad. Second, it feared that "sleeper cells" or other links to foreign terrorist groups had taken root in the United States. Berger then led a formal Millennium after-action review of next steps, culminating in a meeting of the full Principals Committee on March 10.

The principals endorsed a four-part agenda to strengthen the U.S. government's counterterrorism efforts:

- Increase disruption efforts. This would require more resources for CIA operations, to assist friendly governments, and build a stronger capacity for direct action;

- Strengthen enforcement of laws restricting the activity of foreign terrorist organizations in the United States;

- Prevent foreign terrorists from entering the United States by strengthening immigration laws and the capacity of the Immigration and Naturalization Service; and

- Improve the security of the U.S.-Canadian border.

Some particular program ideas, like expanding the number of Joint Terrorism Task Forces across the United States, were adopted. Others, like a centralized translation unit for domestic intercepts, were not. In its January hearing, the Commission reviewed the progress of efforts on border and immigration issues.

Prodded to do more by President Clinton, the NSC staff pursued other initiatives in the spring of 2000. The NSC staff pushed for better technical intelligence collection, working closely with Assistant DCI for Collection Charles Allen and Vice Admiral Scott Fry of the Joint Staff. As we described [previously], this effort spurred use of the Predator reconnaissance aircraft in Afghanistan later in 2000 and produced other innovative ideas. A draft presidential directive on terrorist fundraising apparently did not win approval.

COORDINATING A COUNTERTERRORISM BUDGET

Overall U.S. government spending connected to counterterrorism grew rapidly during the late 1990s. Congress appropriated billions of additional dollars in supplemental appropriations for improvements like building more secure embassies, managing the consequences of a WMD attack, and protecting military forces.

Clarke and others remained frustrated, however, at the CIA's spending on counterterrorism. They complained that baseline spending at headquarters on bin Laden efforts or on operational efforts overseas remained nearly level. The CIA funded an expanded level of activity on a temporary basis with supplemental appropriations, but baseline spending requests, and thus core staffing, remained flat. The CIA told us that Clarke kept promising more budget support, but could never deliver.

The Clinton administration began proposing significant increases in the overall national intelligence budget in January 2000, for Fiscal Year 2001. Until that time, at least, CIA officials have told us that their main effort had been to rebuild the Agency's operating capabilities after what they said had been years of cuts and retrenchment. They believed counterterrorism efforts were relatively well off compared with the needs elsewhere.

In 2000 the budget situation in CIA's counterterrorism effort became critical. The strain on resources from the alert period had nearly exhausted available funds for the current fiscal year. Among counterterrorism officials, frustration with funding levels was growing. In August 1999, the senior Defense Department participant in the CSG noted that it seemed to him the CIA was "underfunding critical programs" in the covert action budget for countering terrorism.

On top of these concerns, the Millennium after-action review recommended significantly more spending. National Security Adviser Berger and DCI Tenet, along with their respective staffs, discussed where the money could be found, on the order of $50–100 million.

Working with senior officials in the White House Office of Management and Budget (OMB), Clarke had devised an innovative process to develop and analyze a counterterrorism budget picture across the government. Spending for the CIA, however, was handled under different procedures over which Clarke had less influence.

The White House initially preferred that the CIA find the money from within its existing funds. The CIA insisted that its other programs were vital too, and that the administration should seek another supplemental appropriation from Congress. The CIA's argument ultimately prevailed, and Congress adopted a supplemental appropriation.

On August 1, 2000, Clarke outlined for Berger a few key goals he hoped the administration could accomplish before it left office: to significantly erode al Qaeda's leadership and infrastructure; to gain the still-pending supplemental appropriations for the counterterrorism effort; and to advance the Predator program.

In August, Clarke urged that the CSG and the Principals Committee be ready for emergency meetings to decide whether to fire cruise missiles if bin Laden were spotted by the Predator. Berger noted to Clarke, though, that before considering any action he would need more than a verified location; he would also need data on a pattern of movements to provide some assurance that bin Laden would stay in place.

In September, Clarke wrote that the drones were providing "truly astonishing" imagery, including a "very high probability" of a bin Laden sighting. Clarke was also more upbeat about progress with disruptions of al Qaeda cells elsewhere. Berger wrote back praising Clarke's and the CSG's performance while observing that this was no time for complacency: "Unfortunately the light at the end of the tunnel is another tunnel."

THE ATTACK ON THE U.S.S. *COLE*

The U.S.S. *Cole* was attacked on October 12 in Yemen. By November 11, Berger and Clarke reported to the President that, while the investigation was continuing, it was becoming increasingly clear that al Qaeda planned and directed the bombing. In an update two weeks later, the President was informed that FBI and CIA investigations had not reached a formal conclusion, but Berger and Clarke expected the investigations would soon conclude that the attack had been carried out by a large cell headed by members of al Qaeda and that most of those involved were trained at bin Laden-operated camps in Afghanistan. So far, bin Laden had not been tied personally to the attacks, but there were reasons to suspect he was involved. In discussing possible responses, Berger stated that inherent in them was the "unproven assumption" that al Qaeda was responsible for the attack.

Berger told us he wanted a more definitive judgment from the DCI before using force. By December 21, the CIA's "preliminary judgment" for principals was that, while al Qaeda appeared to have supported the attack, the CIA still had no definitive answer on the "crucial question" of outside direction of the attack. Clarke added to us that while both the State Department and the Pentagon had reservations about retaliation, the issue never came to a head because the FBI and the CIA had not provided a definitive conclusion about responsibility.

The *Cole* attack prompted renewed consideration of what could be done. Clarke told us that Berger upbraided DCI Tenet so sharply after the *Cole* attack—repeatedly demanding to know why the United States had to put up with such attacks—that it led Tenet to walk out of a Principals Committee meeting. As we mentioned in [a separate] staff statement . . ., Berger obtained a fresh briefing on military options from General Shelton.

In December 2000, the CIA developed initiatives based on the assumption that policy and money were no longer constraints. The result was the "Blue Sky memo," which we discussed [previously]. This was forwarded to the NSC staff.

As the Clinton administration drew to a close, the NSC counterterrorism staff developed another strategy paper, the first such comprehensive effort since the Delenda plan of 1998. The resulting paper, a "Strategy for Eliminating the Threat from the Jihadist Networks of al Qaeda: Status and Prospects," reviewed the threat, the record to date, incorporated the CIA's new ideas from the "Blue Sky" memo, and posed several near-term policy choices. The goal was to "roll back" al Qaeda over a period of three to five years, reducing it eventually to a "rump group" like other formerly feared but now largely defunct terrorist organizations of the 1980s. "Continued anti-al Qaeda operations at the current level will prevent some attacks," Clarke and his staff wrote, "but will not seriously attrit their ability to plan and conduct attacks."

THE BUSH ADMINISTRATION

The Bush administration decided to retain Clarke and his core counterterrorism staff. National Security Adviser [Condoleezza] Rice knew Clarke from prior government experience. She was aware he was controversial, but she and [her deputy] thought they needed an experienced crisis manager in place during the first part of the administration. Working with Clarke, Rice and her deputy, Stephen Hadley, concentrated Clarke's responsibilities on terrorism issues, and planned to spin off some of his office's responsibilities—for cybersecurity, international crime, and consequence management—to other parts of the NSC staff. Clarke in particular wished to elevate the attention being given to the cybersecurity problem. On May 8, President Bush asked Vice President Cheney to chair an effort looking at preparations for managing a WMD attack and problems of national preparedness. It was just getting underway when the 9/11 attack occurred.

Rice and Hadley decided that Clarke's CSG should report to the Deputies Committee, chaired by Hadley, rather than bringing its issues directly to the principals. Clarke would still attend Principals Committee meetings on terrorism, but without the central role he had played in the Clinton-era Small Group. Hadley told us that subordinating the CSG to the Deputies would help resolve counterterrorism issues in a broader context. Clarke protested the change, arguing that it would slow decision-making. Clarke told us that he considered this move a demotion to being a staffer rather than being a de facto principal on terrorism. On operational matters, however, Clarke could and did go directly to Rice.

Clarke and his staff said that the new team, having been out of government for at least eight years, had a learning curve to understand al Qaeda and the new transnational terrorist threat. During the transition, Clarke briefed Secretary of State-designate [Colin] Powell, Rice, and Hadley on al Qaeda, including a mention of "sleeper cells" in many countries, including the United States. Clarke gave a similar briefing to Vice President Cheney in the early days of the administration. Berger said he told Rice during the transition that she would spend more time on terrorism and al Qaeda than on any other issue. Although Clarke briefed President Bush on cybersecurity issues before 9/11, he never briefed or met with President Bush on counterterrorism, which was a significant contrast from the relationship he had enjoyed with President Clinton. Rice pointed out to us that President Bush received his counterterrorism briefings directly from DCI Tenet, who began personally providing intelligence updates at the White House each morning.

Asked by Hadley to offer major initiatives, on January 25, 2001 Clarke forwarded his December 2000 strategy paper, and a copy of his 1998 Delenda plan, to the new national security adviser, Condoleezza Rice. Clarke laid out a proposed agenda for urgent action by the new administration:

- Approval of covert assistance to the Northern Alliance and others.

- Significantly increased funding to pay for this and other CIA activity in preparation of the administration's first budget, for Fiscal Year 2002.

- Choosing a standard of evidence for attributing responsibility for the U.S.S. *Cole* and deciding on a response.

- Going forward with new Predator reconnaissance missions in the spring and preparation of an armed version of the aircraft.

- More work on terrorist fundraising.

Clarke asked on several occasions for early Principals Committee meetings on these issues and was frustrated that no early meeting was scheduled. He wanted principals to accept that al Qaeda was a "first order threat" and not a routine problem being exaggerated by "chicken little" alarmists. No Principals Committee meetings on al Qaeda were held until September 4, 2001. Rice and Hadley said this was because the Deputies Committee needed to work through the many issues related to new policy on al Qaeda. The Principals Committee did meet frequently before 9/11 on other subjects, Rice told us, including Russia, the Persian Gulf, and the Middle East peace process.

Rice and Hadley told us that although the Clinton administration had worked very hard on the al Qaeda problem, its policies on al Qaeda "had run out of gas," as Hadley put it. On March 7, Hadley convened an informal meeting of some of his counterparts from other agencies to discuss al Qaeda. After reviewing the background on the issues, Clarke pressed for immediate decisions on covert assistance to the Northern Alliance and others, as well as for Predator reconnaissance missions. Development of a new presidential directive on terrorism was also discussed.

The proposal for aid to the Northern Alliance was moved into this policy review. This was discussed in more detail [in the staff statement] on diplomacy. In April, the deputies decided not to approve new aid to the Northern Alliance, pending decisions about a broader aid program that would include other opposition groups in Afghanistan.

The administration took action on the intelligence budget for Fiscal Year 2002. It proposed a 27 percent increase in CIA counterterrorism spending.

On the issue of the *Cole*, the Bush administration received essentially the same "preliminary judgment" that had been briefed to the Clinton administration in December. Clarke consistently pressed officials to adopt some standard of evidence that would permit a response. He recommended on January 25 that the United States adopt the approach of responding at a time, place, and manner of its choosing, "and not be forced into a knee-jerk response." Rice agreed with the time, place, and manner point. Hadley added that the discussion of retaliation was less about the evidence and more about what to do. Rice and Hadley told us they did not want to launch cruise missiles in a "tit-for-tat" strike as in 1998, which they considered ineffectual. According to Rice, President Bush had the same reaction: don't do something weak. There was no formal decision not to retaliate. Hadley told us the new administration's response to the *Cole* would take the form of a more aggressive strategy on al Qaeda.

We have discussed the Predator program earlier. . . . Additional policy direction on terrorist fundraising was incorporated in the planned presidential directive.

As spring turned to summer, Clarke was impatient for decisions on aid to the Northern Alliance and on the Predator program, issues managed by Hadley and the Deputies Committee. Clarke and others perceived the process as slow. Clarke argued that the policy on Afghanistan and Pakistan did not need to be settled before moving ahead against al Qaeda. Hadley emphasized to us the time needed to get new officials confirmed and in place. He told us that they moved the process along as fast as they could. The Deputies Committee met seven times from April to September 10 on issues related to al Qaeda, Afghanistan, and Pakistan.

Rice recalled that in May 2001, as threats of possible terrorist attacks came up again and again in DCI Tenet's morning discussions with President Bush, the President expressed impatience with "swatting flies" and pushed his advisers to do more. Rice and

Tenet met at the end of May, along with their counterterrorism advisers, to discuss what Rice at the time called "taking the offensive" against al Qaeda. This led to a discussion about how to break the back of bin Laden's organization. Within the NSC staff, Clarke was asked to put together a broad policy to eliminate al Qaeda, to be codified in the presidential directive. The Deputies Committee discussed complementary policies that would be adopted on Afghanistan and Pakistan as well.

Clarke and his staff regarded the new approach as essentially similar to the proposal they had developed in December 2000 and had put forward to the new administration in January 2001. Clarke's staff produced a draft presidential directive on al Qaeda. Hadley circulated it to his counterparts in early June as "an admittedly ambitious program."

The draft had the goal of eliminating the al Qaeda network as a threat over a multi-year period. It had headings such as "No Sanctuaries" and "No Financial Support." The draft committed the administration to providing sufficient funds to support this program in its budgets from Fiscal Year 2002 to Fiscal Year 2006. Specific annexes dealt with activities to be undertaken by the CIA and planning to be done by the Defense Department.

From April through July, alarming threat reports were pouring in. Clarke and the CSG were consumed with coordinating defensive reactions. In late June, Clarke wrote Rice that the threat reporting had reached a crescendo. Security was stepped up for the G–8 summit in Genoa, including air-defense measures. U.S. embassies were temporarily closed. Units of the Fifth Fleet were redeployed from usual locations in the Persian Gulf. Administration officials, including Vice President Cheney, Secretary Powell, and DCI Tenet, contacted foreign officials to urge them to take needed defensive steps.

On July 2, the FBI issued a national threat advisory. Rice recalls asking Clarke on July 5 to bring additional law enforcement and domestic agencies into the CSG threat discussions. That afternoon, officials from a number of these agencies met at the White House, following up with alerts of their own, including FBI and FAA [Federal Aviation Administration] warnings.

The next day, the CIA told CSG participants that al Qaeda members "believe the upcoming attack will be a 'spectacular,' qualitatively different from anything they have done to date." On July 27 Clarke reported to Rice and Hadley that the spike in intelligence indicating a near-term attack appeared to have ceased, but he urged them to keep readiness high; intelligence indicated that an attack had been postponed for a few months.

In early August, the CIA prepared an article for the president's daily intelligence brief on whether or how terrorists might attack the United States. Neither the White House nor the CSG received specific, credible information about any threatened attacks in the United States. Neither Clarke nor the CSG were informed about the August 2001 investigations that produced the discovery of suspected al Qaeda operatives in the United States. Nor did the group learn about the arrest or FBI investigation of [student pilot] Zacarias Moussaoui in Minnesota.

Arguments about flying the Predator continued. Rice and Hadley, contrary to Clarke's advice, acceded to the CIA view that reconnaissance flights should be held off until the armed version was ready. Hadley sent a July 11 memo to his counterparts at the CIA and the Defense Department directing them to have Predators capable of being armed ready to deploy no later than September 1.

At the beginning of August Rice and Hadley again reviewed the draft presidential directive on al Qaeda. Rice commented that it was "very good," and principals needed to discuss it briefly, just for closure, before it was submitted to President Bush. This meeting was scheduled for September 4.

The directive envisioned an expanded covert action program against al Qaeda, including significantly increased funding and more support for the Northern Alliance, anti-Taliban Pashtuns, and other groups. But the authorities for this program had not yet been approved, and the funding to get this program underway still had not been found. Although the administration had proposed a larger covert action budget for [Fiscal Year] '02, the Congress had not yet appropriated the money and the fiscal year had not begun. The planned covert action program would need funds going well beyond what had already been budgeted for the current fiscal year, including the supplemental passed at the end of 2000. This budget problem was not resolved before 9/11.

The policy streams converged at a meeting of the Principals Committee, the Administration's first such meeting on al Qaeda issues, on September 4. Before this meeting, Clarke wrote to Rice summarizing many of his frustrations. He urged policymakers to imagine a day after a terrorist attack, with hundreds of Americans dead at home and abroad, and ask themselves what they could have done earlier. He criticized the military for what he called its unwillingness to retaliate for the *Cole* attack or strike Afghan camps. He accused senior CIA officials of trying to block the Predator program. He warned that unless adequate funding was found for the planned effort, the directive would be a hollow shell. He feared, apparently referring to President Bush's earlier comment, that Washington might be left with a modest effort to swat flies, relying on foreign governments while waiting for the big attack.

Rice chaired the meeting of principals. They apparently approved the draft directive. As discussed earlier . . ., they agreed that the armed Predator capability was needed, leaving open issues related to command and control. DCI Tenet was also pressed to reconsider his opposition to starting immediately with reconnaissance flights and, after the meeting, Tenet agreed to proceed with such flights.

Various follow-up activities began in the following days, including discussions between Rice and Tenet, Hadley's September 10 directive to Tenet to develop expanded covert action authorities, and, that same day, further Deputies Committee consideration of policy toward Afghanistan and Pakistan. Then came the attacks on September 11.

Warren Bass, Michael Hurley, Alexis Albion, and Dan Marcus did much of the investigative work reflected in this statement. The Executive Office of the President, the Central Intelligence Agency, and other government agencies have made the material available to us for the preparation of this statement.

Excerpts of testimony from Samuel Berger, Richard Clarke, Richard Armitage, and Condoleezza Rice

EXCERPTS OF TESTIMONY FROM SAMUEL BERGER, FORMER NATIONAL SECURITY ADVISER

"There could not have been any doubt about what President Clinton's intent was after he fired 60 Tomahawk cruise missiles at bin Laden in August '98. I assure you they were not delivering an arrest warrant. The intent was to kill bin Laden."

What were the elements of our counterterrorism strategy? First, as our understanding of bin Laden evolved in the mid-1990s, from one of many financiers of terrorist groups to a galvanizer of anti-American hatred, our focus on him and his network increased. We established a dedicated CIA cell for tracking his activities after the bombings of our embassies in Kenya and Tanzania in August 1998, the first time we had established bin Laden's role in attacks against Americans. Getting bin Laden and stopping al Qaeda became a top priority.

It has been reported the president gave the CIA broad, lethal and unprecedented authorities regarding bin Laden and his lieutenants. The president's willingness to destroy Osama bin Laden and his lieutenants was made unmistakably clear in August 1998, the one time we had actionable intelligence as to bin Laden's whereabouts. The president ordered a cruise missile attack against him. According to the intelligence community, at the time, 20 to 30 al Qaeda lieutenants were killed, but bin Laden was missed by a few hours.

For the rest of our term, we tried continually to obtain actionable intelligence on bin Laden and other top operatives. Unfortunately, such intelligence never emerged again. And it was our judgment that to attack primitive camps and fail to destroy bin Laden or other al Qaeda leaders would strengthen al Qaeda and make us look weak. President Clinton pressed often for special forces options to get bin Laden; boots on the ground. The military seriously considered such missions. But, before 9/11, with no regional support or bases, daunting operational obstacles, and no lead time intelligence on bin Laden's whereabouts, the military leadership concluded any such mission likely would fail. Nonetheless, we continued to seek the whereabouts of bin Laden and his lieutenants, and we were ready to act if we could locate them.

QUESTIONS FROM COMMISSIONERS

RICHARD BEN-VENISTE: With respect to the authorization for the use of force given to Director Tenet, he was reluctant to go into specifics but he did say that there was no request for authority that was denied by President Clinton. Could you shed light on that as well?

BERGER: I will try, Mr. Commissioner. I've read some of these reports in the press and otherwise. Let me say, first of all, there could not have been any doubt about what President Clinton's intent was after he fired 60 Tomahawk cruise missiles at bin Laden in August '98. I assure you they were not delivering an arrest warrant. The intent was to kill bin Laden.

Number one, his overall intent was manifest in August '98. Number two, I believe the director understood and I think he reiterated it today that we wanted him to use the full measure of the CIA's capabilities. Only the CIA can judge what its capabilities are, and that then defines the scope of the authorization. We gave the CIA every inch of authorization that it had asked for. If there was any confusion down the ranks it was never communicated to me nor to the president. And if any additional authority had been requested, I am convinced it would have been given immediately.

BEN-VENISTE: Yesterday, the secretary of defense indicated that missile attacks against al Qaeda in its location in Afghanistan would have been—I think he used the term "bouncing the rubble." Did you regard the missile attack which you just described to be bouncing the rubble?

BERGER: The missile attack in August of '98 was attempting to be bouncing bin Laden into rubble. We had specific intelligence that a large gathering would be there, that probably bin Laden would be there. We struck with the intent of killing bin Laden and/or his operatives. I deeply regret that we did not succeed. . . .

BEN-VENISTE: Moreover, let me just add, in doing so, it would be important—would it not—to advise [India and Pakistan] that the missile that we were sending, for the purpose of eliminating bin Laden, was not coming from either of them against the other.

BERGER: It's a very important point you raise, Mr. Ben-Veniste. When we attacked in August '98, we obviously did not want to give them advance notice, because we, quite honestly, didn't trust the Pakistani army to not be penetrated. The Pakistani army was the midwife of the Taliban. There were very close relationships. We sent General [Joseph] Ralston to go have dinner, as I recall, with General [Jahangir] Karamat, the head of the Pakistani military. And as those missiles were heading into Pakistani airspace, General Ralston said, by the way, General Karamat, at this moment missiles are coming over your airspace, so that the Pakistanis would not read those as incoming missiles from India with nuclear warheads and we'd start a nuclear war. . . .

BEN-VENISTE: When you say that the Pakistani military was behind the Taliban in its creation, this was a significant problem from a diplomacy standpoint to deal with. Not only was the Taliban in control in Afghanistan and protecting bin Laden, but the situation in Pakistan was not particularly conducive to assisting the United States and eliminating bin Laden, was it?

BERGER: I think that's a very important point, if I can take one minute on it. I believe we put as much pressure on Pakistan to put pressure on the Taliban as we possibly could, through every means available to us. We didn't have any sticks. Because of the nuclear weapon sanctions, because of the other sanctions, there was nothing we could say, "We'll take this away from you," because we weren't giving them anything. But we leaned on them very heavily. We had the Saudis lean on them very, very heavily. The only thing we could have done, I think, that we didn't do was cut off their access to IMF [International Monetary Fund] loans, which would have collapsed Pakistan, and we would have had a failed nuclear state in South Asia, which probably would not have been the best thing for the United States.

· · ·

JOHN F. LEHMAN: So let me just start with some of the key milestones in the terror attacks as they developed against the United States, starting with the '93 attempt by Saddam to assassinate President Bush. According to testimony that we've had, the response of President Clinton was to take very strong action. And indeed, a whole broad series of targets were selected and the direction was given to implement that retaliatory plan. But, in fact, because [Secretary of State] Warren Christopher and some others argued strongly against that strong an attack, it ended up being reduced to a small cruise missile attack against the Iraqi intelligence headquarters in the middle of the night so nobody would be there. Tell us about your impression and what went on and what happened with that particular crisis. . . .

BERGER: With respect to the bombing of the intelligence headquarters, . . . I don't believe it's accurate that those were scaled back because of Secretary Christopher's reservations. This was what the chairman of the joint chiefs of staff, Chairman Powell, and the other national security principals recommended. We took down their intelligence headquarters. It's like them taking down Langley. And I suspect if somebody took down Langley, we would not call that a pin prick. And we said at the same time to them that if they ever try terrorism again against the United States, the consequences will be severe. And as far as I know, from 1993 on, they never did.

.   .   .

EXCERPTS OF TESTIMONY FROM RICHARD CLARKE, FORMER NATIONAL COORDINATOR FOR COUNTERTERRORISM

"I believe the Bush administration in the first eight months considered terrorism an important issue, but not an urgent issue. [T]here was a process under way to address al Qaeda. But although I continued to say it was an urgent problem, I don't think it was ever treated that way."

[From his written statement:] Although there were people in the FBI, CIA, Defense Department, State Department, and White House who worked very hard to destroy al Qaeda before it did catastrophic damage to the U.S., there were many others who found the prospect of significant al Qaeda attacks remote. In both CIA and the military there was reluctance at senior career levels to fully utilize all of the capabilities available. There was risk aversion. FBI was, throughout much of this period, organized, staffed, and equipped in such a way that it was ineffective in dealing with the domestic terrorist threat from al Qaeda.

At the senior policy levels in the Clinton Administration, there was an acute understanding of the terrorist threat, particularly al Qaeda. That understanding resulted in a vigorous program to counter al Qaeda, including lethal covert action, but it did not include a willingness to resume bombing of Afghanistan. Events in the Balkans, Iraq, the Peace Process, and domestic politics occurring at the same time as the anti-terrorism effort played a role.

The Bush Administration saw terrorism policy as important but not urgent, prior to 9/11. The difficulty in obtaining the first Cabinet level (Principals) policy meeting on terrorism and the limited Principals' involvement sent unfortunate signals to the bureaucracy about the Administration's attitude toward the al Qaeda threat.

The U.S. response to al Qaeda following 9/11 has been partially effective. Unfortunately, the U.S. did not act sufficiently quickly to insert U.S. forces to capture or kill the al Qaeda leadership in Afghanistan. Nor did we employ sufficient U.S. and Allied forces to stabilize that country. In the ensuing 30 months, al Qaeda has morphed into a decentralized network, with its national and regional affiliates operating effectively and independently. There have been more major al Qaeda related attacks globally in the 30 months since 9/11 than there were in the 30 months preceding it. Hostility toward the U.S. in the Islamic world has increased since 9/11, largely as a result of the invasion and occupation of Iraq. Thus, new terrorist cells are likely being created, unknown to U.S. intelligence.

To address the continuing threat from radical Islamic terrorism, the U.S. and its allies must become increasingly focused and effective in countering the ideology that motivates that terrorism.

· · ·

[From his opening statement:] I welcome these hearings because of the opportunity that they provide to the American people to better understand why the tragedy of 9/11 happened and what we must do to prevent a reoccurrence.

I also welcome the hearings because it is finally a forum where I can apologize to the loved ones of the victims of 9/11.

To them who are here in the room, to those who are watching on television, your government failed you, those entrusted with protecting you failed you and I failed you. We tried hard, but that doesn't matter because we failed.

And for that failure, I would ask—once all the facts are out—for your understanding and for your forgiveness.

QUESTIONS FROM COMMISSIONERS

TIMOTHY J. ROEMER: . . . Was fighting al Qaeda a top priority for the Clinton administration from 1998 to the year 2001? How high a priority was it in that Clinton administration during that time period?

CLARKE: My impression was that fighting terrorism, in general, and fighting al Qaeda, in particular, were an extraordinarily high priority in the Clinton administration—certainly no higher priority. There were priorities probably of equal importance such as the Middle East peace process, but I certainly don't know of one that was any higher in the priority of that administration.

ROEMER: With respect to the Bush administration, from the time they took office until September 11, 2001, you had much to deal with: Russia, China, G–8, Middle East. How high a priority was fighting al Qaeda in the Bush administration?

CLARKE: I believe the Bush administration in the first eight months considered terrorism an important issue, but not an urgent issue. Well, President Bush himself says as much in his interview with Bob Woodward in the book "Bush at War." He said, "I didn't feel a sense of urgency." George Tenet and I tried very hard to create a sense of urgency by seeing to it that intelligence reports on the al Qaeda threat were frequently given to the president and other high-level officials. And there was a process under way to address al Qaeda. But although I continued to say it was an urgent problem, I don't think it was ever treated that way.

ROEMER: [Y]ou've issued some blistering attacks on the Bush administration. But you've not held those criticisms from the Clinton administration, either. We heard from Mr. Berger earlier that you were critical of the Clinton administration on two areas: not providing aid to the Northern Alliance, and not going after the human conveyor belts of jihadists coming out of the sanctuaries in Afghanistan. Are there more in the Clinton administration years—the U.S.S. *Cole*, the response there?

CLARKE: Well, I think first of all, Mr. Berger is right to say that almost everything I ever asked for in the way of support from him or from President Clinton, I got. We did enormously increase the counterterrorism budget of the federal government, initiated many programs, including one that is now called Homeland Security. Mr. Berger is also right to note that I wanted a covert action program to aid Afghan factions to fight the Taliban, and that was not accomplished. He's also right to note that on several occasions, including after the attack on the *Cole*, I suggested that we bomb all of the Taliban and al Qaeda infrastructure, whether or not it would succeed in killing bin Laden. I thought that was the wrong way of looking at the problem. I think the answer is essentially Mr. Berger got it right.

ROEMER: . . . On January 25th, we've seen a memo that you've written to Dr. Rice urgently asking for a principals' review of al Qaeda. You include helping the Northern Alliance, covert aid, significant new '02 budget authority to help fight al Qaeda and a response to the U.S.S. *Cole*. You attach to this document both the Delenda Plan of 1998 and a strategy paper from December 2000. Did you get a response to this urgent request for a principals' meeting on these? And how does this affect your time frame for dealing with these important issues?

CLARKE: I did get a response, and the response was that in the Bush administration I should, and my committee, counterterrorism security group, should report to the deputies committee, which is a sub-Cabinet level committee, and not to the principals and that, therefore, it was inappropriate for me to be asking for a principals' meeting. Instead, there would be a deputies meeting.

ROEMER: So does this slow the process down to go to the deputies rather than to the principals or a small group as you had previously done?

CLARKE: It slowed it down enormously, by months. First of all, the deputies committee didn't meet urgently in January or February. Then when the deputies committee did meet, it took the issue of al Qaeda as part of a cluster of policy issues, including nuclear proliferation in South Asia, democratization in Pakistan, how to treat the various problems, including narcotics and other problems in Afghanistan, and launched on a series of deputies meetings extending over several months to address al Qaeda in the context of all of those interrelated issues. That process probably ended, I think, in July of 2001. So we were ready for a principals' meeting in July. But the principals' calendar was full and then they went on vacation, many of them in August, so we couldn't meet in August, and therefore the principals met in September.

ROEMER: So as the Bush administration is carefully considering from bottom up a full review of fighting terrorism, what happens to these individual items like a response to the U.S.S. *Cole*, flying the Predator? Why aren't these decided in a shorter time frame as they're also going through a larger policy review of how this policy affects Pakistan and other countries—important considerations, but why can't you do both?

CLARKE: The deputies committee, its chairman, Mr. Hadley, and others thought that all these issues were sufficiently inter-related, that they should be taken up as a set of issues, and pieces of them should not be broken off.

ROEMER: Did you agree with that?

CLARKE: No, I didn't agree with much of that.

ROEMER: Were you frustrated by this process?

CLARKE: I was sufficiently frustrated that I asked to be reassigned.

ROEMER: When was this?

CLARKE: Probably May or June. Certainly no later than June. And there was agreement in that time frame, in the May or June time frame, that my request would be honored and I would be reassigned on the 1st of October to a new position to deal with cybersecurity, a position that I requested be created.

ROEMER: So you're saying that the frustration got to a high enough level that it wasn't your portfolio, it wasn't doing a lot of things at the same time, it was that you weren't getting fast enough action on what you were requesting?

CLARKE: That's right. My view was that this administration, while it listened to me, didn't either believe me that there was an urgent problem or was unprepared to act as though there were an urgent problem. And I thought, if the administration doesn't believe its national coordinator for counterterrorism when he says there's an urgent problem and if it's unprepared to act as though there's an urgent problem, then probably I should get another job. I thought cybersecurity was and I still think cybersecurity is an extraordinarily important issue for which this country is very underprepared. And I thought perhaps I could make a contribution if I worked full time on that issue.

ROEMER: You then wrote a memo on September 4th to Dr. Rice expressing some of these frustrations several months later, if you say the time frame is May or June when you decided to resign. A memo comes out that we have seen on September the 4th. You are blunt in blasting DOD [Department of Defense] for not willingly using the force and the power. You blast the CIA for blocking Predator. You urge policymakers to imagine a day after hundreds of Americans lay dead at home or abroad after a terrorist attack and ask themselves what else they could have done. You write this on September the 4th, seven days before September 11th.

CLARKE: That's right.

ROEMER: What else could have been done, Mr. Clarke?

CLARKE: Well, all of the things that we recommended in the plan or strategy—there's a lot of debate about whether it's a plan or a strategy or a series of options. But all of the things we recommended back in January were those things on the table in September. They were done. They were done after September 11th. They were all done. I didn't really understand why they couldn't have been done in February.

ROEMER: Well, let's say, Mr. Clarke—I think this is a fair question—let's say that you asked to brief the president of the United States on counterterrorism.

CLARKE: Yes.

ROEMER: Did you ask that?

CLARKE: I asked for a series of briefings on the issues in my portfolio, including counterterrorism and cybersecurity.

ROEMER: Did you get that request?

CLARKE: I did. I was given an opportunity to brief on cybersecurity in June. I was told I could brief the president on terrorism after this policy development process was complete and we had the principals meeting and the draft national security policy decision that had been approved by the deputies committee. . . .

ROEMER: Let me ask you . . . a question about the summer 2001 alert. You were saying, the CIA was saying, everybody was saying something spectacular is about to happen. Spiking in intelligence, something terrible is about to happen. You've told us in some of our interviews you only wish you would have known at that time in that summer what the FBI knew with regard to Moussaoui, the

Phoenix memo [urging an investigation on possible terrorists in U.S. flight schools], and terrorists in the United States. What could you have done with some of that information, with the spiked alerts, with the spectacular attack on the horizon in the summer of 2001?

CLARKE: Congressman, it is very easy in retrospect to say that I would have done this or I would have done that. And we'll never know. I would like to think that had I been informed by the FBI that two senior al Qaeda operatives who had been in a planning meeting earlier in Kuala Lumpur were now in the United States and we knew that and we knew their names—and I think we even had their pictures—I would like to think that I would have released, or would have had the FBI release, a press release with their names, with their descriptions, held a press conference, tried to get their names and pictures on the front page of every paper, "America's Most Wanted," the evening news, and caused a successful nationwide manhunt for those two of the 19 hijackers, but I don't know because you're asking me a hypothetical and I have the benefit now of 20/20 hindsight.

.   .   .

SLADE GORTON: In August of 1998, did you recommend a longer-lasting military response [to the attack on two U.S. embassies in Africa] or just precisely the one that, in fact, took place?

CLARKE: I recommended a series of rolling attacks against the infrastructure in Afghanistan. Every time they would rebuild it, I proposed that we blow it up again much like, in fact, we were doing in Iraq, where we had a rolling series of attacks on their air defense system.

GORTON: And shortly after that, you came up with the so-called Delenda Plan, as I understand it. And is our staff report accurate in saying that it had four principal approaches—diplomacy, covert action, various financial members and military action? Is that a reasonable summary?

CLARKE: Yes, sir.

GORTON: Also, is our staff accurate in saying that the strategy was never formally adopted, but that you were authorized in effect to go ahead with the first three, but not with the fourth?

CLARKE: Yes, sir.

GORTON: And at various times thereafter you did recommend specific military responses under specific circumstances, did you not?

CLARKE: Yes, sir.

GORTON: Each of which was rejected for one reason or another?

CLARKE: That's correct.

GORTON: Then in the early winter of 1999, when the CIA came up with a plan to attack a hunting camp in Afghanistan, which it felt that Osama bin Laden was present or was not present, that recommendation, or that plan, was ultimately aborted. Did you recommend against that plan?

CLARKE: Yes, Senator. What I did was to call the Director of Central Intelligence and say that I had finally been presented with satellite photography of the facility. And it was very clear to me that this looked like something other than a terrorist camp. It looked like a luxury hunting trip. And I asked him to look into it, personally. When he did, he called back and he said that he was no longer recommending the attack.

GORTON: OK. So you never recommended either for or against an attack on that camp?

CLARKE: Well, I think—I don't want to split hairs. By calling the Director of Central Intelligence and suggesting to him that this did not look to me like a terrorist facility and urging him to look into it, he certainly had the impression that I wasn't in favor of it. Absolutely.

GORTON: Well, did it make any difference as to what kind of camp it was, if it was likely that Osama bin Laden was there?

CLARKE: After the bombings in 1998, we kept submarines off the coast of Pakistan, loaded with cruise missiles, for the purpose of launching a follow-on attack when we could locate bin Laden. The intelligence that we got about where bin Laden was, was very poor. The DCI, Mr. Tenet, characterized that intelligence himself on repeated occasions as very poor. On one occasion, we thought we knew where he was, and there were two problems. One, the intelligence was poor, according to George Tenet. And two, the collateral damage would have been great, according to the Pentagon.

When I looked at this facility, it looked to me like the intelligence was, again, poor, because it didn't look like a terrorist camp. And the probability of collateral damage would have been high, I thought, since I believed, based on the satellite photography, that people other than terrorists were there. The decision ultimately was George Tenet's, and George Tenet recommended no action be taken. I don't know, in retrospect—your staff might—but I don't know, in retrospect, whether it proved to be true that bin Laden was in the vicinity or not.

GORTON: In any event, every recommendation for military action or covert action, from late 1998 until the year 2000, ran up against the objection of actionable—that it was not based on actionable intelligence, that wonderful phrase we've heard in the last two days. Is that not correct, because of the uncertainty as to whether bin Laden was present, uncertainty about collateral damage, et cetera?

CLARKE: That's true in describing actions aimed at Osama bin Laden himself. There were other covert action activities taken which we obviously can't go into here. But, there was a pre-existing finding on terrorism under which CIA was operating. And the CIA was able to do some things outside of Afghanistan against the al Qaeda network using that authority.

GORTON: And at the very end of the Clinton administration after the attack on the *Cole*, there was triggered, either by the *Cole* or by everything else, a new set of initiatives resulting in what is called a Blue Sky memo, is that correct?

CLARKE: That's right.

GORTON: And were you a part of that? Did you draft it? Was it your plan?

CLARKE: The Blue Sky memo I believe you're referring to was part of an overall update of the Delenda Plan. And it was in part generated by the Central Intelligence Agency. We, my staff, generated the rest of the update.

GORTON: And the goal of that plan was to roll back al Qaeda over a period of three to five years, reducing it eventually to a rump group like other terrorist organizations around the world.

CLARKE: Our goal was to do that to eliminate it as a threat to the United States, recognizing that one might not ever be able to totally eliminate everybody in the world who thought they were a member of al Qaeda. But if we could get it to be as ineffective as the Abu Nidal organization was toward the end of its existence; it didn't pose a threat to the United States. That's what we wanted. The CIA said that if they got all the resources they needed, that might be possible over the course of three years at the earliest.

GORTON: And then Delenda and that Blue Sky proposal, I take it, were pretty much the basis of what you recommended to Condoleezza Rice in January of 2001: covert assistance to the Northern Alliance, you know, more money for CIA activities, something called choosing a standard of evidence for attributing responsibility for the *Cole*, new Predator reconnaissance missions and more work on funding?

CLARKE: That's right, Senator. The update to the Delenda Plan that we did in October, November, December of 2000 was handed to the new national security adviser in January of 2001. It formed the basis of the draft national security presidential directive that was then discussed in September of 2001 and signed by President Bush as NSPD [National Security Presidential Directive]–9, I believe, later in September.

GORTON: What do you mean by a standard of evidence? I'm troubled by this fuzzy phrase, "actionable intelligence." And let's take the *Cole* from that. As we've heard from Director Tenet in November and then more precisely in December of 2000, they pretty much concluded that the *Cole* took place through al Qaeda people, but they couldn't prove that it had been directed by Osama bin Laden. Was the amount of intelligence available in November, December of 2000 and 2001, in your view, actionable intelligence that could have been the appropriate basis for a specific response to the *Cole*?

CLARKE: The phrase that you read, "the standard for actionable," was a way of my addressing this problem. And I wanted to get us away from having to prove either in a court of law legal standard or even in some fancy intelligence community standard that went through a prolonged process that took months.

I thought we could disassociate the attack on the *Cole* from any attacks that we did on the Taliban and al Qaeda. If people wanted to further study who was guilty of attacking the *Cole*—and the FBI had deployed hundreds of people to do that, and CIA was saying that there were some people involved who might have been al Qaeda—I thought fine. If you want to have that kind [of] standard and you want to have that kind of process, fine. Then let's separate that and let's bomb Afghanistan anyway and not tie the two together.

But it seemed to my staff, looking at the same intelligence that the CIA was looking at, it seemed to us within two days of the attack on the *Cole* that we could put together an intelligence case that this was an al Qaeda attack by the local al Qaeda cell in Yemen. And that is, of course, the conclusion that the CIA came to in January or February of the next year based on pretty much nothing but the evidence that we had available to us within two days.

GORTON: . . . Assuming that the recommendations that you made on January 25th of 2001, based on Delenda, based on Blue Sky, including aid to the Northern Alliance, which had been an agenda item at this point for two and a half years without any action, assuming that there had been more Predator reconnaissance missions, assuming that that had all been adopted say on January 26th, year 2001, is there the remotest chance that it would have prevented 9/11?

CLARKE: No.

GORTON: It just would have allowed our response, after 9/11, to be perhaps a little bit faster?

CLARKE: Well, the response would have begun before 9/11.

GORTON: Yes, but there was no recommendation, on your part or anyone else's part, that we declare war and attempt to invade Afghanistan prior to 9/11?

CLARKE: That's right.

. . .

THOMAS H. KEAN: . . . I'm trying to find not only what we could have done, but what should we be doing perhaps in the future? Because we were beaten. I mean, we were really beaten by these guys, and 3,000 people died. And is there anything you can think of in that long period, had we done differently as a country, as a policy, what have you, that could have made a difference? . . .

CLARKE: I think al Qaeda probably came into existence in 1988 or in 1989, and no one in the White House was ever informed by the intelligence community that there was an al Qaeda until probably 1995. The existence of an organization like that was something that members of the National Security Council staff suspected in 1993. National Security Adviser Anthony Lake urged CIA to create a special program to investigate whether there was some organization centered around bin Laden. It was not done because CIA decided there was probably an organization, it was done because the national security adviser thought there was probably an organization.

Had we a more robust intelligence capability in the late 1980s and early 1990s, we might have recognized the existence of al Qaeda relatively soon after it came into existence. And if we recognized its existence and if we knew its philosophy and if we had a proactive intelligence covert action program—so that's both more on the collection side and more on the covert action side—then we might have been able to nip it in the bud. But as George Tenet I think explained this morning, our HUMINT program, our spy capability, had been eviscerated in the 1980s and early 1990s. And there was no such capability either to even know that al Qaeda existed, let alone to destroy it.

And there is something else that I think we need to understand about the CIA's covert action capabilities. For many years, they were roundly criticized by the Congress and the media for various covert actions that they carried out at the request of people like me and the White House—not me, but people like me. And many CIA senior managers were dragged up into this room and others and berated for failed covert action activities, and they became great political footballs. Now, if you're in the CIA and you're growing up as a CIA manager over this period of time and that's what you see going on and you see one boss after another, one deputy director of operations after another being fired or threatened with indictment, I think the thing you learn from that is that covert action is a very dangerous thing that can damage the CIA as much as it can damage the enemy.

Robert Gates, when he was deputy director of CIA, and when he was director of CIA, and when he was deputy national security adviser, Robert Gates repeatedly taught the lesson that covert action isn't worth doing. It's too risky. That's the lesson that the current generation of directorate of operations managers learned as they were growing up in the agency.

Now, George Tenet says they're not risk-averse, and I'm sure he knows better than I do. But from the outside, working with the DOD over the course of the last 20 years, it certainly looks to me as though they were risk-averse, but they had every reason to be risk-averse, because the Congress, the media, had taught them that the use of covert action would likely blow up in their face.

.   .   .

RICHARD BEN-VENISTE: . . . I want to focus on the role of the national security adviser and your relationship with the national security adviser in the Clinton administration as compared with the Bush administration. Can you point to any similarities or differences?

CLARKE: Well, I think the similarity is that under all four national security advisers for whom I worked, I was told by each of the four, beginning with Brent Scowcroft, that if I ever had any—I hate to use the word, Senator, "actionable intelligence," the phrase—if I ever had reason to believe that there was something urgent that they could act on that I could interrupt anything that they were doing, that I had an open door any time I needed it day or night if there was something about to happen.

I think the difference between the two national security advisers in the Clinton administration and the national security adviser in the Bush administration is that on policy development, I dealt directly with the national security advisers in the Clinton administration. But policy development on counterterrorism I was told would be best done with the deputy national security adviser. So I spent less time talking about the problems of terrorism with the national security adviser in this administration. . . .

BEN-VENISTE: . . . Is it fair to say that in the summer of 2001, the threat level either approached or exceeded anything that you had previously been receiving?

CLARKE: I think it exceeded anything that George Tenet or I had ever seen.

BEN-VENISTE: And I think the phrase which has received some currency in our hearings of someone's hair being on fire originated with you, saying that basically you knew that something drastic was about to happen and that the indicators were all consistent in that regard.

CLARKE: That's right.

BEN-VENISTE: Did you make a determination that the threat was going to come from abroad, as an exclusive proposition? Or did you understand that given the fact that we had been attacked before and that the plans had been interrupted to attack us before that the potential existed for al Qaeda to strike at us in our homeland?

CLARKE: The CIA said in their assessments that the attack would most likely occur overseas, most probably in Saudi Arabia, possibly in Israel. I thought, however, that it might well take place in the United States based on what we had learned in December '99, when we rolled up operations in Washington state, in Brooklyn, in Boston.

The fact that we didn't have intelligence that we could point to that said it would take place in the United States wasn't significant in my view, because, frankly, sir—I know how this is going to sound but I have to say it—I didn't think the FBI would know whether or not there was anything going on in the United States by al Qaeda.

BEN-VENISTE: Well, the FBI was a principal agency upon which you had to rely, is that not the case?

CLARKE: It is.

BEN-VENISTE: Now, with respect to what you were told—you

were the principal coordinator for counterterrorism for the chief executive flowing up and down through you, correct?

CLARKE: Yes, sir.

BEN-VENISTE: Did you know that the two individuals who had been identified as al Qaeda had entered the United States and were presently thought to be in the country?

CLARKE: I was not informed of that, nor were senior levels of the FBI.

BEN-VENISTE: Had you known that these individuals were in the country, what steps, with the benefit of hindsight, but informed hindsight, would you have taken, given the level of threat?

CLARKE: To put the answer in context, I had been saying to the FBI and to the other federal law enforcement agencies and to the CIA that because of this intelligence that something was about to happen that they should lower their threshold of reporting, that they should tell us anything that looked the slightest bit unusual. In retrospect, having said that over and over again to them, for them to have had this information somewhere in the FBI and not told to me, I still find absolutely incomprehensible.

BEN-VENISTE: . . . Was the information with respect to Moussaoui and his erratic behavior in flight school ever communicated to you?

CLARKE: Not to me. . . .

BEN-VENISTE: . . . An FAA advisory went out. The FAA advised on the potential for domestic hijackings.

CLARKE: I asked them to.

BEN-VENISTE: And had you known on top of that that there was a jihadist who was identified, apprehended in the United States before 9/11 who was in flight school acting erratically . . .

CLARKE: I would like to think, sir, that even without the benefit of 20/20 hindsight, I could have connected those dots.

. . .

JAMES R. THOMPSON: Mr. Clarke, as we sit here this afternoon, we have your book and we have your press briefing of August 2002. Which is true?

CLARKE: Well, I think the question is a little misleading. The press briefing you're referring to comes in the following context: *Time* magazine had published a cover story article highlighting what your staff briefing talks about. They had learned that, as your staff briefing notes, that there was a strategy or a plan and a series of additional options that were presented to the national security adviser and the new Bush team when they came into office. *Time* magazine ran a somewhat sensational story that implied that the Bush administration hadn't worked on that plan. And this, of course, coming after 9/11 caused the Bush White House a great deal of concern.

So I was asked by several people in senior levels of the Bush White House to do a press backgrounder to try to explain that set of facts in a way that minimized criticism of the administration. And so I did. Now, we can get into semantic games of whether it was a strategy, or whether it was a plan, or whether it was a series of options to be decided upon. I think the facts are as they were outlined in your staff briefing.

THOMPSON: Well, let's take a look, then, at your press briefing, because I don't want to engage in semantic games. You said, the Bush administration decided, then, you know, mid-January— that's mid-January, 2001—to do 2 things: one, vigorously pursue the existing policy—that would be the Clinton policy—including all of the lethal covert action findings which we've now made public to some extent. Is that so? Did they decide in January of 2001 to vigorously pursue the existing Clinton policy?

CLARKE: They decided that the existing covert action findings would remain in effect.

THOMPSON: OK. The second thing the administration decided to do is to initiate a process to look at those issues which had been on the table for a couple of years and get them decided. Now, that seems to indicate to me that proposals had been sitting on the table in the Clinton administration for a couple of years, but that the Bush administration was going to get them done. Is that a correct assumption?

CLARKE: Well, that was my hope at the time. It turned out not to be the case.

THOMPSON: Well, then why in August of 2002, over a year later, did you say that it was the case?

CLARKE: I was asked to make that case to the press. I was a special assistant to the president, and I made the case I was asked to make.

THOMPSON: Are you saying to me you were asked to make an untrue case to the press and the public, and that you went ahead and did it?

CLARKE: No, sir. Not untrue. Not an untrue case. I was asked to highlight the positive aspects of what the administration had done and to minimize the negative aspects of what the administration had done. And as a special assistant to the president, one is frequently asked to do that kind of thing. I've done it for several presidents.

THOMPSON: Well, OK, over the course of the summer, they developed implementation details. The principals met at the end of the summer, approved them in their first meeting, changed the strategy by authorizing the increase in funding five-fold. Did they authorize the increase in funding five-fold?

CLARKE: Authorized but not appropriated.

THOMPSON: Well, but the Congress appropriates, don't they, Mr. Clarke?

CLARKE: Well, within the executive branch, there are two steps as well. In the executive branch, there's the policy process which you can compare to authorization, which is to say we would like to spend this amount of money for this program. And then there is the second step, the budgetary step, which is to find the offsets. And that had not been done. In fact, it wasn't done until after September 11th.

THOMPSON: Changing the policy on Pakistan, was the policy on Pakistan changed?

CLARKE: Yes, sir it was.

THOMPSON: Changing the policy on Uzbekistan, was it changed?

CLARKE: Yes, sir.

THOMPSON: Changing the policy on the Northern Alliance assistance, was that changed?

CLARKE: Well, let me back up. I said yes to the last two answers. It was changed only after September 11th. It had gone through an approvals process. It was going through an approvals process with the deputies committee. And they had approved it—the deputies had approved those policy changes. It had then gone to a principals committee for approval, and that occurred on September 4th. Those three things which you mentioned were approved by the principals. They were not approved by the president, and therefore the final approval hadn't occurred until after September 11th.

THOMPSON: But they were approved by people in the administration below the level of the president, moving toward the president. Is that correct?

CLARKE: Yes, so over the course of many, many months, they went through several committee meetings at the sub-Cabinet level. And then there was a hiatus. And then . . . finally on September 4th, a week before the attacks, they went to the principals for their approval. Of course, the final approval by the president didn't take place until after the attacks.

THOMPSON: Well, is that eight-month period unusual?

CLARKE: It is unusual when you are being told every day that there is an urgent threat.

THOMPSON: Well, but the policy involved changing, for example, the policy on Pakistan, right? So you would have to involve those people in the administration who had charge of the Pakistani policy, would you not?

CLARKE: The secretary of state has, as a member of the principals committee, that kind of authority over all foreign policy issues.

THOMPSON: Changing the policy on the Northern Alliance assistance, that would have been DOD?

CLARKE: No. Governor, that would have been the CIA. But again, all of the right people to make those kinds of changes were represented by the five or six people on the principals committee.

THOMPSON: But they were also represented on the smaller group, were they not, the deputies committee?

CLARKE: But they didn't have the authority to approve it. They only had the authority to recommend it further up the process.

THOMPSON: Well, is policy usually made at the level of the principals committee before it comes up?

CLARKE: Policy usually originates in working groups. Recommendations and differences then are floated up from working groups to the deputies committee. If there are differences there, policy recommendations and differences are then floated up to the principals. And occasionally, when there is not a consensus at the principals level, policy recommendations and options, or differences, go to the president. And the president makes these kinds of decisions. By law, in fact, many of the kinds of decisions you're talking about can only be made by the president.

THOMPSON: And you said that the strategy changed from one of rollback with al Qaeda over the course of five years, which it had been, which I presume is the Clinton policy, to a new strategy that called for the rapid elimination of al Qaeda, that is in fact the time line. Is that correct?

CLARKE: It is, but it requires a bit of elaboration. As your staff brief said, the goal of the Delenda Plan was to roll back al Qaeda over the course of three to five years so that it was just a nub of an organization like Abu Nidal that didn't threaten the United States. I tried to insert the phrase early in the Bush administration in the draft NSPD that our goal should be to eliminate al Qaeda. And I was told by various members of the deputies committee that that was overly ambitious and that we should take the word "eliminate" out and say "significantly erode." And then, following 9/11, we were able to go back to my language of "eliminate," rather than "significantly erode." And so, the version of the national security presidential decision directive that President Bush finally got to see after 9/11, had my original language of "eliminate," not the interim language of "erode."

THOMPSON: And you were asked when was . . . that presented to the president? And you answered: The president was briefed throughout this process.

CLARKE: Yes. The president apparently asked, on one occasion that I'm aware of, for a strategy. And when he asked that, he apparently didn't know there was a strategy in the works. I, therefore, was told about this by the national security adviser. I came back to her and said, well, there is a strategy; after all, it's basically what I showed you in January. It stuck in the deputies committee. She said she would tell the president that, and she said she would try to break it out of the deputies committee.

THOMPSON: So you believe that your conference with the press in August of 2002 is consistent with what you've said in your book and what you've said in press interviews the last five days about your book?

CLARKE: I do. I think the thing that's obviously bothering you is the tenor and the tone. And I've tried to explain to you, sir, that when you're on the staff of the president of the United States, you try to make his policies look as good as possible.

THOMPSON: Well, with all respect, Mr. Clarke, I think a lot of things beyond the tenor and the tone bother me about this.

. . .

JAMIE S. GORELICK: When Dr. Rice writes in the *Washington Post*, "No al Qaeda plan was turned over to the new administration," is that true?

CLARKE: No. I think what is true is what your staff found by going through the documents and what your staff briefing says, which is that early in the administration, within days of the Bush administration coming into office, that we gave them two documents. In fact, I briefed Dr. Rice on this even before they came into office. One was the original Delenda Plan from 1998, and the other document was the update that we did following the *Cole* attack, which had as part of it a number of decisions that had to be taken so that she characterizes as a series of options rather than a plan. I'd like to think of it as a plan with a series of options, but I think we're getting into semantic differences.

GORELICK: Thank you. I'd like to turn to NSPD–9, the document that was wending its way through the process up until September

4th. The document is classified so I can only speak of it in generalities. But as I understand it, it had three stages which were to take place over, according to Steve Hadley, the deputy national security adviser, over a period of three years. The first stage was, we would warn the Taliban. The second stage was we would pressure the Taliban. And the third stage was that we would look for ways to oust the Taliban based upon individuals on the ground other than ourselves, at the same time making military contingency plans. Is that correct?

CLARKE: Well, that's right. The military contingency plans had always been around, but there was nothing in the original draft NSPD that was approved by the principals to suggest U.S. forces would be sent into Afghanistan on the ground.

GORELICK: In addition to that, Director Tenet was asked to draft new additional covert action authorities. Is that right?

CLARKE: That's right, in part because Mr. Hadley found the existing six memorandums of covert action authority to be Talmudic—it's actually I think Mr. Hadley who gets credit for that word. But it wasn't really meant to expand them significantly other than providing direct aid to Afghan factions.

GORELICK: Now you have just described, then, the skeleton, if you will, of what was approved by the administration as of September 4th. And we know that no further action was taken before September 11th. And so I would read to you—and these are questions I would have put to Dr. Rice had she been here, and I will put to the White House designee, Secretary [Richard] Armitage. She says our strategy, which was expected to take years, marshaled all elements of national power to take down the network, not just respond to individual attacks with law enforcement measures. Our plan called for military options to attack al Qaeda and Taliban leadership, ground forces and other targets, taking the fight to the enemy where he lived. Is that an accurate statement, in your view?

CLARKE: No, it's not.

GORELICK: In addition to the items that were left hanging during this period of time that we've talked about, in your view—the Predator, the issue of aid to the Northern Alliance, the response to the *Cole*—the other item that we have heard about that was deferred until the policy emerged was action on the set of covert authorities or the draft of covert authorities that Director Tenet supplied to the NSC in I believe it was March of '01. Is that true?

CLARKE: Yes.

GORELICK: And no action was taken on those until after 9/11. Is that correct?

CLARKE: That's correct.

GORELICK: [Y]ou, above maybe anybody else, saw the systemic problems. I mean you have described, yourself, the problems with the FBI, the wall between the FBI and the CIA. We've heard about the disconnect between the State Department watch list and the FAA no-fly list. We've heard about really the inadequacy of our visa program and our consular effort. So my question for you is this: You had a great shot after the millennium to take a whack at these problems which you no doubt must have seen or maybe—I'll give you the benefit of the doubt—perhaps there are some you hadn't seen. Why was the after-action report, post-millennium, as modest as it was. Why didn't it address these fissures and these gaps in the system?

CLARKE: Well, it made 28 or 29 recommendations. Had all of those recommendations been easy to do, they would have been implemented, before or after the after-action report. Many of the 28 or 29 recommendations were implemented, but some of them weren't, because we went pretty far in the art of the practical, the art of the possible, with those recommendations. That's probably why some of them never got done. And some of them still haven't been done. I've learned over time that if you go for the perfect solution, the best solution, you don't get very far in actually achieving things. You can write nice reports if you're the Brookings commission or something, but if you want to get something done in the real world, you do what is doable and you try to do a little bit more. But you don't shoot for the moon.

And I think some of the systemic things that are obvious to you and—I know they are—were more practical after 9/11 than they were after the millennium. Remember, in the millennium, we succeeded in stopping the attacks. That was good news. But it was not good news for those of us who also wanted to put pressure on the Congress and pressure on OMB and other places because we were not able to point to—and I hate to say this—body bags. You know, unfortunately, this country takes body bags and requires body bags sometimes to make really tough decisions about money and about governmental arrangements.

And one of the things I would hope that comes out of your commission report is a recommendation for a change in the attitude of government about threats, that we be able to act on threats that we foresee, even if acting requires boldness and requires money and requires changing the way we do business, that we act on threats in the future before they happen.

The problem is that when you make that recommendation before they happen, when you recommend an air defense system for Washington before there has been a 9/11, people tend to think you're nuts. And I got a lot of that. You know, when the Clinton administration ended, 35 Americans had died at the hands of al Qaeda over the course of eight years. And a lot of people said, behind my back and some of them to my face, why are you so obsessed with this organization? It's only killed 35 Americans over the course of eight years. Why are you making such a big deal over this organization?

That's the kind of mind-set that made it difficult for us, even though the president, the national security adviser, and others, the DCI, knew there was a problem and were supporting me. But the institutional bureaucracy and the FBI and DOD and then CIA and OMB and on the Hill—because I spent a lot of time up here trying to get money and trying to change authorities—couldn't see the threat because it hadn't happened.

. . .

JOHN F. LEHMAN: [B]ecause of my real genuine long-term admiration for you, I hope you'll resolve that credibility problem [created by anti-Bush writings], because I'd hate to see you become totally shoved to one side during a presidential campaign as an active partisan selling a book.

CLARKE: Let me talk about partisanship here, since you raise it. I've been accused of being a member of John Kerry's campaign team several times this week, including by the White House. So let's just lay that one to bed. I'm not working for the Kerry campaign. Last time I had to declare my party loyalty, it was to vote in the Virginia primary for president of the United States in the year 2000. And I asked for a Republican ballot. I worked for Ronald Reagan with you. I worked for the first President Bush. And he nominated me to the Senate as an assistant secretary of state, and I worked in his White House, and I've worked for this President Bush. And I'm not working for Senator Kerry. . . .

The White House has said that my book is an audition for a high-level position in the Kerry campaign. So let me say here as I am under oath, that I will not accept any position in the Kerry administration, should there be one—on the record, under oath.

Now, as to your accusation that there is a difference between what I said to this commission in 15 hours of testimony and what I am saying in my book and what media outlets are asking me to comment on, I think there's a very good reason for that. In the 15 hours of testimony, no one asked me what I thought about the president's invasion of Iraq. And the reason I am strident in my criticism of the president of the United States is because by invading Iraq—something I was not asked about by the commission, it's something I chose to write about a lot in the book—by invading Iraq the president of the United States has greatly undermined the war on terrorism.

. . .

ROEMER: On the FBI, you've said that the FBI did not do a very good job. I think I'm paraphrasing you in much easier language than you have used. But that during the millennium, which may be the exception to the rule, they performed extremely well in sharing information. How do we get the FBI to do this on a regular basis? We . . . do know something for certain, and that is that groups like al Qaeda want to get dirty bombs, they want to get chemical and biological weapons, and they want to come after America. So how do we get this situation solved, Mr. Clarke? What do we do with the FBI? What's your recommendation?

CLARKE: In the perfect world, I believe we could create a domestic intelligence service that would have sufficient oversight that it would not infringe on our civil liberties. In a perfect world, I would create that domestic intelligence service separately from the FBI. In the world in which we live, I think that would be a difficult step to go directly to. And so what I proposed, instead, is that we create a domestic intelligence service within the FBI and, as fast as we could, develop it into an autonomous agency.

I am very fearful that such an agency would have potential to infringe on our civil liberties. And therefore, I think we would have to take extraordinary steps to have active oversight of such an agency. And we would have to explain to the American people in a very compelling way why they needed a domestic intelligence service, because I think most Americans would be fearful of a secret police in the United States. But frankly, the FBI culture, the FBI organization, the FBI personnel are not the best we could do in this country for a domestic intelligence service.

. . .

GORTON: OK. We talked a little bit in my earlier round of questioning about this frustrating phrase "actionable intelligence." And one of your recommendations to the new administration, according to our staff report, was to choose a standard of evidence for attributing responsibility for the *Cole* and deciding on a response. Did that express a frustration that you had had, now, for the previous several years, that the phrase "actionable intelligence" often seemed to be an excuse for people not doing anything, that perhaps they had other reasons for not wanting to do?

Did you want a broader definition, either of how much intelligence was needed, or how broad action should be?

CLARKE: Yes.

GORTON: Yes to both?

CLARKE: OK.

GORTON: Could you tell me what your previous frustrations had been, and what kind of test you would have imposed?

CLARKE: Well, I think if you go back to 1993, when the attempted assassination on the first President Bush occurred in Kuwait, the process we put in place then was to ask the FBI, working with the Secret Service, to develop a set of evidence and CIA to develop separately an intelligence case. And that took from February of '93 through the end of May. And it was done in a way that was reminiscent of a criminal process, at least the FBI case was. The CIA case was an intelligence case and had different sources of information, different standards for what was admissible and a more lenient standard for making a determination.

Well, I think beginning then, I was frustrated by that kind of evidentiary process. . . . So what I was suggesting there and what I am suggesting here now is that while Sandy Berger is right and we should not rush to judgment after a terrorist attack as to who did it until there is ample intelligence evidence—not criminal evidence—on the other hand, we should feel free to attack terrorist groups without waiting for them to attack us if we make a policy and an intelligence judgment that they pose a threat.

GORTON: One follow-up question on that. Between January and September of 2001, was there any actionable intelligence under either the narrow or broader definition that caused you to recommend an immediate military response to some provocation?

CLARKE: I suggested, beginning in January of 2001, that the *Cole* case was still out there and that by now, in January of 2001, CIA had finally gotten around to saying it was an al Qaeda attack, and that therefore there was an open issue which should be decided about whether or not the Bush administration should retaliate for the *Cole* attack. Unfortunately, there was no interest, no acceptance of that proposition. And I was told on a couple of occasions, "Well, you know, that happened on the Clinton administration's watch." I didn't think it made any difference. I thought the Bush administration, now that it had the CIA saying it was al Qaeda, should have responded.

.   .   .

ROEMER: As you know, the Predator [unmanned aircraft] first came out of use in Kosovo, and it was used in various activities, with a laser on it, to track Serb tanks, to help us go after those tanks. It was flown in 2000 in the Clinton administration as a recon vehicle, unmanned recon vehicle. In 2001, we had a debate, a complex debate, that I can understand both sides of. Took several months to try to resolve it. There are two issues here: on the recon Predator and on the armed Predator. Mr. Tenet said that they were not blocking the armed Predator. You have said that they were blocking the armed Predator. How do we reconcile these two?

CLARKE: Let me begin in the first few months of the year 2000. President Clinton was enormously frustrated because he had authorized, in effect, the assassination of bin Laden and his lieutenants by CIA. He had also authorized, in principle, the use of military forces, cruise missiles, to attack and kill bin Laden and his lieutenants. And none of this had happened because the CIA had been unable to use its human intelligence resources in Afghanistan to provide—I'm sorry, Senator—actionable intelligence.

On the occasions when we had things that looked like actionable intelligence, the three or four occasions, the director of CIA himself said the intelligence wasn't good enough. So the president was very mad and he asked Sandy Berger and me to come up with a better way.

I asked the director of the joint staff, Admiral Fry, and the associate DCI, Charlie Allen, to form a task force to come up with a better way. They proposed flying the Predator in Afghanistan. CIA's Directorate of Operations, the director of the Directorate of Operations, opposed the use of Predator in 2000 for reconnaissance purposes. He said that if there were additional resources available to pay for the Predator operation, he would prefer to use them on human intelligence.

ROEMER: And how much are we talking about, Mr. Clarke?

CLARKE: Pennies, relatively.

ROEMER: Hundreds of thousands of dollars?

CLARKE: Some of it cost hundreds of thousands. The whole program was in the low millions, I think.

In any event, this slowed things down, obviously. Mr. Berger took up my cause with the Director of Central Intelligence and got their agreement that they would fly the reconnaissance version. It was flown in September and October of 2000, 11 flights. And the Directorate of Operations put a lot of restrictions on those flights, in part because they were afraid that the aircraft would be shot down and they would have to pay for it. . . .

In any event, during those flights, at CIA's insistence, they were designed as a proof-of-concept operation, meaning that we could not have cruise missiles, other military activity, other covert action capabilities cued to this so that when the Predator did see bin Laden, as it did I think on three occasions, but clearly on one in that time frame, there were no military assets available, there were no covert action assets available, at the insistence of the CIA, because they wanted this only as a proof-of-concept operation.

Fast forward to 2001: The flights had been suspended because of the winter during which they couldn't fly. We then became aware that there was a long-term program in the Air Force to arm the Predator. Johnny Jumper, the head of the Air Force, thought that it might be possible to crash—probably the wrong word—to accelerate this program and arm the Predator right away. General Jumper directed that happening. It happened in a matter of months, not a matter of years. And it appeared to work in tests in the western United States. When on September 4th we held the principals meeting that's been discussed, the issue on the table was: Would CIA fly the armed Predator?

And CIA took the view, in the principals meeting, that it was not their job to fly armed [unmanned aircraft]. They did not want to fly the armed Predator under their authority. I was informed by people who were in the CIA that during the discussions inside CIA, people in the Directorate of Operations had raised objections—saying, for example that if CIA flies the armed Predator, and it kills bin Laden, then CIA agents all around the world will be at risk of retaliation attacks by al Qaeda. I didn't think that was a very persuasive reason because I thought CIA agents were already at risk of attack by al Qaeda.

In any event, as the September 4th principals meeting ended, CIA had not agreed to fly the mission. September 11th happened. CIA then agreed to fly the armed Predator mission. It went into operation very quickly in Afghanistan. It found the military commander of al Qaeda. And because it was armed, then, it could not only find things, it could kill them. And it launched a missile, a Hellfire missile, at the military commander of al Qaeda and killed him and his associates.

.   .   .

EXCERPTS FROM TESTIMONY FROM RICHARD ARMITAGE, DEPUTY U.S. SECRETARY OF STATE

"[T]he words of Samuel Clemens come to mind, and that is that even though you're on the right track you can get run over if you're not going fast enough. And I think it is the case, it's certainly in hindsight, that we weren't going fast enough."

The president said that he was tired of swatting flies. He gave us a little more strategic direction. It was clear to us that roll-back was no longer a sufficient strategy and that we had to go to the elimination of al Qaeda. To that end, at least through the deputies prior to the horror of September 11th, decisions were approved to arm the Predator, to increase the assistance to Uzbekistan, to work with the Northern Alliance in a bigger way, to try to reinvigorate what was going on with Pakistan. And certainly in order to bring some stability to South Asia we had to have a different relationship with India and one that's not hyphenated, Indo-Pak.

So I saw in both administrations a lot of people working terrifically hard doing the best jobs they could. But a lot of people in successive administrations working just as hard as they can on the issue is not a source of any satisfaction for anyone. I don't think any of us, or anyone who's worked on these issues, can feel any sense of satisfaction with 3,000 of our fellow citizens horribly murdered.

So the inevitable evisceration of Osama bin Laden personally will be a very good thing, but in itself it's not going to bring any satisfaction or justice. True satisfaction and true justice, in my belief, will only come for Americans—and for that matter now for Spaniards and Turks and Saudis and Moroccans—when we've put an end to terrorism. The terrible thing is, I'm afraid that's going to be at some far-out date in the future, and we just have to steel ourselves for it.

QUESTIONS FROM COMMISSIONERS

JAMES R. THOMPSON: Both in his book and in his testimony here today, Mr. Clarke complained that the eight-month gap between the time the administration took office in January of 2001, and the time that the NSPD was produced in September—I believe September 4th of 2001—was an inordinately long time to formulate a process. Do you agree with that?

ARMITAGE: No, I don't. But I'd like to say that—the words of Samuel Clemens come to mind, and that is that even though you're on the right track you can get run over if you're not going fast enough. And I think it is the case, it's certainly in hindsight, that we weren't going fast enough.

Now, you can make your own judgments about whether we were moving faster or slower than other administrations. But there were are a lot of complex issues and we thought we were getting or trying to get our arms around all of them and not just pieces of them.

· · ·

JAMIE S. GORELICK: . . . You just said that you might have suggested, and I don't want to put words in your mouth, that the president could have, should have, advocated to Congress and to policymakers putting boots on the ground. I don't see any boots on the ground in NSPD–9. Is that correct?

ARMITAGE: First, it's not necessarily correct that I would advocate putting boots on the ground.

GORELICK: I didn't mean to put words in your mouth.

ARMITAGE: No, but it's an important point. As far as this citizen is concerned the decision to commit men and women, who are also sons and daughters, to combat is an extraordinarily important one and not to be done to just feel good; to be done to absolutely accomplish a mission. Now, sometimes I'm accused of being a foot-dragger, not wanting to go along with the force. But I'm sorry, that's my view.

Having said that, the Taliban, for a lot of reasons we were handling them somewhat gently. Some of our citizens were still there. Some of our NGOs [Non-Governmental Organizations] were the only thing keeping some segments of the Afghan population alive and feed programs and things of that nature. So you don't want to throw the baby out with the bath water, generally. And so the question of the Taliban is a tough one. There was no question about, I think, in anybody's mind about the desirability of putting soldiers on the ground if we could catch or capture or kill bin Laden. But as a discreet element.

. . .

TIMOTHY J. ROEMER: . . . You said that the deputies process has not worked, quote "speedily before or since 9/11" unquote. Can you expand on that a little bit?

ARMITAGE: I've long held the view and it's well known to the administration, as I said. We ought to have less meetings and be more crisp. I missed some things, but I'm fairly crisp. I was impatient on this and other issues. But I think all of my colleagues wanted to get it exactly right.

. . .

EXCERPTS OF TESTIMONY FROM CONDOLEEZZA RICE, NATIONAL SECURITY ADVISER

"[U.S. counterterrorism forces staged] intense activity in the high threat period of the summer of 2001. Yet . . . there was no silver bullet that could have prevented the 9/11 attacks."

The terrorist threat to our nation did not emerge on September 11, 2001. Long before that day, radical, freedom-hating terrorists declared war on America and on the civilized world. The attack on the Marine barracks in Lebanon in 1983, the hijacking of the *Achille Lauro* in 1985, the rise of al Qaeda and the bombing of the World Trade Center in 1993, the attacks on American installations in Saudi Arabia in 1995 and 1996, the East Africa bombings of 1998, the attack on the U.S.S. *Cole* in 2000—these and other atrocities were part of a sustained, systematic campaign to spread devastation and chaos and to murder innocent Americans.

The terrorists were at war with us, but we were not yet at war with them. For more than 20 years, the terrorist threat gathered, and America's response across several administrations of both parties was insufficient. Historically, democratic societies have been slow to react to gathering threats, tending instead to wait to confront threats until they are too dangerous to ignore or until it is too late. Despite the sinking of the *Lusitania* in 1915 and continued German harassment of American shipping, the United States did not enter the First World War until two years later. Despite Nazi Germany's repeated violations of the Versailles treaty and provocations throughout the mid-1930s, the western democracies did not take action until 1939. The U.S. government did not act against the growing threat from imperial Japan until it became all too evident at Pearl Harbor. And tragically, for all the language of war spoken before September 11th, this country simply was not on war footing.

Since then, America has been at war and under President Bush's leadership, we will remain at war until the terrorist threat to our nation has ended. The world has changed so much that it is hard to remember what our lives were like before that day. But I do want to describe some of the actions that were taken by the administration prior to September 11th. After President Bush was elected, we were briefed by the Clinton administration on many national security issues during the transition. The president-elect and I were briefed by George Tenet on terrorism and on the al Qaeda network. Members of Sandy Berger's NSC staff briefed me, along with other members of the national security team, on counterterrorism and al Qaeda. This briefing lasted for about an hour, and it reviewed the Clinton administration's counterterrorism approach and the various counterterrorism activities then under way. Sandy and I personally discussed a variety of other topics, including North Korea, Iraq, the Middle East and the Balkans.

Because of these briefings, and because we had watched the rise of al Qaeda over many years, we understood that the network posed a serious threat to the United States. We wanted to ensure that there was no respite in the fight against al Qaeda. On an operational level, therefore, we decided immediately to continue to pursue the Clinton administration's covert action authority and other efforts to fight the network. President Bush retained George Tenet as director of central intelligence, and Louis Freeh remained the director of the FBI. And I took the unusual step of retaining Dick Clarke and the entire Clinton administration's counterterrorism team on the NSC staff. I knew Dick Clarke to be an expert in his field, as well as an experienced crisis manager. Our goal was to ensure continuity of operations while we developed new policies.

At the beginning of the administration, President Bush revived the practice of meeting with the director of central intelligence almost every day in the Oval Office, meetings which I attended, along with the vice president and the chief of staff. At these meetings, the president received up-to-date intelligence and asked questions of his most senior intelligence officials. From January 20th through September 10th, the president received at these daily meetings more than 40 briefing items on al Qaeda, and 13 of those were in response to questions he or his top advisers posed. In addition to seeing DCI Tenet almost every morning, I generally spoke by telephone to coordinate policy at 7:15 with Secretaries Powell and Rumsfeld on a variety of topics, and I also met and spoke regularly with the DCI about al Qaeda and terrorism.

Of course, we did have other responsibilities. President Bush had set a broad foreign policy agenda. We were determined to confront the proliferation of weapons of mass destruction. We were improving America's relations with the world's great powers. We had to change an Iraq policy that was making no progress against a hostile regime which regularly shot at U.S. planes enforcing U.N. Security Council resolutions. And we had to deal with the occasional crisis, for instance, when the crew of a Navy plane was detained in China for 11 days.

We also moved to develop a new and comprehensive strategy to try and eliminate the al Qaeda network. President Bush understood the threat, and he understood its importance. He made clear to us that he did not want to respond to al Qaeda one attack at a time. He told me he was tired of swatting flies.

This new strategy was developed over the spring and summer of 2001 and was approved by the president's senior national security officials on September 4th. It was the very first major national security policy directive of the Bush administration—not Russia, not missile defense, not Iraq, but the elimination of al Qaeda. Although this national security presidential directive was originally a highly classified document, we've arranged for portions to be declassified to help the commission in its work, and I will describe some of it today.

The strategy set as a goal the elimination of the al Qaeda network and threat and ordered the leadership of relevant U.S. departments and agencies to make the elimination of al Qaeda a high priority and to use all aspects of our national power—intelligence, financial, diplomatic and military—to meet that goal. And it gave Cabinet secretaries and department heads specific responsibilities. For instance, it directed the secretary of state to work with other countries to end all sanctuaries given to al Qaeda. It directed the secretaries of the treasury and state to work with foreign governments to seize or freeze assets and holdings of al Qaeda and its benefactors. It directed the director of central intelligence to prepare an aggressive program of covert activities to disrupt al Qaeda and provide assistance to anti-Taliban groups operating in Afghanistan. It tasked the director of OMB with ensuring that sufficient funds were available in budgets over the next five years to meet the goals laid out in the strategy. And it directed the secretary of defense to, and I quote, "ensure that contingency planning processes include plans against al Qaeda and associated terrorist facilities in Afghanistan, including leadership, command/control and communications, training, and logistics facilities, and against Taliban targets in Afghanistan, including leadership, command/control, air and air defense, ground forces, and logistics; and to eliminate weapons of mass destruction which al Qaeda and associated terrorist groups may acquire or manufacture, including those stored in underground bunkers."

This was a change from the prior strategy—Presidential Decision Directive 62, signed in 1998—which ordered the secretary of defense to provide transportation to bring individual terrorists to the U.S. for trial, to protect DOD forces overseas, and to be prepared to respond to terrorist and weapons-of-mass-destruction incidents.

More importantly, we recognized that no counterterrorism

strategy could succeed in isolation. As you know from the Pakistan and Afghanistan strategy documents that we have made available to the commission, our counterterrorism strategy was a part of a broader package of strategies that addressed the complexities of the region. Integrating our counterterrorism and regional strategies was the most difficult and the most important aspect of the new strategy to get right. Al Qaeda was both a client of and a patron to the Taliban, which, in turn, was supported by Pakistan. Those relationships provided al Qaeda with a powerful umbrella of protection, and we had to sever that. This was not easy.

Not that we hadn't tried. Within a month of taking office, President Bush sent a strong private message to [Pakistan's] President [Pervez] Musharraf, urging him to use his influence with the Taliban to bring bin Laden to justice and to close down al Qaeda training camps. Secretary Powell actively urged the Pakistanis, including Musharraf himself, to abandon support for the Taliban. I remember well meeting with the Pakistani foreign minister— and I think I referred to this meeting in my private meeting with you—in my office in June of 2001, and I delivered what I considered to be a very tough message. He met that message with a rote answer and with an expressionless response.

America's al Qaeda policy wasn't working because our Afghanistan policy wasn't working, and our Afghanistan policy wasn't working because our Pakistan policy wasn't working. We recognized that America's counterterrorism policy had to be connected to our regional strategies and to our overall foreign policies. To address these problems, I had to make sure that key regional experts were involved, not just counterterrorism experts. I brought in Zalmay Khalilzad, an expert on Afghanistan, who, as a senior diplomat in the 1980s, had worked closely with the Afghan mujahedeen, helping them to turn back the Soviet invasion. I also ensured the participation of the NSC experts on South Asia, as well as the secretary of state and his regional specialists.

Together, we developed a new strategic approach to Afghanistan. Instead of the intense focus on the Northern Alliance, we emphasized the importance of the south, the social and political heartland of the country. Our new approach to Pakistan combined the use of carrots and sticks to persuade Pakistan to drop its support for the Taliban. And we began to change our approach to India to preserve stability on the continent.

While we were developing this new strategy to deal with al Qaeda, we also made decisions on a number of specific anti-al Qaeda initiatives that had been proposed by Dick Clarke to me in an early memorandum after we had taken office. Many of these ideas had been deferred by the last administration, and some had been on the table since 1998. We increased counterterrorism assistance to Uzbekistan. We bolstered the Treasury Department's activities to track and seize terrorist assets. We increased funding for counterterrorism activities across several agencies. And we moved to arm Predator unmanned surveillance vehicles for action against al Qaeda.

When threat reporting increased during the spring and summer of 2001, we moved the U.S. government at all levels to a high state of alert and activity. Let me clear up any confusion about the relationship between the development of our new strategy and the actions that we took to respond to the threats of the summer. Policy development and crisis management require different approaches. Throughout this period, we did both simultaneously. For the essential crisis-management task, we depended on the Counterterrorism Security Group, chaired by Dick Clarke, to be the interagency nerve center. The CSG consisted of senior counterterrorism experts from the CIA, the FBI, the Department of Justice, the Defense Department—including the Joint Chiefs of Staff—the State Department and the Secret Service.

The CSG had met regularly for many years, and its members had worked through numerous periods of heightened threat activity. As threat information increased, the CSG met more frequently, sometimes daily, to review and analyze the threat reporting and to coordinate actions in response. CSG members also had ready access to their Cabinet secretaries and could raise any concerns that they had at the highest levels.

The threat reporting that we received in the spring and summer of 2001 was not specific as to time, nor place, nor manner of attack. Almost all of the reports focused on al Qaeda activities outside the United States, especially in the Middle East and North Africa. In fact, the information that was specific enough to be actionable referred to terrorist operations overseas. Most often, though, the threat reporting was frustratingly vague. Let me read you some of the actual chatter that was picked up in that spring and summer:

"Unbelievable news coming in weeks," said one.

"Big event—there will be a very, very, very, very big uproar."

"There will be attacks in the near future."

Troubling, yes. But they don't tell us when; they don't tell us where; they don't tell us who; and they don't tell us how.

In this context, I want to address in some detail one of the briefing items that we did receive, since its content has been frequently mischaracterized. On August 6, 2001, the president's intelligence briefing included a response to questions that he had earlier raised about any al Qaeda intentions to strike our homeland. The briefing team reviewed past intelligence reporting, mostly dating from the 1990s, regarding possible al Qaeda plans to attack inside the United States. It referred to uncorroborated reporting from 1998 that a terrorist might attempt to hijack a U.S. aircraft in an attempt to blackmail the government into releasing U.S.-held terrorists who had participated in the 1993 World Trade Center bombing. This briefing item was not prompted by any specific threat information. And it did not raise the possibility that terrorists might use airplanes as missiles.

Despite the fact that the vast majority of the threat information we received was focused overseas, I was concerned about possible threats inside the United States. And on July 5th, Chief of Staff Andy Card and I met with Dick Clarke, and I asked Dick to make sure that domestic agencies were aware of the heightened threat period and were taking appropriate steps to respond, even though we did not have specific threats to the homeland. Later that same day, Clarke convened a special meeting of his CSG, as well as representatives from the FAA, the INS [Immigration and Naturalization Service], Customs and the Coast Guard. At that meeting, these agencies were asked to take additional measures to increase security and surveillance.

Throughout the period of heightened threat information, we worked hard on multiple fronts to detect, protect against and disrupt any terrorist plans or operations that might lead to an attack. For instance, the Department of Defense issued at least five urgent warnings to U.S. military forces that al Qaeda might be planning a near-term attack and placed our military forces in certain regions on heightened alert. The State Department issued at least four urgent security advisories and public worldwide cautions on terrorist threats, enhanced security measures at certain embassies, and warned the Taliban that they would be held responsible for any al Qaeda attack on U.S. interests. The FBI issued at least three nationwide warnings to federal, state and law enforcement agencies and specifically stated that, although the vast majority of the information indicated overseas targets, attacks against the homeland could not be ruled out. The FBI tasked all 56 of its U.S. field offices to increase surveillance of known suspects of terrorism and to reach out to known informants who might have information on terrorist activities. The FAA issued at least five civil aviation security information circulars to all U.S. airlines and airport security personnel, including specific warnings about the possibility of hijacking.

The CIA worked around the clock to disrupt threats worldwide. Agency officials launched a wide-ranging disruption effort against al Qaeda in more than 20 countries. And during this period, the vice president, Director Tenet and members of my staff called senior foreign officials, requesting that they increase their intelligence assistance and report to us any relevant threat information.

This is a brief sample of our intense activity in the high threat period of the summer of 2001. Yet, as your hearings have shown, there was no silver bullet that could have prevented the 9/11 attacks. In hindsight, if anything might have helped stop 9/11, it would have been better information about threats inside the United States—something made very difficult by structural and legal impediments that prevented the collection and sharing of information by our law enforcement and intelligence agencies.

So the attacks came. A band of vicious terrorists tried to decapitate our government, destroy our financial system and break the spirit of America. And as an officer of government on duty that day, I will never forget the sorrow and the anger that I felt, nor will I forget the courage and resilience of the American people, nor the leadership of the president that day.

Now we have an opportunity and an obligation to move forward together. Bold and comprehensive changes are sometimes only possible in the wake of catastrophic events—events which create a new consensus that allows us to transcend old ways of thinking and acting. And just as World War II led to a fundamental reorganization of our national defense structure and the creation of the National Security Council, so has September 11th made possible sweeping changes in the ways we protect our homeland.

President Bush is leading the country during this time of crisis and change. He has unified and streamlined our efforts to secure the American homeland by creating the Department of Homeland Security; established a new center to integrate and analyze terrorist threat information; directed the transformation of the FBI into an agency dedicated to fighting terror; broken down the bureaucratic walls and legal barriers that prevent the sharing of vital information between our domestic law enforcement and foreign intelligence agencies; and, working with the Congress, given officials new tools, such as the Patriot Act, to find and stop terrorists. And he has done this in a way that is consistent with protecting America's cherished civil liberties and with preserving our character as a free and open society.

But the president recognizes that our work is far from complete. More structural reform will likely be necessary. Our intelligence gathering and analysis have improved dramatically in the last two years, but they must be stronger still. The president and all of us in his administration welcome new ideas and fresh thinking. We are eager to do whatever it is that will help to protect the American people. And we look forward to receiving this commission's recommendations.

We are at war, and our security as a nation depends on winning that war. We must, and we will, do everything we can to harden terrorist targets within the United States. Dedicated law enforcement and security professionals continue to risk their lives every day to make us all safer, and we owe them a debt of gratitude. And let's remember that those charged with protecting us from attack have to be right 100 percent of the time. To inflict devastation on a massive scale, the terrorists only have to succeed once. And we know that they are trying every day. That is why we must address the source of the problem. We must stay on the offensive to find and defeat the terrorists wherever they live, hide and plot around the world. If we learned anything from September 11th, it is that we cannot wait while dangers gather.

After the September 11th attacks, our nation faced hard choices: We could fight a narrow war against al Qaeda and the Taliban, or we could fight a broad war against a global menace. We could seek a narrow victory, or we could work for a lasting peace and a better world. President Bush has chosen the bolder course. He recognizes that the war on terror is a broad war. Under his leadership, the United States and our allies are disrupting terrorist operations, cutting off their funding and hunting down terrorists one by one. Their world is getting smaller. The terrorists have lost a home base and training camps in Afghanistan. The governments of Pakistan and Saudi Arabia now pursue them with energy and force.

We are confronting the nexus between terror and weapons of mass destruction. We are working to stop the spread of deadly weapons and to prevent them from getting into the hands of terrorists, seizing dangerous materials in transit, where necessary. Because we acted in Iraq, Saddam Hussein will never again use weapons of mass destruction against his people or his neighbors, and we have convinced Libya to give up all its weapons-of-mass-destruction-related programs and materials.

And as we attack the threat at its source, we are also addressing its roots. Thanks to the bravery and skill of our men and women in uniform, we have removed from power two of the world's most brutal regimes—sources of violence and fear and instability in the world's most dangerous region. Today, along with many allies, we are helping the people of Iraq and Afghanistan to build free societies. And we are working with the people of the Middle East to spread the blessings of liberty and democracy as alternatives to instability and hatred and terror.

This work is hard and it is dangerous, yet it is worthy of our effort and sacrifice. The defeat of terror and the success of freedom in those nations will serve the interests of our nation and inspire hope and encourage reform throughout the greater Middle East.

In the aftermath of September 11th, those were the right choices for America to make—the only choices that can ensure the safety of our nation for decades to come.

QUESTIONS FROM COMMISSIONERS

THOMAS H. KEAN: I've got a question now I'd like to ask you. It was given to me by a number of members of the families. Did you ever see or hear from the FBI, from the CIA, from any other intelligence agency, any memos or discussions or anything else between the time you got into office and 9/11 that talked about using planes as bombs?

RICE: Let me address this question because it has been on the table. I think that concern about what I might have known or we might have known was provoked by some statements that I made in a press conference. I was in a press conference to try and describe the August 6th memo, which I've talked about here in my opening remarks and which I talked about with you in the private session. And I said at one point, that this was a historical memo, that it was—it was not based on new threat information. And I said, "No one could have imagined them taking a plane, slamming it into the Pentagon"—I'm paraphrasing now—"into the World Trade Center, using planes as a missile." As I said to you in the private session, I probably should have said, "I could not have imagined," because within two days, people started to come to me and say, "Oh, but there were these reports in 1998 and 1999. The intelligence community did look at information about this."

To the best of my knowledge, Mr. Chairman, this kind of

analysis about the use of airplanes as weapons actually was never briefed to us. I cannot tell you that there might not have been a report here or a report there that reached somebody in our midst. Part of the problem is—and I think Sandy Berger made this point when he was asked the same question—that you have thousands of pieces of information—car bombs and this method and that method—and you have to depend to a certain degree on the intelligence agencies to sort, to tell you what is actually relevant, what is actually based on sound sources, what is speculative. And I can only assume or believe that perhaps the intelligence agencies thought that the sourcing was speculative.

All that I can tell you is that it was not in the August 6th memo, using planes as a weapon. And I do not remember any reports to us, a kind of strategic warning, that planes might be used as weapons. In fact, there were some reports done in '98 and '99. I was certainly not aware of them at the time that I spoke.

KEAN: You didn't see any memos to you or any documents to you?

RICE: No, I did not.

KEAN: Some Americans have wondered whether you or the president worried too much about Iraq in the days after the 9/11 attack and perhaps not enough about the fight ahead against al Qaeda. We know that at the Camp David meeting on the weekend of September 15th and 16th, the president rejected the idea of immediate action against Iraq. Others have told that the president decided Afghanistan had to come first.

We also know that, even after those Camp David meetings, the administration was still readying plans for possible action against Iraq. So can you help us understand where, in those early days after 9/11, the administration placed Iraq in the strategy for responding to the attack?

RICE: Certainly. Let me start with the period in which you're trying to figure out who did this to you. And I think, given our exceedingly hostile relationship with Iraq at the time—this is, after all, a place that tried to assassinate an American president, was still shooting at our planes in the no-fly zone—it was a reasonable question to ask whether, indeed, Iraq might have been behind this. I remember, later on, in a conversation with [Britain's] Prime Minister [Tony] Blair, President Bush also said that he wondered could it have been Iran, because the attack was so sophisticated, was this really just a network that had done this.

When we got to Camp David—and let me just be very clear: In the days between September 11th and getting to Camp David, I was with the president a lot. I know what was on his mind. What was on his mind was follow-on attacks, trying to reassure the American people. . . . [B]y the time that we got to Camp David and began to plan for what we would do in response, what was rolled out on the table was Afghanistan—a map of Afghanistan. And I will tell you, that was a daunting enough task to figure out how to avoid some of the pitfalls that great powers had in Afghanistan, mostly recently the Soviet Union and, of course, the British before that.

There was a discussion of Iraq. I think it was raised by Don Rumsfeld. It was pressed a bit by Paul Wolfowitz. Given that this was a global war on terror, should we look not just at Afghanistan but should we look at doing something against Iraq? There was a discussion of that. The president listened to all of his advisers. I can tell you that when he went around the table and asked his advisers what he should do, not a single one of his principal advisers advised doing anything against Iraq. It was all to Afghanistan.

When I got back to the White House with the president, he laid out for me what he wanted to do. And one of the points, after a long list of things about Afghanistan, a long list of things about protecting the homeland, the president said that he wanted contingency plans against Iraq should Iraq act against our interests. There was a kind of concern that they might try and take advantage of us in that period. They were still—we were still patroling no-fly zones. And there was also, he said, in case we find that they were behind 9/11, we should have contingency plans. But this was not along the lines of what later was discussed about Iraq, which was how to deal with Iraq on a grand scale. This was really about—we went to planning Afghanistan, you can look at what we did. From that time on, this was about Afghanistan.

. . .

Lee H. Hamilton: You know very well that the commission is focusing on this whole question of, what priority did the Clinton administration and the Bush administration give to terrorism. . . . The deputy director for Central Intelligence, Mr. [John] McLaughlin, told us that he was concerned about the pace of policymaking in the summer of 2001, given the urgency of the threat. The deputy secretary of state, Mr. Armitage, was here and expressed his concerns about the speed of the process. And if I recall, his comment is that, "We weren't going fast enough." I think that's a direct quote.

There was no response to the *Cole* attack in the Clinton administration and none in the Bush administration. Your public statements focused largely on China and Russia and missile defense. You did make comments on terrorism, but they were connected—the link between terrorism and the rogue regimes, like North Korea and Iran and Iraq. And General Shelton, who was chairman of the Joint Chiefs, said that terrorism had been pushed farther to the back burner.

Now, this is what we're trying to assess. We have your statements. We have these other statements. And I know . . . how difficult the role of the policymaker is and how many things press upon you. But I did want to give you an opportunity to comment on some of these other matters.

Rice: The quotes by others about how the process is moving, again, it's important to realize that had parallel tracks here. We were continuing to do what the Clinton administration had been doing under all the same authorities that were operating. George Tenet was continuing to try to disrupt al Qaeda. We were continuing the diplomatic efforts. But we did want to take the time to get in place a policy that was more strategic toward al Qaeda, more robust. It takes some time to think about how to reorient your policy toward Pakistan. It takes some time to think about how to have a more effective policy toward Afghanistan. It particularly takes some time when you don't get your people on board for several months.

So I understand that there are those who have said they felt it wasn't moving along fast enough. I talked to George Tenet about this at least every couple of weeks, sometimes more often. How can we move forward on the Predator? What do you want to do about the Northern Alliance? So I think we were putting the energy into it.

And I should just make one other point, Mr. Hamilton, if you don't mind, which is that we also moved forward on some of the specific ideas that Dick Clarke had put forward prior to completing the strategy review. We increased assistance to Uzbekistan, for instance, which had been one of the recommendations. We moved along the armed Predator, the development of the armed Predator. We increased counterterrorism funding.

But there were a couple of things that we did not want to do. I'm now convinced that, while nothing in this strategy would have done anything about 9/11, if we had, in fact, moved on the things that were in the original memos that we got from our counterterrorism people, we might have even gone off course, because it was very Northern Alliance-focused. That was going to cause a huge problem with Pakistan. It was not going to put us in the center of action in Afghanistan, which is the south.

And so, we simply had to take some time to get this right. But I think we need not confuse that with either what we did during the threat period where we were urgently working the operational issues every day or with the continuation of the Clinton policy.

. . .

RICHARD BEN-VENISTE: I want to ask you some questions about the August 6, 2001, PDB [Presidential Daily Brief]. We had been advised in writing by CIA on March 19, 2004, that the August 6th PDB was prepared and self-generated by a CIA employee. Following Director Tenet's testimony on March 26th before us, the CIA clarified its version of events, saying that questions by the president prompted them to prepare the August 6th PDB. Now, you have said to us in our meeting together earlier in February, that the president directed the CIA to prepare the August 6th PDB.

The extraordinarily high terrorist attack threat level in the summer of 2001 is well-documented. And Richard Clarke's testimony about the possibility of an attack against the United States homeland was repeatedly discussed from May to August within the intelligence community, and that is well-documented. You acknowledged to us in your interview of February 7, 2004, that Richard Clarke told you that al Qaeda cells were in the United States. Did you tell the president, at any time prior to August 6th, of the existence of al Qaeda cells in the United States?

RICE: First, let me just make certain . . .

BEN-VENISTE: If you could just answer that question, because I only have a very limited . . .

RICE: I understand, Commissioner, but it's important . . .

BEN-VENISTE: Did you tell the president . . .

RICE: . . . that I also address . . . It's also important that, Commissioner, that I address the other issues that you have raised. So I will do it quickly, but if you'll just give me a moment.

BEN-VENISTE: Well, my only question to you is whether you . . .

RICE: I understand, Commissioner, but I will . . .

BEN-VENISTE: . . . told the president.

RICE: If you'll just give me a moment, I will address fully the questions that you've asked. First of all, yes, the August 6th PDB was in response to questions of the president—and that since he asked that this be done, it was not a particular threat report. And there was historical information in there about various aspects of al Qaeda's operations.

Dick Clarke had told me, I think in a memorandum—I remember it as being only a line or two—that there were al Qaeda cells in the United States. Now, the question is, what did we need to do about that? And I also understood that that was what the FBI was doing, that the FBI was pursuing these al Qaeda cells. I believe in the August 6th memorandum it says that there were 70 full field investigations under way of these cells. And so there was no recommendation that we do something about this; the FBI was pursuing it. I really don't remember, Commissioner, whether I discussed this with the president.

BEN-VENISTE: Thank you.

RICE: I remember very well that the president was aware that there were issues inside the United States. He talked to people about this. But I don't remember the al Qaeda cells as being something that we were told we needed to do something about.

BEN-VENISTE: Isn't it a fact, Dr. Rice, that the August 6th PDB warned against possible attacks in this country? And I ask you whether you recall the title of that PDB?

RICE: I believe the title was, "Bin Laden Determined to Attack Inside the United States." Now, the . . .

BEN-VENISTE: Thank you.

RICE: No, Mr. Ben-Veniste . . .

BEN-VENISTE: I will get into the . . .

RICE: I would like to finish my point here.

BEN-VENISTE: I didn't know there was a point.

RICE: Given that—you asked me whether or not it warned of attacks.

BEN-VENISTE: I asked you what the title was.

RICE: You said, did it not warn of attacks. It did not warn of attacks inside the United States. It was historical information based on old reporting. There was no new threat information. And it did not, in fact, warn of any coming attacks inside the United States.

BEN-VENISTE: Now, you knew by August 2001 of al Qaeda involvement in the first World Trade Center bombing, is that correct? You knew that in 1999, late '99, in the millennium threat period, that we had thwarted an al Qaeda attempt to blow up Los Angeles International Airport and thwarted cells operating in Brooklyn, New York, and Boston, Massachusetts. As of the August 6th briefing, you learned that al Qaeda members have resided or traveled to the United States for years and maintained a support system in the United States. And you learned that FBI information since the 1998 blind sheikh warning of hijackings to free the blind sheikh indicated a pattern of suspicious activity in the country up until August 6th consistent with preparation for hijackings. Isn't that so?

RICE: Do you have other questions that you want me to answer as a part of the sequence?

BEN-VENISTE: Well, did you not—you have indicated here that this was some historical document. And I am asking you whether it is not the case that you learned in the PDB memo of August 6th that the FBI was saying that it had information suggesting that preparations—not historically, but ongoing, along with these numerous full field investigations against al Qaeda cells—that preparations were being made consistent with hijackings within the United States.

RICE: What the August 6th PDB said, and perhaps I should read it to you . . .

BEN-VENISTE: We would be happy to have it declassified in full at this time, including its title.

RICE: I believe, Mr. Ben-Veniste, that you've had access to this PDB. But let me just . . .

BEN-VENISTE: But we have not had it declassified so that it can be shown publicly, as you know.

RICE: I believe you've had access to this PDB—exceptional access. But let me address your question.

BEN-VENISTE: Nor could we, prior to today, reveal the title of that PDB.

RICE: May I address the question, sir? The fact is that this August 6th PDB was in response to the president's questions about whether or not something might happen or something might be planned by al Qaeda inside the United States. He asked because all of the threat reporting or the threat reporting that was actionable was about the threats abroad, not about the United States.

This particular PDB had a long section on what bin Laden had wanted to do—speculative, much of it—in '97, '98; that he had, in fact, liked the results of the 1993 bombing. It had a number of discussions of—it had a discussion of whether or not they might use hijacking to try and free a prisoner who was being held in the United States—Ressam. It reported that the FBI had full field investigations under way. And we checked on the issue of whether or not there was something going on with surveillance of buildings, and we were told, I believe, that the issue was the courthouse in which this might take place.

Commissioner, this was not a warning. This was a historic memo—historical memo prepared by the agency because the president was asking questions about what we knew about the inside.

BEN-VENISTE: . . . Let me ask you a general matter, beyond the fact that this memorandum provided information, not speculative, but based on intelligence information, that bin Laden had threatened to attack the United States and specifically Washington, D.C. There was nothing reassuring, was there, in that PDB?

RICE: Certainly not. There was nothing reassuring. But I can also tell you that there was nothing in this memo that suggested that an attack was coming on New York or Washington, D.C. There was nothing in this memo as to time, place, how or where. This was not a threat report to the president or a threat report to me.

BEN-VENISTE: We agree that there were no specifics. Let me move on, if I may.

RICE: There were no specifics, and, in fact, the country had already taken steps through the FAA to warn of potential hijackings. The country had already taken steps through the FBI to task their 56 field offices to increase their activity. The country had taken the steps that it could given that there was no threat reporting about what might happen inside the United States.

BEN-VENISTE: We have explored that and we will continue to with respect to the muscularity and the specifics of those efforts. The president was in Crawford, Texas, at the time he received the PDB; you were not with him, correct?

RICE: That is correct.

BEN-VENISTE: Now, was the president, in words or substance, alarmed or in any way motivated to take any action, such as meeting with the director of the FBI, meeting with the attorney general, as a result of receiving the information contained in the PDB?

RICE: I want to repeat that when this document was presented, it was presented as, yes, there were some frightening things—and by the way, I was not at Crawford, but the president and I were in contact and I might have even been, though I can't remember, with him by video link during that time. The president was told this is historical information. I'm told he was told this is historical information and there was nothing actionable in this. The president knew that the FBI was pursuing this issue. The president knew that the director of central intelligence was pursuing this issue. And there was no new threat information in this document to pursue.

. . .

JAMIE S. GORELICK: Now, you say that—and I think quite rightly—that the big problem was systemic, that the FBI could not function as it should, and it didn't have the right methods of communicating with the CIA and vice versa. . . . Now, you have said to us that your policy review was meant to be comprehensive. You took your time because you wanted to get at the hard issues and have a hard-hitting, comprehensive policy. And yet there is nothing in it about the vast domestic landscape that we were all warned needed so much attention. Can you give me the answer to the question why?

RICE: I would ask the following. We were there for 233 days. There had been recognition for a number of years before—after the '93 bombing, and certainly after the millennium—that there were challenges, if I could say it that way, inside the United States, and that there were challenges concerning our domestic agencies and the challenges concerning the FBI and the CIA. We were in office 233 days. It's absolutely the case that we did not begin structural reform of the FBI.

Now, the vice president was asked by the president, and that was tasked in May, to put all of this together and to see if he could put together, from all of the recommendations, a program for protection of the homeland against WMD, what else needed to be done. And in fact, he had hired Admiral Steve Abbot to do that work. And it was on that basis that we were able to put together the Homeland Security Council, which Tom Ridge came to head very, very quickly.

But I think the question is, why, over all of these years, did we not address the structural problems that were there, with the FBI, with the CIA, the homeland departments being scattered among many different departments? And why, given all of the opportunities that we'd had to do it, had we not done it? And I think that the unfortunate—and I really do think it's extremely tragic—fact is that sometimes until there is a catastrophic event that forces people to think differently, that forces people to overcome all customs and old culture and old fears about domestic intelligence and the relationship, that you don't get that kind of change.

. . .

SLADE GORTON: One subject that certainly any administration in your place would not like to bring up but I want to bring up in any event is, the fact is that we've now gone two and a half years and we have not had another incident in the United States even remotely comparable to 9/11. There have been many such horrific incidents in other parts of the world, from al Qaeda or al Qaeda look-alikes. In your view, have the measures that have been taken here in the United States actually reduced the amount of terrorism, or simply displaced it and caused it to move elsewhere?

RICE: I believe that we have really hurt the al Qaeda network. We have not destroyed it. And it is clear that it was much more entrenched and had relationships with many more organizations than I think people generally recognize. I don't think it's been displaced. But they realize that they are in an all-out war. And so you're starting to see them try to fight back. And I think that's one reason that you're getting the terrorist attacks that you are. But I don't think it's been displaced; I think it's just coming to the surface.

GORTON: Well, maybe you don't understand what I mean by displacement. Do you not think that al Qaeda and these terrorist entities are now engaged in terrorism where they think it's easier than it would be in the United States? That's what I mean about displacement.

RICE: Oh, I see. I'm sorry. I didn't understand the question. I think that it is possible that they recognize the heightened security profile that we have post-September 11th, and I believe that we have made it harder for them to attack here. I will tell you that I get up every day concerned because I don't think we've made it impossible for them. We're safer, but we're not safe.

. . .

BOB KERREY: You've used the phrase a number of times, and I'm hoping with my question to disabuse you of using it in the future. You said the president was tired of swatting flies. Can you tell me one example where the president swatted a fly when it came to al Qaeda prior to 9/11?

RICE: I think what the president was speaking to was . . .

KERREY: No, no. What fly had he swatted?

RICE: Well, the disruptions abroad was what he was really focusing on . . .

KERREY: No, no . . .

RICE: . . . when the CIA would go after [al Qaeda leader] Abu Zubaydah . . .

KERREY: He hadn't swatted . . .

RICE: . . . or go after this guy . . .

KERREY: Dr. Rice, we didn't . . .

RICE: That was what was meant.

KERREY: We only swatted a fly once on the 20th of August 1998. We didn't swat any flies afterwards. How the hell could he be tired?

RICE: We swatted at—I think he felt that what the agency was doing was going after individual terrorists here and there, and that's what he meant by swatting flies. It was simply a figure of speech.

KERREY: Well, I think it's an unfortunate figure of speech because I think, especially after the attack on the *Cole* on the 12th of October, 2000, it would not have been swatting a fly. It would not have been—we did not need to wait to get a strategic plan. . . . So I just—why didn't we respond to the *Cole*?

RICE: Well, we . . .

KERREY: Why didn't we swat that fly?

RICE: I believe that there's a question of whether or not you respond in a tactical sense or whether you respond in a strategic sense; whether or not you decide that you're going to respond to every attack with minimal use of military force and go after every—on a kind of tit-for-tat basis . . . .

Yes, the *Cole* had happened. We received, I think on January 25th, the same assessment—or roughly the same assessment—of who was responsible for the *Cole* that Sandy Berger talked to you about. It was preliminary. It was not clear. But that was not the reason that we felt that we did not want to, quote, "respond to the *Cole*." We knew that the options that had been employed by the Clinton administration had been standoff options—meaning missile strikes or perhaps bombers would have been possible, long-range bombers, although getting in place the apparatus to use long-range bombers is even a matter of whether you have basing in the region.

We knew that Osama bin Laden had been, in something that was provided to me, bragging that he was going to withstand any response and then he was going to emerge and come out stronger.

KERREY: But you're figuring this out. You've got to give a very long answer.

RICE: We simply believed that the best approach was to put in place a plan that was going to eliminate this threat, not respond to an attack.

KERREY: Let me say, I think you would have come in there if you said, "We screwed up. We made a lot of mistakes." You obviously don't want to use the M-word in here. And I would say fine, it's game, set, match. I understand that. But this strategic and tactical, I mean, I just—it sounds like something from a seminar. It doesn't . . . I do not believe to this day that it would have been a good thing to respond to the *Cole*, given the kinds of options that we were going to have. And with all due respect to Dick Clarke, if you're speaking about the Delenda plan, my understanding is that it was, A, never adopted, and that Dick Clarke himself has said that the military portion of this was not taken up by the Clinton administration.

Let me move into another area.

RICE: So we were not presented—I just want to be very clear on this, because it's been a source of controversy—we were not presented with a plan.

KERREY: Well, that's not true. It is not . . .

RICE: We were not presented. We were presented with . . .

KERREY: I've heard you say that, Dr. Clarke [sic], that 25 January, 2001, memo was declassified, I don't believe . . .

RICE: That January 25 memo has a series of actionable items having to do with Afghanistan, the Northern Alliance.

KERREY: Let me move to another area.

RICE: May I finish answering your question, though, because this is an important . . .

KERREY: I know it's important. Everything that's going on here is important. But I get 10 minutes.

RICE: But since we have a point of disagreement, I'd like to have a chance to address it.

KERREY: Well, no, no, actually, we have many points of disagreement, Dr. Clarke [sic], but we'll have a chance to do those in closed session. Please don't filibuster me. It's not fair. It is not fair. I have been polite. I have been courteous. It is not fair to me. I understand that we have a disagreement.

RICE: Commissioner, I am here to answer questions. And you've asked me a question, and I'd like to have an opportunity to answer it. The fact is that what we were presented on January the 25th was a set of ideas and a paper, most of which was about what the Clinton administration had done and something called the Delenda plan which had been considered in 1998 and never adopted. We decided to take a different track. We decided to put together a strategic approach to this that would get the regional powers—the problem wasn't that you didn't have a good counterterrorism person. The problem was you didn't have an approach against al Qaeda because you didn't have an approach against Afghanistan. And you didn't have an approach against Afghanistan because you didn't have an approach against Pakistan. And until we could get that right, we didn't have a policy.

KERREY: Thank you for answering my question.

RICE: You're welcome.

JOHN F. LEHMAN: Dr. Rice, I'd like to ask you whether you agree with the testimony we had from Mr. Clarke that, when asked whether if all of his recommendations during the transition or during the period when his, quote, "hair was on fire," had been followed immediately, would it have prevented 9/11, he said no. Do you agree with that?

RICE: I agree completely with that.

LEHMAN: In a way, one of the criticisms that has been made—or one of the, perhaps, excuses for an inefficient hand-off of power at the change, the transition, is, indeed, something we're going to be looking into in depth. Because of the circumstances of the election, it was the shortest handover in memory. But in many ways, really, it was the longest handover, certainly in my memory. Because while the Cabinet changed, virtually all of the national and domestic security agencies and executive action agencies remained the same. . . . Now, that raises . . . a whole series of questions. First, during the short or long transition, were you told before the summer that there were functioning al Qaeda cells in the United States?

RICE: In the memorandum that Dick Clarke sent me on January 25th, he mentions sleeper cells. There is no mention or recommendation of anything that needs to be done about them. And the FBI was pursuing them. And usually when things come to me, it's because I'm supposed to do something about it, and there was no indication that the FBI was not adequately pursuing the sleeper cells.

LEHMAN: Were you told that there were numerous young Arab males in flight training, had taken flight training, were in flight training?

RICE: I was not. And I'm not sure that that was known at the center.

LEHMAN: Were you told that the U.S. Marshal program had been changed to drop any U.S. marshals on domestic flights?

RICE: I was not told that.

LEHMAN: Were you told that the red team in FAA—the red teams for 10 years had reported their hard data that the U.S. airport security system never got higher than 20 percent effective and was usually down around 10 percent for 10 straight years?

RICE: To the best of my recollection, I was not told that.

LEHMAN: Were you aware that INS had been lobbying for years

to get the airlines to drop the transit-without-visa loophole that enabled terrorists and illegals to simply buy a ticket through the transit-without-visa waiver and pay the airlines extra money and come in?

RICE: I learned about that after September 11th.

LEHMAN: Were you aware that the INS had quietly, internally, halved its internal security enforcement budget?

RICE: I was not made aware of that. I don't remember being made aware of that, no.

LEHMAN: Were you aware that it was the U.S. government-established policy not to question or oppose the sanctuary policies of New York, Los Angeles, Houston, Chicago, San Diego for political reasons, which policy in those cities prohibited the local police from cooperating at all with federal immigration authorities?

RICE: I do not believe I was aware of that.

LEHMAN: Were you aware—to shift a little bit to Saudi Arabia— were you aware of the program that was well established that allowed Saudi citizens to get visas without interviews?

RICE: I learned of that after 9/11.

LEHMAN: Were you aware of the activities of the Saudi ministry of religious affairs here in the United States during that transition?

RICE: I believe that only after September 11th did the full extent of what was going on with the ministry of religious affairs become evident.

LEHMAN: Were you aware of the extensive activities of the Saudi government in supporting over 300 radical teaching schools and mosques around the country, including right here in the United States?

RICE: I believe we've learned a great deal more about this and addressed it with the Saudi government since 9/11.

· · ·

TIMOTHY J. ROEMER: You had an opportunity, I think, with Mr. Clarke, who had served a number of presidents going back to the Reagan administration; who you'd decided to keep on in office; who was a pile driver, a bulldozer, so to speak—but this person who you, in the Woodward interview—he's the very first name out of your mouth when you suspect that terrorists have attacked us on September the 11th. You say, I think, immediately it was a terrorist attack; get Dick Clarke, the terrorist guy. Even before you mentioned Tenet and Rumsfeld's names, "Get Dick Clarke." Why don't you get Dick Clarke to brief the president before 9/11? Here is one of the consummate experts that never has the opportunity to brief the president of the United States on one of the most lethal, dynamic and agile threats to the United States of America. Why don't you use this asset? Why doesn't the president ask to meet with Dick Clarke?

RICE: Well, the president was meeting with his director of central intelligence. And Dick Clarke is a very, very fine counterterrorism expert—and that's why I kept him on. And what I wanted Dick Clarke to do was to manage the crisis for us and help us develop a new strategy. And I can guarantee you, when we had that new strategy in place, the president—who was asking for it and wondering what was happening to it—was going to be in a position to engage it fully.

The fact is that what Dick Clarke recommended to us, as he has said, would not have prevented 9/11. I actually would say that not only would it have not prevented 9/11, but if we had done everything on that list, we would have actually been off in the wrong direction about the importance that we needed to attach to a new policy for Afghanistan and a new policy for Pakistan. Because even though Dick is a very fine counterterrorism expert, he was not a specialist on Afghanistan. That's why I brought somebody in who really understood Afghanistan. He was not a specialist on Pakistan. That's why I brought somebody in to deal with Pakistan. He had some very good ideas. We acted on them. Dick Clarke—let me just step back for a second and say we had a very—we had a very good relationship.

ROEMER: Yes. I'd appreciate it if you could be very concise here, so I can get to some more issues.

RICE: But all that he needed—all that he needed to do was to say, "I need time to brief the president on something." But . . .

ROEMER: I think he did say that. Dr. Rice, in a private interview to us he said he asked to brief the president . . .

RICE: Well, I have to say—I have to say, Mr. Roemer, to my recollection . . .

ROEMER: You say he didn't.

RICE: . . . Dick Clarke never asked me to brief the president on counterterrorism. He did brief the president later on cybersecurity, in July, but he, to my recollection, never asked. And my senior directors have an open door to come and say, "I think the president needs to do this. I think the president needs to do that. He needs to make this phone call. He needs to hear this briefing." It's not hard to get done.

·   ·   ·

JAMES R. THOMPSON: The *Cole*—why didn't the Bush administration respond to the *Cole*?

RICE: I think Secretary Rumsfeld has perhaps said it best. We really thought that the *Cole* incident was passed, that you didn't want to respond tit-for-tat. As I've said, there is strategic response and tactical response. And just responding to another attack in an insufficient way we thought would actually probably embolden the terrorists. They had been emboldened by everything else that had been done to them. And that the best course was to look ahead to a more aggressive strategy against them. I still believe to this day that the al Qaeda were prepared for a response to the *Cole* and that, as some of the intelligence suggested, bin Laden was intending to show that he survived yet another one, and that it might have been counterproductive.

THOMPSON: I've got to say that answer bothers me a little bit because of where it logically leads, and that is—and I don't like "what if" questions, but this is a "what if" question. What if, in March of 2001, under your administration, al Qaeda had blown up another U.S. destroyer? What would you have done and what—would that have been tit-for-tat?

RICE: I don't know what we would have done, but I do think that we were moving to a different concept that said that you had to hold at risk what they cared about, not just try and punish them, not just try to go after bin Laden. I would like to think that we might have come to an effective response. I think that in the context of war, when you're at war with somebody, it's not an issue of every battle or every skirmish; it's an issue of, can you do strategic damage to this organization? And we were thinking much more along the lines of strategic damage.

THOMPSON: Well, I'm going to sound like my brother Kerrey, which terrifies me somewhat. But blowing up our destroyers is an act of war against us, is it not? I mean, how long would that have to go on before we would respond with an act of war?

RICE: We'd had several acts of war committed against us. And I think we believed that responding kind of tit-for-tat, probably with inadequate military options because, for all the plans that might have been looked at by the Pentagon or on the shelf, they were not connected to a political policy that was going to change the circumstances of al Qaeda and the Taliban and therefore the relationship to Pakistan.

Staff Statement No. 9

Law Enforcement, Counterterrorism, and Intelligence Collection in the United States Prior to 9/11

The FBI played the lead role in the government's domestic counterterrorism strategy before September 11. In the 1990s, the FBI's counterterrorism efforts against international terrorist organizations included both intelligence and criminal investigations. Consistent with its traditional law enforcement approach, most of the FBI's energy during this period was devoted to after-the-fact investigations of major terrorist attacks in order to develop criminal cases.

Investigating these attacks always required an enormous amount of resources. As most of these attacks occurred overseas, many of the FBI's top terrorism investigators were deployed abroad for long periods of time. New York was the "Office of Origin" for the al Qaeda program and consequently where most of the FBI's institutional knowledge on al Qaeda resided. Working closely with the Office of the U.S. Attorney for the Southern District of New York, the Department of Justice, and the U.S. Intelligence Community, the FBI's New York field office was often successful in these investigations, and many of the perpetrators of these plots were identified, arrested, prosecuted, and convicted. We will summarize a few of the major episodes.

World Trade Center Bombing. On February 26, 1993, six people were killed and over a thousand injured when a truck bomb exploded in the basement of the World Trade Center. The FBI was able to identify the perpetrators of the attack as radical Islamists who were followers of the "Blind Sheikh," Omar Abd al Rahman. Through an international effort, the attack's mastermind, Abdul Basit Mahmoud Abdul Karim (better known by his alias, Ramzi Yousef), was brought back to the United States to stand trial, and he, like some of his co-conspirators, was convicted.

Landmarks Plot. Later in 1993, the FBI disrupted the "Day of Terror" plot which followers of Sheikh Rahman were in the midst of planning. Their plan was to blow up landmarks in the New York City area, including the Lincoln and Holland Tunnels, the George Washington Bridge, the United Nations, and the New York FBI Office. The FBI was able to prevent this attack by reactivating a source who had previously infiltrated this particular cell.

Manila Airlines Plot. In January 1995, the Philippine police uncovered the plot to blow up 12 airplanes bound for the United States. Two of the perpetrators had also discussed the possibility of flying a small plane into the headquarters of the CIA. The FBI, working with the Philippine government, was able to determine that Ramzi Yousef was involved in this attack, as was Khalid Sheikh Mohammed, the eventual mastermind of the September 11, 2001 attacks.

Khobar Towers Bombing. On June 25, 1996, terrorists attacked Khobar Towers in Saudi Arabia, killing 19 U.S. military personnel and wounding hundreds more. The FBI mounted a full-scale criminal investigation, deploying several hundred FBI personnel to Saudi Arabia to investigate the attack. The investigation resulted in the indictment of 13 individuals in June 2001.

East Africa Embassy Bombings. On August 7, 1998, al Qaeda operatives bombed the U.S. Embassies in Kenya and Tanzania, in nearly simultaneous attacks. Twelve Americans and more than 200 Kenyans and Tanzanians were killed, and over 4,000 were injured. The FBI deployed hundreds of agents and other personnel to Africa to investigate the attacks. Osama bin Laden and 22 other individuals were indicted for their role in these attacks. Four of these individuals were caught and convicted.

Millennium Plot. On December 13, 1999, Ahmed Ressam was detained by an alert U.S. Customs agent as he attempted to cross the border from Canada into the United States. During interviews later with the FBI, Ressam acknowledged that he was planning to conduct an attack at the Los Angeles International Airport. Based on information derived from both Ressam's arrest and the arrests in Jordan associated with a planned attack on an American-owned hotel, the CIA and FBI were mobilized to prevent a terrorist attack within the United States.

U.S.S. Cole *Bombing.* On October 12, 2000, terrorists conducted a suicide attack against the U.S.S. *Cole,* a U.S. naval warship stationed in the port of Aden, Yemen. Seventeen sailors were killed, and 39 were injured. The FBI deployed scores of agents and other personnel to Yemen, and determined that al Qaeda operatives were behind the attacks.

APPROACH TO COUNTERTERRORISM

The FBI took a traditional law enforcement approach to counterterrorism. Its agents were trained to build cases. Its management was deliberately decentralized to empower the individual field offices and agents on the street.

The Bureau rewarded agents based on statistics reflecting arrests, indictments, and prosecutions. As a result, fields such as counterterrorism and counterintelligence, where investigations generally result in fewer prosecutions, were viewed as backwaters.

Agents developed information in support of their own cases, not as part of a broader, more strategic effort. Given the poor state of the FBI's information systems, field agents usually did not know what investigations agents in their own office, let alone in other field offices, were working on. Nor did analysts have easy access to this information. As a result, it was almost impossible to develop an understanding of the threat from a particular international terrorist group.

Agents investigated their individual cases with the knowledge that any case information recorded on paper and stored in case files was potentially discoverable in court. Thus, there was a disincentive to share information, even with other FBI agents and analysts. Analysts were discouraged from producing written assessments which could be discoverable and used to attack the prosecution's case at trial.

In the investigative arena, the field office had primacy. Counterterrorism investigations were run by the field, not headquarters. Moreover, the field office that initiated a case maintained control over it, an approach the FBI called the "Office of Origin" model. This decentralized management structure allowed field offices to set their own priorities with little direction from headquarters.

MANAGEMENT PRIORITIES AND CHALLENGES

The FBI determined early in the 1990s that a preventive posture was a better way to counter the growing threat from international terrorism. In its first budget request to Congress after the 1993 World Trade Center bombing, the FBI stated that, "merely solving this type of crime is not enough; it is equally important that the FBI thwart terrorism before such acts can be perpetrated."

The FBI made several organizational changes at headquarters during the 1990s, including the creation of a Counterterrorism Center, the exchange of senior FBI and CIA counterterrorism officials, and the creation of a unit focused exclusively on Osama bin Laden. The FBI also expanded its overseas Legal Attaché program during this period, largely to improve its liaison with foreign governments on terrorism.

By the late 1990s, the FBI recognized that certain limitations undermined a preventive counterterrorism strategy, and it initiated several significant reforms to address them. These broad efforts were focused on intelligence collection and analysis, counterterrorism expertise and training, information technology, and the counterterrorism capacity of field offices.

Yet the FBI's leadership confronted two fundamental challenges in countering terrorism. First, the FBI had to reconcile this new priority with its existing agenda. This immediately required choices about whether to divert experienced agents or scarce resources from criminal or other intelligence work to terrorism. As the terrorism danger grew, Director [Louis] Freeh faced the choice of whether to lower the priority the FBI attached to work on general crime, including the war on drugs, and allocate these resources to terrorism.

The Department of Justice Inspector General found that when the FBI designated "national and economic security" as its top priority in 1998, it did not shift its human resources accordingly. Although the FBI's counterterrorism budget tripled during the mid-1990s, FBI counterterrorism spending remained fairly constant between fiscal years 1998 and 2001. The Inspector General's 2003 report stated that prior to 9/11, "the Bureau devoted significantly more special agent resources to traditional law enforcement activities such as white collar crime, organized crime, drug, and violent crime investigations than to domestic and international terrorism issues." According to another external review of the FBI, by 2000 there were twice as many agents devoted to drug enforcement matters as to counterterrorism. On September 11, 2001, only about 1,300 agents, or six percent of the FBI's total personnel, worked on counterterrorism.

Former FBI officials told us that prior to 9/11, there was not sufficient national commitment or political will to dedicate the necessary resources to counterterrorism. Specifically, they believed that neither Congress nor the Office of Management and Budget fully understood the FBI's counterterrorism resource needs. Nor did the FBI receive all it requested from the [Clinton administration's] Department of Justice, under Attorney General Janet Reno.

Reno told us that the Bureau never seemed to have sufficient resources given the broad scope of its responsibilities. She said in light of the appropriations FBI received, it needed to prioritize and put counterterrorism first. She also said that Director Freeh seemed unwilling to shift resources to terrorism from other areas such as violent crime. Freeh said that it was difficult to tell field executives that they needed to do additional counterterrorism work without additional resources.

Finally, even though the number of agents devoted to counterterrorism was limited, they were not always fully utilized in the field offices. We learned through our interviews that prior to 9/11, field agents often were diverted from counterterrorism or other intelligence work in order to cover major criminal cases.

The second core challenge was a legal issue that became a management challenge as well. Certain provisions of federal law had been interpreted to limit communication between agents conducting intelligence investigations and the criminal prosecution units of the Department of Justice. This was done so that the broad powers for gathering intelligence would not be seized upon by prosecutors trying to make a criminal case. The separation of intelligence from criminal investigations became known as the "wall." New procedures issued by Attorney General Reno in 1995 required the FBI to notify prosecutors when "facts and circumstances are developed" in a foreign intelligence or foreign counterintelligence investigation that "reasonably indicate a significant federal crime has been, is being, or may be committed." The procedures, however, prohibited the prosecutors from "directing or controlling" the intelligence investigation.

Over time, the wall requirement came to be interpreted by the Justice Department, and particularly the Foreign Intelligence Surveillance Court, as imposing an increasingly stringent barrier to communications between FBI intelligence agents and criminal prosecutors. Despite additional guidance on information sharing issued by Attorney General Reno in February 2000 and by Deputy Attorney General Larry Thompson in August 2001, the wall remained a source of considerable frustration and concern within the Justice Department. Justice Department prosecutors and FBI criminal agents were responsible for large criminal cases, like the Embassy bombings. The intelligence side of the FBI, though, had the legal tools that were essential for domestic intelligence work, such as FISA [Foreign Intelligence Surveillance Act] surveillance. In this environment, domestic counterterrorism efforts were impaired.

ATTEMPTS AT REFORM

The 1998 Strategic Plan. The FBI issued a five-year strategic plan in May 1998 that was spearheaded by Deputy Director Robert Bryant. With this plan, the FBI designated national and economic security, including counterterrorism, as its top priority for the first time in the Bureau's history. The plan emphasized that the FBI's goal in the counterterrorism arena was "to prevent horrific acts" such as the 1993 World Trade Center and 1995 Oklahoma City bombings. The plan recognized that the Bureau needed to substantially enhance its collection, analysis, and dissemination of intelligence in order to understand the terrorist threat, and thus become more proactive on national security issues.

The plan mandated development of a strong intelligence base, including human sources, intelligence collection, and reporting requirements. It called for implementation of a nationwide automated system to facilitate intelligence collection, analysis, and dissemination. It envisioned creation of a professional intelligence cadre of experienced and trained agents and analysts. It hoped for partnerships with intelligence community and national and local law enforcement agencies to leverage their expertise. As a result of the Strategic Plan, the FBI created an Office of Intelligence that was superseded by a new Investigative Services Division created in 1999.

The Investigative Services Division. That Division was intended to strengthen the FBI's strategic analysis capability across the spectrum of traditional criminal, counterintelligence, and counterterrorism cases. Thus, for the first time, the strategic analysis function was made independent of the operational divisions.

The Investigative Services Division also was intended to increase the professional stature of analysts. An internal review of the FBI's intelligence analysis function at this time found that 66 percent of the Bureau's analysts were not qualified to perform analytical duties. The review made recommendations for improvements. It appears that these recommendations were either not implemented or not enforced.

The new Division did not succeed. FBI officials told us that it did not receive sufficient resources, and there was ongoing resistance to its creation from the senior managers in the FBI's operational divisions. Those managers feared losing control. They feared losing resources. They feared they would be unable to get the assistance they wanted from the new Division's analysts.

Director Robert Mueller dismantled the Division soon after the 9/11 attacks. We will discuss his changes in Staff Statement No. 12.

The Counterterrorism Division and MAXCAP 05. In 1999, the FBI also created separate Counterterrorism and Counterintelligence Divisions intended to ensure sufficient focus on these two national security missions. By late 1999 Dale Watson, the first head of the new Counterterrorism Division, recognized the urgent need to elevate the counterterrorism capacity of the FBI organization-wide.

Watson developed a strategy he called MAXCAP 05. His goal was that the Bureau reach its "maximum feasible capacity" in counterterrorism by 2005 through a strategy focused on "intelligence gathering, valid and straightforward reporting and tracking mechanisms, effective interagency liaison and cooperation, and accountable program management."

During July and August of 2000 at four regional conferences, Counterterrorism Division leadership presented the new strategy to all of the FBI's Assistant Directors and Special Agents in Charge of the 56 FBI field offices. Field executives told Watson that they did not have the analysts, linguists, or technically trained experts to carry out the strategy. Watson asked for help from the Training Division and the new Investigative Services Division.

Dale Watson told us that trying to implement this strategy was the hardest thing he had ever done in his life. One year after the regional conferences, almost every FBI field office's counterterrorism program was assessed to be operating at far below "maximum capacity." Watson thought the FBI had to step up to a major choice of mission, perhaps turning over a significant share of narcotics enforcement to the DEA in order to free up resources for countering terrorism. Although he thought FBI Director Freeh was sympathetic, most FBI managers opposed such a fundamental change before 9/11 and none of the pre–9/11 budgets made that choice.

The FBI's new counterterrorism strategy was not a focus of the Justice Department in 2001. Attorney General [John] Ashcroft told us that upon his arrival at the Department, he faced a number of challenges that signaled the need for reform at the FBI. He mentioned the Ruby Ridge and Waco incidents, the Wen Ho Lee investigation, FBI agent Robert Hanssen's espionage, the late discovery of FBI documents related to the Timothy McVeigh case, and public disclosures about lost laptops and firearms.

The new Bush administration proposed an 8 percent increase in overall FBI funding for fiscal year 2002. This included the largest proposed percentage increase in the FBI's counterterrorism program since fiscal year 1997. On May 9, 2001, Attorney General John Ashcroft testified at a hearing on U.S. federal efforts to combat terrorism. He testified that the Justice Department had no higher priority than to protect citizens from terrorist attacks.

On May 10, 2001, the Department issued guidance for developing the fiscal year 2003 budget that made reducing the incidence of gun violence and reducing the trafficking of illegal drugs priority objectives. Watson told us that he almost fell out of his chair when he saw the memo, because it made no mention of counterterrorism. The Department prepared a budget for fiscal year 2003 that did not increase counterterrorism funding over its pending proposal for fiscal year 2002. It did include an enhancement for the FBI's information technology program intended to support the collection, analysis, and rapid dissemination of information pertinent to FBI investigations. Acting FBI Director Thomas Pickard, [who served from June 25 until September 4, 2001,] told us he made an appeal to Attorney General Ashcroft for further counterterrorism enhancements not included in this budget proposal. On September 10, the Attorney General rejected that appeal.

Despite recognition by the FBI of the growing terrorist threat, it was still hobbled by significant deficiencies.

INTELLIGENCE COLLECTION

Intelligence collection efforts should begin with a strategy to comprehend what is being collected, identify the gaps, and push efforts toward meeting requirements identified by strategic analysis. Prior to 9/11 the FBI did not have a process in place to effectively manage its intelligence collection efforts. It did not identify intelligence gaps.

Collection of useful intelligence from human sources was limited. By the mid-1990s senior FBI managers became concerned that the Bureau's statistically-driven performance system had resulted in a roster of mediocre sources. The FBI did not have a formal mechanism for validating source reporting, nor did it have a system for adequately tracking and sharing such reporting, either internally or externally.

The "wall" between criminal and intelligence investigations apparently caused agents to be less aggressive than they might otherwise have been in pursuing Foreign Intelligence Surveillance Act (FISA) surveillance powers in counterterrorism investigations. Moreover, the FISA approval process involved multiple levels of review, which also discouraged agents from using such surveillance. Many agents also told us that the process for getting FISA packages approved at FBI Headquarters and the Department of Justice was incredibly lengthy and inefficient. Several FBI agents added that, prior to 9/11, FISA-derived intelligence information was not fully exploited but was collected primarily to justify continuing the surveillance.

The FBI did not dedicate sufficient resources to the surveillance or translation needs of counterterrorism agents. The FBI's surveillance personnel were more focused on counterintelligence and drug cases. In fact, many field offices did not have surveillance squads prior to 9/11. Similarly, the FBI did not have a sufficient number of translators proficient in Arabic and other languages useful in counterterrorism investigations, resulting in a significant backlog of untranslated FISA intercepts by early 2001.

FBI agents received very little formalized training in the counterterrorism discipline. Only three days of the 16-week new agents course were devoted to national security matters, including counterterrorism and counterintelligence, and most subsequent counterterrorism training was received on an ad hoc basis or "on the job."

Additionally, the career path for agents necessitated rotations between headquarters and the field in a variety of work areas, making it difficult for agents to develop expertise in any particular area, especially counterterrorism and counterintelligence. We were told that very few FBI field managers had any counterterrorism experience, and thus either were not focused on the issue or did not have the expertise to run an effective program.

Finally, agents' investigative activities were governed by Attorney General Guidelines, first put in place in 1976 and revised in 1995, to guard against misuse of government power. The Guidelines limited the investigative methods and techniques available to agents conducting preliminary investigations of potential terrorist activities or connections. They prohibited the use of publicly available source information, such as that found on the Internet, unless specified criteria were present. These restrictions may have had the unintended consequence of causing agents to avoid legitimate investigative activity that might conceivably be viewed as infringing on religious liberties or lawful political protest. Agents we interviewed believed these limitations were too restrictive and adversely affected their counterterrorism intelligence investigations.

STRATEGIC ANALYSIS

It is the role of the strategic analyst to look across individual operations and cases to identify trends in terrorist activity and develop broad assessments of the terrorist threat to U.S. interests. The goal is not abstract. Such analysis drives collection efforts. It is the only way to evaluate what the institution does not know. The FBI had little understanding of, or appreciation for, the role of strategic analysis in driving investigations or allocating resources.

The role of the tactical analyst, on the other hand, is geared toward providing direct support to investigations. Agents viewed tactical analysts as performing duties that advanced their cases. They failed to see the value of strategic analysis, finding it too academic and therefore irrelevant. Creation of the ill-fated Investigative Services Division may have worsened this attitude by distancing strategic analysts from agents in the operational divisions.

Moreover, strategic analysts had difficulty getting access to the FBI and Intelligence Community information they were expected to analyze. The poor state of the FBI's information systems meant that analysts' access to information depended in large part on their personal relationships with individuals in the operational units or squads where the information resided. In short, analysts didn't know what they didn't know. As a result, prior to 9/11 relatively few strategic counterterrorism analytical products had been completed. Indeed, the FBI had never completed an assessment of the overall terrorist threat to the U.S. homeland. According to the Department of Justice Inspector General, FBI officials were comfortable relying on their individual professional judgment regarding the terrorist threat and "did not value a formal written assessment that uses a structured methodology."

Compounding this situation was the FBI's tradition of hiring analysts from within the agency rather than recruiting individuals with the relevant educational background and expertise. In our field visits, we encountered several situations in which poorly qualified administrative personnel were promoted to analyst positions, in part as a reward for good performance in other positions. When the FBI hired or promoted people with appropriate analytical skills and experience, the Bureau's lack of a long-term career path and a professional training program caused many capable individuals to leave the Bureau or move internally to other positions. In addition, managers often did not use qualified analysts effectively, especially in the field. Some field analysts we interviewed told us they were viewed as "über-secretaries," expected to perform any duty that was deemed non-investigative, including data entry and answering phones. Headquarters managers often did not have sufficient staff support, so they, too, turned to analysts to perform policy-oriented and programmatic duties that were not analytic in nature.

KNOWLEDGE MANAGEMENT

Prior to 9/11, the FBI did not have an adequate ability to know what it knew. In other words, the FBI did not have an effective mechanism for capturing or sharing its institutional knowledge. FBI agents did create records of interviews and other investigative efforts, but there were no reports officers to condense the information into meaningful intelligence that could be retrieved and disseminated.

The FBI's primary information management system, designed using 1980s technology already obsolete when installed in 1995, limited the Bureau's ability to share its information internally and externally. The FBI did not have an effective system for storing, searching, or retrieving information of intelligence value contained in its investigative files.

Director Freeh told us that he went before congressional staff and members twice a year "begging and screaming" for funds to improve the FBI's information technology infrastructure. Former Department of Justice and FBI officials told us that the FBI lacked personnel with the necessary expertise leading its information technology improvement efforts, increasing Congress's reluctance to support funding proposals in this area.

Once Freeh brought former 30-year IBM executive Robert Dies on board in 2000, the Bureau developed a comprehensive information technology plan that Congress supported. The FBI received congressional approval in late 2000 for the "Trilogy" project, a 36-month plan for improving its networks, systems, and software. Dies told us that given the enormity of the task at hand, his goal was merely to "get the car out of the ditch." As of September 2001, the project was underway but by no means fully implemented.

The FBI's Joint Terrorism Task Forces (JTTFs) were the primary mechanism for sharing counterterrorism information with other law enforcement agencies in the field. The FBI expanded the number of JTTFs throughout the 1990s, and by 9/11 there were 35.

The JTTFs, while useful, had limitations. The JTTFs set their own priorities in accordance solely with regional and field office concerns, and most were not fully staffed. Many state and local entities believed they would gain little from having a representative on a JTTF. Most detailees performed primarily a liaison function rather than serving as full working members of the JTTFs, and many did not have access to either FBI information systems or their own home agency systems while in the FBI workspace. Moreover, the supervisors in their home agency chains of command often did not have security clearances, making it difficult to share important intelligence information.

We were told that at headquarters, information sharing between the FBI and CIA improved greatly when the agencies began exchanging senior counterterrorism officials in 1996. After serving on rotation, senior officials better understood the other agency's mission and capabilities. As will be discussed in the next staff statement, however, there were other problems with information sharing between the FBI and the CIA. The FBI's inability or unwillingness to share information reportedly frustrated White House national security officials. According to former

National Counterterrorism Coordinator Richard Clarke, the National Security Council [NSC] never received anything in writing from the FBI whatsoever. Former Deputy National Security Adviser James Steinberg stated that the only time that the FBI provided the National Security Council with relevant information was during the Millennium crisis. Clarke told us that Attorney General Reno was notified that the National Security Council could not run an effective counterterrorism program without access to FBI information.

The Justice Department representative on Clarke's interagency group, the Counterterrorism and Security Group, has told us, however, that—to his knowledge—neither Clarke nor anyone else at the NSC raised any systemic issue of FBI information sharing as a policy issue or a matter to be considered by the Attorney General. Reno, in any case, initiated biweekly briefings of National Security Adviser Samuel Berger with FBI Director Freeh.

Reno told us that she was very concerned about the Bureau's information sharing and intelligence capabilities. In 2000, Reno sent several memoranda to Director Freeh expressing these concerns. One memo stated that "it is imperative that the FBI immediately develop the capacity to fully assimilate and utilize intelligence information currently collected and contained in FBI files and use that knowledge to work proactively to identify and protect against emerging national security threats." Reno's requirements involved improved information sharing, improved counterterrorism training, a threat assessment, and a strategy to counter that threat. It is not clear what actions the FBI took in response to these directives from the Attorney General.

TERRORIST FINANCING

The FBI worked hard on terrorist financing investigations. The Bureau primarily utilized an intelligence approach to these investigations. Agents in a number of field offices gathered intelligence on a significant number of suspected terrorist financing organizations. Prior to September 11, these FBI offices had been able to gain a basic understanding of some of the largest and most problematic terrorist financing conspiracies that have since been identified. The agents understood that there was a network of extremist organizations operating within the United States supporting a global Islamic jihad movement. They did not know the degree to which these extremist groups were associated with al Qaeda. It was also unclear whether any of these groups were sending money to al Qaeda. The FBI operated a web of informants, conducted electronic surveillance, and had opened investigations in a number of field offices. Numerous field offices, including New York, Chicago, Detroit, San Diego, and Minneapolis, had significant intelligence investigations into groups that appeared to be raising money for Islamic extremist groups. Many of these groups appeared to the FBI to have some connection to either al Qaeda or Osama bin Laden.

The problems in the FBI's counterterrorism program affected these fundraising investigations as well. The FBI was hampered by an inability to develop an endgame. Its agents continued to gather intelligence with little hope that they would be able to make a criminal case or otherwise disrupt the operation. Agents were stymied by rules regarding the distinction between intelligence and criminal cases, in part due to the "wall" then in place between criminal and intelligence investigations, described above.

Making a terrorist financing case was at least as difficult, and perhaps more so, than other similarly complex international financial criminal investigations. The money inevitably moved overseas. Once that occurred, the money was much harder to track, and the agents were at a dead end. In addition, due to the FBI's inadequate information management systems, strategic analysis, and information sharing capabilities prior to 9/11, the FBI lacked a fundamental strategic understanding of the nature and extent of the al Qaeda fundraising problem within the United States. As a result, the FBI could not fulfill its responsibility to provide intelligence on domestic terrorist financing to government policymakers, and did not contribute to national policy coordination on this issue. Instead, FBI agents simply kept tabs on these fundraisers, even as millions of dollars flowed to foreign Islamic extremists.

CONCLUSION

- From the first World Trade Center attack in 1993, FBI and Department of Justice leadership in Washington and New York became increasingly concerned about the terrorist threat from Islamic extremists to U.S. interests both at home and abroad.

- Throughout the 1990s, the FBI's counterterrorism efforts against international terrorist organizations included both intelligence and criminal investigations. The FBI's approach to investigations was case-specific, decentralized, and geared toward prosecution. Significant FBI resources were devoted to after-the-fact investigations of major terrorist attacks, resulting in several prosecutions.

- The FBI attempted several reform efforts aimed at strengthening its ability to prevent such attacks, but these reform efforts failed to effect change organization-wide.

- On September 11, 2001, the FBI was limited in several areas critical to an effective, preventive counterterrorism strategy. Those working counterterrorism matters did so despite limited intelligence collection and strategic analysis capabilities, a limited capacity to share information both internally and externally, insufficient training, an overly complex legal regime, and inadequate resources.

Caroline Barnes, Christine Healey, Lance Cole, Michael Jacobson, Peter Rundlet, and Doug Greenburg did most of the investigative work reflected in this statement. We were fortunate in being able to build upon strong investigative work done by the Congressional Joint Inquiry and by the Department of Justice's Office of the Inspector General. We have obtained excellent cooperation from the FBI and the Department of Justice, both in Washington and in six FBI field offices across the United States.

Excerpts of testimony from Louis J. Freeh and Janet Reno

EXCERPTS OF TESTIMONY FROM LOUIS J. FREEH, FORMER DIRECTOR, FEDERAL BUREAU OF INVESTIGATION

"We weren't fighting a real war. . . . [W]e were using grand jury subpoenas and arrest warrants to fight an enemy that was using missiles."

I think the point that I would like to make is that it is imperative, in my view, that the commission distinguish between the period before September 11 and the period after September 11; that this is, I would respectfully suggest, a central question for the commission and for the American people. And I think the inability to focus on that question leaves not only a lot of speculation, but I think a lot of misinformation about some of the activities and some of the dynamics here involved. I guess my view is that al Qaeda declared war on the United States in 1996. That's when bin Laden issued his first fatwa. The 1998 fatwa was much more specific. It directed his followers to kill Americans anywhere. That was followed by attacks against American soldiers in Yemen in 1992, which was actually the subject of a Southern District of New York FBI indictment returned in June of 1998 prior to the attacks against the embassies in East Africa. The attacks upon the

American soldiers in Somalia, Project Restore Hope, was an activity sponsored by and directed by al Qaeda soldiers. That, as you know, was one of the overt acts publicly identified in the New York City indictment with respect to bin Laden. The attacks against the embassies in 1998: acts of war against the United States. The attacks against our warship in 2000: acts of war against the United States.

I remember briefing Senator [Bob] Kerrey and Senator [Richard] Shelby after one of these attacks—it was the embassy attacks—and he asked me a very good question, a question that I think is maybe more relevant today than it was then. And he said, Why is the FBI over in East Africa, hundreds of FBI agents sifting through a crime scene maintaining chain of custody, talking to people and giving them their Miranda rights, when this is an act of war against the United States? And my response then, as it would be now, is that, absent a declaration of war backed by the United States against al Qaeda, against this very competent and very dangerous terrorist organization, we were left with the tools that were available to fight terrorism and to neutralize and incapacitate, not just bin Laden, but many of his operatives and allied organizations. The point there is not that anybody in the FBI or anybody in the United States thought that investigating these cases was the best response to a war that was declared against the United States. You could poll any FBI agent, any jury that tried and convicted many of the people in these cases and they would tell you absolutely not. An arrest warrant, two of them for bin Laden in the Southern District of New York, was not going to deter him from what happened on September 11th.

But the point of these investigations was in the absence of invading Afghanistan, in the absence of armed Predator missiles seeking out our enemies, in the absence of all the things that were appropriately done after September 11th, when the United States declared war back on al Qaeda, we were left with alternatives which were better than no alternatives. . . . [B]efore September 11th most of the information that was residing in the United States government with respect to al Qaeda came from FBI investigations, not from intelligence operations, not from collection. It came from the cooperating witnesses that we found in 1993, after the World Trade bombing in February. The FBI conducting an investigation but an investigation that went to the identification of the people who might have been involved in supporting that attack led to, if you recall, the prevention—and I stress that word—the prevention of a second major terrorist attack against the United States in New York City which was called the Day of Terror. And the organization was going to blow up tunnels and bridges and the United Nations and federal office buildings, killing potentially thousands and thousands of Americans.

It was the investigation of the World Trade tower that prevented that and also gave us an arrest warrant for one Ramzi Yousef. Ramzi Yousef, related to Khalid Sheikh Mohammed, one of the architects of the September 11th attack. He was found in Pakistan, staying in an al Qaeda guest house, by FBI agents who had an arrest warrant, and without that arrest warrant, he would never have been brought back to the United States. Why was it important to have an arrest warrant? Because incapacitating him would prevent him from further attacks against the United States. As you know, in 1995, he and others—Khalid Sheikh Mohammed being one of them—were planning to blow up 12 U.S. airliners over the Pacific Ocean, killing hundreds of Americans. That was aborted due to a series of events, but precisely the FBI criminal investigation served to prevent that from happening. My point is that these investigations or projects that seek to gather maximum amount of information so the organization can be stopped from committing future acts of terrorism. It was never our notion in the FBI that criminal prosecutions of terrorists and investigations of their organizations was a substitute for military action, for foreign policy action, for the United States doing what it did on September 11th, declaring war on an enemy that had declared war on us many years ago. The point of it is that these investigations, as they existed, prevented acts of terrorism.

With very limited resources. The FBI, as you know, before September 11, had 3.5 percent of the federal government's anti-terrorism budget. And it's no news to anybody that for many, many years, as your executive director recounted, the resource issue and the legal authority issue certainly limited what we were able to do before September 11th. In the budget years 2000, 2001, 2002, we asked for 1,895 people: agents, linguists, analysts. We got a total of 76 people during that period. That's not to criticize the Congress, it's not to criticize the Department of Justice, it is to focus on the fact that that was not a national priority. It's to repeat what we saw in the 2000 presidential election. Terrorism was not discussed. This was not an issue that candidates talked about, that the American people talked about during that period. And this was right after the attack on the U.S.S. *Cole*. For many, many years, a lack of these resources and, maybe more importantly, a lack of legal authority prevented us from doing what was easily done after September 11th. . . . The Patriot Act, the November 18, 2002 decision by the court of review, which threw out a 20-year interpretation of the FISA statute. The court said to the judges, to the Department of Justice, to the FBI, to the intelligence community, You've been misreading the statute for 20 years. Not only does the Patriot Act provide for this, but the actual statute provides for that. So this wall that had been erected was a self-erected wall by the United States government, confirmed by interpretations, by the FISA court.

All of these things being said, the point I guess I want to make to you this morning and which I tried to make in my statement, is that we had a very effective program with respect to counterterrorism before September 11th given the resources in my view and given the authorities that we had. Bin Laden was indicted in June of 1998. He was indicted again after the African bombings. He was put on our top 10 list. [CIA Director] George Tenet and I reviewed plans to have him arrested and taken into custody in Afghanistan and brought back to the United States. I went over to see [Pakistan's] then-chief executive [Pervez] Musharraf in 2002 and made the case for him that this person be thrown out of Afghanistan; that he help us take him into custody so we could bring him back to the United States. All of the other things that were being done were being done in a limited framework, given, again, lack of resources and, maybe more importantly, the legal authorities that we had to live with.

QUESTIONS FROM COMMISSIONERS

RICHARD BEN-VENISTE: Let me turn to the subject of the state of the intelligence community's knowledge regarding the potential for the use of airplanes as weapons, a subject of obvious interest to this commission. Did the subject of planes as weapons come up in planning for security of the Olympics held in Atlanta in 1996?

FREEH: Yes, I believe it came up in a series of these, as we call them, special events. These were intergovernmental planning strategy sessions and operations. And I think in the years 2000, 2001, even going back maybe to the 2000 Olympics, that was always one of the considerations in the planning. And resources were actually designated to deal with that particular threat.

BEN-VENISTE: So it was well-known in the intelligence community that one of the potential areas or devices to be used by terrorists, which they had discussed, according to our intelligence information, was the use of airplanes, either packed with explosives or otherwise, in suicide missions?

FREEH: That was part of the planning for those events, that's correct.

BEN-VENISTE: Did that come up, the same subject, come up again? I know you carried on from the Clinton administration through six months, more or less, of the Bush administration. Did that subject come up again in the planning for the G–8 summit in Italy?

FREEH: I don't recall that it did, but I would not have been involved in that planning. The FBI would not have been involved in that particular planning.

BEN-VENISTE: We were advised that there was a CAP or no-fly zone imposed over first Naples, in the preplanning session, and then Genoa during the meeting of the eight heads of state. And that subsequently it was disclosed that President [Hosni] Mubarak of Egypt had warned of a potential suicide flight using explosive-packed airplanes to fly into the summit meeting.

FREEH: I don't dispute that. But that planning would be done by the Secret Service, probably the Department of Defense. We would not have been involved in that event outside the United States in terms of the special planning, although we probably detailed some people there.

BEN-VENISTE: Let me ask you this: To your knowledge, coming back to the United States, was the intelligence information accumulated by the year 2001 regarding various plots, real or otherwise, to crash planes using suicide pilots integrated into any air defense plan for protecting the homeland, and particularly our nation's capital?

FREEH: I'm not aware of such a plan.

BEN-VENISTE: Can you explain why it was, given the fact that we knew this information, and given the fact that, as we know now, our air defense system on 9/11 was looking outward in a Cold War-posture, rather than inward, in a protective posture, that we didn't have such a plan? Was that a failure of the Clinton administration, was that a failure of the Bush administration, given all of the information that we had accumulated at that time?

FREEH: Well, I mean, I don't know that I would characterize it as a failure by either administration. I know, you know, by that time there were air defense systems with respect to the White House. There were air defense systems that the military command in the Washington, D.C., area, you know, had incorporated. I don't think there were probably—at least I never was aware of a plan that contemplated commercial airliners being used as weapons after a hijacking. I don't think that was integrated in any plan. But with respect to air defense issues and that threat, it was clearly known and it was incorporated, as I mentioned, into standard special events planning.

.   .   .

THOMAS H. KEAN: Now, I read our staff statement as an indictment of the FBI over a long period of time. You know, when I read things like that 66 percent of your analysts weren't qualified, that you didn't have the translators necessary to do the job, that you had FISA difficulties, that you had all the information on the fund-raising but you couldn't find a way to use it properly to stop terrorism. And that's without counting, of course, the things that were going on at the same time: Ruby Ridge, Waco, the Wen Ho Lee case, the Hanssen case, the lost laptops and firearms and all of the rest. The present director, your successor, has a whole series of reforms that he is trying to put to make the agency work better. You tried reforms. You tried very hard to reform the agency. According to our staff report, those reforms failed. I guess my question to you is, looking at this director's efforts to reform the agency, can those reforms work or should there be some more fundamental changes to the agency and the way we get our intelligence?

FREEH: Well, first of all, I take exception to your comment that your staff report is an indictment of the FBI. I think your staff report evidences some very good work and some very diligent interviews and a very technical, almost auditing, analysis of some of the programs. I think the centerpiece of your executive director's report, as I heard it, came down to resources and legal authorities.

So I would ask that you balance what you call an indictment, and which I don't agree with at all, with the two primary findings of your staff. One is that there was a lack of resources; and two, there were legal impediments. With respect to your question, I certainly support and applaud the director's efforts. The Patriot Act, the court of review, a couple of billion dollars is certainly a big help when we're talking about changes. With respect to the jurisdiction of the FBI, I do not believe that we should establish a separate domestic intelligence agency with respect to counterterrorism. I think that would be a huge mistake for the country for a number of reasons. One, I don't think in the United States we will tolerate very well what, in effect, is a state secret police even with all of the protections and the constitutional entitlements that we would subscribe it with. Americans, I don't think, like secret police. And you would, in effect, be establishing a secret police. Secondly, if you look at the models around the world where this has been tried, it hasn't worked very well, in my opinion. The other thing, it would take a long time to integrate. If the Homeland Security Department and 170,000 people to be integrated is going to take a couple of years; standing up a brand new domestic intelligence agency would take a decade and we would lose very precious time at a very dangerous time for the United States.

If you look at some the analyses of MI–5 operations, and you can look at the Bishop Gate bombing, you can look at the Dockland's bombing . . . it's been found to be not very effective. In fact, one of the studies that I know your staff has looked at in the United Kingdom that looked at this actually said the FBI was a preferred model because it breaks down the barriers between enforcement and intelligence. A lot of the good work of this commission has been to identify the barriers that existed—and still exist—between intelligence and law enforcement. Standing up a separate intelligence agency will just increase those barriers. And if you thought the wall was a big one, that's a fortress in my view and will make for a very ineffective counterterrorism program and, I think, expose the country to dangers.

So I think we ought to have the Department of Justice, supervised by the attorney general, FBI agents who are schooled in the Constitution, who have a transparent operation with respect to oversight by courts, as well as by Congress. Give them the tools, give them the legal authority, give them the budget, and they'll do this job very well. It's not very different from looking at organized crime, from looking at counterintelligence, which, in my view, the bureau has done exceptionally well for decades. The difficulty with the wall was that the wall that was set up in Janet Reno's guidelines of July 19th were completely appropriate with respect to counterintelligence cases because counterintelligence cases happen in two dynamics. One, there is an investigation, and then there is either an indictment or an expulsion. Counterterrorism cases are completely different. Because of the threat, there is always an ongoing need to act and to use the intelligence to prevent attacks from taking place. So the wall is not an appropriate one with respect to counterterrorism, and that's been repaired both by the Patriot Act and the court of review.

. . .

BOB KERREY: . . . In an otherwise, I thought, exceptional staff report, the staff, I think, incorrectly describes the seven cases that you were involved with, saying that most of those were overseas. In truth, three of them were domestic, and four of them were overseas. World Trade Center number one, landmarks plot number one, the millennium, and indeed if you include the threats against the city of New York during the 2001 trial, there were four domestic attacks and/or efforts. Did the FBI ever produce an evaluation of the threat to the homeland during this period to the president? Or was there one requested of you?

FREEH: There was none requested, that I'm aware of. I don't think we ever furnished a national threat report to the president with respect to homeland security.

KERREY: I mean, of all the facts that—in this whole process, that have just caused scales to fall from my eyes was listening to Betty Ong, a flight attendant on flight 11, talk to the ground and hear the ground surprised by a hijacking. I mean, not only were we not at a high state of alert in our airports, we were at ease. We stacked arms. I mean, we weren't prepared at all. And it's baffling to me why some alert wasn't given to the airlines to alter their preparedness and to go to a much higher state of alert. It seems to me a lot of things would have changed if that would have happened. . . .

FREEH: Well, Senator, I served on the Gore commission, as your staff may know. . . . We spent many, many months writing detailed recommendations that asked for passenger screening, asked for many, many things which were never implemented. The whole purpose and the conclusions of that report, if you read it, was that the airline industry and operations were vulnerable at multi points with respect to hijackings and terrorist attacks. So I agree with you, there was no . . .

KERREY: But I mean, you said that, you know, we couldn't have had a declaration of war because public opinion wasn't there. I probably would disagree with that. Public opinion wasn't on the side of the Bosnian war or the Iraq war in the beginning either, and the president made a determination in both cases to come to the American people and say, There's a crisis. But even absent a declaration of war, why did we let their soldiers into the United States? Because that's what the al Qaeda men were, they were soldiers. They were part of an Islamic army called the jihad to come into the United States. Why did we let them into the United States? Why didn't President Clinton and/or President Bush issue an order to change the FISA procedures and other orders to INS, et cetera, to make sure that their soldiers couldn't get into America? Why did we let them in?

FREEH: Well, again, I think part of my answer is that we weren't fighting a real war. We hadn't declared war on these enemies in the manner that you suggest that would have prevented entry had we taken war measures and put the country and its intelligence and law enforcement agencies on a war footing. The Joint Intelligence Committee, in one of their reports—I think I excerpted the conclusion in my statement—said that neither administration put its intelligence agencies or law enforcement agencies on a war footing. A war footing means we seal borders. A war footing means we detain people that we're suspicious of. A war footing means that we have statutes like the Patriot Act, although with time set provisions, give us new powers.

We weren't doing that. Now, whether there was a political will for it or not, I guess we could debate that. But the fact of the matter is we didn't do it and we were using grand jury subpoenas and arrest warrants to fight an enemy that was using missiles and suicide boats to attack our warships.

.   .   .

EXCERPTS OF TESTIMONY FROM
JANET RENO,
FORMER U.S. ATTORNEY GENERAL

"What I lacked confidence in was in knowing what [the FBI] had. And the second thing was, if it knew what it had, sharing what it had."

First of all, I am so proud of the FBI. The agents that I've worked with, I've seen so many in action. I've seen them do incredible things. I've seen them risk their lives. And I have a profound respect for all the people that I have worked with in the bureau. But quickly, when I came into office, I learned that the FBI didn't know what it had. We found stuff in files here that the right hand didn't know what the left hand was doing. And it was obvious that the development of a computer system and a system of automation would be very helpful to it. But it was also important for people to begin to look at manually what they could do to find out what they had and what they didn't have, and we proceeded in that direction. Sometimes I thought we had made progress, but then we'd find something else that we didn't know we didn't have. . . .

Director Freeh has suggested that there were two other issues that were problems: resources and legal authorities. . . . As Director Freeh pointed out, everybody knows that we're competing for limited resources in the budget process and people ask for more than they know they're going to receive. But I worked very closely with Director Freeh to try to make sure that we properly pursued a request that reflected the needs of the bureau. . . .

[W]hen I came into office, I was told that the FBI had come out of the Cold War. They now had agents who needed something to do, and they had been assigned to and were involved in fighting street crime. Well, America has a lot of resources committed to fighting street crime now. Community police officers were hired, other steps were taken, crime is down, and state and local law enforcement can do that or at least do a very good job of it. If we needed to reprogram, I told Director Freeh, let's do it and get these people into counterterrorism. We have a drug enforcement agency. If we need to do it, let's get these people into counterterrorism. Yes, it's sometimes difficult to get reprogramming approval from Congress. But if we have people who work with the Department of Justice, do it the right way, come forward in clear statements, I think we can do a lot more in terms of reprogramming. . . . .

With respect to sharing, one of the frustrations is that the bureau even when it finds that it has something doesn't share, and it says it doesn't share because the legal authorities prohibit it from sharing. But I haven't been able to find . . . what prevented anybody from sharing. Many of these issues will or have been resolved by the passage of the Patriot Act or other statements. But I think it is extremely important that the director or whoever leads the FBI understands that you've got to repeat the message again and again. . . .

They say they can't exchange information with the CIA, but it's all in the context of cases where the FBI and the CIA have been exchanging information. What suddenly prevents them in one situation and not in the other? We can't be selective. Again we have got to change. . . .

A lot of talk about a new agency. Don't create another agency, or recommend it. The worst thing you can do is create another agency and then we'll be back talking about whether they can share here or there or what. Let's try to work through it.

QUESTIONS FROM COMMISSIONERS

TIMOTHY J. ROEMER: Did you lack confidence in the FBI's ability to accumulate information due to these technological problems?

RENO: I didn't lack confidence in its ability to accumulate it. It accumulated more information than—I mean, it was . . .

ROEMER: How about share it?

RENO: Knowing my—what I lacked confidence in was in knowing

what it had. And the second thing was, if it knew what it had, sharing what it had.

ROEMER: Now, you said in your statement that, Shortly after he took office, Attorney General Ashcroft invited me to lunch with him, and you gave him these same sets of memoranda. Did you feel like there was some progress then, after you gave these same pieces of paper to General Ashcroft; that he was going to implement this change and do something different from what the FBI had done or not done leading up to that time?

RENO: I had obviously left office by that point and was no longer briefed or privy to what was going to be done, so I don't know what was done. And I apologize to everybody concerned if I've been presumptuous in suggesting what Director Mueller needs, because I haven't really been involved. But I'm giving my historical perspective of the time. And I think Attorney General Ashcroft was very gracious and said, This is very interesting. And I don't know what happened after that.

ROEMER: Let's stay on the topic of your relationship to the new attorney general. In the transition period, were you able to brief Attorney General Ashcroft as to your concerns on counterterrorism? And did al Qaeda come up in that briefing?

RENO: I don't know whether al Qaeda came up in the briefing or not. I cannot recall whether I specifically talked to him about al Qaeda. But what I did talk about was reflected in the memos which I gave him, which is: If we don't put the pieces together and connect the dots, there's going to be something that happens. And there is so much information out there, it is so important that we get this done. And that's the reason I brought the memos with me.

ROEMER: Do you recall—and excuse me for pushing you on this— but do you recall mentioning al Qaeda, Osama bin Laden, domestic cells of terrorists in the United States to the new attorney general?

RENO: No, I don't.

ROEMER: You don't recall that. Do you recall being briefed on that type of domestic threat by FBI personnel sometime in the 1990s?

RENO: Cells—what I was briefed on was what the bureau had under way. I don't recall a briefing on cells in the United States.

ROEMER: So all throughout the 1990s, when you had people like Dale Watson or Director Freeh, your contacts with the National Security Council, they never briefed you on al Qaeda cells or the presence of al Qaeda in the United States—'98, '99, 2000—sometime in that period?

RENO: They briefed me on the presence of al Qaeda in the United States. But in terms of cells and where they were, I don't recall such a briefing.

ROEMER: And therefore, you had no specifics at that point, so you did not brief the new attorney general on something like that?

RENO: What I thought was important was with respect to all terrorism issues. I told him that it was, to me, one of the most important issues. And one of the things that is critically important, I never focused just on al Qaeda, because I stood there and watched the Murrah building in rubble just as we saw it—the beginnings of the Oklahoma bombing on CNN, and tended to jump to conclusions. You can't jump to conclusions. You can't say that one thing is going to be our overriding issue. I think one other recommendation I would make is we have got to be prepared for terrorism in any form. And a focus on one is going to make it difficult.

ROEMER: I want to push back a little bit on the Clinton administration here, and the priority on terrorism. You say in your statement, priority of counterterrorism efforts, counterterrorism was a top priority for the Department of Justice. This priority was reflected in the department's strategic plan. Now, if it's a top priority for you and your administration, wouldn't that be one of the first things that you briefed to the new attorney general: counter-terrorism, al Qaeda, the domestic threat?

RENO: Which I did, and which I did in—the point that I thought most important to make was if we were going to protect this nation's economic and national security, we had to be prepared at the bureau in terms of the information-sharing, organization, training of people, and that was the point I was making.

Staff Statement No. 10

Threats and Responses in 2001

For years the U.S. government had experienced surges of threat reports. Significant surges had been experienced, for example, at the end of 1999 as part of a more generalized fear of attacks associated with Millennium events. There had been other surges in threat reporting during the summer of 2000 and in the Ramadan period at the end of 2000. But until 2001 the Millennium had set a kind of benchmark, and so it is worth recalling that episode.

In early December 1999, Jordanian authorities discovered a cell planning attacks on a hotel and other tourist sites. The CIA learned of links between this cell and people living in Boston and Los Angeles. Then, in mid-December, U.S. border inspectors caught Ahmed Ressam at the Canadian border trying to smuggle explosives into the United States. Investigators later learned his true target was the Los Angeles International Airport. The FBI linked Ressam to a terrorist cell in Montreal that, in turn, had links to individuals in Brooklyn. NSC [National Security Council] Counterterrorism Coordinator Richard Clarke told us that at that point the U.S. government went to what we would now call an "orange" alert. In an extraordinary effort, spurred by Attorney General Janet Reno, the FBI mobilized its field offices nationwide to prevent an attack.

Beginning in December, there was an intense period with frequent phone calls and meetings among cabinet-level principals. The FBI asked for and obtained an extraordinary number of FISA [Foreign Intelligence Surveillance Act] warrants. Principals participated directly in tracking the progress of various domestic investigations. [National Security Adviser Samuel] Berger, in particular, met or spoke constantly with [CIA Director George] Tenet and Attorney General Reno. He visited the FBI and the CIA on Christmas Day 1999 to raise the morale of exhausted officials. After the Millennium passed, a more normal work pace returned. But, as Tenet recalled to us, the Millennium was followed by the October 2000 *Cole* bombing, then threats during the Ramadan period at the end of 2000. "You're running like hell" during this entire period, he said. Until officials live through one of these periods, he added, they cannot understand what it is like.

In spring 2001, the level of reporting on terrorist threats and planned attacks began to increase dramatically, representing the most significant spike in activity since the Millennium. At the end of March the Intelligence Community disseminated a Terrorist Threat Advisory, indicating there was a heightened threat of Sunni extremist terrorist attacks against U.S. facilities, personnel, and other interests in the coming weeks. In April and May 2001 the drumbeat of reporting increased. Articles presented to top officials contained headlines such as: "Bin Laden planning multiple operations." "Bin Laden public profile may presage attack." "Bin Laden network's plans advancing." By late May there were reports of a hostage plot against Americans to force the release of prisoners, including Sheikh Omar Abd al Rahman, the "Blind Sheikh," who was serving a life sentence for his role in the 1993 plot to blow up sites in New York City. The reporting noted that the operatives may opt to hijack an aircraft or storm a U.S. embassy. The reporting also mentioned that [al Qaeda leader] Abu Zubaydah was planning an attack and expected to carry out more if things went well. The U.S. government redoubled efforts, ongoing since late 1999, to capture Abu Zubaydah. National Counterterrorism Coordinator Clarke also called National Security Adviser Condoleezza Rice's attention to possible plots in Yemen and Italy, and by an alleged cell in Canada that might be planning an attack against the United States.

Reports similar to these were made available to President Bush in morning meetings with DCI [Director of Central Intelligence] Tenet, usually attended by Vice President Cheney and National Security Adviser Rice as well. None of these reports mentioned that the attacks might occur in the United States. At the end of May, Counterterrorist Center (CTC) Chief Cofer Black, [who served in that position from 1999 to 2002,] told Rice that the current threat level was a "7" on a scale of 10, as compared to an "8" during the Millennium.

The threat reports surged again in June and July, reaching an even higher peak of urgency. A Terrorist Threat Advisory in late June indicated that there was a high probability of near-term "spectacular" terrorist attacks resulting in numerous casualties. Headlines from intelligence reports were stark: "Bin Laden threats are real." "Bin Laden planning high profile attacks." The intelligence reporting consistently described the upcoming attacks as occurring on a catastrophic level, indicating that they would cause the world to be in turmoil, consisting of possible multiple—but not necessarily simultaneous—attacks. A late June report stated that bin Laden operatives expect near-term attacks to have dramatic consequences of catastrophic proportion.

Rice told us Clarke and his Counterterrorism Security Group (CSG) were "the nerve center" in coordinating responses but that principals were also involved. In addition to his daily meetings with President Bush, and weekly meetings to go over other issues with National Security Adviser Rice, Tenet continued his regular meetings with Secretary [of State Colin] Powell and Secretary [of Defense Donald] Rumsfeld. The foreign policy principals talked on the phone every day on a variety of subjects, including the threat. The summer threats seemed to be focused on Saudi Arabia, Israel, Bahrain, Kuwait, Yemen, and possibly Rome, but the danger could be anywhere—including a possible attack on the G–8 summit in Genoa, where air defense measures were taken. Disruption operations were launched involving twenty countries. Several terrorist operatives were detained by foreign governments, possibly disrupting operations in the Gulf and Italy and perhaps averting attacks against two or three U.S. embassies. U.S. armed forces in at least six countries were placed on higher alert. Units of the Fifth Fleet were redeployed. Embassies were alerted. Vice President Cheney contacted Crown Prince Abdullah to get more Saudi help. DCI Tenet phoned or met with approximately twenty top security officials from other countries. Deputy National Security Adviser [Stephen] Hadley apparently called European counterparts. Clarke worked with senior officials in the Gulf.

At Rice's request, on July 5 the CIA briefed Attorney General John Ashcroft on the al Qaeda threat, warning that a significant terrorist attack was imminent, and a strike could occur at any time. That same day, officials from domestic agencies, including the FAA [Federal Aviation Administration], met with Clarke to discuss the current threat. Rice worked directly with Tenet on security issues for the G–8 summit. In addition to the individual reports, on July 11 top officials received a summary recapitulating the mass of al Qaeda-related threat reporting on several continents. Tenet told us that in his world "the system was blinking red," and by late July it could not have been any worse. Tenet told us he felt that President Bush and other officials grasped the urgency of what they were being told.

On July 27 Clarke informed Rice and Hadley that the spike in signals intelligence about a near-term attack had stopped. He urged keeping readiness high during the August vacation period, warning that another report suggested an attack had just been postponed for a few months. On August 3 the Intelligence Community issued a Threat Advisory warning that the threat of impending al Qaeda attacks would likely continue indefinitely. The advisory cited threats in the Arabian Peninsula, Jordan, Israel, and Europe, and suggested that al Qaeda was lying in wait and searching for gaps in security before moving forward with the planned attacks.

During the spring and summer of 2001, President Bush had occasionally asked his briefers whether any of the threats pointed to the United States. Reflecting on these questions, the CIA decided to write a briefing article summarizing its understanding of this danger. The article, which the President received on August 6, is attached to this staff statement.

Despite the large number of threats received, there were no specifics regarding time, place, method, or target. Disruption efforts continued. An al Qaeda associate from North Africa, connected to Abu Zubaydah, was arrested in the United Arab Emirates on August 13. He had apparently been planning an attack against the U.S. Embassy in Paris.

CIA analysts who have recently reviewed the threat surge of the summer of 2001 told us they believe it may have been related to a separate stream of events. These threats may have been referring to the 9/11 attack, the planned assassination of Northern Alliance leader Ahmed Shah Massoud, or other operations.

In July 2001, the CSG alerted federal law enforcement agencies and asked the FAA to send out security advisories. Beginning on July 27 the FAA issued several security directives to U.S. air carriers prior to September 11. In addition, the FAA issued a number of general warnings about potential threats, primarily overseas, to civil aviation. None of these warnings required the implementation of additional aviation security measures. They urged air carriers to be alert.

Although there was no credible evidence of an attack in the United States, Clarke told us, the CSG arranged for the CIA to brief senior intelligence and security officials from the domestic agencies. The head of counterterrorism at the FBI, Dale Watson, said he had many discussions about possible attacks with Cofer Black at the CIA. They had expected an attack on July 4. Watson said he felt deeply that something was going to happen. But he told us the threat information was "nebulous." He wished he had known more. He wished he had had "500 analysts looking at Osama bin Laden threat information instead of two."

Rice and Hadley told us that, before 9/11, they did not feel they had the job of handling domestic security. They felt that Clarke and the CSG were the NSC's bridge between foreign and domestic threats.

In late August, working-level CIA and FBI officials realized that one or more al Qaeda operatives might be in the United States. We have found no evidence that this discovery was ever briefed to the CSG, to principals, or to senior counterterrorism officials at the FBI or the CIA. Nor was the White House told about the arrest of Zacarias Moussaoui [a student at a Minnesota flight school].

We investigated awareness of the terrorist threat within the Department of Justice and the FBI during the spring and summer of 2001. Rice told us that she believed the FBI had tasked its 56 U.S. field offices to increase surveillance of suspected terrorists and to reach out to informants who might have information about terrorist plots. An NSC document at the time describes such a tasking having occurred in late June, although it does not indicate whether the tasking was generated by the NSC or the FBI.

At this point we have found the following: On April 13 FBI Headquarters alerted field offices to a heightened threat from al Qaeda against U.S. interests. The communication detailed the threats against U.S. interests abroad, but made no mention of any possible threat inside the United States. The field offices were asked to "task all resources to include electronic databases and human sources for any information pertaining to the current operational activities relating to Sunni extremism."

On July 2 the FBI Counterterrorism Division sent a message to federal agencies and state and local law enforcement agencies that summarized information regarding threats against U.S. interests from bin Laden. The message reported that there was an increased volume of threat reporting indicating a potential for attacks against U.S. targets abroad from groups "aligned with or sympathetic to Osama bin Laden." It further stated, "[t]he FBI has no information indicating a credible threat of terrorist attack in the United States." However, it went on to emphasize that the possibility of attack in the United States could not be discounted. It also noted that the July 4 holiday might heighten the threats. The report asked the recipients to "exercise vigilance" and "report suspicious activities" to the FBI.

[Former] Acting FBI Director Thomas Pickard recently told

us that during his summer telephone calls with Special Agents in Charge of each FBI field office, he mentioned to each the heightened threat, among other subjects. He also told us that he had a conference call with all Special Agents in Charge on July 19 in which he discussed a variety of subjects. He said one of the items he mentioned was that they needed to have their evidence response teams ready to move at a moment's notice in case they needed to respond to an attack.

We found in our field office visits last fall, however, that a number of FBI personnel—with the exception of those in the New York field office—did not recall a heightened sense of threat from al Qaeda within the United States in summer 2001. For example, an international terrorism squad supervisor in the Washington Field Office told us he was neither aware in summer 2001 of an increased threat, nor did his squad take any special steps or actions. The Special Agent in Charge of the Miami Field Office told us he did not learn of the high level of threat until after September 11.

Pickard said in late June and through July he met with Attorney General Ashcroft once a week. He told us that although he initially briefed the Attorney General regarding these threats, after two such briefings the Attorney General told him he did not want to hear this information anymore. The Justice Department has informed us that Attorney General Ashcroft, his former deputy, and his chief of staff deny that the Attorney General made any such statement to Pickard.

Ashcroft told us that he asked Pickard whether there was intelligence about attacks in the United States. Pickard said he replied that he could not assure Ashcroft that there would be no attacks in the United States, although the reports of threats were related to overseas targets. Ashcroft said he therefore assumed that the FBI was doing what it needed to do. He acknowledged that, in retrospect, this was a dangerous assumption.

Prior to 9/11 neither Ashcroft nor his predecessors received a copy of the President's Daily Brief. After 9/11 Ashcroft began to receive portions of the brief that relate to counterterrorism.

AL MIHDHAR AND AL HAZMI CONTINUED

While top officials in Washington were receiving and reacting to various threat reports, we need to step further down into the bureaucracy to trace a now significant story of how particular al Qaeda associates were addressed by lower-level officials. In [an earlier] staff statement, we discussed the complex story of successes and failures in tracking and identifying hijackers Khalid al Mihdhar, Nawaf al Hazmi, Nawaf's brother Salem al Hazmi, and the *Cole* bomber "Khallad."

Those efforts had trailed off in January 2000. No one at CIA headquarters reacted to the March 2000 cable from Bangkok that someone named Nawaf al Hazmi had traveled to the United States. But there were three episodes in 2001 when the CIA and/or the FBI had apparent opportunities to refocus on the significance of al Hazmi and al Mihdhar and reinvigorate the search for them. As in the 2000 story, the details are complex.

JANUARY 2001:
IDENTIFICATION OF KHALLAD

Almost one year after the original trail had been lost in Bangkok, the January 2000 rendezvous of suspected terrorists in Kuala Lumpur resurfaced. The FBI and the CIA learned from a conspirator in the U.S.S. *Cole* attack in Yemen that a person he knew as "Khallad" had helped direct the *Cole* bombing. One of the members of the FBI's investigative team in Yemen realized that he had previously heard of Khallad from a joint FBI/CIA source, who had said Khallad was close to bin Laden. Khallad was also linked to the East Africa embassy bombings in 1998.

The FBI agent obtained, from a foreign government, a photo of the person believed to have directed the *Cole* bombing. The joint source confirmed that the man in that photograph was the same Khallad he had described.

In December 2000, based on some analysis of information associated with Khalid al Mihdhar, the CIA's Bin Laden Station speculated that Khallad and Khalid al Mihdhar might be one and the same. So the CIA asked that a Kuala Lumpur surveillance photo of al Mihdhar be shown to the joint source who had already identified an official photograph of Khallad.

In early January 2001 two photographs from the Kuala Lumpur meeting were shown to the joint source. One was a known photograph of al Mihdhar, the other a photograph of an unknown subject. The joint source did not recognize al Mihdhar. But he indicated he was ninety percent certain that the other individual was Khallad.

This meant that Khallad and al Mihdhar were two different people. But the fact that both had attended the meeting in Kuala Lumpur also meant that there was a link between Khallad, a suspected leader in the *Cole* bombing, the Kuala Lumpur meeting, and al Mihdhar. Despite this new information, we found no effort by the CIA to renew the long-abandoned search for al Mihdhar or his travel companions.

In addition, we found that the CIA did not notify the FBI of this identification until late August. DCI Tenet and Cofer Black testified before the Joint Inquiry that the FBI had access to this identification from the beginning. But based on an extensive record, including documents that were not available to CIA personnel who drafted that testimony, we conclude they were in error. The FBI's primary *Cole* investigators had no knowledge of Khallad's possible participation in the Kuala Lumpur meeting until after the September 11 attacks.

This is an example of how day-to-day gaps in information sharing can emerge even in a situation of goodwill on all sides. The information was from a joint FBI/CIA source. The source spoke essentially no English. The FBI person on the scene overseas did not speak the languages the source spoke. Due to travel and security issues, the amount of time spent with the source was necessarily kept short. As a result, the CIA officer usually did not simultaneously translate either the questions or the answers for his accompanying FBI colleague, and friend.

For interviews without such simultaneous translation, the FBI agent on the scene received copies of the reports that the CIA disseminated to other agencies, but he was not given access to the CIA's internal operational traffic that contained more detail. The information regarding the January 2001 identification of Khallad was only reported in operational traffic to which the relevant FBI investigators did not have access. The CIA officer does not recall this particular identification and thus cannot say why it was not shared with his FBI colleague. But he may have misunderstood the possible significance of the new identification.

Al Mihdhar left the United States in June 2000. It is possible that if, in January 2001, agencies had resumed their search for him or placed him on the TIPOFF watchlist, they might have found him before or at the time al Mihdhar applied for a new visa in June 2001. Or they might have been alerted to him when he returned to the United States the following month. We cannot know.

SPRING 2001:
LOOKING AGAIN AT KUALA LUMPUR

By mid-May 2001, as the threat reports were surging again, a CIA official detailed to the International Terrorism Operations Section at the FBI wondered where the attacks might occur. We will call him John. John recalled the Kuala Lumpur travel of al Mihdhar and his associates around the Millennium. He searched the CIA's databases for information regarding the travel. On May 15 he and an official at CIA reexamined many of the old cables from early 2000, including the information that al Mihdhar had a U.S. visa, and that al Hazmi had come to Los Angeles on January 15, 2000.

The CIA official who reviewed the cables took no action regarding these cables. She cannot recall this work. John, however, began a lengthy exchange with a CIA analyst to figure out what these cables meant. He recognized the relationship to the bombing case, and he was aware that someone had identified Khallad in one of the surveillance photographs from the Malaysia meeting. He concluded that "something bad was definitely up." Despite the U.S. links evident in this traffic, John did not raise that aspect with his FBI counterparts. He was focused on Malaysia.

John's focus on the overseas target area might be understood from his description of the CIA as an agency that tended to play a "zone defense." In contrast, he said, the FBI tends to play "man-to-man." Desk officers at the CIA's Bin Laden Station did not have "cases" in the same sense as an FBI agent who works something beginning to end. Thus, when the trail went cold after the Kuala Lumpur meeting in January 2000, the desk officer moved on to different things. By the time the March 2000 cable arrived with information that one of the travelers had flown to Los Angeles, the case officer was not responsible for following up that information. While several individuals at the Bin Laden Station opened the cable when it arrived in March 2000, it was no one's concern, and no action was taken. We discussed some of the management issues raised by this in [an earlier] staff statement.

The CIA's zone defense concentrated on "where," not "who." Had its information been shared with the FBI, a combination of the CIA's zone defense and the FBI's man-to-man approach might have been far more productive.

AUGUST 2001:
THE SEARCH FOR AL MIHDHAR
AND AL HAZMI BEGINS AND FAILS

During the summer of 2001 John asked an FBI official detailed to the CIA to review all of the Kuala Lumpur materials one more time. We will call her Mary. He asked her to do the research in her free time. She began her work on July 24. That day she found the cable reporting that al Mihdhar had a visa to the United States. A week later she found the cable reporting that al Mihdhar's visa application—what was later discovered to be his first application—listed New York as his destination. On August 21 she located the March 2000 cable that "noted with interest" that al Hazmi had flown to Los Angeles in January 2000. She grasped the significance of this information.

Mary and an FBI analyst working the case, whom we will call Jane, promptly met with an INS [Immigration and Naturalization Service] representative at FBI Headquarters. On August 22 INS told them that al Mihdhar had entered the United States on January 15, 2000, and again on July 4, 2001. Jane and Mary also learned that there was no record that al Hazmi had left since January 2000, but they were not certain if he was still here and assumed that he had left with al Mihdhar in June 2000. They decided that if al Mihdhar was in the United States, he should be found.

They divided up the work. Mary asked the Bin Laden Station to draft a cable requesting that al Mihdhar and al Hazmi be put on the TIPOFF watchlist. Jane took responsibility for the search effort inside the United States. As the information indicated that al Mihdhar had last arrived in New York and this was determined to be related to the bin Laden case in New York, she began drafting a lead for the FBI's New York field office. She called an agent in New York to give him a "heads up" on the matter, but her draft lead was not sent until August 28. Her e-mail told the New York agent that she wanted him to get started on this as soon as possible, but she labeled the lead as "Routine." A "Routine" designation informs the receiving office that it has thirty days to respond to the lead.

The agent who received the lead forwarded it to his squad supervisor. That same day the supervisor forwarded the lead to an intelligence agent to open an intelligence case. He also sent it to the *Cole* case agents and an agent who had spent significant time in Malaysia searching for another Khalid—Khalid Sheikh Mohammed.

The suggested goal of the investigation was to locate al Mihdhar, determine his contacts and reasons for being in the United States, and possibly conduct an interview. Before sending the lead, Jane had discussed it with John, the CIA official on detail to the FBI, and with the acting head of the FBI's Bin Laden Unit. The discussion apparently was limited to whether the search should be classified as an intelligence investigation or as a criminal one, a legally important distinction for reasons we explained earlier. . . . Neither of those individuals apparently disagreed with the analyst's proposed plan. No one apparently felt they needed to inform higher levels of management in either the FBI or CIA about the case.

One of the *Cole* case agents read the lead with interest and contacted Jane to obtain more information. Jane took the position, however, that because the agent was a designated "criminal" agent, the "wall" kept him from participating in any search for al Mihdhar. In fact, she felt he had to destroy his copy of the lead because it contained information she believed could not be shared with any criminal agents. The Joint Inquiry covered the details of their heated exchanges, and we will not repeat them here. The result was that criminal agents who were knowledgeable about the *Cole* and experienced with criminal investigative techniques, including finding suspects and possible criminal charges, were excluded from the search.

Many witnesses have suggested that even if al Mihdhar had been found, there was nothing the agents could have done except follow him onto the plane. We believe this is incorrect. Both al Hazmi and al Mihdhar could have been held for immigration violations or as material witnesses in the *Cole* bombing case. Investigation or interrogation of these individuals, and their travel and financial activities, also may have yielded evidence of connections to other participants in the 9/11 plot. In any case, the opportunity did not arise.

Notably, the lead did not draw any connections between the threat reporting that had been coming in for months and the presence of two possible al Qaeda operatives in the United States. Moreover, there is no evidence that the issue was substantively discussed at any level above deputy chief of a section within the Counterterrorism Division at FBI headquarters.

The search was assigned to one FBI agent for whom this was his very first counterterrorism lead. By the terms of the lead, he was given 30 days to open an intelligence case and make some unspecified efforts to locate al Mihdhar. He started the process a week later. He checked local New York indices for criminal record and driver's license information and checked the hotel listed on al Mihdhar's U.S. entry form. On September 11 the agent sent a lead to Los Angeles based on the fact that al Mihdhar had initially arrived in Los Angeles in January 2000. Time had run out on the search.

THE PHOENIX MEMO

The Phoenix Memo was investigated at length by the Joint Inquiry. We will recap it briefly here. In July 2001, an FBI agent in the Phoenix field office sent a memo to FBI headquarters and to two agents on international terrorism squads in the New York field office advising of the "possibility of a coordinated effort by Osama bin Laden" to send students to the United States to attend civil aviation schools. The agent based his theory on the "inordinate number of individuals of investigative interest" attending such schools in Arizona.

The agent made four recommendations to FBI headquarters: to compile a list of civil aviation schools, to establish liaison with those schools, to discuss his theories about bin Laden with the Intelligence Community, and to seek authority to obtain visa information on persons applying to flight schools. His recommendations were not acted upon prior to September 11. His memo was forwarded to one field office. Managers of the Osama bin Laden unit and the Radical Fundamentalist Unit at FBI headquarters were addressees, but did not even see the memo until after September 11. No managers at headquarters saw the memo before September 11. The New York field office took no action. It was not shared outside the FBI.

As its author told us, the Phoenix Memo was not an alert about suicide pilots. His worry was more about a Pan Am 103 scenario in which explosives were placed on an aircraft. The memo's references to aviation training were broad, including electronics and aircraft maintenance.

MOUSSAOUI

On August 15, 2001, the Minneapolis FBI field office initiated an intelligence investigation on Zacarias Moussaoui. He had entered the country on February 23, 2001, and began flight lessons at Airman Flight School in Oklahoma City. He began flight training at the Pan American flight training school in Minneapolis on August 13. Moussaoui had none of the usual qualifications for flight training on Pan Am's Boeing 747 flight simulators. Contrary to popular belief, Moussaoui did not say he was not interested in learning how to take off or land. Instead, he stood out because, with little knowledge of flying, he wanted to learn how to take off and land a Boeing 747.

The FBI agent who handled the case in conjunction with the INS representative on the Minneapolis Joint Terrorism Task Force suspected Moussaoui of wanting to hijack planes. Because Moussaoui was a French national who had overstayed his visa, he was detained by the INS.

The FBI agent sent a summary of his investigation to FBI headquarters on August 18. In his message he requested assistance from the FBI field office in Oklahoma City and from the FBI legal attaché in Paris. Each of these offices responded quickly. By August 24 the Minneapolis agent had also contacted an FBI detailee and a CIA analyst at the Counterterrorist Center about the case. DCI Tenet was briefed about the Moussaoui case. He told us that no connection to al Qaeda was apparent to him before 9/11.

Moussaoui had lived in London, so the Minneapolis agent also requested assistance from the legal attaché in London. The legal attaché promptly prepared a written request of the British government for information concerning Moussaoui and hand-delivered the request on August 21. He informed the British of developments in the case on September 4. The case, though handled expeditiously at the American end, was not handled by the British as a priority amid a large number of other terrorist-related inquiries. On September 11, after the attacks, the legal attaché renewed his request for information.

After 9/11 the British government, in response to U.S. requests, supplied some basic biographical information about Moussaoui. The British government has informed us that it also tasked intelligence collection facilities for information potentially relating to Moussaoui. On September 13, the British received new, sensitive intelligence that Moussaoui had attended an al Qaeda training camp in Afghanistan. It passed this intelligence the same day to the United States.

Had this information been available in late August 2001, the Moussaoui case would almost certainly have received intense and much higher-level attention. Prior to 9/11, there was a continuing dispute between FBI agents in Minneapolis and supervisors at headquarters about whether evidence had been sufficient to seek a FISA warrant to search Moussaoui's computer hard drive and belongings. After 9/11, the FBI learned that Millennium terrorist Ressam, who was cooperating with investigators, could have recognized Moussaoui from the Afghan camps. Either the British information or the Ressam identification would have broken the logjam. A maximum U.S. effort to investigate Moussaoui could conceivably have unearthed his connections to the Hamburg cell, though this might have required an extensive effort, with help from foreign governments. The publicity about the threat also might have disrupted the plot. But this would have been a race against time.

INFORMATION ISSUES

We have identified several major issues that had a detrimental impact on the information flow between the agencies that caused the missed opportunities described above.

- There were organizational restrictions on information sharing. We heard numerous complaints regarding the lack of authorization to share information. This lack of authorization was not limited to low-level employees. Tom Pickard, who was acting director of the FBI in the summer of 2001, told us Dale Watson briefed him that the CIA was taking a second look at the Kuala Lumpur meeting. Pickard thought that concern about the meeting was driving the higher threat levels that summer. Pickard said that Watson told him this information was "close hold." Pickard said he understood this to mean that he had no authority to brief the Attorney General about the meeting.

- There were misunderstandings regarding responsibility for information sharing. The CIA has repeatedly argued that it did not withhold information from the FBI because it gave FBI detailees access to critical databases. The CIA believed the detailees were responsible for identifying and communicating information of interest to the FBI. The FBI did not understand this to be the case. There were no memoranda of understanding regarding the roles of detailees and no management direction overseeing them. The individuals who filled the roles did not view their primary roles to be information sharers. The problems of information flow also worked in reverse. The CIA complained its detailees did not get meaningful access to FBI's automated case system.

- There were different views on classification levels for identical information. We found that the CIA classified identical information at a significantly higher level than the FBI. This precluded important information from being available on the FBI agents' computers.

- We found there was an underlying concern by the CIA that information it shared with the FBI might be disclosed in the course of the discovery process or at trial.

- There were significant problems sharing information within the FBI, including the "wall" between criminal and intelligence investigations. . . .

IMMEDIATE RESPONSE TO 9/11

We conclude our statement with preliminary findings to date on two post–9/11 events: the flights of Saudi nationals departing the United States, and preventive detentions and other immigration law enforcement initiatives.

The Saudi Flights

National air space was closed on September 11. Fearing reprisals against Saudi nationals, the Saudi government asked for help in getting some of its citizens out of the country. We have not yet identified whom they contacted for help. But we have found that the request came to the attention of Richard Clarke and that each of the flights we have studied was investigated by the FBI and dealt with in a professional manner prior to its departure.

No commercial planes, including chartered flights, were permitted to fly into, out of, or within the United States until September 13, 2001. After the airspace reopened, six chartered flights with 142 people, mostly Saudi Arabian nationals, departed from the United States between September 14 and 24. One flight, the so-called bin Laden flight, departed the United States on September 20 with 26 passengers, most of them relatives of Osama bin Laden. We have found no credible evidence that any chartered flights of Saudi Arabian nationals departed the United States before the reopening of national airspace.

The Saudi flights were screened by law enforcement officials, primarily the FBI, to ensure that people on these flights did not pose a threat to national security, and that nobody of interest to the FBI with regard to the 9/11 investigation was allowed to leave the country. Thirty of the 142 people on these flights were interviewed by the FBI, including 22 of the 26 people (23 passengers and 3 private security guards) on the bin Laden flight. Many were asked detailed questions. None of the passengers stated that they had any recent contact with Osama bin Laden or knew anything about terrorist activity.

The FBI checked a variety of databases for information on the bin Laden flight passengers and searched the aircraft. It is unclear whether the TIPOFF terrorist watchlist was checked. At our request, the Terrorist Screening Center has rechecked the names of individuals on the flight manifests of these six Saudi flights against the current TIPOFF watchlist. There are no matches.

The FBI has concluded that nobody was allowed to depart on these six flights whom the FBI wanted to interview in connection with the 9/11 attacks, or who the FBI later concluded had any involvement in those attacks. To date, we have uncovered no evidence to contradict this conclusion.

Immigration Law Enforcement Initiatives

Beginning on September 11, 2001, Attorney General Ashcroft, with the FBI and, at times, with other cabinet departments, initiated a series of immigration-related programs to disrupt terrorist activities in the United States. We report preliminarily on four of them. We will report later on two other important initiatives—the voluntary interview program and the special registration program.

The "Special Interest" Detainees. Beginning on September 11, 2001, INS agents working in cooperation with the FBI began arresting individuals for immigration violations based on leads in the PENTTBOM case. Eventually, 768 so-called "special interest" aliens were detained. Attorney General Ashcroft told us that he saw his job in directing this effort as "risk minimization," both to find out who committed the attacks and to prevent a subsequent attack. His policy was that no "special interest" alien should be granted bond. Rather, they should be held until they were "cleared" of terrorist connections by the FBI and other agencies. Ashcroft also ordered all "special interest" immigration hearings closed to the public and press. INS attorneys charged with prosecuting the immigration violations had difficulty getting information about the detainees, and their terrorist connections, from the FBI. The "clearance" process approved by the Justice Department was involved and time consuming, lasting on average 80 days. We continue to investigate what counterterrorism benefits and costs were associated with these detentions.

Twenty-Day Hold. After September 11, the Department of Justice pressed the State Department to reduce the number of visas issued to individuals from countries with significant Muslim populations. Justice Department proposals included stopping the issuance of all visas, suspending visa issuance entirely to nationals of selected countries, and requiring that the FBI and CIA check each applicant from certain countries before a visa is issued. Effective November 14, 2001, the State Department issued a blanket 20-day hold before any visa could be issued to males 16 to 45 years old from 26 countries in the Middle East and North Africa, plus Bangladesh, Malaysia and Indonesia. This program was discontinued in October 2002. Records we have reviewed suggest it yielded no useful anti-terrorist information and led to no visa denials.

The Visas Condor Program was initiated on January 26, 2002. It mandated additional screening by the FBI and other agencies for certain visa applicants from 26 predominantly Muslim countries. However, neither the FBI nor the CIA was able to process these visa applicants in a timely fashion because of their other burgeoning responsibilities after the September 11 attacks. In July 2002, the FBI acknowledged it could not meet the agreed upon 30-day target for name checks, and the State Department agreed to place these visa applicants on indefinite hold until the FBI responded. In September 2002 the CIA withdrew from the program because it had uncovered no significant information from these visa applicants. The CIA was already placing all important information into the TIPOFF terrorist watchlist, used by the State Department to screen these same applicants at the outset. Approximately 130,000 name checks have been completed. At present, there are nearly 1,700 checks that have been pending for more than 30 days, almost 1,100 for more than four months. No terrorists have been uncovered by the Visas Condor program.

Absconder Apprehension Initiative. Absconders are non-citizens who fail to depart the United States after receiving a final order of deportation from an Immigration Judge. After September 11, INS Commissioner [James] Ziglar proposed the inclusion of the names of 314,000 absconders in the National Crime Information Center database. Attorney General Ashcroft decided to start a program called the Absconder Apprehension Initiative targeting a smaller number of citizens from countries where there has been al Qaeda terrorist presence or activity, to locate and remove them. The INS mounted a nationwide search for over 5,000 non-citizens under this program. By early 2003, 1,139 had been apprehended, of whom 803 had been deported, 224 were in custody awaiting deportation, and U.S. Attorneys were criminally prosecuting 45. So far, we have not learned that any of the absconders were deported under a terrorism statute, prosecuted for terrorist related crimes, or linked in any way to terrorism. Our investigation continues.

Barbara Grewe, Michael Jacobson, Thomas Eldridge, and Susan Ginsburg did much of the work reflected in this statement. We have built upon the substantial work carried out by the Joint Inquiry of the House and Senate Intelligence Committees. We have obtained excellent cooperation from the CIA, FBI, and the Office of Inspector General of the Department of Justice. They made significant material available for the preparation of this statement.

The Presidential Daily Brief, August 6, 2001

Here is the text of the CIA report prepared at President Bush's request and delivered to the president at his ranch in Crawford, Texas on August 6, 2001. Portions identifying foreign intelligence sources were deleted by the White House. A facsimile of the Presidential Daily Brief is included in the Appendix of this book.

BIN LADEN DETERMINED TO STRIKE IN U.S.

Clandestine, foreign government, and media reports indicate bin Laden since 1997 has wanted to conduct terrorist attacks in the U.S. Bin Laden implied in U.S. television interviews in 1997 and 1998 that his followers would follow the example of World Trade Center bomber Ramzi Yousef and "bring the fighting to America."

After U.S. missile strikes on his base in Afghanistan in 1998, bin Laden told followers he wanted to retaliate in Washington, according to a [deleted] service.

An Egyptian Islamic Jihad (E.I.J.) operative told an [deleted] service at the same time that bin Laden was planning to exploit the operative's access to the U.S. to mount a terrorist strike.

The millennium plotting in Canada in 1999 may have been part of bin Laden's first serious attempt to implement a terrorist strike in the U.S. Convicted plotter Ahmed Ressam has told the F.B.I. that he conceived the idea to attack Los Angeles International Airport himself, but that bin Laden lieutenant Abu Zubaydah encouraged him and helped facilitate the operation. Ressam also said that in 1998 Abu Zubaydah was planning his own U.S. attack.

Ressam says bin Laden was aware of the Los Angeles operation.

Although bin Laden has not succeeded, his attacks against the U.S. embassies in Kenya and Tanzania in 1998 demonstrate that he prepares operations years in advance and is not deterred by setbacks. Bin Laden associates surveilled our embassies in Nairobi and Dar es Salaam as early as 1993, and some members of the Nairobi cell planning the bombings were arrested and deported in 1997.

Al Qaeda members—including some who are U.S. citizens— have resided in or traveled to the U.S. for years, and the group apparently maintains a support structure that could aid attacks. Two al Qaeda members found guilty in the conspiracy to bomb our embassies in East Africa were U.S. citizens, and a senior E.I.J. member lived in California in the mid-1990s.

A clandestine source said in 1998 that a bin Laden cell in New York was recruiting Muslim-American youth for attacks.

We have not been able to corroborate some of the more sensational threat reporting, such as that from a [deleted] service in 1998 saying that bin Laden wanted to hijack a U.S. aircraft to gain the release of "Blind Sheik" Omar Abd al Rahman and other U.S.-held extremists.

Nevertheless, F.B.I. information since that time indicates patterns of suspicious activity in this country consistent with preparations for hijackings or other types of attacks, including recent surveillance of federal buildings in New York.

The F.B.I. is conducting approximately 70 full field investigations throughout the U.S. that it considers bin Laden-related. C.I.A. and the F.B.I. are investigating a call to our embassy in the U.A.E. in May saying that a group of bin Laden supporters was in the U.S. planning attacks with explosives.

·   ·   ·

Excerpts of testimony from Thomas J. Pickard, J. Cofer Black, and John Ashcroft

_____

EXCERPTS OF TESTIMONY FROM THOMAS J. PICKARD, FORMER ACTING DIRECTOR, FEDERAL BUREAU OF INVESTIGATION

"The attorney general on May 10th issued budget guidance for us and I did not see [terrorism] as a top item on his agenda."

No one knows how deeply many employees of the FBI are troubled by the haunting events leading up to that day. In my view, the tragedy of 9/11 clearly demonstrates the high costs for the collective failure of the U.S. government to penetrate the inner workings of al Qaeda or to deal with terrorism, as it was then, as it is now, a war against the United States, intended to inflict as many American casualties as possible. For many complex reasons we did not develop the necessary intelligence, either through our own resources or through foreign resources, to sufficiently understand and react to their planning, communications, control and capacity to do us harm. I was the acting director of the FBI in the summer of 2001. The intelligence and the experience I had available to me at the time were what I acted upon. As I recall, during the period January to September 2001, the FBI received over 1,000 threats. Many of these threats had great specificity and others were very general in nature.

All were taken seriously, but the volume was daunting. The increase in the chatter was by far the most serious, but it was also the most difficult to deal with. There was no specificity as to what, where and when. We knew the who, but only that it was al Qaeda. I had regular conversations with the director of CIA and his deputy and the attorney general and his deputy about the threats we were receiving and to learn if there was anything more that would help us understand the fragmentary information we had. The only news I received was that the chatter subsided in August 2001.

Further, I personally spoke, both collectively and individually, with each of the special agents in charge of the FBI's 56 field offices and with the assistant directors at FBI headquarters about what we knew and what we should be doing. Most of what I heard pointed overseas. For example, at the recommendation of the assistant director of New York and the head of counterterrorism, I removed the agents from Yemen due to the threat level and the chatter. During the summer, we continued to pursue our investigations of the bombing of the African embassies and the U.S.S. Cole. These were not just investigations to bring people responsible to justice, but they were also giving us valuable intelligence on al Qaeda. These investigations did more than advance the prosecution of these matters; they provided some of the best intelligence the U.S. government possessed about al Qaeda. Many of those arrested and brought back to the United States started to cooperate with the FBI. They provided us not only information about the bombings, but also became valuable resources in identifying al Qaeda members to U.S. intelligence. They gave us unique insights into al Qaeda's command and control.

We also exploited their pocket letter, cell phones, calling cards, credit cards and hotel registrations for links to other members. The agents were tireless in pursuing these bits and pieces of information. The New York office of the FBI, the Joint Terrorism Task Force and the U.S. attorney's office in the Southern District of New York had become very knowledgeable and adept at exploiting these investigations. The FBI also had Foreign Intelligence Surveillance Act coverage on individuals in the United States, which has recently been discussed. This too gave us links to other possible members of al Qaeda. These investigations and coverages were the direct result of FBI investigations, as well as coming from the United States and foreign intelligence communities.

None of what we knew or learned pointed to what was about to happen on 9/11. To the contrary, all of these steps were not enough given what we had learned about the 19 hijackers since September 11th. The plot was hatched probably in Afghanistan, it was honed in Germany and was financed in the Middle East. Each of the hijackers was selected to ensure that he could come and go into the United States without attracting attention, not a difficult thing to do with our open and overwhelmed borders. They did not receive support knowingly from anyone in the United States, nor did they contact known al Qaeda sympathizers in the United States. They utilized publicly accessible Internet connections, prepaid calling cards to communicate and to escape detection by U.S. authorities. These 19 acted flawlessly in their planning and execution. They successfully exploited every weakness from our borders to our cockpit doors.

The members of al Qaeda are a formidable enemy. I have personally met with Ramzi Yousef, the mastermind of the 1993 World Trade Center attack. He is poised, articulate, well educated. He speaks English with a British accent as well as six other languages. He has degrees in chemistry and electrical engineering. And in 1995 he utilized a laptop computer with an encryption program on it. I have also led two separate teams overseas to return Eyad Mahmoud Ismail Najim, who drove the van into the World Trade Center in 1993, and Wali Khan, who was part of the Manila Air plot, back to the United States to stand trial. Both were fairly well-educated, poised young men dedicated to a jihad in America. I've used the word enemy to describe them because that's what they are. They are dedicated terrorists willing to even commit suicide for their beliefs. The camps in Afghanistan and elsewhere were graduating thousands like them who are educated, committed and even computer savvy. Al Qaeda was turning out five times more graduates from their camps than the CIA and the FBI were graduating from their training schools. I could only utilize handcuffs on them. President Bush and the U.S. military gave them something more effective—bombs, bullets and bayonets.

QUESTIONS FROM COMMISSIONERS

JOHN F. LEHMAN: [In the August 6 Presidential Daily Brief] the presumably FBI sources report and tell the president that there are some 70 full field investigations going on. We previously had testimony from Mr. Berger that, in response to queries to the FBI on al Qaeda, the response was, We got it covered. There have been reports . . . that Attorney General Ashcroft, when querying about the terrorist threat, the FBI response was essentially, We've got it covered. This PDB has the same tone. We're doing 70 field investigations on suspected al Qaeda personnel in the United States. We've got it covered. And our understanding is that this was, to put it nicely, a bit of an exaggeration, because 70 full field investigations have the aura of being a major, massive, going to battle stations, where in fact it really referred to every single individual that was under investigation. So it was an exaggeration which gave a wrong perception at a time when the threat that we now know was really much further along. . . . Could you address that?

PICKARD: Mr. Lehman, you're correct with approximately 70 full field investigations. They focused on 70 individuals, give or take some. But, first off, I did not have access to the PDB. I had never seen a PDB until September 11th. So the FBI did not get to vet the article. I would find it a mischaracterization to say that anyone in the FBI said, We've got them covered. We only knew what we knew. The intelligence we had led us to these 70 individuals and we worked on them as best we could. . . . Those 70 in the United States, they were partly a result of FBI investigations, but credit has to be given very greatly to the CIA for giving us the information and for the other members of the intelligence community that they provided us with information to direct us to look at these individuals. Otherwise, we're operating in a vacuum where we don't know who to be on. We cannot, by any stretch, target any persons of a particular faith just because they belong to a faith. We're trying to identify people who are al Qaeda operatives who might give either some kind of support, whether it's financial or otherwise, to these individuals.

· · ·

TIMOTHY J. ROEMER: . . . Did you brief the attorney general on terrorism?

PICKARD: Yes, I did.

ROEMER: And what—how many times did you brief him on terrorism?

PICKARD: After Director [Louis] Freeh left the FBI, the attorney general had me come in on June 22nd to meet with him and he appointed me as the acting director of the FBI. And then on June 28th I had a meeting with the attorney general, the deputy attorney general, and I believe his chief of staff was in parts of that meeting as well as Assistant Director [Ruben] Garcia.

ROEMER: So what would you guess, Mr. Pickard? How many times did you brief . . .

PICKARD: At least three times.

ROEMER: Three times. And what were the attorney general's priorities with respect to terrorism? Was it a top tier priority for the attorney general?

PICKARD: It was a top tier for the FBI. The attorney general on May 10th issued budget guidance for us and I did not see that as a top item on his agenda.

ROEMER: Did you take that to the attorney general that you were concerned that that was not a top item for him? . . .

PICKARD: . . . I spoke to the attorney general briefly and asked him if I could appeal it and he told me, yes, I could; put it in writing. I had our finance and counterterrorism people put together an appeal of that decision. And then on September 12th, I read the denial of that appeal from the attorney general.

ROEMER: So you had a May 10th memo on the attorney general's priorities that you objected to. And then you had a meeting in August where you personally appealed to the attorney general and received a letter from him saying no to the increases that you received on what date?

PICKARD: I received that on September 12th, that denial.

ROEMER: So what does this say about counterterrorism as a priority for the attorney general? Do you think it was not the priority that you hoped it would be, commensurate with the FBI's?

PICKARD: I only had the perspective to see it from my view of the FBI. I don't know all that the attorney general had to look at with the hundred thousand employees of the Department of Justice.

. . .

RICHARD BEN-VENISTE: [A]ccording to our staff report, you told them that in June 2001, you met with Attorney General Ashcroft and he told you that you would be the acting FBI director.

PICKARD: That's correct.

BEN-VENISTE: You had some seven or eight meetings with the attorney general?

PICKARD: Somewhere in that number. I have the exact number, but I don't know the total.

BEN-VENISTE: And according to the statement that our staff took from you, you said that you would start each meeting discussing either counterterrorism or counterintelligence. At the same time the threat level was going up and was very high. Mr. Watson had come to you and said that the CIA was very concerned that there would be an attack. You said that you told the attorney general this fact repeatedly in these meetings. Is that correct?

PICKARD: I told him at least on two occasions.

BEN-VENISTE: And you told the staff according to this statement that Mr. Ashcroft told you that he did not want to hear about this anymore. Is that correct?

PICKARD: That is correct.

BEN-VENISTE: Let me ask you about this PDB. You never vetted the PDB. You never saw the PDB. You never knew that it was going to be produced. Correct?

PICKARD: That's correct.

BEN-VENISTE: And it would appear that the author or the individual at CIA who edited this PDB by entitling the PDB Bin Laden Determined to Strike in the United States wanted to get the president's attention because most of the threat reporting seemed to be that the heightened alert reflected the potential for a threat overseas. And that this was perhaps the same syndrome as the white van in the sniper case that we saw, where everybody's looking in one direction for one thing, but not looking in the other direction where something might occur. Condoleezza Rice said that when she saw this PDB, it was certainly not reassuring. And quite clearly we know, whether the information was right, wrong, or in the middle somewhere, this author was prescient. The attack came in the United States. Now my question to you, sir, is that if you had the information that the president of the United States was requesting what information the FBI had up to that moment about the potentiality for a strike by bin Laden in the United States, would you not have pulsed the FBI to determine from every FBI agent in this country what information they had at that moment that might indicate the possibility of a terrorist attack here?

PICKARD: Yes, I would have.

BEN-VENISTE: And you learned on September 11th three things, if I understand your testimony. Number one, you learned about Moussaoui.

PICKARD: Right.

BEN-VENISTE: Number two, you learned about the Phoenix memo. Number three, you learned about two of the hijackers who were in the United States, who the FBI was looking for. Had you learned that information soon after August the 6th, was there not a possibility that you could have utilized that information, connected the information, put it together with what you already knew and taken some action?

PICKARD: I don't know. Moussaoui was arrested on August 15th. The information about the other two hijackers came to the FBI's attention, I believe, August 23rd, and later on, on August 27th. To bring these three diverse pieces of information together, absent the afternoon of September 11th, I don't know, with all of the information the FBI collects, whether we would have had the ability to hone in specifically on those three items.

BEN-VENISTE: Certainly if you knew that the president of the United States was asking . . .

PICKARD: I was not informed that the president was asking.

BEN-VENISTE: . . . Let me ask you this. Did the president or the attorney general of the United States ever ask to meet with you following August 6th?

PICKARD: No. There was a policy that I was not to go to the White House unless the attorney general or the deputy attorney general or someone from the Department of Justice, either I had informed them or they went with me . . . .

.   .   .

EXCERPTS OF TESTIMONY FROM
J. COFER BLACK,
FORMER DIRECTOR,
CIA COUNTERTERRORIST CENTER

"We approached almost two dozen cooperative services to go after Osama bin Laden-related targets worldwide. At best we were hoping to delay any attack to buy ourselves more time to find out what was planned."

2001 started out with many distinct terrorist threats that required our attention. Again, this is a highly classified area. I'll attempt to summarize what I can tell you. CTC was continuing to work with the FBI on the U.S.S. *Cole* attack, working to follow through on a major multi-country takedown of terrorist cells in Southeast Asia, responding to a hostage situation in Ecuador, dealing with another hostage crisis in the Philippines. Overshadowing all this was the rising volume of threat reporting. By the summer of 2001, we were seeing an increased amount of so-called chatter alluding to a massive terrorist strike.

We were receiving this intelligence not only from our own sources, but also from the liaison. Human intelligence was providing the same kinds of insights. Disruption efforts and detentions were also corroborating our concerns about a coming attack. None of this, unfortunately, specified method, time or place. Where we had clues, it looked like planning was under way for an attack in the Middle East or Europe. At the same time, we were working on two tracks: to go after al Qaeda and to disrupt the terrorist attacks.

In going after the organization, we were doing several things simultaneously. First we had to penetrate the threat. To do this, we needed to penetrate both the al Qaeda safe haven in Afghanistan and the organization itself to collect enhanced human and technical intelligence on its activities and to understand it well enough to conduct offensive operations against it. Second, we had to look for opportunities to take down al Qaeda cells. With the intelligence we collected, we worked to create plans to disrupt or degrade al Qaeda. Make no mistake: This was a hard mission with a low probability for success in the near term. Finally, we were developing new capabilities to enable us to penetrate and take down the organization. These ranged from Predator to developing new approaches for going after the Afghan safe haven, by working with groups within the country and with any cooperative service in neighboring countries. A number of these initiatives were also included in the so-called December 2000 Blue Sky memo and in follow-on discussions in the CSG process that had been previously discussed by others and in your staff statements.

In order to disrupt, we approached almost two dozen cooperative services to go after Osama bin Laden-related targets worldwide. At best we were hoping to delay any attack to buy ourselves more time to find out what was planned. We were looking for every opportunity to go on the offensive against al Qaeda. Where we did not have enough information, we warned. We produced CIA and community analysis that examined the heightened threat situation. Your staff's statement this morning ran titles of a number of these documents. More broadly, I also want to emphasize that CTC and the intelligence community produced significant strategic analysis that examined the growing threat from the international jihadist networks and al Qaeda. I believe that the record shows that the U.S. government understood the nature of the threat.

This understanding was the result of a range of products we produced or contributed to, including: personal interaction via participation in the Counterterrorism Security Group; periodic stand-back assessments on OBL and Sunni extremist-related topics; contributing to the annual Patterns of Global Terrorism; and outside the executive branch, activities such as the DCI's worldwide threat briefings; support for the Bremer commission on terrorism; and briefings for the HPSCI Terrorism Subcommittee. But ultimately, we were not able to stop what happened on 9/11 despite our actions and our warnings. I promised to be brief, so I'll close with a final thought. What I have been largely talking about is what the Counterterrorism Center can and has done, but ultimately what we at the agency do is deal with the symptoms of terrorism at a tactical level. As long as there are people who are not happy with their lot in life, as long as the United States is perceived to somehow be the cause of this unhappiness, there will be terrorism. No matter how many plots we uncover . . . .

Mr. Chairman, we need to remind the American public of this reality. Those like the families who have lived through the horrors of 9/11 will never forget. But I fear sometimes, that the rest of the country is losing sight of the long and hard way ahead. At the more strategic level, the only way to address terrorism is to deal with the issues that create terrorism, to resolve them where possible, and where that's not possible to ensure that there is an alternative to violence. And that is not something that the Counterterrorism Center or CIA can do. That is a mission for the broader United States government. Prior to this hearing, I contacted former Counterterrorism Center colleagues at our headquarters here in Virginia and those that are overseas and now in harm's way. I asked them the question, What am I going to tell these people? It should not be my words alone, but it should be ours. And hauntingly, all of my CTC friends, independently, said exactly the same thing. They used the same words and they said them in the same order: We are profoundly sorry. We did all we could. We did our best. And they said make them understand how few we were and what we had to deal with. The shortage of money and people seriously hurt our operations and analysis.

. . .

EXCERPTS OF TESTIMONY FROM
JOHN ASHCROFT, ATTORNEY GENERAL

"Let our money do the talking. In the budgets proposed prior to September 11th, the total [counterterrorism] increases were 72 percent greater than the total increases for drugs and gun prosecutions combined."

[F]or the time being, al Qaeda's slaughter has ceased on America's soil. We've been aggressive, we've been tough and we've suffered no small amount of criticism for being tough in our tough tactics. We accept this criticism for what it is: the price we are privileged to pay for our liberty. Had I known a terrorist attack on the United States was imminent in 2001, I would have unloaded our full arsenal of weaponry against it. Despite the inevitable criticism, the Justice Department's warriors, our agents and our prosecutors, would have been unleashed. Every tough tactic we have deployed since the attacks would have been deployed before the attacks. But the simple fact of September 11th is this: We did not know an attack was coming because for nearly a decade our government had blinded itself to its enemies. Our agents were isolated by government-imposed walls, handcuffed by government-imposed restrictions and starved for basic information technology. The old national intelligence system in place on September 11th was destined to fail. This commission can serve a noble purpose. Your responsibility is to examine the root causes of September 11th and to help the United States prevent another terrorist attack. . . .

In February 2001, shortly after becoming attorney general, I reviewed [covert action authorities directed at Osama bin Laden prior to 2001]. Let me be clear: My thorough review revealed no covert action program to kill bin Laden. There was a covert action program to capture bin Laden for criminal prosecution, but even this program was crippled by a snarled web of requirements, restrictions and regulations that prevented decisive action by our men and women in the field. When they most needed clear, understandable guidance, our agents and operatives were given instead the language of lawyers. Even if they could have penetrated bin Laden's training camps they would have needed a battery of attorneys to approve the capture.

With unclear guidance, our covert action teams' risk of injury may have exceeded the risk to Osama bin Laden. On March 7, 2001, I met with National Security Adviser Condoleezza Rice. I recommended that the covert action authorities be clarified and be expanded to allow for decisive, lethal action. We should end the failed capture policy, I said. We should find and kill bin Laden. I recall that Dr. Rice agreed and gave Director Tenet the responsibility for drafting, clarifying and expanding the new authorities. My second point today goes to the heart of this commission's duty to uncover the facts. The single greatest structural cause for the September 11th problem was the wall that segregated or separated criminal investigators and intelligence agents. Government erected this wall, government buttressed this wall and before September 11th government was blinded by this wall. In 1995, the Justice Department embraced flawed legal reasoning, imposing a series of restrictions on the FBI that went beyond what the law required.

The 1995 guidelines and the procedures developed around them imposed draconian barriers, barriers between the law enforcement and intelligence communities. The wall effectively excluded prosecutors from intelligence investigations. The wall left intelligence agents afraid to talk with criminal prosecutors or agents. In 1995, the Justice Department designed a system that was destined to fail. In the days before September 11th, the wall specifically impeded the investigation of Zacarias Moussaoui, investigation of Khalid al Mihdhar and Nawaf al Hazmi. After the FBI arrested Moussaoui, agents became suspicious of his interest in commercial aircraft and sought approval for a criminal search warrant to search his computer. The warrant was rejected because FBI officials feared breaching the wall. When the CIA finally told the FBI that al Mihdhar and al Hazmi were in the country in late August, agents in New York searched for the suspects. But because of the wall, FBI headquarters refused to allow criminal investigators who knew the most about recent al Qaeda attacks to join the hunt for suspected terrorists. At that time, a frustrated FBI investigator wrote headquarters, and I'm quoting: Whatever has happened to this, some day somebody— someone will die. And, wall or not, the public will not understand why we were not more effective in throwing every resource we had at certain problems. Let's hope the National Security Law Unit [NSLU] will stand behind their decision then, especially since the biggest threat to us, OBL, is getting the most protection. FBI headquarters responded, and I quote: We're all frustrated with this issue. These are the rules. NSLU does not make them up. But somebody did make these rules. Somebody built this wall.

The basic architecture for the wall in the 1995 guidelines was contained in a classified memorandum entitled Instructions for Separation of Certain Foreign Counterintelligence and Criminal Investigations. The memorandum ordered FBI Director Louis Freeh and others, quote, We believe that it is prudent to establish a set of instructions that will more clearly separate the counterintelligence investigation from the more limited, but continued criminal investigations. These procedures, the memo went on to say, which go beyond what is legally required, will prevent any risk of creating an unwarranted appearance that FISA is being used to avoid procedural safeguards which would apply in a criminal investigation. This memorandum laid the foundation for a wall separating the criminal and intelligence investigations, as a matter of fact, established the wall following the 1993 World Trade Center attack, which at the time was the largest international terrorism attack on American soil, the largest prior to September 11th.

Although you understand the debilitating impact of the wall, I cannot imagine that the commission knew about this memorandum. So I have had it declassified for you and the public to review. Full disclosure compels me to inform you that the author of this memorandum is a member of the commission. By 2000, the Justice Department was so addicted to the wall it actually opposed legislation to lower the wall. Finally, the USA Patriot Act tore down this wall between our intelligence and law enforcement personnel in 2001. And when the Patriot Act was challenged, the FISA court of review upheld the law, ruling that the 1995 guidelines were required by neither the Constitution nor the law.

QUESTIONS FROM COMMISSIONERS

JAMES R. THOMPSON: Acting Director Pickard testified this afternoon that he briefed you twice on al Qaeda and Osama bin Laden and when he sought to do so again you told him you didn't need to hear from him again. Can you comment on that please?

ASHCROFT: First of all, Acting Director Pickard and I had more than two meetings. We had regular meetings. Secondly, I did never speak to him saying that I did not want to hear about terrorism. I care greatly about the safety and security of the American people and was very interested in terrorism and specifically interrogated him about threats to the American people and domestic threats in particular. One of the first items which came to my attention—which I mentioned in my opening remarks—was the question of whether we wanted to capture or find and kill bin Laden.

I carried that immediately to the national security adviser and expressed myself in that matter. Together with the vice president of the United States, we got a briefing at FBI headquarters regarding terrorism. And I asked the question, Why can't we arrest these people because I believe an aggressive arrest and prosecution model is the way to disrupt terrorism? These are things about which I care deeply. When the Senate Appropriations Committee met on May the 9th, in the summer of 2001, I told the committee that my number one priority was the attack against terror; that we would protect Americans from terror. I wrote later to them a confirming letter saying that we had no higher priority. These are the kinds of things that I did in order to communicate very clearly my interest in making sure that we would be prepared against terror. In addition when we went for the largest increase in counterterrorism budgeting before 9/11, in the last five years, that signaled a priority in that respect. And when we, for the next year, had a 13 percent higher counterterrorism budget than was provided in the last year of the Clinton administration, it was also a signal that counterterrorism was a matter of great concern to us and that we would treat it seriously. . . .

THOMPSON: . . . Sometimes in this country we fall victim to the notion of fighting the last war. And my guess is Osama bin Laden and al Qaeda are not going to fight the last war, they're going to fight a new war, perhaps, in the future. We've responded with greatly increased security precautions to the hijackings that took place on September 11th. But who in the government, who in the

Bush administration, is worrying about the next war and other means that al Qaeda may use to attack us—or other groups, Hezbollah, Hamas, other groups—on our soil, on other portions of our infrastructure besides aircraft and airports? Our food supply. Our water supply. Our oil pipelines. Our railroads. Our chemical factories. Who's worrying about that, and how are they worrying about that? And what assurance do the American people have that somebody is indeed worrying about the next war?

ASHCROFT: Well, frankly, there are a number of us who are worrying about the next war, and we understand that al Qaeda is very likely to change its method of operation and its style to avoid detection. And it's something when we have to understand the nature of this enemy that we face. It's an enemy that is not stupid. This is not some garden variety criminal who is robbing a 7-Eleven. They plan well. They undertake actions that last for years. They seek to inflict mass casualties. We understand that they might seek to use a different style of individual, individuals who would come from different countries, that it's clear that we know that they have interest in poisons, that they have interest in toxicity, in evil chemistry and evil biology, as well as the interest which they have had in explosives.

We've seen a wide variety of explosives used around the world in the proliferation of terrorism that has followed 9/11. It's not been used here and we're grateful that we've been successful in keeping it from happening here. But this administration has tasked every quadrant of the administration to be alert. In agriculture, I know very much the concerns of Secretary [Ann] Veneman. I know in transportation, the concerns of Secretary [Norman] Mineta. And I know in energy the kinds of concerns that have been expressed by Secretary [Spencer] Abraham, and the list could go on completely. I guess I would say that we need to continue to do everything possible. When you look around the world and we see that even in cultures that are very attuned and very focused on disrupting terrorism that they are not always successful, and so we have to be at the highest level of readiness and anticipation.

. . .

RICHARD BEN-VENISTE: . . . Let me ask you about the August 6th PDB memorandum, sir. It is correct, is it not, that you did not receive that document contemporaneously?

ASHCROFT: I did not receive that document in the August 2001 timeframe.

BEN-VENISTE: When was the first you had seen it?

ASHCROFT: I think I saw that in the last several days.

BEN-VENISTE: And so, unlike in the previous administration, the attorney general of the United States in the Bush administration was not a recipient of the PDB memorandum; is that correct?

ASHCROFT: Not prior to 9/11.

BEN-VENISTE: 9/11. That has changed since?

ASHCROFT: I am involved regularly with briefing of the president in regard to terrorist threats. And I accompany the director of the FBI to a morning briefing with the president, which briefing is attended by the director of the CIA and other officials, including director of homeland security. And I think you're familiar with that, I need not . . .

BEN-VENISTE: Yes, I am, sir. If you put yourself back in time to early August of 2001, aside from not receiving the PDB, were you made aware from any source that the president of the United States had requested a briefing with respect to the potential for an attack by bin Laden in the United States?

ASHCROFT: This was the kind of information I was asking when I was briefed by the CIA and when I was briefed by the FBI. I was not aware that the president of the United States had made a request in that respect.

BEN-VENISTE: Had you been aware, would you not have made sure that the president received a comprehensive report from the FBI?

ASHCROFT: Any time the president would ask for information from the FBI it would have been my intention to provide the president with a comprehensive report from the FBI. We were not into giving the president less than comprehensive . . .

BEN-VENISTE: I understand that, sir.

ASHCROFT: . . . responses. And had the president asked the FBI for information and I'd been aware of it—and I would have expected to be aware of it—I would have encouraged the FBI to be comprehensive. . . .

BEN-VENISTE: I'm pleased to have been able to give you the opportunity to clarify that issue for all who have written to this commission and communicated in other ways about their questions about that, sir. Let me also give you the opportunity to respond to Mr. Pickard's testimony just a little while ago about a statement which he claims that you made with respect to priorities. And in that regard, it is correct, is it not—because we have looked at the May 10th, 2001, guidance for preparing fiscal year 2003 budgets in which you indicate your priorities—there are five goals, strategic goals laid out there? It does not appear that terrorism was one of them. Is that correct?

ASHCROFT: Let me make an explanation here, because I welcome, as well, this opportunity. The date preceding, on May the 9th, I met with the Senate Appropriations Committee and was asked about my priorities. I said my number one priority was to protect the people of the United States against terrorism. The Department of Justice, required by the Congress to have a strategic plan, followed that plan. The plan was developed in the year 2000 by my predecessor and had a set of strategic goals. They're listed here early in the book and they are similar to the goals—they are, as a matter of fact, the goals which were used in large measure for the May 10th memorandum. And they cite some additional goals to terrorism. There's no question about that. Let me just go—because our time is limited . . .

Ben-Veniste: I'm sorry. Did you say in the prior plan there were citations to counterterrorism?

Ashcroft: Well, there was no major goal of counterterrorism, but under . . . the Keep America Safe by enforcing federal criminal laws, [former Attorney General Janet Reno] did have deter and detect terrorist incidents. And this is the kind of—let me just cut to the chase here to see where we were. Let our money do the talking. In the budgets proposed prior to September 11th, the total CT increases were 72 percent greater than the total increases for drugs and gun prosecutions combined. Now, those were the other issues that were listed as priorities of the department.

What we had was a combined total of increases of $683.1 million for drugs and gun prosecutions. We had a combined counterterrorism-related budget increase of $1,175.2 million, 72 percent higher for counterterrorism-related items than for items related to the other priorities which we had stated, drug interdiction and the prosecution of gun criminals. Now I don't mean to discount those priorities. Thousands of people die on our streets as a result of gun crimes. And we are very grateful for our record there. But let the record be clear that when it comes to where the appropriation was, that we had a $1.175 billion increase for counterterrorism in those first two budgets, a $0.683 billion, or $683 million increase on drugs and guns.

.   .   .

Jamie S. Gorelick: . . . You said in response to—I think it was Commissioner Ben-Veniste's question—that you, indeed, had been struck from the list of senior executives in the administration who got the presidential daily brief. I think you said you did not get it. And that is curious, I think, given Dr. Rice's testimony that the domestic aspect of our national security was largely in the

Department of Justice and FBI bailiwick. You, when you were interviewed by our staff with regard to the adequacy of the FBI's response to the intelligence that was coming out in the summer of '01, said that you accepted the FBI's assurance that the threats were overseas and, sort of, assumed that things must be in hand and that whatever they were doing was adequate to respond. And then you said, I think quite candidly, that this was a dangerous assumption to make. Now here is my question: You did not get the presidential daily brief, but you did get the senior executive intelligence brief that was provided to the next rung of the government. Is that correct? You got that daily?

Ashcroft: The SEIB . . .

Gorelick: The SEIB.

Ashcroft: . . . was available to me.

Gorelick: On August 7, 2001, an SEIB that reflected much of—although it was not identical to—much of the content of the August 6th presidential daily brief came out. And I would like to ask you if you remember seeing a document headed, Terrorism: Bin Laden Determined To Strike In The United States, in the SEIB.

Ashcroft: I do not remember seeing that. I was in—I believe I was in Chicago speaking at the American Bar Association meeting, I believe, at the time. So I do not have a recollection of seeing that.

Gorelick: Did your staff regularly brief you on the intelligence when you returned?

Ashcroft: I was briefed, and items of interest were noted for me from time to time by my staff.

Gorelick: Would something like this, which is a memorandum

that is going out to your colleagues, hundreds of your colleagues in the government, saying that bin Laden is determined to strike in the United States, been an item of significance that you would think would have been briefed to you?

ASHCROFT: These items had been briefed to me. They had been briefed to me by the FBI, they have been briefed to me by the CIA. The administration asked me to get briefings when appropriate in regard to these measures. I remember Ms. Rice, for example, early in July, during the threat period and the heightened and elevated threat, asking me if I would receive a briefing from the CIA because she thought it important. It's that kind of briefing that I received early. The CIA, we have reconstructed it from the slides they used, talked a lot about the threat overseas. And we, obviously, were aware of the historical information that Osama bin Laden had issued statements years before, much of which is in the SEIB and was in the August 6th PDB, which I have now read. But we inquired of the CIA and the FBI: Are there domestic threats that require—is there any evidence of domestic threat? And they both said no. I might add that for the CIA, I inquired of them: Are there things we can do additionally by way of FISA to assist you in making sure that we have all the information necessary to be aware of those threats? And they assured me that if they needed additional help, they would ask for it.

GORELICK: So you were aware in early August—by at least early August of '01—that in addition to the fatwas and the statements of intention by bin Laden, that there was evidence that he intended to strike in the United States. Is that correct?

ASHCROFT: Well, I don't know if in addition to the fatwas and his statement of intention. We were aware that he had stated his intention, of the historical items mentioned in the SEIB and I believe also mentioned in the PDB. We were aware that those kinds of historical references had been made. And it was with that in mind, in conjunction with our understanding of what he had done in terms of the bombings in Nairobi and Dar es Salaam, that we understood him to be a very serious individual and we should take him seriously.

GORELICK: As a result of your awareness of this domestic threat, did you review with Acting Director Pickard the specific actions that he had taken to ensure that information in the possession of agents of the FBI across America relating to bin Laden's threats, his capacity, his ability to strike us, activities that might be going on in the United States, that that information would be flowing up to you?

ASHCROFT: I queried the director on numbers of occasions about threats in the United States that would require our attention. I expected those queries to result in the kind of activity which we saw in the FBI across the summer—not only in the face-to-face inquiries at the SAC meetings, but in the telephone inquiries and in the communications—through the electronic communication as well as the inlets—which shared those awarenesses with the rest of the law enforcement community in the country. We viewed inlets as a force multiplier because we got away from just the 12,000 FBI agents to the 700,000 or so law enforcement officials in the country. And we wanted those to be pulsed, as well.

GORELICK: Do you know if any of the inlets actually produced any information to the FBI?

ASHCROFT: I do not know and would not be expecting to know what 700,000 or so law enforcement officials might be saying to the people in the FBI Joint Terrorism Task Forces around the country. And I'm sure they were saying lots of things. But obviously I wouldn't be aware of those.

Staff Statement No. 11

The Performance of the Intelligence Community

[In an earlier staff statement] we discussed our initial findings on the work of the CIA as an instrument of national policy, in the areas of clandestine and covert action. [Now] we focus on intelligence analysis and warning, the collection of intelligence, and the overall management of the Intelligence Community before September 11, 2001.

THE INTELLIGENCE COMMUNITY AND TERRORISM

Today's Intelligence Community is a collection of agencies which were largely created to help wage the Cold War. The Central Intelligence Agency was created in 1947. The Department of Defense was created in the same legislation. The signals intelligence agencies were in the armed services and were unified under the National Security Agency [NSA] in 1952, yet stayed in the Defense Department.

The National Security Act forbids the CIA from performing any internal security functions. Internal security is the province of the FBI. In contrast, the CIA collects foreign intelligence focused on human sources outside of the United States. The CIA is also responsible for analyzing information from all sources to provide objective intelligence for the President and policymakers.

The Defense Department (DOD) conducts the vast majority of technical intelligence collection. The National Security Agency, located in that Department, intercepts communications. The recently renamed National Geospatial-Intelligence Agency, also located in DOD, analyzes photographs and other imagery and prepares needed maps. These agencies are supported by the National Reconnaissance Office, which acquires, launches, and manages systems that orbit the earth, and is another DOD agency.

Each of the executive departments involved in national security has its own intelligence agency or bureau. These include the Defense Intelligence Agency, the intelligence branches of the military services, the intelligence divisions of the FBI, and the Bureau of Intelligence and Research within the Department of State.

The United States spends more on intelligence than most nations spend on national security as a whole. Most of this money is spent on intelligence collection, much of it on very expensive hardware, such as systems based in space. Most of the Intelligence Community's budget is spent in the Department of Defense, in part because the collection systems are mainly managed by agencies set up in that Department and in part because of the substantial intelligence organizations created to support the armed forces and the operations of the unified military commands around the world.

The Director of Central Intelligence [DCI] has two sets of responsibilities. First, he leads a particular agency, the CIA. The CIA has special responsibilities for clandestine intelligence collection and covert action, and for independent analysis of foreign developments. Second, as the DCI he has the responsibility to coordinate the efforts of the entire Intelligence Community, this loose collection of federal agencies and parts of agencies, so that it purposefully and efficiently supports broad national priorities set by the President, the National Security Council, and the Congress. The DCI controls the CIA, but other cabinet secretaries and the FBI Director direct their parts of the Intelligence Community.

One of the Intelligence Community's priorities in the 1970s and 1980s was the danger posed by international terrorism. In that era terrorism was seen as tied to regional conflicts, mainly in the Middle East, and many of the terrorist groups were sponsored by governments. In 1985 President Reagan created a presidential task force to review U.S. efforts to combat terrorism. The task force was chaired by Vice President Bush. One of its recommendations was to establish an "all source intelligence fusion center for international terrorism."

The CIA then created a Counterterrorist Center, or CTC. In 1989, DCI [William] Webster expanded the scope of the CTC beyond CIA to make it a "DCI Center" with responsibilities for overseeing the intelligence effort across all the intelligence agencies. Employees were detailed to the CTC from across the Intelligence Community. DCI Webster created additional mission-oriented Intelligence Community centers such as the Counternarcotics and Counterintelligence Centers. DCI [Robert] Gates added a Non-Proliferation Center, and other DCIs have devised more Centers to try to cope with transnational challenges.

The CTC was organized to combat mainly regional terrorist organizations and the states that supported them. Therefore its focus tended to be traditional, on collection of intelligence in and against particular states. That intelligence would then inform the foreign policy choices about engagement or coercion to influence the behavior of countries like Libya, Lebanon, Syria, Iran, and Iraq. As the CIA and the rest of the Community struggled to reorient its priorities during the early 1990s, the CTC began to observe a disturbing new trend of shadowy new groups as illustrated by those involved with Ramzi Yousef in the 1993 attack on the World Trade Center.

ANALYSIS OF A NEW DANGER

Information comes to intelligence agencies from many sources. These sources include the reports from other U.S. government agencies such as the State Department, from counterparts in foreign security agencies, from human agents, from signals intelligence such as communications, from imagery, and from open sources like foreign newspapers. The CIA was originally created, in large part, to sort through all such sources and offer unbiased assessments to the nation's leaders. In other words, although the CIA became and remains a principal collector and operator in its own right, its first duty was to provide integrated analysis.

Analysis is more than a news report. Tactical analysis studies a particular case involving an individual or group as a guide to specific operations. Strategic analysis looks beyond the particular in order to see patterns, notice gaps, or assemble a larger picture on a wider timeframe to guide the development of national policy.

Budget cuts in the national foreign intelligence program from fiscal years 1990 to 1996, and essentially flat budgets from fiscal years 1996 to 2000 (except for the so-called "Gingrich Supplemental" of [Fiscal Year] 1999) caused significant staffing reductions that constrained the numbers and training of analysts. Analysis was already a relatively minor part of intelligence budgets devoted mainly to collection and operations.

Meanwhile, during the 1990s, the rise of round the clock news shows and the Internet reinforced pressure on the diminishing number of intelligence analysts to pass along fresh reports to policymakers at an ever faster pace, trying to add context or supplement what their policy consumers were receiving from the media. Many officials told us that the demands of providing "current intelligence" and briefings to more and more consumers, both in the executive branch and in Congress, drained scarce resources away from systematic, reflective strategic analysis.

In the late 1990s, weaknesses in all-source and strategic analysis were spotlighted by independent panels critiquing the Intelligence Community's failure to foresee the India-Pakistan nuclear weapons tests in 1998, and its limited ability to assess the ballistic missile threat to the United States in 1999. The first panel was led by Admiral David Jeremiah; the second by Donald Rumsfeld. Both panels called attention to the dispersal of effort on too many priorities, declining attention to the craft of strategic analysis, budget constraints, sophisticated denial and deception efforts by adversaries, and security rules that prevented adequate sharing of information. We found similar shortcomings with the quality of finished intelligence on transnational terrorism prior to 9/11.

While we now know that al Qaeda was formed in 1988, at the end of the Soviet occupation of Afghanistan, the Intelligence Community did not describe this organization, at least in documents we have seen, until 1999. As late as 1997, the CTC characterized Osama bin Laden as a financier of terrorism. This was at a time when the Intelligence Community had recently received a major input of new information revealing that bin Laden headed his own terrorist organization, with its own targeting agenda and operational commanders. This new information also revealed the previously unknown involvement of bin Laden's organization in the 1992 attack on the Yemen hotel quartering U.S. military personnel and the 1993 shootdown of U.S. Army Blackhawk helicopters in Somalia; and quite possibly in the 1995 Riyadh bombing of the American training mission to the Saudi Arabian National Guard. Nor had analysts worked through answers to questions about links between bin Laden and his associates with the bombing of the World Trade Center in 1993 and the Manila airlines plot of 1994.

The most impressive piece of analysis on the emerging transnational terrorist threat was the 1995 National Intelligence Estimate [NIE] entitled: *The Foreign Terrorist Threat in the United States*. It judged at the time that: "[T]he most likely threat of an attack in the United States would be from transient groupings of individuals similar to those drawn together by Ramzi Yousef. Such groupings lack strong organization but rather are loose affiliations."

The NIE warned of terrorist attacks in the United States over the following two years. It was updated in 1997. As we mentioned [previously], by early 1997 the United States had received dramatic new information about the organization of al Qaeda and its efforts to mount catastrophic attacks against the United States. The 1997 update failed to reflect this new information. No comprehensive national estimates were subsequently produced on terrorism prior to the attacks of 9/11.

Thousands of particular reports were circulated. A number of very good analytical papers were distributed on specific topics such as bin Laden's political philosophy, his command of a global network, analysis of information from terrorists captured in Jordan in December 1999, al Qaeda's operational style, and on the evolving goals of the international extremist movement. Hundreds of articles for morning briefings were prepared for the highest officials in the government with titles such as "Bin Laden Threatening to Attack US Aircraft [with anti-aircraft missiles]" (June 1998), "OBL Plans for Reprisals Against U.S. Targets, Possibly in U.S." (September 1998), "Strains Surface Between Taliban and bin Laden" (January 1999), "Terrorist Threat to US Interests in Caucasus" (June 1999), "Bin Laden to Exploit Looser Security During Holidays" (December 1999), "Bin Laden Evading Sanctions" (March 2000), "Bin Laden's Interest in Biological and Radiological Weapons" (February 2001), "Taliban Holding Firm on Bin Laden for Now" (March 2001), "Terrorist Groups Said Cooperating on US Hostage Plot" (May 2001), and "Bin Laden Determined to Strike in US" (August 2001).

Despite such reports, and a 1999 paper on bin Laden's command structure for al Qaeda, there were no complete authoritative portraits of his strategy and the extent of his organization's involvement in past terrorist attacks. Nor had the community provided an authoritative depiction of his organization's relationships with other governments, or the scale of the threat his organization posed to the United States.

A few analysts within the CTC were dedicated to working on bin Laden. One of them had developed a lengthy comprehensive paper on his organization by 1998. Her supervisor did not consider the paper publishable and broke the topic down into four papers assigned to four other available analysts. As an indicator of the scarcity of analysts and the press of current intelligence reporting work, it took more than two years for two of these papers to be published at all. The other two were not finished until after 9/11.

Some officials, including Deputy DCI John McLaughlin, are skeptical about the importance of comprehensive estimates. McLaughlin has been in charge of the estimate process. He told us such estimates are time-consuming to prepare. Judgments are watered down in negotiations. Conclusions may duplicate those already circulated in more specific papers. He and others said that key policymakers understood the threat.

Other officials, however, stress the importance of such estimates as a process that surfaces and clarifies disagreements. Through coordination and vetting views, the Community comes to a collective understanding of the nature of the threat it faces—what is known, unknown, and a discussion of how to close these gaps.

Most important, our interviews of senior policymakers in both administrations revealed a fundamental uncertainty about how to regard the threat posed by bin Laden and al Qaeda. After 9/11, the catastrophic character of the threat seems obvious. It is hard now to recapture the old conventional wisdom before 9/11. For example, a *New York Times* investigation in April 1999 sought to debunk claims that bin Laden was a terrorist leader, with the headline: "U.S. Hard Put to Find Proof Bin Laden Directed Attacks." The head of analysis at the CTC until 1999 regarded the bin Laden danger as still in the realm of past experience, discounting the alarms about a catastrophic threat as relating only to the danger of chemical, biological, or nuclear attack which he downplayed, referring in 2001—before 9/11—to "overheated rhetoric" on the subject.

In other words, before the attack we found uncertainty among senior officials about whether this was just a new and especially venomous version of the ordinary terrorist threat America had lived with for decades, or was radically new, posing a threat beyond any yet experienced. Some pointed out to us that, before 9/11, al Qaeda was considered responsible for the deaths of less than fifty Americans, all of them overseas. Former officials, including an NSC [National Security Council] staffer working for Richard Clarke, told us the threat was seen as one that could cause hundreds of casualties, not thousands. Such differences affect calculations about whether or how to go to war. Even officials who acknowledge a vital threat intellectually may not be ready to act upon such beliefs at great cost or at high risk.

Therefore, the government experts who believed there was such a danger needed a process that could win and acknowledge broad support for their views or at least spotlight the areas of dispute. Such a process could also prompt action across the government. The national estimate process has often played this role, and is sometimes controversial for this very reason. It played no role in judging the threat posed by al Qaeda.

In the CTC, priority was given to tactical analysis to support operations. Although the CTC formally reports to the DCI, the Center is effectively embedded in the CIA's Directorate of Operations. The Center had difficulty attracting talented analysts from their traditional billets in the Agency's Directorate of Intelligence. The CTC also was especially vulnerable to the pressures that placed reporting ahead of research and analysis. Strategic analysis was a luxury the strained cadres of analysts in the Center could rarely indulge.

In late 2000 DCI [George] Tenet recognized the deficiency of strategic analysis against al Qaeda. He appointed a senior manager to tackle the problem within the CTC. In March 2001 this manager briefed DCI Tenet on "creating a strategic assessment capability." The CTC established a new strategic assessments branch during July 2001. The decision to add about ten analysts to this effort was seen as a major bureaucratic victory. The CTC labored to find analysts to serve in this office. The new chief of this branch reported for duty on September 10, 2001.

WARNING AND THE CASE OF
AIRCRAFT AS WEAPONS

Since the Pearl Harbor attack of 1941, the Intelligence Community has devoted generations of effort to understanding the problem of warning against surprise attack. Rigorous analytic methods were developed, focused in particular on the Soviet Union. Several leading practitioners within the Intelligence Community discussed them with us. They have been articulated in many ways, but almost all seem to have at least four elements in common: (1) think about how surprise attacks might be launched; (2) identify telltale indicators connected to the most dangerous possibilities; (3) where feasible, collect intelligence against these indicators; and (4) adopt defenses to deflect the most dangerous possibilities or at least get more warning.

Concern about warning issues arising after the end of the Gulf War led to a major study conducted for DCI Robert Gates in 1992 which recommended several measures, including a stronger National Intelligence Officer for Warning. We were told that these measures languished under Gates's successors. The National Intelligence Officer for Warning yielded responsibility to the CTC in handling warnings related to a terrorist attack. Those responsibilities were passed to an Intelligence Community Counterterrorism Board that would issue periodic threat advisories.

With the important exception of analysis of al Qaeda efforts in chemical, biological, radiological, and nuclear weapons, we did not find evidence that this process regularly applied the methods to avoid surprise attack that had been so laboriously developed over the years. There was, for example, no evident Intelligence Community analysis of the danger of boat bombs before the attack on the U.S.S. *Cole* in October 2000, although expertise about such means of attack existed within the Community, especially at the Office of Naval Intelligence.

Amid the thousands of threat reports, some mentioned aircraft in the years before 9/11. The most prominent hijacking threat report came from a foreign government source in late 1998 and discussed a plan for hijacking a plane in order to gain hostages and bargain for the release of prisoners such as the "Blind Sheikh." As we mentioned [earlier], this 1998 report was the source of the allusion to hijacking in the President's Daily Brief article provided to President Bush in August 2001.

Other threat reports mentioned the possibility of using an aircraft laden with explosives. Of these the most prominent asserted a possible plot to fly an explosives-laden aircraft into a U.S. city. This report was circulated in September 1998 and originated from a source who walked into an American consulate in East Asia. Neither the source's reliability nor the information could be corroborated. In addition, an Algerian group hijacked an airliner in 1994 in order to fly it into the Eiffel Tower, but they could not fly the plane. There was also in 1994 the private airplane crashing into the White House south lawn. In early 1995, Abdul Hakim Murad—Ramzi Yousef's accomplice in the Manila airlines bombing plot—told Philippine authorities that he and Yousef had discussed flying a plane into CIA headquarters. A 1996 report asserted that Iranians were plotting to hijack a Japanese plane and crash it in Tel Aviv.

These past episodes suggest possibilities. Alone, they are not warnings. But, returning to the four elements mentioned above:

- The CTC did not analyze how a hijacked aircraft or other explosives-laden aircraft might be used as a weapon. If it had done so, it could have identified that a critical obstacle would be to find a suicide terrorist able to fly large jet aircraft. This had never happened before 9/11.

- The CTC did not develop a set of tell-tale indicators for this means of attack. For example, one such indicator might be the discovery of terrorists seeking or taking flight training to fly large jet aircraft, or seeking to buy advanced flight simulators.

- The CTC did not propose, and the Intelligence Community collection management process did not set, collection requirements against such telltale indicators. Therefore the warning system was not looking for information such as the July 2001 FBI report of terrorist interest in various kinds of aircraft training in Arizona, or the August 2001 arrest of Zacarias Moussaoui because of his suspicious behavior in a Minnesota flight school. In late August, the Moussaoui arrest was briefed to the DCI and other top CIA officials under the heading, "Islamic Extremist Learns to Fly." The news had no evident effect on warning.

- Neither the Intelligence Community nor the NSC policy process analyzed systemic defenses of aircraft or against suicide aircraft. The many threat reports mentioning aircraft were passed to the FAA [Federal Aviation Administration]. We discussed the problems at that agency in [earlier] staff statements. . . . Richard Clarke told us that he was concerned about this threat in the context of protecting the Atlanta Olympics of 1996, the White House complex, and the 2001 G–8 summit in Genoa. But he attributed his awareness to novels more than any warnings from the Intelligence Community. He did not pursue the systemic issues of defending aircraft from suicide hijackers or bolstering wider air defenses.

INTELLIGENCE COLLECTION

The CTC and the larger Intelligence Community tried to understand the emerging terrorist threat with their traditional collection methods of human source collection, or the use of informants; information provided by foreign intelligence services; signals collection, or the intercept of communications; and open sources, or the systematic collection of print, broadcast, and, in the late 1990s, Internet information. Imagery intelligence was extremely valuable for targeting cruise missiles, interpreting Predator [unmanned aircraft] videos, and identifying training camps in Afghanistan. This form of intelligence collection worked well. But its sustained effectiveness depended on cues provided by other sources of intelligence.

Human source intelligence is conducted by both the CIA and the Defense Intelligence Agency (DIA). Gaining access to organizations or individuals who have access to terrorist groups has proven extremely difficult for both the CIA and the DIA. This has led to a heavy reliance on "walk-ins" and foreign intelligence services.

Often, CIA's best sources of information on terrorist organizations have been volunteers or "walk-ins," who approach U.S. personnel at embassies and other places for a variety of reasons. But, evaluating these volunteers and walk-ins is a time consuming and sometimes risky proposition. The ratio of valuable information providers to charlatans, fabricators, or double agents is about 1 to 10. That is, for every ten walk-ins only one produces information of value to the Intelligence Community and U.S. policymakers. Yet some of the best sources on al Qaeda during the 1990s were walk-ins. One of these individuals, Jamal al Fadl, began providing information in 1996 and has testified in open court.

Foreign security services also play a critical role in understanding the terrorist threat. The United States government relied, and relies, heavily on this assistance. A major function of the Intelligence Community is the development and maintenance of these information sharing relationships, which may include expenditures to help the foreign agency improve its own capabilities. Before 9/11 the U.S. government developed especially helpful relationships with several governments in the Middle East and Southeast Asia. Where these relationships work, the local services have an enormous advantage in collecting intelligence. Of course, the quality of these relationships varied.

The German government provided the U.S. government information on an individual named "Marwan" who was acquainted with the target of a German investigation. This common first name and a phone number in the United Arab Emirates [U.A.E.] were provided as a possible lead in 1999. The CTC pursued this lead for a short time but, with the scant information provided, the CTC found nothing to provoke a special effort on this lead. The CIA did not ask any other agency in the intelligence community for assistance. We now know that "Marwan" was Marwan al Shehhi, who later piloted United Airlines flight 175 into the South Tower of the World Trade Center. He used the UAE telephone number in the period before the 9/11 attacks. We are continuing to investigate this episode.

We also corroborated that some countries did not support U.S. efforts to collect intelligence information on terrorist cells in their countries, or did not share the American assessments of the threat. According to a former Chief of the CTC, before 9/11 many liaison services were "highly skeptical," and "frankly thought we were crazy." They saw [Osama bin Laden] as more an "oddball" than a real terrorist threat. This was especially true for some of the European services.

Most importantly, from our interviews it is clear that the Community has no comprehensive and integrated foreign liaison strategy. Each agency pursues foreign partnerships unilaterally, and has done so for many years with minimal interagency coordination.

Signals intelligence has been another source of terrorist-related information. The United States spends a great deal on signals intelligence capabilities. Signals intelligence provides global reach through land, air, sea and space-based systems. But U.S. capabilities have been challenged by the use of modern systems and the operational security practiced by the current generation of terrorists. Moreover, serious legal and policy challenges arise for foreign intelligence agencies when dealing with communications between the U.S. and foreign countries. The NSA is also prohibited from collecting intelligence on people residing in the United States, whether they are U.S. citizens or not, without a warrant under the Foreign Intelligence Surveillance Act.

Signals intelligence is a source of measuring "chatter," which is an indicator of terrorist activity. Interpreting chatter is difficult. For example, the press reported that the Congressional Joint Inquiry was told about intercepted communications collected on September 10, 2001, saying "tomorrow is zero hour," and about the imminent beginning of "the match." Additional information later came to light within the Intelligence Community, however, that suggested this information was connected with the opening of the Taliban and al Qaeda military offensive in Afghanistan against the Northern Alliance, following on the September 9 al Qaeda assassination of the Northern Alliance's leader, rather than the 9/11 attacks.

Finally, open sources—the systematic collection of foreign media—have always been a bedrock source of information for intelligence. Open sources remain important, including among terrorist groups that use the media and the Internet to communicate leadership guidance. This mission was performed by the Foreign Broadcast Information Service. During the early 1990s that service had been "shredded," as one official put it to us, by budget cuts. But, by 2001, the FBIS had built a significant translation effort for terrorism-related media. The FBIS believes its charter bars open source collection of foreign language media within the United States.

The management of the Intelligence Community's collection efforts is critical. Beginning in 1999, both Assistant DCI for Collection Charles Allen and CTC Director Cofer Black devoted significant attention to improving the collection of intelligence against the al Qaeda sanctuary in Afghanistan. [W]e mentioned "The Plan" developed to energize the recruitment of human agents. These efforts complemented ingenious efforts already underway to improve the collection of signals intelligence. In these SIGINT efforts the CIA relied heavily on its own efforts, sometimes working well with NSA and sometimes quarreling. But they ultimately failed to achieve an adequate combined effort.

There were some commendable initiatives. Backed by the White House, Assistant DCI Allen worked with military officers in the Joint Staff during the spring and summer of 2000 to come up with innovative collection ideas. One of these was the Predator drone that first flew over Afghanistan in September 2000.

Strategic collection management depends upon strategic analysis to define the baseline of what is known, and what is not known, and to guide the setting of clear, agreed requirements. This process did not occur. Assistant DCI Allen concentrated on day-to-day collection challenges with enormous energy and dedication. However, there was no comprehensive collection strategy to pull together human sources, imagery, signals intelligence, and open sources. Even "The Plan" was essentially a CIA plan, not one for the Intelligence Community as a whole.

Collection was focused in a way that led analysts to look for the next attack to occur overseas. That was where the CIA and the

NSA collected. The FBI, on the other hand, acquired little information on U.S. based individuals and groups. What was acquired was often not shared with other members of the Community. . . .

Human intelligence relied heavily on [proxies], on foreign liaison, and on walk-ins. The CIA did not send its own officers into Afghanistan to unilaterally collect intelligence themselves. The CIA's capabilities for such direct action overseas were very limited. The military's special operations capabilities to perform such tasks were more formidable, but were not utilized to collect intelligence in Afghanistan.

Signals intelligence collection against terrorism, while significant, did not have sufficient funding within the NSA. The NSA's slow transformation meant it could not keep pace with advances in telecommunications.

One final point on collection. We have devoted most of our attention to organizations in Washington. Tackling terrorist cells, however, takes place in the field. A few examples illustrate the challenges and dangers of working the terrorist target:

- In 2000 and again in 2001 CIA officers clandestinely flew into Afghanistan's Panjshir Valley on old Soviet helicopters to forge intelligence partnerships with Northern Alliance leaders.

- Also in 2000 and 2001, officers from the FBI and the CIA met repeatedly in a dangerous location overseas with an al Qaeda foot soldier who traveled in and out of the Afghan training camps carrying critical information on al Qaeda personnel, training, and capabilities. The CIA and FBI officers never knew whether the source might lure them into an ambush; they had to come armed, expecting the worst.

Unfortunately, the problems of coordination and sharing we found in Washington are sometimes replicated overseas as well.

DCI TENET'S "WAR"

On December 4, 1998 DCI Tenet issued a directive to several CIA officials and the DDCI for Community Management stating: "We are at war. I want no resources or people spared in this effort, either inside CIA or the Community." Unfortunately, we found the memorandum had little overall effect on mobilizing the CIA or the Intelligence Community.

The memo was addressed only to CIA officials and the Deputy DCI for Community Management, Joan Dempsey. She faxed the memo to the heads of the major agencies. Almost all our interviewees had never seen the memo or only learned of it after 9/11. The NSA Director at the time, Lieutenant General Kenneth Minihan, told us he believed the memo applied only to CIA and not NSA since no one had informed him of any NSA shortcomings. On the other hand, CIA officials thought the memorandum was intended for the rest of the Community given the fact that they were already doing all they could and they thought that the Community needed to pull its weight.

The episode indicates some of the limitations of the DCI's authority over the direction and priorities of the Intelligence Community. Congress attempted to strengthen his authority in 1996 by creating the positions of Deputy DCI for Community Management and Assistant DCIs for Collection, Analysis and Production, and Administration. Perhaps their authority is not great enough. Perhaps it is not used enough. The vision of central coordination has not been realized.

The DCI did not develop a management strategy for a war against terrorism before 9/11. Such a management strategy would define the capabilities the Intelligence Community must acquire for such a war—from language training to collection systems to analysts. Such a management strategy would necessarily extend beyond the CTC to the components that feed its expertise and support its operations, linked transparently to counterterrorism objectives. It would then detail the proposed expenditures and organizational changes required to acquire and implement these capabilities.

DCI Tenet and the CIA's Deputy Director for Operations told us they did have a management strategy for war on terrorism. It was called: Rebuilding the CIA. They said the CIA as a whole had been badly damaged by prior budget constraints and that capability needed to be restored across the board. Indeed, the CTC had survived the budget cuts with less damage than many other components within the Agency. By restoring funding across the CIA, a rising tide would lift all boats. They also stressed the synergy between improvements of every part of the Agency and the capabilities that the CTC or stations overseas could draw upon in the war on terror.

As some officials pointed out to us, the tradeoff of this management approach is that by attempting to rebuild everything, the highest priority efforts might get only an average share, not maximum support. Further, this approach tended to take relatively strong outside support for combating terrorism and tried to channel this support into backing for across the board funding increases. Proponents of the counterterrorism agenda might be less inclined to loosen the purse strings than they would have been if offered a convincing counterterrorism budget strategy. The DCI's management strategy was also primarily focused on the CIA.

DCI Tenet and his predecessors had not developed the management and administrative tools to run the Intelligence Community that most federal departments use to monitor and rationalize their resources against priorities. The Intelligence Community did not have a financial accounting system, a chief financial officer, or a comptroller. The CIA had these tools for its own operations; the Intelligence Community did not. Instead, to manage the Community as a whole, the DCI relied on a variety of financial systems maintained by different agencies and without standardized definitions for expenditures.

Lacking a management strategy for the war on terrorism or ways to see how funds were being spent across the Community, it was difficult for DCI Tenet and his aides to develop an overall Intelligence Community budget for a war on terrorism.

The Administration and the Congress relied on supplemental appropriations to increase counterterrorism funding. While supplementals were a useful one-time plus-up, the DCI was not able to build long-term capabilities.

The Community lacked a common information architecture that would help to ensure the integration of counterterrorism data across CIA, NSA, DIA, the FBI, and other agencies. In 1998, DCI Tenet called for such integration in his *Strategic Intent for the Intelligence Community* with a vision of greater unity and horizontal integration across the Community, but the Intelligence Community did not develop a plan to achieve it before 9/11.

Finally, the Community had not institutionalized a process for learning from its successes and failures. We did not find any after-action reviews sponsored by the Intelligence Community after surprise terrorist attacks such as the Embassy bombings of August 1998 or the U.S.S. *Cole* attack of October 2000. The Community participated in Inspector General inquiries conducted by individual agencies, but these reviews were perceived as fault-finding, without enough constructive emphasis on learning lessons and discovering best practices. What we did not find was anything between the extremes of no investigation at all, and an adversarial inquiry triggered by a public outcry. We did not find an institution or culture that provided a safe outlet for admitting errors and improving procedures.

CONCLUSION

Our investigation so far has found the Intelligence Community struggling to collect on and analyze the phenomena of transnational terrorism through the mid- to late 1990s. While many dedicated officers worked day and night for years to piece together the growing body of evidence on al Qaeda and to understand the threats, in the end it was not enough to gain the advantage before the 9/11 attacks.

- While there were many reports on bin Laden and his growing al Qaeda organization, there was no comprehensive estimate of the enemy, either to build consensus or clarify differences.

- With the important exception of attacks with chemical, biological, radiological, or nuclear weapons, the methods developed for decades to warn of surprise attacks were not applied to the problem of warning against terrorist attacks.

- In intelligence collection, despite many excellent efforts, there was not a comprehensive review of what the Community knew, what it did not know, followed by the development of a community-wide plan to close those gaps.

- The DCI labored within—and was accountable for—a Community of loosely associated agencies and departmental offices that lacked the incentives to cooperate, collaborate, and share information. Like his predecessors, he focused his energies on where he could add the greatest value—the CIA, which is a fraction of the nation's overall intelligence capability. As a result, a question remains: Who is in charge of intelligence?

Kevin Scheid, Lorry Fenner, Gordon Lederman, Lloyd Salvetti, and Doug MacEachin did much of the investigative work reflected in this statement. We built upon the very significant work done on this topic in 2002 by the Congressional Joint Inquiry. All the agencies of the Intelligence Community made the necessary documents and witnesses available to us, often with a considerable investment of time and effort.

Excerpts of testimony from George J. Tenet, Director, Central Intelligence Agency

"I would tell you that the lesson is, yes, of course, we need more change. . . . I've been evolutionary in terms of the [intelligence] community. Maybe I should have been more revolutionary."

By the mid-1990s, the intelligence community was operating with a significant erosion in resources and people and was unable to keep pace with technological change. When I became DCI, I found a community in the CIA whose dollars were declining and whose expertise was ebbing. We lost close to 25 percent of our people and billions of dollars in capital investment. The pace of technological change challenged the National Security Agency's ability to keep up with the increasing volume and velocity of modern communications. The infrastructure to recruit, train and sustain officers for our clandestine services, the nation's human intelligence capability, was in disarray. We were not hiring new analysts, emphasizing the importance of expertise, or giving the analysts the tools they needed. I also found that the threats to the nation had not declined or even stabilized, but had grown more complex and dangerous. The rebuilding of the intelligence community across the board became my highest priority. We had to invest in the transformation of the National Security Agency to attack modern communications. We had to invest in a future imagery architecture. We had to overhaul our recruitment, training and deployment strategy to rebuild our human intelligence critical to penetrating terrorist cells. And we had to invest in our people. And while we were rebuilding across the board, we ensured that investments in counterterrorism continued to grow while other priorities either stayed flat or were reduced. . . .

Building our overall capabilities would be instrumental in how we positioned ourselves against al Qaeda, its terrorist organizations that represented a worldwide network in 68 countries and operated out of a sanctuary in Afghanistan. We also needed an integrated operations and collection plan against al Qaeda. We had one. I have previously testified about the 1999 strategy that we called The Plan. The Plan required that collection disciplines be integrated to support worldwide collection and disruption and penetration operations inside Afghanistan and other terrorist sanctuaries. In 1998, after the East Africa bombings, I directed the assistant director of central intelligence for collection to ensure that all elements of intelligence in the community had the right assets focused on the right problem with respect to al Qaeda and bin Laden. We convened frequent meetings with the most senior collection specialists in the community to develop a comprehensive approach to support the Counterterrorism Center's operations against bin Laden. He told me that, despite progress, we needed a sustained, longer-term effort if the community was to penetrate deeply into the Afghan sanctuary.

We established an integrated community collection cell focused on tracking al Qaeda leaders, identifying their facilities and activities in Afghanistan. The cell, which often met daily, included analysts, operations officers, imagery officers and officers from the National Security Agency. We used these sessions to drive signals and imagery collection against al Qaeda and to build innovative capabilities to target bin Laden and the al Qaeda organization. We moved to satellite to increase our coverage of Afghanistan. CIA and NSA designed and employed a clandestine collection system inside Afghanistan. The imagery agency intensified its efforts across Afghanistan and more imagery analysts were moved to cover al Qaeda. The imagery agency gave al Qaeda interest in targets its highest priority in the intense daily competition for overhead imagery resources. We established an integrated community collection cell that focused on tracking al Qaeda leaders and identifying and characterizing their facilities. When the Predator began flying in the summer of 2000, we opened it in a fused, all-source environment within the Counterterrorism Center. . . .

Between 1999 and 2001, our human agent base against the terrorist target grew by over 50 percent. We ran over 70 sources and sub-sources, 25 of whom operated inside of Afghanistan. We received information from eight separate Afghan tribal networks. We forged strategic relationships consistent with our plan with liaison services that, because of their regional access and profile, could enhance our reach. They ran their own agents into Afghanistan and around the world in response to our tasking. The period of early September 2000 to 2001 was also characterized by an important increase in our unilateral capability. Almost half of these assets and programs in place in Afghanistan were developed in the preceding 18 months. By September 11th, a map would show that these collection programs and human networks were operating throughout Afghanistan. This array meant that when the military campaign to topple the Taliban and destroy al Qaeda began in October, we were already on the ground supporting it with a substantial body of data and a large stable of assets. . . . How do I assess our performance? The intelligence that we provided our senior policymakers about the threat al Qaeda posed, its leadership and its operational span across over 60 countries and the use of Afghanistan as a sanctuary was clear and direct. . . . The warning was well understood, even if the timing and method of attacks were not.

The intelligence community had the right strategy and was making the right investments to position itself for the future against al Qaeda. We made good progress across intelligence disciplines. Disruptions, renditions and sensitive collection activities no doubt saved lives. However, we never penetrated the 9/11 plot overseas. While we positioned ourselves very well with extensive human and technical penetrations to facilitate the take-down of the Afghan sanctuary, we did not discern the specific nature of the plot. We made mistakes. Our failure to watchlist al Hazmi and al Mihdhar [9/11 terrorists under CIA surveillance in Malaysia] in a timely manner or the FBI's inability to find them in the narrow window at the time afforded them showed systemic weaknesses and the lack of redundancy. There were at least four separate terrorist identity databases at the State, CIA, the Department of Defense and the FBI. None were interoperable or broadly accessible. There were dozens of watch lists, many haphazardly maintained. There were legal impediments to cooperation across the continuum of criminal intelligence operations. It was not a secret at all that we understood it, but in truth, all of us took little action to create a common arena of criminal and intelligence data that we could all access.

Most profoundly, we lacked a government-wide capability to integrate foreign and domestic knowledge, data, operations and analysis. Warning is not good enough without the structure to put it into action. We all understood bin Laden's attempt to strike the homeland, but we never translated this knowledge into an effective defense of the country. Doing so would have complicated the terrorist calculation of the difficulty in succeeding in a vast open society that, in effect, was unprotected on September 11th. During periods of heightened threat, we undertook smart, disciplined actions. But ultimately all of us acknowledge that we did not have the data, the span of control, the redundancy, the fusion or the laws in place to give us the chance to compensate for the mistakes that will always be made in any human endeavor. . . .

I wanted to close just on four or five points about the future of intelligence and issues that you might want to consider as you think ahead to structures you may want to propose. The first thing I would say is, we've spent an enormous amount of time and energy transforming our collection, operational and analytical capabilities. The first thing I would say to the commission is that the care and nurturing of these capabilities is absolutely essential. It will take us another five years to have the kind of clandestine service our country needs. There is a creative, innovative strategy to get us there that requires sustained commitment, leadership and funding. The same can be said for our other disciplines. Something has to be said about the importance of intelligence and how we look at this discipline for the country quite publicly. Second, we have created an important paradigm in the way we have made changes in the foreign intelligence and law enforcement communities beginning with the Counterterrorism Center and evolving through the creation of TTIC [Terrorist Threat Integration Center] with the fusion of all-source data in one place against a critical mission area. This approach could serve as a model for the intelligence community to organize our most critical missions around centers where there's an emphasis on fusion, the flow of data, the fluid integration of analytical and operational capabilities. Capabilities are important. The organization around missions where those capabilities are fully integrated in whatever structure you want to create I think is the way ahead in the future and that's the way we're moving.

Third, in the foreign intelligence arena, the most important relationship—aside from the president—that a DCI has, is with the secretary of defense. Rather than focus on a zero-sum game of authorities, the focus should be on ensuring that the DCI and the secretary of defense work together on investments tied to mission. Why? Because the investments that we make together in accounts that we don't jointly manage I believe have enormous power when they're synchronized, and the secretary of defense and I have been working just to achieve that. Fourth, the DCI has to have an operational and analytical span of control that allows him or her to inform the president authoritatively about covert action and other sensitive activities. Finally, our oversight committees should begin a systematic series of hearings to examine the world we will face over the next 20 or 30 years, the operational end state we want to achieve in terms of structure, and the statutory changes that may need to be made to achieve these objectives. And none may be required, but I believe some will be.

QUESTIONS FROM COMMISSIONERS

JOHN F. LEHMAN: [A]ll I have to do is reread the PDB [Presidential Daily Brief] which the agency resisted so strongly our declassifying, and the key line is, We have not been able to corroborate some of the more sensational threat reporting, like the intention of bin Laden to hijack U.S. aircraft. All the king's horses and all the king's men in CIA could not corroborate what turned out to be true, and told the president of the United States almost a month before the attack that they couldn't corroborate these reports. That's an institutional failure. And I'm here to tell you, and I'm sure you've heard it before, there is a train coming down the track. There are going to be very real changes made. And you are an invaluable part of helping us come to the right conclusions on that. So now I have a few questions. First, why shouldn't we have a DCI who worries about the community with the authorities to do that, without having to worry about the day-to-day running of the CIA?

TENET: First of all, I want you to know that I have serious issues with the staff statement as it was written today. I have serious issues about how the DCI's authorities have been used to integrate collection, operations. When the staff statement says the DCI had no strategic plan to manage the war on terrorism, that's flat wrong. When the staff statement says I had no program or strategic direction in place to integrate, correlate data and move data across the community, that's wrong. I just want to say to you that I would like to come back to the committee and give you my sense of it, at the same time telling you, it ain't perfect. And by no stretch of the imagination am I going to tell you that I've solved all the problems of the community in terms of integrating and in lashing it up. But we've made an enormous amount of progress.

I would tell you also that—this is the perspective I lived. Nobody else can live what I lived through. I believe that if you separate—if you separate the DCI from troops, from operators and analysts, I have a concern about his or her effectiveness, his or her connection. Now, you may want to have a different structure. You may want to have a different CIA, sir, in terms of how you manage it, so there may be some things we can do there. But I wouldn't separate the individual from the institution. You may manage it differently, because I believe that one of the concerns I have is, if you create another layer and another staff between something that's supposed to provide central organization, all-source analysis and operations, we've created another gap and a distance.

So I wouldn't design America's intelligence community 56 years later the way the National Security Act designed it. I would recognize that the key operational principle is not who is in charge of the wire diagrams, but the way data flows, is integrated between analysis and operations. And in the 21st century, technology is your friend, not an enemy, and from a security perspective, it also makes your life easier. I would be very focused on organizing around missions and ensuring the capabilities were built, but the mission focused and centers drove the way we operated against the things that mattered most to us in terms of the foreign intelligence target. You can structure on top of that. You can lay anything you want on top of that, sir. But I think that that integration is what's key. And you can figure out the wire diagrams and the authorities any way you want.

I would tell you that the lesson is, yes, of course, we need more change. . . . I've been evolutionary in terms of the [intelligence] community. Maybe I should have been more revolutionary. I sit back at night and look at a war in Iraq, a war on terrorism, conflict in Afghanistan and all the things I have to do and recognize, you know, no single human being can do all these things. I understand that. So maybe some structure is required. But I would also urge the commission—and I will come back to you formally—to take a look at some significant things that have happened in the management of the community, of our resources, of our people, of our collection, of our training, of our education because they are building blocks that, quite frankly, I'm proud of.

LEHMAN: Well, I think that you're really making my point. I think that my experience in this town has been, there are only two things that matter in doing management and oversight because everybody makes the same amount of money. You can't give bonuses to people and your hiring and firing is somewhat limited. You've got the ability to hire and fire the top people if they don't perform and pick the ones that do perform and promote the ones that do perform, and you've got appropriations power. And neither of those things do you have for the responsibilities of cross-community. You've wielded them very well within your agency, but all you have for cross-agency—cross-community—is exhortation and the power of your logic, which has been powerful, but not powerful enough against big bureaucracy. So why shouldn't you—let's step into my Alice in Wonderland and you've been detached from CIA. You don't have to run it anymore. You are now a DCI who is principally seized of solving the problems that we have identified and you've struggled with for these years. Why shouldn't you have the power to hire and fire—more importantly—the head of NSA, the head of the FBI intelligence section, or a separate MI–5, the head of the CIA, the head of all of the alphabet soup that are really national intelligence assets? Why shouldn't you have that?

TENET: Well, let me talk to you about my Alice in Wonderland— just to talk through this a little bit. You could do that, sir, but I want to bring back an issue that I think is quite important here. We need to understand the relationship between the DCI and the secretary of defense in a very, very fundamental way. Why? You have an organizational structure today that basically has—three or four of the major organizations are combat support organizations. They provide tactical support to the military as well as support the national intelligence needs. And somehow in the structure that you create, he must be a partner in designing this framework to ensure that we don't miss—or don't crack a seam that we're trying to build together—because he executes tactical and other programs that in effect add to the power of what the DCI can do. But we have to wrestle with that in some way.

So everybody wants to empower this individual with all kinds of powers. And all I'm asking is: Yes, could a DCI be more powerful? Have more executive authority? Execute budgets, joint personnel policies? You know, the question ultimately is: Is there a Goldwater-Nichols framework here [referring to the law that consolidated Pentagon operations] that works? Is there some new framework that we have to put in place? All I want to focus on is: Don't throw the baby out with the bath water. Don't miss the capabilities that have to be grown. Don't separate those capabilities from a chain of command that can only execute them and then figure out how that mesh works. Now, the person you describe probably would survive for about 20 minutes in terms of what's going on in this town. And you probably went a little bit too far, but look—we have to be open to thinking like this. I've done it one way. It ain't the perfect way—and within the structure that I lived in, the power of persuasion and cajoling is absolutely important.

Because you know at the end of the day you still have to lead. You can have all the authority you want. It may not matter. So it's a little bit more complicated but all of it should be on—all I'm saying to you commissioners, it should all be on the table. But before we rush to a judgment don't we want to know what the world's going to look like? Don't we want to understand, with some precision, where do you want to end up? And I think you have to focus on that fusion of capabilities around mission first and foremost, and then decide the rest. It will flow from there. The power of forcing that collaboration in and of itself breaks down the walls.

· · ·

TIMOTHY J. ROEMER: . . . In the Woodward book, you say, immediately upon learning of the 9/11 attacks, that it's al Qaeda and you mention somebody in a flight school. I assume that's Moussaoui. Is that correct?

TENET: These are words attributed to me. I don't recall that piece of it, but I know I got up immediately and said, It's got to be al Qaeda.

ROEMER: And do you have the information at that point on Moussaoui?

TENET: Yes, I was briefed on Moussaoui in late August.

ROEMER: August what?

TENET: I believe it's the 23rd or the 24th. . . .

ROEMER: Now, do you all share this information, then, with other people at CTC and FBI and other places? What do you do with this information?

TENET: I believe that the context of the information—and again, I've got to go back and review all of this carefully. The context of this information is, it came to us from one of our domestic field stations, who was asked to provide some assistance in dealing with this FISA [Foreign Intelligence Surveillance Act] request. That's the context it came to us. And I believe in that time period we immediately tried to undertake a way to figure out how to help the FBI get data and deal with this particular problem. But I'd really want to go back and check records.

ROEMER: With this interesting, curious, fascinating piece of data, do you share this data at the September 4th principals' meeting with other people in the room at that point when you're discussing this policy that has taken seven months to make its way through the process on al Qaeda?

TENET: It wasn't discussed at the principals' meeting since we were having a separate agenda. My assumption at the time was, Mr. Roemer, that this was something that would be laid down in front of the CSG and people working this at the time.

ROEMER: Why would you assume that that would be . . .

TENET: Because all terrorist . . .

ROEMER: Why not bring it up to the principals? This is the first principals' meeting in seven months on terrorism. Why wouldn't that be something that you would think would be interesting to this discussion?

TENET: The nature of the discussion we had that morning was on the Predator, how we would fly it, whether we . . .

ROEMER: But it's an overall policy discussion about al Qaeda and how we fight al Qaeda.

TENET: Well, it just wasn't—for whatever reason, all I can tell you is just it wasn't the appropriate place. I just can't take you any farther than that.

ROEMER: Would it have made any difference if you had mentioned—did you ever mention it, for instance, to the president—your briefing the president from August 6th on?

TENET: I didn't see the president. I was not in briefings with him during this time. He was on vacation. I was here.

ROEMER: You didn't see the president between August 6, 2001, and September 10th?

TENET: Well, no. Before—saw him after Labor Day, to be sure.

ROEMER: So you saw him September 4th—at the principals' meeting?

TENET: It was not at a principals' meeting.

ROEMER: Well, you don't see him . . .

TENET: . . . I saw him in this time frame, to be sure.

ROEMER: OK. I'm just confused. You see him on August 6th with the PDB.

TENET: No, I do not, sir. I'm not there.

ROEMER: OK. You're not—when do you see him in August?

TENET: I don't believe I do.

ROEMER: You don't see the president of the United States once in the month of August?

TENET: He's in Texas and I'm either here or on leave for some of that time, so I'm not here.

ROEMER: So who's briefing him on the PDBs?

TENET: The briefer, himself. We have a presidential briefer.

ROEMER: But you never get on the phone or in any kind of conference with him to talk at this level of high chatter and huge warnings during the spring and summer to talk to him through the whole month of August?

TENET: We talked to him directly throughout the spring and early summer almost every day.

ROEMER: But not in August?

TENET: In this time period, I'm not talking to him, no.

ROEMER: Does he ever say to [National Security Adviser Condoleezza] Rice or somebody else, I want to talk to Tenet. Tenet is a guy that knows this situation, has been briefing me all through the spring and the summer. Tenet understands this stuff. His hair's been on fire. He's been worried about this stuff. Is that ever asked? Or are you ever called on to . . .

TENET: I don't have a recollection of being called, Mr. Roemer. But I'm sure that if I wanted to make a phone call because I had my hair on fire, I would have picked up the phone and talked to the president.

ROEMER: It was just never made.

TENET: No.

[Editor's note: The CIA later corrected Tenet's testimony. The director met with Bush twice in August 2001: once at the president's Texas ranch, and once in Washington after Bush had returned from vacation.]

Staff Statement No. 12

Reforming Law Enforcement, Counterterrorism and Intelligence Collection in the United States

It is important for us to emphasize that during the course of our investigation we met outstanding FBI and Department of Justice [DOJ] employees—including analysts, agents, translators, and surveillance specialists, among others—who strive daily to overcome great obstacles for little recognition in order to safeguard our country. Their dedication, effort, and sacrifice are remarkable.

On September 4, 2001, Robert Mueller became the Director of the FBI. Soon after the attacks, Director Mueller began to announce and to implement an ambitious series of reforms aimed at, in his words, "transforming the Bureau into an intelligence agency." The FBI's leadership has set in motion an impressive number of potentially significant reforms. We believe the FBI is a stronger counterterrorism agency than it was before 9/11.

Most of the proposed reforms are a work in progress. Institutional change takes time. In field visits last summer and fall, two years after 9/11, we found there was a gap between the announced reforms at FBI headquarters and the reality in the field. There may have been additional progress since then.

We divide our discussion of these reforms and the FBI's current capacity to detect and prevent terrorist attacks in the United

States into the following four broad areas . . .: management priorities and strategy; intelligence collection and processing; strategic analysis; and knowledge management.

MANAGEMENT PRIORITIES AND STRATEGY

After 9/11, the FBI abandoned its former opaque structure of "tiered" priorities in favor of a short, clear list of priorities. It made "protecting the United States from terrorist attack" the number one priority. It downgraded the priority attached to once sacrosanct parts of the Bureau's mission, including general crimes and narcotics enforcement, which are being left more to state and local agencies or the Drug Enforcement Administration.

FBI leadership also moved quickly to centralize the management of the counterterrorism program. This centralization represents a shift away from the pre–9/11 "Office of Origin" model in which the field office that initiated a case maintained control over it. All significant international terrorism cases and operations are directed from FBI headquarters. Director Mueller explained that "counterterrorism has national and international dimensions that transcend field office territorial borders and require centralized coordination to ensure that the individual pieces of an investigation can be assembled into a coherent picture."

Director Mueller has also endeavored to transform the reactive, law enforcement culture of the FBI. In the course of announcing reforms in May 2002, Director Mueller said, "What we need to do better is be predictive. We have to be proactive."

Along with these changes, the FBI has received large increases in funding since 2001. Appropriations to the FBI's National Security program have nearly doubled between September 11 and today. The FBI reports that the number of counterterrorism agents has increased from about 1,350 on 9/11 to nearly 2,400 today. It has also increased the number of analysts and language translators supporting the counterterrorism mission. The FBI has also created a number of specialized counterterrorism units at its headquarters. These include a unit to analyze electronic and telephone communications, a unit to exploit intelligence gleaned from documents or computers seized overseas by intelligence agencies, a surge capacity to augment local field investigative capabilities with specialized personnel, and a section to focus on the financial aspects of terrorism investigations.

Because of Director Mueller's efforts, there is widespread understanding that counterterrorism is the FBI's number one priority. However, many agents in the field were offended by the Director's statements that the FBI needs a new, proactive culture. Some agents who had worked counterterrorism cases before 9/11 felt prevention had always been part of their mission. We also found resistance to running counterterrorism cases out of FBI headquarters. Many field agents felt the supervisory agents in the Counterterrorism Division at headquarters lacked the necessary experience in counterterrorism to guide their work. In addition, because the organizational chart for the Counterterrorism Division has changed many times since 9/11, some field office personnel told us that they no longer have any idea who is their primary point of contact at headquarters.

The expertise of agents, analysts, linguists, and surveillance personnel contribute to effective counterterrorism operations. However, FBI personnel continue to be pulled away from counterterrorism to assist on criminal investigations. At present, the FBI attempts to address field office reassignments and disruptions primarily through its inspection process.

Director Mueller believes that, while counterterrorism is the number one priority, all agents should have training and experience in traditional criminal matters. The Director expects to implement by October a special agent career track that requires new agents to start at a small FBI office and be exposed to each of the FBI's four program areas for their first three years. The programs are counterterrorism/counterintelligence; cyber; criminal investigative; and intelligence. Thereafter, agents will be transferred to one of the largest field offices with a primary assignment in an area of specialization. The FBI will also require agents who seek to be promoted to Assistant Special Agent in Charge or Section Chief to have an intelligence officer certification.

INTELLIGENCE COLLECTION
AND PROCESSING

The FBI is widely regarded as one of the best post-event investigative agencies in the world. Many outside experts spoke to us
about the FBI's incredible forensic abilities, as illustrated by the
Lockerbie case, which enable agents to piece together evidence of
a crime. The question after 9/11 has been whether the FBI can
also collect intelligence that will lead to the prevention of attacks.

Director Mueller's articulation of priorities has reached the
field. FBI personnel consistently told us the current policy is that
no counterterrorism lead will go unaddressed, no matter how
minor or far-fetched. They also told us that there should be no
backlog on translations for international terrorism cases.

Many agents in the field told us that there is a new aggressiveness in pursuing international terrorism cases and a new push for
agents to recruit more sources and assets. Agents are no longer
required to open parallel intelligence and criminal cases for each
terrorism investigation. The "wall" is down. All international terrorism cases are now treated simply as counterterrorism investigations.

The USA PATRIOT Act, passed by Congress approximately
six weeks after 9/11, provided additional investigative tools and
has lowered or removed legal hurdles that were widely believed
to have hindered the FBI's intelligence investigations. The Attorney General Guidelines, which set forth the standards and
parameters of the FBI's investigative authority, have also been
changed by Attorney General John Ashcroft. These Guidelines
now allow for greater flexibility in employing investigative methods, such as permitting agents to attend public events and to
search the Internet, including publicly available subscription
services, before opening an investigation. These legal and policy
changes have prompted significant public debate about the
appropriate balance of civil liberties, privacy, and security. . . .

Nearly all FBI personnel we interviewed praised these legal
and policy changes. When pressed to describe which of the new
authorities are most helpful to them and how they employ them,
however, there was much less certainty. In fact, there appears to

be widespread confusion—even among DOJ and FBI personnel—over what the PATRIOT Act actually allows. Although the
FBI has revamped and increased its training programs, the FBI's
General Counsel recently conceded that much more training and
guidance must be provided to personnel in the field.

Many agents in the field told us that although there is now less
hesitancy in seeking approval for electronic surveillance under
the Foreign Intelligence Surveillance Act (or FISA), the application process nonetheless continues to be long and slow. Requests
for such approvals are overwhelming the ability of the system to
process them and to conduct the surveillance. The Department
of Justice and FBI are attempting to address bottlenecks in the
process.

To develop a collection strategy, FBI headquarters has recently
undertaken an Intelligence Capabilities Survey of field office
intelligence collection derived from all sources. This survey is an
appropriate first step in an effort to obtain a comprehensive view
of the FBI's capability to collect intelligence against its investigative priorities and to identify the critical gaps in collection.

Recruitment of sources has increased, but agents recognize
more sources are needed. Michael Rolince, who at the time was
Acting Assistant Director of the Washington field office, told us
that although the FBI knows "ten times" more now about the
radical Islamic community in his territory than it did before 9/11,
its knowledge is at about 20 on a scale of 1 to 100. A supervisor of
an international terrorism squad told us the FBI has not adequately reached out to the communities in which it should be
developing sources. He believes that while agents are complying
with the FBI's policy that they investigate any lead that comes in,
other systematic collection work is left undone. There have not
been many instances in which the FBI has been able to recruit an
asset to go abroad with specific collection requirements. Despite
the widespread view that assets and informants are the best
source of intelligence on where potential terrorists are and what
they are doing, many agents complained to us that the training
they received on how to recruit, validate, and maintain assets was
inadequate.

Another ongoing problem is the shortage of qualified language specialists to translate the intercepts. While highest priority cases are supposed to be translated within 24 hours, the FBI cannot translate all it collects. According to a recent report by the Department of Justice Inspector General, "the FBI shortages of linguists have resulted in thousands of hours of audiotapes and pages of written material not being reviewed or translated in a timely manner." The choice is between forgoing access to potentially relevant conversations and obtaining such conversations that remain untranslated. Despite the recent hire of 653 new linguists, demand exceeds supply. Shortages of translators in languages such as Arabic, Urdu, Farsi, and Pashto remain a barrier to the FBI's understanding of the terrorist threat.

In addition, language specialists suffer from not being part of an integrated intelligence program. During our field visits, language specialists told us that their summaries and translations are usually not disseminated broadly, not uploaded into a searchable database, and not systematically analyzed for intelligence value. The individual case agent has the responsibility for determining whether the information should be disseminated and to whom. Several language specialists expressed concern that neither the case agents nor the analysts coordinate with them sufficiently. As a result, the language specialists often lack the proper context to understand the significance of otherwise innocuous references they hear or read. Moreover, we have learned that if a language specialist mishandles a translation, there are few checks to catch the error.

Finally, at every office we visited, we heard that there were not enough surveillance personnel to cover the requests to conduct live physical surveillance of identified terrorist suspects. Like the language specialists, surveillance personnel are not treated as part of an integrated intelligence program. In most cases, their logs are not searchable electronically and they do not meet regularly with case agents to learn about the targets and the broader investigation.

STRATEGIC ANALYSIS

In response to widely recognized shortcomings, an Analysis Branch was created in the Counterterrorism Division soon after 9/11 with the mission of producing strategic assessments of the terrorist threat to the United States. The College of Analytical Studies also was created at the FBI's Quantico training facility to improve the quality of training for new analysts.

On January 30, 2003, Director Mueller announced what FBI leadership has described as the "centerpiece" of its effort to improve intelligence analysis: the establishment of the Executive Assistant Director for Intelligence. Mueller stated that "the directed and purposeful collection and analysis of intelligence has not previously been a primary mission focus of the FBI." The position was created to provide one official with direct authority and responsibility for the FBI's national intelligence program. The many responsibilities assigned to the new Executive Assistant Director fall into four general areas: intelligence collection, analysis, dissemination, and intelligence program management.

In April 2003, Director Mueller appointed Maureen Baginski, a former executive of the National Security Agency [NSA], to this new position. Under Baginski, the FBI has embarked on a series of proposals designed to integrate intelligence into the FBI's operations. She has directed that each field office create a centralized intelligence component called the Field Intelligence Group. FBI leadership is also striving to professionalize and elevate the status of analysts.

Agents and analysts in the field had heard of these changes. But many were still confused by the pace and number of changes and are uncertain about their titles and roles. We question whether the new intelligence program has enough staff and resources to serve as an engine of reform. It is too early to judge whether the Field Intelligence Groups will develop into the centralized intelligence components they are intended to become.

We are concerned whether the qualifications, status, and role of most analysts in the field have changed in practice. In the past, analysts were often promoted from secretarial and administrative positions, and they too often served as "catch-all" support personnel.

We spoke with analysts who were discouraged by the pace of reform. Indeed, we heard from many analysts who complain that they are able to do little actual analysis because they continue to be assigned menial tasks, including covering the phones at the reception desk and emptying the office trash bins. As a consequence, many of the agents have very low expectations about the type of assistance they can get from analysts. Furthermore, there appears to be no process for evaluating and reassigning unqualified analysts. To retain analysts, the FBI will have to provide them with opportunities comparable to those offered by other intelligence agencies.

The FBI reports that its Counterterrorism Analysis Branch at headquarters has produced more than 70 strategic assessments. The demand for tactical analysis and executive-level briefings, however, has made it difficult for senior managers to focus their resources sufficiently on strategic analysis.

KNOWLEDGE MANAGEMENT

The terrorist attacks of September 11 revealed significant deficiencies in the FBI's information sharing capabilities and processes—both with respect to sharing information internally with FBI components, as well as externally with intelligence and law enforcement partners at the federal, state, and local levels. While progress has been made in addressing these deficiencies, problems remain.

Information Sharing within the FBI

Although there are many explanations for the failure to share information internally, one of the most common is the FBI's outdated information technology, the Automated Case Support system in particular. It employs 1980s-era technology that is by all accounts user-unfriendly. More troubling, the system cannot be used to store or transmit top secret or sensitive compartmented information.

For a variety of reasons, significant information collected by the FBI never gets uploaded into the Automated Case Support system, or it gets uploaded long after it is learned. One of the reasons for this is the traditional approach to cases, in which information is treated as "owned" by the case agent and maintained in a paper case file. One official told us that headquarters personnel visiting the field have been amazed at the information they found in the paper files.

Agent after agent told us that the primary way information gets shared is through personal relationships. There does not appear to be any recognition that this system fails in the absence of good personal relationships.

Some steps to address these ongoing problems have been taken. The attempt to centralize control over the field offices has been made, in part, to ensure that all of the counterterrorism information collected is brought together in one place and disseminated. These steps, driven in part by the Director's responsibility since 9/11 to brief the President daily on terrorist threats, have helped get information from the field to headquarters.

However, improvements have been slow. Many current officials told us that the FBI still does not know what information is in its files. Furthermore, the Department of Justice's Inspector General reported in December 2003 that the FBI had not established adequate policies and procedures for sharing intelligence.

The FBI has had a longstanding plan to upgrade its information technology systems. The FBI has upgraded desktop terminals, established new networks, and consolidated databases. However, the replacement of the antiquated Automated Case Support system has been delayed once again. The Director recently told us that the new Virtual Case File system, which is supposed to enhance internal FBI information sharing, should be ready by the end of the year.

Information Sharing with the Intelligence Community

As we described yesterday, while top-level officials had frequent contacts and exchanges of information, the overall performance of the FBI and other intelligence community agencies in sharing information was troubled. A tradition of protecting information in order to preserve it for trial, concerns about compromising sources and methods, the absence of a reports officer function, and the lack of sophisticated information technology systems have all contributed to the FBI's reputation of being what one former [National Security Council] official called an information "black hole."

In July 2002, the FBI created the new National Joint Terrorism Task Force at headquarters to "enhance communication, coordination and cooperation between federal, state and local government agencies." At present, this headquarters task force consists of 38 government agencies. Similarly, the FBI has increased the number of Joint Terrorism Task Forces (JTTFs) in the field from 35 before 9/11 to 84 today, with more than 1,500 outside representatives participating on a full-time basis. Although the JTTFs vary in size and focus from office to office, they are designed to be "force multipliers," pooling the expertise from many agencies to assist in the collection and sharing of intelligence related to counterterrorism.

The FBI has also begun to hire and train reports officers. Reports officers glean intelligence from case files, briefing notes and elsewhere; summarize the information; and format it for dissemination to the intelligence and law enforcement communities. Although filling these new positions has gone slowly—indeed none of the field offices we visited had permanent reports officers in place at the time of our visits—the program is now underway.

The passage of the USA PATRIOT Act also has facilitated greater information sharing. The Act provides for the sharing of intelligence information obtained under FISA with FBI criminal agents and Department of Justice prosecutors. The Act also requires the expeditious disclosure of foreign intelligence information acquired during the course of a criminal investigation to the Director of Central Intelligence.

Despite all of these efforts, it is clear that gaps in intelligence sharing still exist. Michael Rolince, the acting Assistant Director of the Office of Intelligence, put it more bluntly: We are kidding ourselves if we think that there is seamless integration among all of the agencies. Former Acting FBI Director Thomas Pickard told us that the most difficult thing about information sharing is trying to figure out what information will actually be important to someone else. John Brennan, the Director of the Terrorist Threat Integration Center, told us that he is seeing a "cacophony of activities" within the Intelligence Community but no strategy and planning. Coordination and collaboration are insufficient, he told us. A fundamental strategy for joint work, for integration, is key. This is a problem neither the FBI nor the CIA nor any other agency can solve on its own. We found there is no national strategy for sharing information to counter terrorism.

In the field, JTTF members cannot easily obtain needed information from intelligence agencies. They are expected to go through FBI and CIA headquarters. For example, the process of obtaining name traces from the Intelligence Community is slow and unsatisfactory.

Compounding the problem of inadequate coordination at the field level is the lack of access by field agents to information systems that operate at the top secret level or above. Very few field agents or analysts have access to Intelink, a worldwide web of information classified at the top secret level. Such terminals have to be maintained in Sensitive Compartmented Information Facilities and such spaces in FBI field offices are extremely limited. To get access to such systems, for instance, many agents and analysts on the New York JTTF have to leave their building, cross the street and enter a separate building. They must then go to the secure room, which is barely large enough to accommodate a few people comfortably. Keep in mind that before 9/11, the New York office was the key FBI office working on international terrorism.

Basic connectivity is still a problem for some FBI field offices. The then-acting Director of the Washington field office told us last August that he still could not e-mail anyone at the Department of Justice from his desk. He said that the Washington field office, which is the second largest field office in the country, still has only one Internet terminal on each floor.

Information Sharing with State and Local Law Enforcement

The FBI also needs to be able to coordinate effectively with the hundreds of thousands of state and local law enforcement officers around the country to prevent terrorist attacks. In recognition of the need to work better with state and local law enforcement, Director Mueller announced the creation of the Office of Law Enforcement Coordination in December 2001. The FBI also sends an unclassified weekly Intelligence Bulletin to over 17,000 law enforcement agencies in the United States. The FBI has granted clearances to many police chiefs and other law enforcement officials to increase information sharing.

We spoke with several state and local law enforcement officials who told us that the FBI is doing a much better job sharing threat-related information. However, the Inspector General for the Department of Justice found that the reports "varied as to content and usefulness." We heard complaints that the FBI still needs to share much more operational, case-related information. The NYPD's Deputy Commissioner for Counterterrorism, Michael Sheehan, speculated that one of the reasons for deficiencies in this information sharing may be that the FBI does not always recognize what information might be important to others. For example, if a source mentions something about New York City to an FBI agent in Seattle, this information could be relevant for the NYPD and should be shared immediately. Los Angeles Police Department officials complained to us that they receive watered-down reports from the FBI. They said FBI agents have been told for years that their careers would be at stake if they improperly shared information. In their view, despite recent progress this attitude will take a long time to change. We have been told that the FBI plans to move toward a "write to release" approach that would allow for more immediate and broader dissemination of intelligence on an unclassified basis.

Central to the effort to coordinate with state and local officials is the expansion of the JTTFs that now exist in every field office. Indeed, Larry Mefford, the FBI's former Executive Assistant Director for Counterterrorism and Counterintelligence, called the JTTF structure "the foundation of the Bureau's information sharing efforts." All of the outside representatives on the JTTFs have top secret security clearances, just as all FBI agents do, and they may pass along certain information to their home agencies on a cleared and need-to-know basis.

We found, however, that the role of agency representatives varies from office to office. Information sharing is often ad hoc and depends upon the personalities involved. Although the representatives bring additional personnel to the FBI, the JTTF structure has not produced the full cooperation between the FBI and state and local law enforcement.

Most outside representatives on these task forces have an understanding of terrorism that is limited to the cases they are working on. Thus, they can not reasonably be expected to be the conduit for all threat and case information that may be important to their home agency.

One state counterterrorism official told us only a very small percentage of state and local police officers serve on the JTTFs and that "important information obtained from these national investigations does not reach the officers responsible for patrolling the cities, towns, highways, villages, and neighborhoods of our country." We heard this concern from other state and local counterterrorism officials. As a result, several state and local law enforcement agencies have begun to develop their own counter-terrorism efforts, separate and apart from the FBI.

LOOKING AHEAD

Two-and-a-half years after 9/11, it is clear that the FBI is an institution in transition. We recognize Director Mueller's genuine attempts to transform the FBI into an agency with the capacity to prevent terrorism. He has made progress. Important structural challenges remain to be addressed in order to improve the flow of information and to enhance the FBI's counterterrorism effectiveness. These challenges include:

- The relationship between headquarters and field offices;

- The relationship between the FBI, the JTTFs, and state and local law enforcement;

- The place of the FBI in the overall Intelligence Community; and

- The respective roles of the FBI, the new Department of Homeland Security, and the Terrorist Threat Integration Center.

———————

Peter Rundlet, Christine Healey, Caroline Barnes, Lance Cole, and Michael Jacobson did most of the work reflected in this statement. We were fortunate in being able to build upon strong investigative work done by the Congressional Joint Inquiry and by the Department of Justice's Office of the Inspector General. We have obtained excellent cooperation from the FBI and the Department of Justice, both in Washington and in six FBI field offices across the United States.

Excerpts of testimony from Robert S. Mueller III, Director, Federal Bureau of Investigation

"I do believe that creating a separate agency to collect intelligence in the United States would be a grave mistake. Splitting the law enforcement and the intelligence functions would leave both agencies fighting the war on terrorism with one hand tied behind their backs."

Prior to September 11th, there were various walls that existed. . . . The legal walls between intelligence and law enforcement operations thankfully have been broken down. Those walls handicapped us before September 11th, but they have now been eliminated. We are now able to fully coordinate operations within the bureau and within the intelligence community. And with these changes, we in the bureau can finally take full operational advantage of our dual role as both a law enforcement and an intelligence agency.

We are eliminating the wall that historically stood between us and the CIA. The FBI and the CIA started exchanging senior personnel in 1996, and we have worked hard to build on that effort. Today the FBI and the CIA are integrated at virtually every level of our operation, and this integration will be further enhanced later this year when our counterterrorism division co-locates with the CIA's counterterrorist center and the Terrorist Threat Integration Center [TTIC] at a new facility in Virginia.

We have also worked hard to break down the walls that have at times hampered coordination with our 750,000 partners in state and local law enforcement, and more than doubled the number of joint terrorism task forces since September 11th. Removing these walls has been part of a comprehensive plan to strengthen the ability of the FBI to predict and to prevent terrorism; we developed this plan immediately after the September 11th attacks and with the participation and strong support of the Department of Justice and the attorney general. We have been steadily and methodically implementing it ever since. . . .

The last crucial element of our transformation has been to develop our strategic analytic capability, while at the same time integrating intelligence processes into all of our investigative operations. We needed to dramatically expand our ability to convert our investigative information into strategic intelligence that could guide our operations. And to build that capacity, we have been steadily increasing the size and the caliber of our analytical corps. And we established an intelligence program to manage the intelligence process throughout the bureau. And to oversee this effort, last May I appointed Maureen Baginski, who is with me today, a 25-year analyst and executive from the National Security Agency, to serve as the bureau's first executive assistant director for intelligence. . . .

I'm sure the question will be asked today as to my views on the need to establish a separate domestic intelligence agency, so let me address that now. I do believe that creating a separate agency to collect intelligence in the United States would be a grave mistake. Splitting the law enforcement and the intelligence functions would leave both agencies fighting the war on terrorism with one hand tied behind their backs. The distinct advantage we gain by having intelligence and law enforcement together would be lost in more layers and greater stovepiping of information, not to mention the difficulty of transitioning safely to a new entity while terrorists seek to do us harm. The FBI's strength has always been, is, and will be in the collection of information. Our weakness has been in the integration, analysis and dissemination of that information. And we are addressing these weaknesses. The country has a tremendous resource in the FBI. We want to make the FBI better, we want to improve it so that we can fulfill our mission to protect America.

QUESTIONS FROM COMMISSIONERS

SLADE GORTON: [T]ry to imagine that we really were starting all over again without existing institutions in this field, as to whether or not your ideals in law enforcement and intelligence would be the two agencies that we have at the present time: one, law enforcement and domestic intelligence and one foreign intelligence; two, separate entities, one law enforcement and one all intelligence, both domestic and foreign; three, one for each of these; or one in which foreign and domestic intelligence were united together with law enforcement itself.

MUELLER: Well, let me start from the premise that you were working on a clean sheet of paper . . .

GORTON: That's what I would like you to do in this case.

MUELLER: . . . and working on a clean sheet of paper, if we go back all of those years and put history behind us, I think there are benefits to a separate intelligence organization where you have recruiting for intelligence and you focus on intelligence. I think that's an argument that we have to give. But then you look at the other side. And in order to deter attacks in the future, it cannot be one agency, particularly when you're looking domestically in the United States. And it's not just the FBI. What we have to do is leverage ourselves with every police department, state and local law enforcement, in order to gather the intelligence, the information in our communities, have it passed up so that we can be more predictive. And what the FBI brings to that intelligence gathering capacity is the 56 field offices we have around the country, more than 400 satellite offices in just about every one of our communities who have intersected over the years with state and local law enforcement in a wide variety of undertakings and developed the relationships that are so important to leveraging that throughout the United States. So that's number one.

The second point I think is very important is to reflect upon where we were before September 11th with the wall; where you had the divorcing of intelligence and criminal which was often tremendously artificial. And there were a number of contributing factors to that, but that was a fact of life before. What we have done since September 11th is broken down those walls, broken down that artificial determination of whether something's intelligence versus criminal. And what you have now is integrated in one agency within the United States, the ability—looking at it with state and local law enforcement—to push the intelligence aspects of any set of facts so long as you can gather more intelligence, identify more persons, identify more telephone numbers, identify more e-mail addresses, identify the networks here in the United States. But then when you have to neutralize that individual in the sense of taking action, we have the ability to take that action at the appropriate time. And the decisionmaker has all those facts in front of him. I think that is tremendously important to our effectiveness.

If you look at the other scenario that one of them—that you postulate—and that is: Well should you have a combined domestic and foreign intelligence? And I go back to what George [Tenet, CIA director,] said this morning that I think is on mark. One of the things that cannot be lost, I do not believe, when we address terrorism, is the importance of on the one hand protecting our civil liberties. We don't want to look down or have historians in the future look back at us and say, OK, you won the war on terrorism, but you sacrificed your civil liberties.

We operate within the rule of law. The FBI has always been trained operating within the Constitution, [underscoring] the importance within the United States of gathering information according to predication, according to guidelines, whether it be the attorney general, the statutes and the like. And that is the way we operate in the United States. And that is the way we should operate in the United States because we are called upon to gather information and intelligence on United States citizens. It is far different than what we're able to do overseas. And we have grown up with two different entities: one for overseas collection of information and one for domestic collection of information. And when it comes to collection—collection of information, I think it is important that we have that separation. That is not the separation that we need when we come to analyzing, integrating that information, and that is where we did not have the capacity before September 11th. That is where we have put up that capacity in TTIC, and we have to improve that capacity.

GORTON: Thank you. I gather I can summarize your answer, that even if we were starting all over again, you'd like the present division. But we're not starting all over again. And so the argument is overwhelming on one side. But I want to follow up on one thing that you said about recruitment. Now, I'm a young man just having graduated from law school, maybe one or two years of experience. But all through my youth, you know, I've watched television and what I really want to be is an intelligence agent. That's my real ambition. Why am I going to apply to the FBI, where I don't know what my career will be after three years, rather than the CIA, where I do?

MUELLER: As we build up our specialization—your staff statement described the specialization that we anticipate putting into place later this year and beginning of next year. You will come into the FBI, if you want, with a background or the desire to become an intelligence officer. And if you have the aptitude to do it, what we want you to do is understand the full scope of what the FBI can do, all of its capabilities, both on the criminal side and the intelligence side, so we put you through three years in a smaller office. Thereafter, you will specialize. You will specialize as an intelligence officer. You will have a designation as an intelligence officer. It will be the same type of designation that you have as an intelligence officer if it's the CIA, the DIA [Defense Intelligence Agency] or the NSA.

We hope to replicate that. But let me just go one step further and say that there are some persons that would want to come into the FBI and not wear a badge and a gun, not be an agent—a sharp individual who comes out of Middle East language studies and wants to direct collection. Institute requirements. We are building up and what we hope to do and are doing now is building up our analytical capability so that a person can come in as an analyst and become an intelligence officer without ever having to wear a gun or wear a badge and carry a gun. We want those people. We want those people within the bureau. And we want to give them the stature that has not always been there in the bureau.

. . .

JAMIE S. GORELICK: [W]ho is driving our strategy against al Qaeda? [W]ho is personally responsible for bringing all the information together and getting it from the constituent parts, et cetera? [A]bove your pay grade, is there someone who is our quarterback against an agile and entrepreneurial enemy, who brings together the strategy and capabilities of our country to fight this enemy?

MUELLER: Yes, I think there is. And I do believe it's the [National Security Council] and the Homeland Security Council and the staff for the overarching strategy. In other words, the overarching strategy against al Qaeda in my mind is established at that coordinated level and in much the same way our foreign policy is developed, where you have a number of different agencies that have a role, whether it be the department of—whether it be the State Department, the CIA, the Department of Defense. And I believe that the strategy is set there where there is a particular raising of the threat. The integration of the information and the taskings is there. And that's where we are at this point in time.

Now is there another model that might work better? I really don't know because I'm not all that familiar with all aspects of the intelligence community. I will tell you that in terms of developing intelligence and then pursuing the tasking, certainly domestically, I believe that we along with Homeland Security work closely together to do that. And internationally, George Tenet has the responsibility and the capability of understanding, developing the intelligence and doing the taskings.

And where, as I pointed out before, where the gaps existed before are all on the issues where you have a transnational intelligence operation. And the importance for us after September 11th is to assure that we fill those gaps where there is intelligence overseas and intelligence domestically that intersects. And we have addressed that problem by establishing teams whenever we have that type of information and working it jointly. And it has been tremendously effective. Much of it I cannot talk about here today. But when we say that substantial numbers of al Qaeda leadership have been detained overseas, it is because exactly of that integration, that teamwork that we have in those transnational intelligence operations.

And the last point I would make on that is: I do not think you can underestimate the impact of having us together. . . . Having us in the same building with separate collection responsibilities but then close to each other and close to TTIC is going to make a tremendous difference in terms of solidifying those relationships and easing that exchange of information between two components.

GORELICK: Are you a member of the National Security Council?

MUELLER: I am a principal for many—I'm generally a principal for anything having to do with terrorism and law enforcement. I certainly am not a member of the National Security Council for military actions, that kind of thing.

GORELICK: Are you a member of the Homeland Security Council?

MUELLER: Yes.

GORELICK: Do you need two councils?

MUELLER: Yes.

GORELICK: Because?

MUELLER: Well, because, I think, when you look at homeland

security you have something like an anthrax scare, it's very important that Governor [James] Thompson be sitting at the table. If you're looking at transportation within the United States, it's very important that Secretary [Norman] Mineta be sitting at the table. I don't think it's important for those individuals necessarily to be sitting at the table when the National Security Council is determining what we do vis-à-vis Indonesia or Saudi Arabia or Iraq or what have you, so I do believe . . .

GORELICK: You're not at the table when the National Security Council is looking at Indonesia or Saudi Arabia either. This is a question for me. I think—and we will ask this of [Homeland Security] Secretary [Tom] Ridge. But we have heard from a number of—let's say—alums of the homeland security process, that it functions as a third wheel. But you think it actually adds value?

MUELLER: Yes. . . . We have had, as everybody in the country knows, a number of threats in the last 2.5 years. The threat level has been raised. And the Homeland Security Council brings together those within the administration that play some role in either gathering the intelligence, analyzing the intelligence and then determining what steps need to be taken as a result of that intelligence. And Homeland Security Council is the entity that brings us all together, enables us to make decisions as are made, and make recommendations to the president, to the vice president as to what steps should be taken. So I think it is effective and it is necessary and useful.

GORELICK: As I described to the earlier panel and then our staff statement, you see that John Brennan, the director of TTIC, has said that he is seeing quote/unquote, a cacophony of activities in the intelligence community, but no strategy and planning. Do you think there is a clarity of roles with regard to all of these different centers and coordination entities? Or have we created redundancy in the system? Or to what redundancy? There's always some—too much redundancy in the system?

MUELLER: I do believe there is some clarity, but I also believe there's redundancy. And I do not believe redundancy is bad.

GORELICK: So you think there's not—I know there always has to be some redundancy. Your view is we have just the right amount of redundancy?

MUELLER: No, we are growing. TTIC is growing, the role of TTIC is growing. What is so important about TTIC is, as John Brennan testified before, is TTIC has access to all of our data-bases. As he has indicated, ideally what you would want is the ability to search across all those databases. And we are putting that into place. That will be instrumental in order to be able to quickly pull information out of each of those databases with the same common search tools. So we are growing. As we grow, there will be tensions. There will be overlap. There will be some gray areas. I do not altogether believe that it's bad, because we can look at something one way. John Brennan's people can look at it another way. George's people can look at it another way. And I have always found—and perhaps it's the lawyer in me—that the debate and the dialogue is not altogether bad.

II

Excerpts from the
House-Senate Joint
Inquiry Report on 9/11

SENATE SELECT COMMITTEE ON INTELLIGENCE (SSCI)

107TH CONGRESS

MEMBERSHIP

Bob Graham, D—Florida, Chairman

Richard C. Shelby, R—Alabama, Vice Chairman

Democrats
Carl Levin, Michigan
John D. Rockefeller, West Virginia
Dianne Feinstein, California
Ron Wyden, Oregon
Richard J. Durbin, Illinois
Evan Bayh, Indiana
John Edwards, North Carolina
Barbara Mikulski, Maryland
Al Cumming, *Staff Director*

Republicans
Jon Kyl, Arizona
James M. Inhofe, Oklahoma
Orrin Hatch, Utah
Pat Roberts, Kansas
Mike DeWine, Ohio
Fred Thompson, Tennessee
Richard Lugar, Indiana
William Duhnke,
    Minority Staff Director

HOUSE PERMANENT SELECT COMMITTEE ON INTELLIGENCE (HPSCI)

107TH CONGRESS

MEMBERSHIP

Porter J. Goss, R—Florida, Chairman

Nancy Pelosi, D—California, Ranking Democrat

Republicans
Doug Bereuter, Nebraska
Michael N. Castle, Delaware
Sherwood L. Boehlert, New York
Jim Gibbons, Nevada
Ray LaHood, Illinois
Randy "Duke" Cunningham,
   California
Peter Hoekstra, Michigan
Richard Burr, North Carolina
Saxby Chambliss, Georgia
Terry Everett, Alabama
Timothy R. Sample,
   Staff Director

Democrats
Sanford D. Bishop, Georgia
Jane Harman, California
Gary A. Condit, California
Tim Roemer, Indiana
Silvestre Reyes, Texas
Leonard L. Boswell, Iowa
Collin C. Peterson,
   Minnesota
Bud Cramer, Alabama
Michael W. Sheehy,
   Democratic Counsel

The Attacks of September 11, 2001

EDITOR'S NOTE: Osama bin Laden first appeared on the FBI's radar screen eight years before 9/11. The bureau linked him to the terrorists who bombed the World Trade Center in February 1993, to the fighters who killed eighteen U.S. servicemen in Somalia later that year, to the 1998 bombings of U.S. embassies in Kenya and Tanzania, and to the 2001 suicide attack on the U.S.S. *Cole*. Agents knew he had declared war on America and intended to strike there. So how did they miss bin Laden's big act? Three of the al Qaeda pilots emerged from quiet lives in Hamburg, Germany; the fourth had lived peacefully in America for most of a decade. In the critical months before the attacks on New York and Washington, many of the principals traveled to and from the United States at will as they took flight lessons and meticulously planned their strike. Five months before the hijackings, the anonymous fighters who helped take control of the four passenger flights joined the chief planners in the United States, and in August they began buying tickets for their carefully chosen seats. The Joint Inquiry pieced together the elements of a terrorist strike that took years to assemble and one devastating morning to unleash.

ROOTS OF THE OPERATION

Osama bin Laden came to the FBI's attention after the first attack on the World Trade Center in February 1993. While the FBI has not linked that attack directly to bin Laden, the investigation developed information that Muslim men, including participants in the attack, had been recruited at the al Kifah refugee office in Brooklyn, New York, and sent to training camps in Afghanistan—first to fight the Soviet army and later to engage in a jihad against the United States. In 1993, the FBI also learned of a plot to blow up bridges, tunnels, and landmarks in New York. That investigation led to the conviction of Omar Abd al Rahman, the "Blind Sheikh," for soliciting others to commit all of those acts of terrorism in 1993. Bin Laden's fatwas and press statements later called for avenging the Blind Sheikh's imprisonment.

The FBI has identified at least two bin Laden connections in Ramzi Yousef's 1995 conspiracy, centered in the Philippines, to blow up twelve U.S. airplanes flying East Asian routes to the United States. Mohamed Jamal Khalifah, the alleged financier of the plot, is bin Laden's brother-in-law. Ramzi Yousef was arrested at a bin Laden guesthouse in Pakistan to which Yousef had fled after the plot had been uncovered. Yousef was a principal in the first World Trade Center attacks, for which he was tried and convicted upon being returned to the United States.

George Tenet, the Director of Central Intelligence (DCI), testified that "a common thread runs between the first attack on the World Trade Center in February 1993 and the 11 September attacks." The thread is Khalid Sheikh Mohammed, also known as Mukhtar or "the Brain." According to the DCI, Mohammed, "a high-ranking al Qaeda member," was "the mastermind or one of the key planners of the 11 September operation." The DCI noted that Mukhtar is Ramzi Yousef's uncle, and, after the World Trade Center attack, Mohammed joined Yousef in the 1995 airplane plot, for which Mohammed has been indicted by a federal grand jury.

In August 1996, bin Laden issued the first fatwa declaring jihad against the United States. A second fatwa in February 1998 proclaimed: "to kill the Americans and their allies—civilian and military is an individual duty for every Muslim who can do it in any country in which it is possible to do it." Bin Laden repeated these threats in a May 1998 press interview. The bombings of the U.S. embassies in Kenya and Tanzania followed in August.

In June 1998, the Department of Justice obtained a sealed indictment in the Southern District of New York against bin Laden as the sole named defendant in a "conspiracy to attack defense utilities of the United States." Among other overt acts, the indictment charged that in October 1993 "members of al Qaeda participated with Somali tribesmen in an attack on United States military personnel serving in Somalia [that] killed a total of 18 United States soldiers and wounded 73 others." The indictment was unsealed after the East African embassy bombings and was followed by a series of superseding indictments that charged bin Laden and others with a conspiracy to "murder United States nationals anywhere in the world, including in the United States."

The U.S. Government produced proof in the embassy bombing trials of bin Laden's direct connections to the attacks. Mohamed al Owhali, who was to have been a suicide passenger in the Kenya bombing, ran from the bomb truck moments before it exploded. After his arrest in Kenya, al Owhali confessed and admitted that he had been given a telephone number in Sana'a, Yemen, which he called before and after the bombing. Telephone records for calls to that number led to the bomb factory for the Nairobi attack in a house occupied by a ranking al Qaeda member and training camp veteran. Calls from bin Laden's satellite phone to the Yemen number were made the day of the attack and the day after when al Owhali called that number for help. Al Owhali also confessed that he had asked bin Laden for a mission, a request that led to his being in the bomb truck. According to al Owhali, the suicide driver had been present with him at bin Laden's May 1998 press conference.

U.S. investigators have also described bin Laden's connection to the October 2000 attack on the United States Navy's ship, U.S.S. *Cole*. . . . Tawfiq bin Attash, known as Khallad, who had been a trainer at an al Qaeda camp in Afghanistan, prepared an introduction in the summer of 1999 for Abdel Rahim al Nashiri addressed to Jamal al Badawi, who had trained under Khallad. Al Nashiri is believed to be a long-time bin Laden operative and a first cousin of the suicide driver who attacked the U.S. Embassy in Kenya. Khallad appears to have directed the *Cole* operation from Afghanistan or Pakistan, while al Nashiri was its local manager.

Investigators believe that Khallad's letter set in motion plans to attack another U.S. Navy ship. Following al Nashiri's introduction, Badawi obtained the boat that would be used in the failed attack on U.S.S. *The Sullivans* in January 2000. The same boat was used later that year in the attack against U.S.S. *Cole*.

In testimony to the Joint Inquiry, the DCI explained that, after September 11, 2001, CIA learned that "in 1996, bin Laden's second-in-command, Muhammad Atif, drew up a study on the feasibility of hijacking U.S. planes and destroying them in flight." Khalid Sheikh Mohammed proposed to bin Laden that the World Trade Center "be targeted by small aircraft packed with explosives." Bin Laden reportedly suggested using even larger planes.

According to the DCI, Muhammad Atif "chose the hijackers from young Arab men who had no previous terrorist activities." After bin Laden had approved the selection, Khalid Sheikh Mohammed "trained them and instructed them on acquiring pilot training" and "supervised the 'final touches' of the 11 September operation."

SPRINGBOARDS FOR THE ATTACKS

In addition to Afghani-based al Qaeda roots of the September 11 attacks, the FBI reports that "[t]he operational planning for the September 11th attacks took place in overseas locations, most notably Germany, Malaysia and the United Arab Emirates."

THE MALAYSIA CONNECTION

Two principal hijackers in the September 11 attacks, Khalid al Mihdhar and Nawaf al Hazmi, entered the United States on a flight from Bangkok on January 15, 2000, a week after leaving a meeting in Kuala Lumpur, Malaysia. Three other principals, Mohammed Atta, Marwan al Shehhi, and Ziad Jarrah, entered the United States in May and June 2000 from or through Europe. Atta, al Shehhi, and Jarrah had lived in Hamburg, Germany where they associated with each other in various ways. A sixth principal, Hani Hanjour, had been in the United States off and on since October 1991.

In June 18 testimony at a Joint Inquiry hearing, the DCI described al Hazmi and al Mihdhar as "al Qaeda veterans." They had been involved with al Qaeda for six years before September 11, 2001, "having trained and fought under al Qaeda auspices in three different countries."

Al Hazmi first traveled to Afghanistan in 1993 as a teenager and came into contact with a key al Qaeda facilitator in Saudi Arabia in 1994. In 1995, al Hazmi and al Mihdhar traveled to Bosnia to fight with other Muslims against the Serbs. Al Hazmi probably came into contact with al Qaeda leader Abu Zubaydah when Zubaydah visited Saudi Arabia in 1996 to convince young Saudis to attend al Qaeda camps in Afghanistan. Sometime before 1998, al Hazmi returned to Afghanistan and swore loyalty to bin Laden. He fought against the Northern Alliance, possibly with his brother Salem, another of the hijackers, and returned to Saudi Arabia in early 1999, where . . . he disclosed information about the East Africa embassy bombings.

Al Mihdhar's first trip to the Afghanistan training camps was in early 1996. . . . In 1998, al Mihdhar traveled to Afghanistan and swore allegiance to bin Laden.

In April 1999, Nawaf al Hazmi, Salem al Hazmi, and Khalid al Mihdhar obtained visas through the U.S. Consulate in Jeddah, Saudi Arabia. Al Mihdhar and Nawaf al Hazmi then traveled to Afghanistan and "participated in special training," which, according to the DCI, may have been "facilitated by Khallad" (Tawfiq bin Attash, who also directed the U.S.S. *Cole* operation). A U.S.S. *Cole* suicide bomber also participated in that training.

From Yemen, al Mihdhar traveled to Kuala Lumpur, arriving on January 5, 2000. There he met al Hazmi, who had traveled to Malaysia from Pakistan. In Malaysia, the two met Khallad at a condominium owned by Yazid Sufaat, who later signed letters of introduction on behalf of Zacarias Moussaoui [the student pilot arrested in Minnesota shortly before September 11] that were found in Moussaoui's possessions after the September 11 attacks. Malaysian police arrested Sufaat in December 2001 after they developed information that he had procured four tons of bomb material, ammonium nitrate, for an Indonesian jihad cell.

THE GERMANY CONNECTION

In testimony before the Joint Inquiry, DCI Tenet described the significant characteristics that were shared by Mohammed Atta, Marwan al Shehhi, and Ziad Jarrah—the September 11 hijackers who most likely piloted the airplanes that the groups they were part of commandeered. The three were intelligent, spoke English and were proficient in several other languages, and were familiar with Western society. They were also educated in technical subjects and had mastered skills necessary to pilot planes. Of particular note, the three were part of a group of young Muslim men in Hamburg, Germany, who came from different countries and backgrounds, but attended the same mosques, shared acquaintances, and were drawn together by Islamist views and disenchantment with the West.

Atta was born in Egypt in 1968. He graduated from Cairo University with a degree in Architectural Engineering in 1990 and began attending the Technical University in Hamburg in 1992. Between 1996 and 1998, Atta traveled in the Middle East and then returned to Germany.

Al Shehhi was born in the United Arab Emirates in 1978. A sergeant in the UAE Army, he was sent to Germany for technical studies in 1996. In 1997 and 1998, he studied English at the University at Bonn and electrical engineering at the Technical University in Hamburg.

Jarrah was born in Lebanon in 1975. He attended the Fachhochschule, a technical University in Hamburg from 1996 to 2000, studying aircraft construction and maintenance.

While in Germany, Atta, al Shehhi, and Jarrah, according to FBI documents, kept company with a loosely organized group of associates comprised of roommates, co-workers and mosque colleagues. Three associates, Ramzi Binalshibh, Said Bahaji, and Zakariya Essabar, became subjects of post-September 11 German arrest warrants for alleged membership in a terrorist organization and for murder and aircraft piracy. A fourth, Munir el Motassadeq, is on trial in Hamburg on those charges. [Motassadeq was convicted in Germany on February 19, 2003 of being a member of a terrorist organization and accessory to over 3,000 murders in New York and Washington; a German court, ruling that his first trial had been unfair and ordering a second, released him in April 2004.

Binalshibh, who was born in Yemen in 1972 and entered Germany in 1995, is described as a "supporting conspirator" in the Moussaoui indictment. In August 2000, Jarrah attempted to enroll Binalshibh in the Florida Flight Training Center, where Jarrah was taking lessons. On August 15, Binalshibh sent a $2200 wire transfer to the school for tuition, and in July and September, he transferred funds to al Shehhi in Florida. Between May and October 2000, Binalshibh unsuccessfully attempted four times—three in Germany and once in Yemen—to obtain a visa to travel to the United States. Between December 2 and 9, 2000, Binalshibh was in London. Moussaoui flew from London to Pakistan on December 9.

FBI Director [Robert] Mueller testified that Binalshibh was a "significant money person." The Moussaoui indictment charges that Binalshibh received $15,000 in wire transfers from the UAE on or about July 30 and 31, 2001 and that he wired $14,000 to Moussaoui in Oklahoma on or about August 1 and 3 from train stations in Dusseldorf and Hamburg.

DCI Tenet testified that, after September 11, 2001, CIA received reports identifying Binalshibh "as an important al Qaeda operative." The agency suspects that, "unlike the three Hamburg pilots, he may have been associated with al Qaeda even before moving to Germany in 1995." Binalshibh flew to Spain in early September 2001. He disappeared until an interview with al Jazeera was aired in September 2002, and he was captured in Pakistan on September 11, 2002. Binalshibh is now being held . . . at an undisclosed location.

Atta lived at Marienstrasse 54 in Hamburg with Binalshibh, Essabar, and Bahaji. Director Tenet testified that, after Binalshibh failed to obtain a U.S. visa, "another cell member," Essabar, "tried [on two occasions] and failed to obtain a visa in January 2001" to travel to Florida while Atta and al Shehhi were there. Uncorroborated sources report that Essabar was in Afghanistan in late September 2001. Bahaji left Germany on September 3, 2001 for Pakistan. Uncorroborated sources also placed him in Afghanistan in late September 2001.

DCI Tenet testified that Muhammad Heydar Zammar was an acquaintance of members of Atta's circle in Hamburg, where Zammar lived. Zammar, a German citizen born in Syria in 1961, was described by DCI Tenet as "a known al Qaeda associate," active in Islamic extremist circles since the 1980s, who trained and fought in Afghanistan in 1991 and in Bosnia in 1995 and returned to Afghanistan a number of times between 1995 and 2000.

It has been reported that U.S. and German officials believe that Zammar is a pivotal figure in understanding the genesis of the September 11 attacks. DCI Tenet told the Joint Inquiry that Zammar "was taken into custody by the Moroccans" when he traveled to Morocco to divorce his wife and that he was "moved from Morocco into Syrian custody, where he has remained." It has also been reported that Zammar has provided details about the September 11 attacks to U.S. investigators. According to the DCI, Zammar has said that he met Atta, al Shehhi, and Jarrah in the late 1990s in Hamburg's al Qods mosque and he "persuaded them to travel to Afghanistan to join the jihad."

DCI Tenet testified that Atta may have traveled to Afghanistan for the first time in early 1998. In June 1998, he applied for a new passport in Egypt, although his old one had not expired. This suggested, according to the DCI, "that he might have been trying to hide evidence of his travel to Afghanistan." On November 29, 1999, Atta flew from Hamburg to Istanbul and then to Karachi. He left Pakistan to return to Hamburg on February 25, 2000.

In the fall of 1999, al Shehhi stayed at bin Laden's Kandahar guesthouse while awaiting transportation to Pakistan for medical treatment. He returned to Germany in January 2000. According to FBI information, Atta and al Shehhi "were both present at bin Laden facilities in Kandahar in December 1999." The DCI noted that "Jarrah's travel at this time mirrored Atta's," as Jarrah flew from Hamburg to Karachi on November 25, 1999 and stayed in Pakistan for two months.

There are indications that Binalshibh was in Afghanistan in 1998 and had been seen at the Khalden Camp or guesthouse in late 1998. The Moussaoui indictment alleges that Moussaoui had been present at the Khalden Camp in or about April 1998.

LEARNING TO FLY

On January 15, 2000, one week after leaving Malaysia, Khalid al Mihdhar and Nawaf al Hazmi flew to Los Angeles from Bangkok and settled in the San Diego area. In April 2000, al Hazmi took an introductory flying lesson at the National Air College in San Diego. A week later, al Hazmi received a $5000 wire transfer through a third party sent from the United Arab Emirates. In May, al Mihdhar and al Hazmi took flight training in San Diego, and in June, al Mihdhar left the U.S. on a Lufthansa flight from Los Angeles to Frankfurt, connecting to Oman. Al Mihdhar did not return to the United States until thirteen months later in July 2001.

Al Hazmi remained in the United States, staying in the San Diego area until December 2000 when he moved to Arizona with Hani Hanjour, who had just returned to the United States. The DCI testified that Hanjour went to Afghanistan for six weeks in 1989 when he was 17 to participate in a jihad. He first entered the

United States in October 1991 from Saudi Arabia to attend an English language program at the University of Arizona in Tucson. When he left the U.S. in early 1992 for Saudi Arabia, he was a "different person," according to a brother who spoke to the media. According to the DCI, Hanjour then "wore a full beard, cut his past social ties, and spent most of his time reading books on religion and airplanes." Hanjour returned to the United States in April 1996. After residing in Florida for a month, he moved to Oakland, California, where he took an English language course. In the summer, he began flight training, and in September, he moved to Arizona where he took flight lessons for a month in Scottsdale. Hanjour left the U.S. for Saudi Arabia in November 1996, returning to the United States in November 1997.

Hanjour left the United States again in April 1999, after receiving an FAA [Federal Aviation Administration] commercial pilot certificate. In September, after an initial denial, he obtained a student visa in Jeddah and returned to the United States. Then in November 2000, having stayed in Florida for a month, he met al Hazmi in California and traveled with him to Arizona in early December. On December 12, he took up residence in Mesa, Arizona with al Hazmi and resumed aviation training. He took Boeing groundwork and simulator training in February and March 2001, when he and al Hazmi left Arizona for northern Virginia.

Atta returned to Germany from Afghanistan through Pakistan in February 2000. On March 1, he sent the first of a series of e-mails to pilot training schools in Lakeland, Florida, and Norman, Oklahoma. Claiming that his passport had been lost, Atta obtained a new Egyptian passport in Hamburg in May 2000 and a visa for travel to the United States. He crossed over to the Czech Republic by bus and flew to Newark in June 2000. Al Shehhi had arrived several days earlier on a flight from the United Arab Emirates through Brussels to Newark. He obtained a new passport, apparently in Pakistan before leaving for Germany at the beginning of January 2000. Later that month, he obtained a ten-year multiple entry visa at the U.S. consulate in Dubai. Atta and al Shehhi stayed in the New York area, renting apartments together until the beginning of July when they flew to Oklahoma City for a short visit to the Airman Flight School in Norman. They proceeded to Florida, opened a joint account at Sun Trust Bank (depositing $7000), and began training at Huffman Aviation in Venice.

In the meantime, Jarrah arrived in the U.S. on June 27 at Atlanta, Georgia. Earlier in the year, he reported losing his Lebanese passport, and in May he obtained a five-year B1/B2 multiple entry visa. On arriving in the United States, Jarrah proceeded to Venice, Florida, where he began training at the Florida Flight Training Center.

In Fall 2000, Atta and al Shehhi obtained instrument certifications and commercial pilot licenses while at Huffman Aviation. They also spent a brief period at Jones Aviation in Sarasota, Florida. From December 29 through 31, Atta and al Shehhi received Boeing flight simulator training at Sim Center and Pan Am International in Opalocka, Florida. The FBI reports that both men "requested training on executing turns and approaches" but not other training normally associated with the course. In the meantime, Jarrah continued flight training until December 2000 where he had begun it, the Florida Flight Training Center. In mid-December and in early January 2001, he took Boeing flight simulator lessons at the Aeroservice Aviation Center in Virginia Gardens, Florida.

In December 2000, al Shehhi flew to Hamburg and then on to the United Arab Emirates, returning for the December flight simulator training with Atta. On January 4, 2001, Atta flew from Tampa through Miami to Madrid, returning to Miami on January 10. The DCI testified that the purpose of Atta's trip to Spain "may have been to meet with another al Qaeda operative to pass along an update on the pilots' training progress and receive information on the supporting hijackers who would begin arriving in the U.S. in the spring." DCI Tenet testified that "Atta may also have traveled outside of the U.S. in early April 2001 to meet an Iraqi intelligence officer, although we are still working to corroborate this." Atta may have traveled under an unknown alias: The CIA has been unable to establish that he left the United States or entered Europe in April under his true name or any known alias.

On April 18, al Shehhi, who traveled outside the United States three times, flew to Egypt by way of Amsterdam and returned to Miami from Egypt through Amsterdam on May 2. In Egypt, al Shehhi visited Atta's father and returned to the U.S. with Atta's international driver's license. Apart from that, the DCI testified, "nothing else is known of al Shehhi's activities while traveling outside the U.S." Jarrah traveled even more frequently, taking at least five trips outside the United States to visit his family in Lebanon, and to visit his girl friend in Germany.

After al Shehhi returned from Morocco in January 2001, he and Atta moved to Georgia for flight training. In February, they traveled to Virginia Beach, Virginia, where they opened a mail-box account. A crop duster pilot in Belle Glade, Florida identified Atta as inquiring about the purchase and operation of crop dusters while Atta was living in the Atlanta area.

THE "MUSCLE" ARRIVES

The thirteen remaining hijackers, the "muscle," whose role was to overcome pilots and control passengers, began arriving in the United States in April 2001. Except for one threesome, they arrived in pairs, the last in June. Twelve of the thirteen were from Saudi Arabia, and one was from the United Arab Emirates. Salem al Hazmi, Nawaf's brother, obtained his visa as early as April 1999; seven obtained visas from September to November 2000; three, as late as June 2001. As FBI Director Mueller noted, these hijackers arrived in the United States "within a fairly short window," each transiting through the United Arab Emirates.

Many in the group knew each other. There were two pairs of brothers, the al Hazmis and al Shehris, in addition to networks of friends. Many came from southwest Saudi Arabia, and they represented a range of socioeconomic levels. A few had higher education. Others had little education. Some had struggled with depression or alcohol abuse. Some, according to DCI Tenet, "never exhibited much religious fervor, before apparent exposure to extremist ideas—through family members, friends, or clerics—

led to an abrupt radicalization and separation from their families"; some spoke of "their desire to participate in jihad conflicts such as the war in Chechnya, and some appear to have used this as a cover for traveling to Afghanistan." The DCI also testified that "[a]s part of their commitment to militant Islam, these young Saudis traveled to Afghanistan to train in the camps of their exiled countryman Osama bin Laden." Most supporting hijackers went to Afghanistan for the first time in 1999 or 2000. Notwithstanding the experience in Afghanistan, the CIA does not believe that the supporting hijackers became involved in the plot until late 2000. Their early travel may have "added these young men to the ranks of operatives that al Qaeda could call upon to carry out future missions," but DCI Tenet said he does not believe that al Qaeda leadership wanted the supporting hijackers to know about the plot any sooner than necessary: "they probably were told little more than that they were headed for a suicide mission inside the United States."

Al Mihdhar, who left the United States a year before, obtained a visa in Jeddah in June 2001, using a new Saudi passport. According to DCI Tenet, he "spent the past year traveling between Yemen and Afghanistan, with occasional trips to Saudi Arabia." Al Mihdhar traveled to New York in July 2001 from Saudi Arabia, six days after the last of the supporting hijackers had flown to the United States. FBI Director Mueller testified that "al Mihdhar's role in the September 11 plot between June 2000 and July 2001—before his re-entry into the United States—may well have been that of the coordinator and organizer of the movements of the non-pilot hijackers. This is supported by his apparent lengthy stay in Saudi Arabia and his arriving back in the United States only after the arrival of all the hijackers."

FINAL PREPARATIONS

Beginning in May 2001, each of the four pilot hijackers flew across the United States. FBI Director Mueller described these trips: "With their training complete, it appears that the pilots began conducting possible surveillance flights as passengers aboard cross-country flights transiting between the Northeast United States and California." On May 24, al Shehhi flew from New York to San Francisco on a Boeing 767 (seated in first class), leaving immediately on a Boeing 757 (seated in first class) to Las Vegas. On May 27, al Shehhi left Las Vegas to San Francisco, continuing to New York on a Boeing 767 (seated in first class). On June 7, Jarrah flew from Baltimore via Los Angeles to Las Vegas, returning to Baltimore on June 10. On June 28, Atta flew from Boston to San Francisco, continuing to Las Vegas, departing there on July 1 through Denver to Boston. On August 13, Atta flew a second time across country from Washington to Las Vegas on a Boeing 757 (seated in first class), returning on August 14 to Ft. Lauderdale. On August 13, Hanjour and al Hazmi (seated in first class) flew from Dulles to Las Vegas via Los Angeles. They left Las Vegas on August 14 on a flight to Minneapolis (close to Eagan, Minnesota, where Moussaoui had started flight lessons the day before), connecting an hour and a half later to a flight to Baltimore.

Director Mueller noted the Las Vegas layovers:

Each of the return flights for these hijackers had layovers in Las Vegas. To date, the purpose of these one-to-two day layovers is not known. However, with respect to travel to Las Vegas, we know that at least one hijacker on each of the four hijacked airplanes traveled to Las Vegas, Nevada sometime between May and August of 2001. This travel consisted of an initial transcontinental trip from an east-coast city to a west-coast city, and a connection in that west-coast city to a Las Vegas-bound flight.

Atta flew to Zurich from Miami in July 2001, continuing on to Madrid. He checked out of a Madrid hotel on July 9 and rented a car that he returned on July 19, after having driven 1,908 kilometers. For the days immediately following July 9, Atta's whereabouts are unknown until he checked into a hotel in Tarragona on Spain's east coast on July 16. On July 9, Binalshibh flew from Hamburg to Tarragona, where he checked out of a hotel on July 10.

His whereabouts from July 10 to 16 are unaccounted for, "roughly the same period during which Atta's movements are unknown," suggesting, according to DCI Tenet, that "the two engaged in clandestine meetings on the progress of the plot." Atta returned to the United States on July 19, arriving in Atlanta. Jarrah traveled to Germany from Newark on July 25, returning on August 5, a trip that may have permitted further contact with Binalshibh. Director Mueller also testified that "[d]uring the summer of 2001, some of the hijackers, specifically Mohammed Atta and Nawaf al Hazmi, appear to have met face-to-face on a monthly basis to discuss the status of the operation, and ultimately the final preparation for the attack." In an interview with al Jazeera shortly before his capture, Binalshibh described al Hazmi as Atta's "right hand."

As the supporting hijackers arrived, they divided between Florida and New York before moving to three staging areas. The two who arrived in Virginia and the two who arrived in New York joined Nawaf al Hazmi and Hanjour in Paterson, New Jersey. The four who arrived in Orlando and the five who arrived in Miami joined Atta, al Shehhi, and Jarrah in the Fort Lauderdale, Florida, area.

The nineteen hijackers began to book September 11 flights on August 26. Al Mihdhar and Majed Moqed, hijackers on the Pentagon flight, were unable to buy tickets on August 24 because their address could not be verified. They finally purchased them with cash on September 5 at the American Airlines counter in the Baltimore/Washington International Airport. The hijackers in the Fort Lauderdale area also booked flights to locations in the Boston, Newark, New Jersey, and Washington, D.C. areas where the teams for each September 11 flight assembled.

FINANCING THE TERRORISTS

The FBI estimates that the September 11 attacks cost $175,000 to $250,000. According to Director Mueller and Bureau documents, "the funding mechanism behind the conspiracy appears to center around Marwan al Shehhi and individuals providing financial support primarily" through the "banking and wire service infrastructure" of the United Arab Emirates.

In Hamburg, al Shehhi received substantial transfers from the UAE by wire from Mohamed Yousef Mohamed Alqusaidi, whom the FBI believes to be al Shehhi's brother. In July 1999, al Shehhi opened a checking account in the UAE and soon after granted a power of attorney over the account to Alqusaidi. From July 1999 to November 2000, about $100,000 moved through the account. While they were in Germany, al Shehhi transferred funds to Atta.

In July 2000, al Shehhi and Atta opened a joint account at Suntrust Bank in Venice, Florida, which received, according to the FBI, what appears to be the primary funding for the conspiracy, four transfers from the UAE totaling approximately $110,000 from Ali Abdul Aziz Ali using a variety of aliases. In June 2000, al Shehhi also received $5,000 by Western Union wire from Isam Mansour. In April, Ali wired $5,000 to al Hazmi in San Diego. Several hijackers, including Hanjour and al Mihdhar, supplemented their financing with credit cards drawn on Saudi and UAE banks.

Transfers to Binalshibh on July 30 and 31, 2001, which preceded his transfers to Moussaoui, were from Hashem Abdulraham, whom FBI Director Mueller identified as Khalid Sheikh Mohammed, "the Brain."

There was also an important flow of money back to the UAE immediately before September 11. FBI documents state that funds "were returned to the source because the hijackers would not have wanted to die as thieves, therefore they returned the money that was provided to them." Three hijackers, including Atta and al Shehhi, sent funds to Mustafa Ahmed Alhawsawi in the UAE. Al Hazmi sent an Express Mail package to a UAE post office box rented in Alhawsawi's name that contained al Mihdhar's debit card for an account in which $10,000 remained. Alhawsawi also had power of attorney over accounts of several hijackers in the UAE.

SEPTEMBER 11, 2001

At approximately 7:59 A.M., on September 11, American Airlines Flight 11, bound for Los Angeles, was cleared for takeoff from Logan International Airport in Boston. On board were 81 passengers and 11 crew members. Two hijackers were in the first two seats in First Class, from which the cockpit doors were easily accessible. According to Director Mueller, the hijackers, "apparently using commonly available box cutters," seized the aircraft and diverted its course at about 8:13 A.M. At 8:45 A.M. Flight 11 crashed into the World Trade Center's North Tower, which collapsed at 10:25 A.M.

Atta is believed to have been the pilot because he was the only Flight 11 hijacker known to have had flight training. He spent the night before the attacks in Portland, Maine, flying to Boston on the morning of September 11. Atta's luggage did not make the connection to Flight 11. The FBI Director testified that a search "revealed a three page letter handwritten in Arabic which, upon translation, was found to contain instructions on how to prepare for a mission applicable, but not specific, to the September 11 operation."

At approximately 7:58 A.M., United Airlines Flight 175, also bound for Los Angeles, left Logan with 65 passengers and crew members. At 9:05 A.M., Flight 175 crashed into the World Trade Center's South Tower, which collapsed at 9:55 A.M. Marwan al Shehhi is believed to have been the pilot.

As of December 2002, the Office of the Chief Medical Examiner of the City of New York reported that 2792 persons are reported as missing as a result of the attacks on the World Trade Center, including persons on the ground and passengers and crew of the two planes. [By April 2004, the medical examiner had adjusted the number of deaths to 2749].

At approximately 8:20 A.M., American Airlines Flight 77 left Dulles International Airport for Los Angeles with 58 passengers and six crew members. The last routine radio contact with the plane was at 8:50 A.M. A few minutes later the plane made an unauthorized turn. At 9:39 A.M., Flight 77 crashed into the Pentagon's southwest side. In addition to the passengers and crew, 125 military and civilian Pentagon employees died. The pilot is believed to have been Hani Hanjour. A copy of the letter in Atta's luggage was found in a car registered to al Hazmi that had been parked at Dulles.

At approximately 8:42 A.M., United Airlines Flight 93 left Newark International Airport for San Francisco with 37 passengers and seven crew members. Ziad Jarrah was the only one of four hijackers aboard known to have a pilot's license; therefore, he is believed to have been the pilot. At approximately 10:03 A.M., Flight 93 crashed into the ground at Stoney Creek Township in southwestern Pennsylvania.

Telephone calls from passengers and crew to family and friends described attempts by passengers and crew to retake the plane prior to the crash. One call described three hijackers wearing bandanas and armed with knives, with one hijacker claiming to have a bomb strapped to his waist. Two hijackers entered the cockpit and closed the door behind them. The passengers were herded to the back of the plane. The captain and co-pilot were seen lying on the floor of the First Class section, possibly dead. At the words, "Let's roll," passengers rushed forward. As described by the FBI Director, the cockpit tape-recorder indicates that a hijacker, minutes before Flight 93 hit the ground, "advised Jarrah to crash the plane and end the passengers attempt to retake the airplane."

A copy of the letter found in Atta's baggage and al Hazmi's car was also found at the Flight 93 crash site. The FBI notes that some of the Arabic on the cockpit tape, "such as supplications to Allah, conforms to the suicide preparation instructions" in that letter.

In the UAE, Alhawsawi, the plot financier, consolidated in his bank account funds the hijackers had returned, to which he added funds he withdrew from one of their accounts just hours before the September 11 attacks. He then flew to Karachi, Pakistan. His whereabouts are unknown.

The Intelligence Failures

EDITOR'S NOTE: One twist of fortune and the 9/11 plot could have been crushed in its planning stages. The CIA tracked two hijackers from Malaysia to California, but failed to warn the FBI in time or to ask the State Department to put out a watch for them. FBI agents in Phoenix and Minneapolis uncovered vague outlines of the plot, but nobody at headquarters followed up on their reports in time. The National Security Agency found early links between 9/11 hijackers, but failed to disseminate them. Practically every eye and ear in the U.S. intelligence community picked up signals that bin Laden was planning major mayhem, but most of the warnings seemed aimed at American interests abroad. All the tantalizing near misses, bureaucratic buck-passing and general confusion provided the Joint Inquiry with its most important mandate: to build the foundation for reforming America's intelligence systems. As an important first step, investigators had to unravel how those systems broke down on 9/11.

MISSED SIGNALS IN MALAYSIA

In late 1999, the Intelligence Community launched a worldwide effort to disrupt terrorist operations that were planned to occur during the Millennium celebrations. [The CIA discovered that two men with suspected links to al Qaeda, Khalid al Mihdhar and Nawaf al Hazmi, were planning a trip to Kuala Lumpur, Malaysia.] The intelligence preceding the Malaysian meeting also showed that a person whose first name was Salem would attend. An intelligence analyst observed at the time that "Salem may be Nawaf's younger brother," and that observation was reported to other Intelligence Community agencies.

The Kuala Lumpur meeting took place between January 5 and 8, 2000. There has been no intelligence about what was discussed at the meeting, but, according to [Director of Central Intelligence (DCI) George] Tenet, surveillance . . . that began with al Mihdhar's arrival on January 5 "indicated that the behavior of the individuals was consistent with clandestine activity."

It was later determined that Khallad bin Attash, a leading operative in bin Laden's network, also attended the meeting. According to DCI Tenet, Khallad was "the most important figure at the Kuala Lumpur meeting" and he would later become "a key planner in the October 2000 U.S.S. *Cole* bombing."

DCI Tenet testified that, "[i]n early January 2000, we managed to obtain a photocopy of al Mihdhar's passport as he traveled to Kuala Lumpur." This gave the CIA al Mihdhar's full name, his passport number, and birth information. It also showed that al Mihdhar held a U.S. visa, issued in Jeddah, Saudi Arabia, in April 1999, that would not expire until April 2000. These facts were verified at the U.S. consulate in Jeddah before the meeting started. The DCI told the Joint Inquiry:

We had at that point the level of detail needed to watchlist [al Mihdhar]—that is, to nominate him to State Department for refusal of entry into the US or to deny him another visa. Our officers remained focused on the surveillance operation and did not do so.

Surveillance photographs of the meeting were . . . transmitted to CIA Headquarters. When the meeting ended, al Mihdhar, al Hazmi, and Khallad (under a different name) flew to Thailand seated side by side.

Soon after the travelers left Malaysia on January 8, the CIA received evidence that Nawaf's last name might be al Hazmi when it learned that someone with that last name had been seated next to al Mihdhar on the flight from Malaysia. That information could have led to Nawaf al Hazmi's watchlisting.

Unknown to the CIA, since early 1999 the National Security Agency [NSA] had information associating al Hazmi by his full name with the bin Laden network, information it did not disseminate. NSA Director [Michael] Hayden told the Joint Inquiry:

> At the time of the meeting in Kuala Lumpur, we had the al Hazmi brothers, Nawaf and Salem, as well as Khalid al Mihdhar, in our sights. We knew of their association with al Qaeda, and we shared this information with the Community. I've looked at this closely. If we had handled all of the above perfectly, the only new fact that we could have contributed at the time of Kuala Lumpur was that Nawaf's surname (and perhaps that of Salem, who appeared to be Nawaf's brother) was al Hazmi.

Although NSA did not disseminate this information to the Intelligence Community before September 11, it was available in NSA databases. However, no one at CIA or elsewhere asked NSA before September 11 to review its database for information about Nawaf al Hazmi.

Knowledge of Nawaf's last name also pointed to his brother Salem's last name, which meant that the Intelligence Community had in its grasp the full names of three of the future hijackers. In addition, the State Department had in the records of its Jeddah consulate the fact that Nawaf and Salem al Hazmi had obtained U.S. visas in April 1999, several days before al Mihdhar obtained his U.S. visa at that consulate. . . .

A CIA officer, who was working as a CTC [Counterterrorist Center] Supervisor, testified before the Joint Inquiry that a CTC cable in early 2000 noted that al Mihdhar's passport information had been "passed to the FBI," but the CIA was unable to "confirm either passage or receipt of the information" and, thus, could not identify "the exact details . . . that were passed." The Joint

Inquiry found no record of the visa information at FBI Headquarters.

While the Malaysia meeting was in progress, a CIA employee sent an e-mail to a CIA colleague describing "exactly" the briefings he had given two FBI agents on al Mihdhar's activities. The CIA employee had been assigned to the FBI's Strategic Information Operations Center to deal with problems "in communicating between the CIA and the FBI." The e-mail did not mention that al Mihdhar held a U.S. visa, but did report that the CIA employee told the second FBI agent the following:

> This continues to be an [intelligence] operation. Thus far, a lot of suspicious activity has been observed but nothing that would indicate evidence of an impending attack or criminal enterprise. Told [the first FBI agent] that as soon as something concrete is developed leading us to the criminal arena or to known FBI cases, we will immediately bring FBI into the loop. Like [the first FBI agent] yesterday, [the second FBI agent] stated that this was a fine approach and thanked me for keeping him in the loop.

An e-mail from the second FBI agent to FBI Headquarters discussed the conversation with the CIA employee. This e-mail also did not mention al Mihdhar's visa information. None of the participants in these communications now recalls discussing the visa information.

A TERRORIST TRIP TO AMERICA

For six weeks, CIA sought to locate al Mihdhar in Thailand. It was unsuccessful, however, because, according to a CIA officer's testimony, "[w]hen they arrived [in Thailand] we were unable to mobilize what we needed to mobilize." Nonetheless, in February 2000, CIA rejected a request from foreign authorities to become involved because CIA was in the middle of an investigation "to determine what the subject is up to."

In early March 2000, CIA Headquarters, including CTC and

its bin Laden unit, received a cable from a CIA station . . . noting that Nawaf al Hazmi had traveled to Los Angeles on January 15, 2000. The cable was marked "Action Required: None, FYI [For Your Information]." The following day, another station, which had been copied on the cable by the originating station, cabled CTC's bin Laden unit that it had read the cable "with interest," particularly "the information that a member of this group traveled to the U.S. following his visit to Kuala Lumpur." No action resulted at CIA. [This occurred even though CTC had republished guidance reminding personnel of the importance of watchlisting in December 1999.] . . .

The CIA did not consider the possibility that al Mihdhar and al Hazmi, who had flown together to Thailand, continued on together to the United States. In fact, al Mihdhar had flown with al Hazmi to the United States on January 15, 2000. . . .

By February 2000, al Mihdhar and al Hazmi had settled in San Diego, California where they used their true names on a rental agreement. They did the same in obtaining California driver's licenses. . . .

On June 10, al Mihdhar flew from Los Angeles to Frankfurt, and then on to Oman. Al Hazmi remained in the United States. On July 12, two days before the expiration of the six month visa he had been granted on arriving in January, al Hazmi applied to the INS [Immigration and Naturalization Service] for an extension, using the address of the San Diego apartment he had shared with al Mihdhar.

The INS does not have a record of any additional extension request by al Hazmi, who remained in the United States illegally after his extension expired in January 2001. In December 2000, al Hazmi moved to Mesa, Arizona, with Hani Hanjour, another hijacker. . . .

A LINK TO THE U.S.S. *COLE* BOMBING

On October 12, 2000, two al Qaeda terrorists attacked U.S.S. *Cole* as the destroyer refueled in Yemen. In investigating the attack, the FBI developed information that Khallad bin Attash had been a principal planner of the bombing and that two other participants in the *Cole* conspiracy had delivered money to Khallad in Malaysia at the time of the Malaysia meeting. The FBI shared this information with the CIA, whose analysts decided to conduct a review of what was known about the meeting.

In January 2001, CIA concluded, based on statements by a joint CIA/FBI human source, that Khallad appeared in one of the surveillance photos taken during the Malaysia meeting. The CIA recognized that Khallad's presence at the meeting was significant because it meant that the other attendees, including al Mihdhar and al Hazmi, had been in direct contact with the key planner of the *Cole* attack for bin Laden's network. . . . Although al Mihdhar and al Hazmi had now been "definitively" placed "with a known al Qaeda operative," the CIA once again did not act to add them to the State Department's watchlist. In January 2001, Khalid al Mihdhar was abroad, his visa had expired, and he would have to clear a watchlist check before obtaining a new visa to re-enter the United States.

The day after the photo identification by the joint CIA/FBI human source in January 2001, the asset's identification of Khallad in the photo was reported to CIA Headquarters. However, the Joint Inquiry found no information showing that the FBI representative on the scene, who also worked with that source, was told about the identification or that the information was provided to FBI Headquarters. To the contrary, contemporary documents over the next month strongly suggest that the FBI did not know of this development. It was not until August 30, 2001, that CIA Headquarters transmitted to the FBI a memorandum stating, "We wish to advise you that, during a previously scheduled meeting with our joint source," Khallad was identified in a surveillance photo. . . .

On June 13, 2001, al Mihdhar obtained a new U.S. visa in Jeddah, using a different passport than the one he had used to enter the United States in January 2000. On his visa application, he checked "no" in response to the question whether he had ever been in the United States. On July 4, al Mihdhar re-entered the United States.

SOUNDING THE ALARM—TOO LATE

In early July 2001, the . . . CTC Supervisor located [a message] that contained information the CIA had acquired in January 2001 about Khallad's attending the Malaysia meeting. He told the Joint Inquiry that Khallad's presence at the meeting deeply troubled him and he immediately sent an e-mail from FBI Headquarters to CTC stating, "[Khallad] is a major league killer, who orchestrated the *Cole* attack and possibly the Africa bombings."

A review was launched at CIA of all cables regarding the Malaysia meeting. The task fell largely to an FBI analyst assigned to CTC. On August 21, 2001, the analyst put together two key pieces of information: the intelligence the CIA received in January 2000 that al Mihdhar had a multiple entry visa to the United States, and the information it received in March 2000 that al Hazmi had traveled to the United States. Working with an INS representative assigned to CTC, the analyst learned that al Mihdhar had entered the United States on January 15, 2000, had departed on June 10, and had re-entered the United States on July 4, 2001. Suspicions were further aroused by the fact that al Mihdhar and al Hazmi had arrived in Los Angeles in January 2000, when Ahmed Ressam would have been in Los Angeles to conduct terrorist operations at Los Angeles Airport, but for his apprehension at the U.S./Canada border in December 1999.

On August 23, 2001, the CIA sent a cable to the State Department, INS, Customs, and FBI requesting that "bin Laden-related individuals," al Mihdhar, al Hazmi, Khallad, and one other person at the Malaysia meeting, be watchlisted immediately and denied entry into the United States "due to their confirmed links to Egyptian Islamic Jihad operatives and suspicious activities while traveling in East Asia." Although the CIA believed that al Mihdhar was already in the United States, placing him on the watchlist would enable authorities to detain him if he attempted to leave. The CIA cable stated that al Hazmi had arrived in Los Angeles on January 15, 2000 on the same flight as al Mihdhar and that there was no record of al Hazmi's departure. On August 24, the State Department watchlisted al Mihdhar, al Hazmi, and the others listed in the CIA cable. On August 27, it revoked the visa that al Mihdhar had obtained in June.

FBI Headquarters promptly sent to the FBI New York field office a draft communication recommending the opening of "an intelligence investigation to determine if al Mihdhar is still in the United States." It stated that al Mihdhar's "confirmed association" with various elements of bin Laden's terrorist network, including potential association with two individuals involved in the attack on U.S.S. *Cole*, "make him a risk to the national security of the United States." The goal of the intelligence investigation was to "locate al Mihdhar and determine his contacts and reasons for being in the United States."

That communication precipitated a debate between FBI Headquarters and New York field office personnel as to whether to open an intelligence or criminal investigation on al Mihdhar. A New York FBI agent tried to convince Headquarters to open a criminal investigation, given the importance of the search and the limited resources available in intelligence investigations, but Headquarters declined to do so. An e-mail exchange between Headquarters and the New York agent described the debate:

From FBI Headquarters:
  If al Mihdhar is located, the interview must be conducted by an intel [intelligence] agent. A criminal agent CAN NOT be present at the interview. This case, in its entirety, is based on intel. If at such time as information is developed indicating the existence of a substantial federal crime, that information will be passed over the wall [that legally separated intelligence from criminal investigations] according to the proper procedures and turned over for follow-up criminal investigation. [Emphasis in original.]

From the New York agent:
  Whatever has happened to this—someday someone will die— and wall or not—the public will not understand why we were not more effective and throwing every resource we had at certain 'problems.' Let's hope the [FBI's] National Security Law Unit (NSLU) will stand behind their decisions [about the "wall"] then,

especially since the biggest threat to us now, OBL [Osama bin Laden], is getting the most 'protection.'

The agent was told in response: "we [at Headquarters] are all frustrated with this issue," but "[t]hese are the rules. NSLU does not make them up." . . .

The FBI contacted the Bureau of Diplomatic Security at the State Department on August 27, 2001 to obtain al Mihdhar and al Hazmi's visa information. This was provided to the FBI on August 29 and revealed that, on entering the United States in July 2001, al Mihdhar claimed that he would be staying at a Marriott hotel in New York City. An FBI agent determined on September 5 that al Mihdhar had not registered at a New York Marriott. The agent checked computerized national and New York criminal and motor vehicle indices on al Mihdhar and al Hazmi, but those checks were negative. On September 11, the agent sent an electronic communication to the FBI's Los Angeles Field Office, asking it to look for al Mihdhar and to check airline records. . . .

WHAT THE
NATIONAL SECURITY AGENCY KNEW

In early 1999, NSA analyzed communications involving a suspected terrorist facility in the Middle East, some of which were associated with Nawaf al Hazmi and Khaled . . . , [a man] NSA now believes to have been Khalid al Mihdhar. . . . These communications were the first indication NSA had of a link between al Mihdhar and al Hazmi. They were not disseminated in NSA SIGINT [signals intelligence] reporting because the persons were unknown and the subject matter did not meet NSA reporting thresholds. Those thresholds vary, depending on the judgment of the NSA analyst who is reviewing the intercept and the subject, location, and content of the intercept.

[Later in 1999, the NSA analyzed other communications involving al Mihdhar, Khallad, Nawaf al Hazmi and his brother

Salem.] None of this information was disseminated because the subject matter did not meet NSA reporting thresholds.

In early . . . 2000, NSA analyzed what appeared to be related communications concerning [al Mihdhar]. . . . NSA reported this information in early January to CIA, FBI, and other counterterrorism customers.

After this NSA report . . . , CIA submitted a formal request to NSA in early 2000 for approval to share information in the report with . . . foreign intelligence liaison services, along with the fact that [al Mihdhar] may have been connected to a suspected terrorist facility in the Middle East that had previously been linked to al Qaeda's activities against U.S. interests. CIA wanted to cite these connections to enlist liaison assistance. . . . NSA allowed the information to be released. . . .

THE FBI'S NEAR MISS

During the time they were in San Diego, [hijackers Khalid al Mihdhar and Nawaf al Hazmi] had numerous contacts with a long-time FBI counterterrorism informant. A third hijacker, Hani Hanjour, may have had more limited contact with this individual in December 2000.

CIA and FBI Headquarters had information tying al Mihdhar and al Hazmi to al Qaeda as early as January 2000 and later received information that they were in the United States. The San Diego FBI field office received none of this information before September 11. As a result, the informant was not asked to collect information about the hijackers.

An FBI written response to the Joint Inquiry acknowledges questions about the informant's credibility, but the Administration and the FBI have objected to the Joint Inquiry's request to interview the informant and have refused to serve a Committee subpoena and notice of deposition on the informant. As suggested by the FBI, the Joint Inquiry submitted written interrogatories for response by the informant. Through an attorney, the informant declined to respond and indicated that, if subpoenaed, the informant would require a grant of immunity prior to testifying. Thus, this section has been prepared without access to the informant and in reliance on FBI documents, interviews of FBI personnel, and FBI representations about the informant.

. . . After the September 11 attacks, the informant's FBI handling agent interviewed the informant about contacts with al Hazmi and al Mihdhar. Due to suspicions that the informant might have been involved in the attacks, the informant was interviewed multiple times by a number of FBI agents about the informant's contacts with the hijackers. According to the FBI handling agent, the informant admitted having numerous contacts with al Hazmi and al Mihdhar, but denied knowledge of the plot and initially expressed disbelief that the two were involved.

The informant provided the FBI with information concerning the informant's contacts with al Hazmi and al Mihdhar. The informant subsequently told the FBI slightly different stories concerning the initial contact and provided different dates for the contacts with them.

The informant told the FBI that during the contacts with al Hazmi and al Mihdhar, the informant observed no signs that they were involved in terrorist activity. The informant said that at the time the informant thought that the two were good, religious Muslims. They did not act in a peculiar manner and did nothing to arouse the informant's suspicions. . . .

The informant told the FBI that based on the informant's contacts with al Hazmi and al Mihdhar, they did not work, yet they always seemed to have money. Although they did not fit the profile of rich Saudis, the informant never questioned them about finances. . . .

During one of the informant's final contacts with al Hazmi in San Diego, al Hazmi was with someone the informant had not previously met. The informant described the person as 27 years old, 5'8", 130 to 140 pounds, fair complexion, and of either Saudi or Yemeni ancestry. The FBI has determined that Hani Hanjour, who fits this general description, arrived in San Diego from Dubai on December 8, 2000, and left San Diego with al Hazmi for Arizona several days later. The two future hijackers lived together in Arizona. The informant was shown a picture of Hanjour and stated this was not the person that the informant had met.

After September 11, the informant gave the FBI a list of individuals the informant understood had contacts with al Hazmi and al Mihdhar while they were in San Diego. . . . Four of the persons had been the subject of FBI investigations; three of them had been under active FBI investigation during the time that the future hijackers were in San Diego. The FBI opened counterterrorism investigations on other individuals on the list after September 11. . . .

According to the handling agent, the informant did not mention that al Hazmi was pursuing flight training until after September 11. . . . The FBI handling agent said he "did not document the information provided by the informant on these two persons in FBI files before September 11." This was because the informant "provided this information during a discussion of personal matters and not because the informant believed it had any investigative significance." The handling agent said in Joint Inquiry interviews that none of the information provided by the informant about the hijackers before September 11 raised concerns. The fact that the two individuals were Saudi was not a concern before September 11 because Saudi Arabia was considered an ally. . . .

When the San Diego office realized that the informant had numerous contacts with the two hijackers, FBI personnel became suspicious that the informant may have been involved in the plot. San Diego personnel interviewed by the Joint Inquiry, including senior managers and case agents, now believe that the informant was an unwitting observer with no role in the attacks. [But] based on Joint Inquiry interviews of San Diego FBI personnel involved with the informant before September 11 or in assessing the informant's credibility after the attacks and reviews of thousands of Bureau documents, several unresolved questions about the informant's credibility remain. Although the informant did not recognize hijacker Hani Hanjour in photographs shown to the informant by the FBI after September 11, there are indications that Hanjour was in the San Diego area with al Hazmi in December 2000 and probably met the informant. . . . FBI personnel believe it likely that the informant met Hanjour in December 2000 and are unable to explain why the informant failed to identify Hanjour. . . .

The CIA was aware in January 2000 that al Mihdhar had a U.S. visa and in March 2000 that al Hazmi had traveled to California. The FBI handling agent testified that, if he had access to the CIA intelligence concerning al Mihdhar and al Hazmi when they were in San Diego:

> It would have made a huge difference. We would have immediately opened . . . investigations. We had the predicate for a[n] . . . investigation if we had that information. . . . We would immediately go out and canvas the sources and try to find out where these people were. If we locate them, which we probably would have since they were very close—they were nearby—we would have initiated investigations immediately. . . .We would have done everything. We would have used all available investigative techniques. [We] would have given them the full court press. We would . . . have done everything—physical surveillance, technical surveillance and other assets.

AL QAEDA'S AMERICAN SUPPORT NETWORK

In June 2002 testimony before the Joint Inquiry, DCI Tenet and FBI Director [Robert] Mueller asserted, in explaining how the September 11 hijackers had avoided the notice of the Intelligence Community, that the conspirators intentionally avoided actions or associations that would have attracted law enforcement attention during their time in the United States. The DCI said:

> Once in the U.S., the hijackers were careful, with the exception of minor traffic violations, to avoid drawing law enforcement attention and even general notice that might identify them as extrem-

ists. They dressed in Western clothes, most shaved their beards before entering the U.S., and they largely avoided mosques.

FBI Director Mueller appeared to concur:

While here, the hijackers effectively operated without suspicion, triggering nothing that would have alerted law enforcement and doing nothing that exposed them to domestic coverage. As far as we know, they contacted no known terrorist sympathizers in the United States.

The former Assistant Director for the FBI's Counterterrorism Division also emphasized this point in his testimony:

[T]here were no contacts with anybody we were looking at inside the United States . . . quite honestly, with zero contact in the United States of any of our known people with the 19 persons coming here that we had no information about, intelligence-wise, before, through no one's fault, that's how they did it.

However, the Joint Inquiry review of documents and interviews of FBI personnel indicate that the six hijackers who served as the leaders and facilitators of the September 11 attacks were not isolated in the United States, but instead maintained a number of contacts in the United States before September 11. Although the extent to which the persons with whom they were in contact in the United States were aware of the September 11 plot is unknown, it is clear that those persons provided some of the hijackers with substantial assistance while they prepared for the attacks. These contacts in the United States helped hijackers find housing, open bank accounts, obtain drivers licenses, locate flight schools, and facilitate transactions.

The record of the Joint Inquiry demonstrates that some persons known to the FBI through prior or then-current FBI counterterrorism inquiries and investigations, [including the informant mentioned above,] may have had contact with the hijackers, for example:

- Before September 11, hijackers al Mihdhar, Nawaf al Hazmi, Hanjour, Mohammed Atta, Marwan al Shehhi, and possibly others had contact with people who had come to the FBI's attention during counterterrorism or counterintelligence inquiries or investigations. In all, some of the hijackers were in various degrees of contact with at least fourteen such persons, four of whom were the focus of active FBI investigations, while the hijackers were in the United States.

- Before September 11, al Mihdhar, al Hazmi, Hanjour, Atta, al Shehhi, and possibly other hijackers attended at least seven mosques in California, Florida, Virginia, Arizona, and Maryland, some of which were also attended by persons of interest to the FBI.

The fact that so many persons known to the FBI may have been in contact with the hijackers raises questions as to how much the FBI knew about the activities of Islamic extremist groups in the United States before September 11 and whether the FBI was well-positioned to thwart the attack. Moreover, the extent to which the hijackers interacted with and relied on other persons in the United States is vitally important in understanding the modus operandi of the hijackers and al Qaeda and in preventing future attacks.

At a Joint Inquiry hearing in October 2002, FBI Director Mueller commented on his earlier testimony about the hijackers' conduct in the United States:

> [When] I say that the hijackers did "nothing that exposed them to domestic coverage" . . . [and when I say that] the hijackers "contacted no known terrorist sympathizers in the United States," [I] meant in the context of the hijackers not contacting—before 9/11—terrorist sympathizers on whom we had technical or other form of coverage. . . .

At least one FBI document prepared shortly after the September 11 attacks concluded that the hijackers, rather than operating in isolation, were assisted by "a web of contacts" in the United

States. In an undated draft analysis based on information available as of November 2001, the FBI's Investigative Services Division concluded:

> Initial reporting from observers cast the hijackers as loners who stayed aloof from those around them. While these characterizations remain an accurate appraisal of the hijackers' general orientations toward most persons they came into contact with in the United States, more intensive scrutiny reveals that the hijackers— in particular, the six leaders/facilitators—were involved with a much greater number of associates than was originally suspected. In addition to frequent and sustained interaction between and among the hijackers of the various flights before September 11, the group maintained a web of contacts both in the United States and abroad. These associates, ranging in degrees of closeness, include friends and associates from universities and flight schools, former roommates, people they knew through mosques and religious activities, and employment contacts. Other contacts provided legal, logistical, or financial assistance, facilitated U.S. entry and flight school enrollment, or were known from OBL-related activities or training.

The Intelligence Community had information before September 11 suggesting the existence of a radical Islamic network in the United States that could support al Qaeda and other terrorist operatives. The FBI had focused sources and investigative work to some degree on radical Islamic extremists within the United States before September 11. However, according to former National Security Adviser Sandy Berger [who served in the Clinton administration], the Bureau believed that "al Qaeda had limited capacity to operate in the United States and [that] any presence here was under [FBI] surveillance."

An August 2001 Senior Executive Intelligence Brief, provided to senior U.S. Government officials at the time, noted that al Qaeda members, including some U.S. citizens, resided in or traveled to the United States for years and apparently maintained a support structure here. According to CIA documents, . . . in June

2001 . . . al Qaeda operative Khalid Sheikh Mohammed was recruiting persons to travel to the United States and engage in planning terrorist-related activity here. . . . [T]hese persons would be "expected to establish contact with colleagues already living there." In short, before September 11, the Intelligence Community recognized that a radical Islamic network that could provide support to al Qaeda operatives probably existed in the United States.

The FBI Phoenix field office agent who wrote the "Phoenix communication" [noting the large number of Middle Easterners taking flight lessons and urging an investigation] testified that he believed this type of support network existed in Arizona before September 11:

> I cannot sit here and testify today that [al Qaeda] established a network there. However, looking at things historically in Arizona we have seen persons go to school at the University of Arizona in Tucson who subsequently went on to become rather important figures in the al Qaeda organization . . . [P]rior to al Qaeda even coming into existence these people were living and going to school in Arizona. As al Qaeda formed and took off and became operational, we've seen these people travel back into the State of Arizona. We've seen Osama bin Laden send people to Tucson to purchase an airplane for him [and] it's my opinion that's not a coincidence. These people don't continue to come back to Arizona because they like the sunshine or they like the state. I believe that something was established there and I think it's been there for a long time. We're working very hard to try to identify that structure. So I cannot say with a degree of certainty that one is in place there. But . . . that's my investigative theory. . . .

THE HIJACKERS' SUSPECTED ASSOCIATES

On January 15, 2000, following an important meeting of al Qaeda operatives in Malaysia, hijackers al Hazmi and al Mihdhar arrived in Los Angeles, where they remained for approximately two-and-a-half weeks. At one point, they met Omar al Bayoumi. A person the FBI interviewed after September 11 says that he was with al Bayoumi when the latter met al Hazmi and al Mihdhar. This person says that al Bayoumi invited him to travel to Los Angeles, explaining that he had business at the Saudi Consulate. When they arrived at the consulate, al Bayoumi met with someone behind closed doors. Al Bayoumi and the person with whom he had traveled to Los Angeles went to a restaurant, where they met al Hazmi and al Mihdhar. Al Bayoumi struck up a conversation with al Hazmi and al Mihdhar after he heard them speaking Arabic, and he invited them to move to San Diego. Al Bayoumi returned to San Diego after leaving the restaurant, and al Hazmi and al Mihdhar arrived in San Diego shortly thereafter.

According to several FBI agents, the meeting at the restaurant may not have been accidental. In fact, the FBI's written response to the Joint Inquiry refers to the restaurant encounter as a "somewhat suspicious meeting with the hijackers." According to another person the FBI interviewed after September 11, al Bayoumi said before his trip that he was going to Los Angeles to pick up visitors.

When al Hazmi and al Mihdhar moved to San Diego, al Bayoumi gave them considerable assistance. They stayed at al Bayoumi's apartment for several days, until he was able to find them an apartment. Al Bayoumi co-signed their lease and paid their first month's rent and security deposit. The FBI noted in a written response to the Joint Inquiry that "financial records indicate a cash deposit of the same amount as the cashier's check into al Bayoumi's bank account on the same day, which suggests that the hijackers reimbursed him." However, another FBI document appears to reach a different conclusion: "a review of Khalid al Mihdhar and Nawaf al Hazmi's bank records indicate [sic] there is no bank documentation that supports the reimbursement of [the rent money], or any monies to Omar al Bayoumi from al Hazmi or al Mihdhar."

After the hijackers moved into their own apartment, al Bayoumi organized and hosted a party to welcome them to the San

Diego community. He also tasked . . . another member of the Islamic Center of San Diego to help them become acclimated to the United States. . . .

Since September 11, the FBI has learned that al Bayoumi has connections to terrorist elements. He has been tied to an Imam abroad who has connections to al Qaeda. Further, the FBI's Executive Assistant Director for Counterterrorism and Counterintelligence described in testimony before the Joint Inquiry FBI contacts "with the . . . government about collection on a person . . . who has ties to al Qaeda, who has ties to al Bayoumi." According to FBI documents, [the person] was also in the Phoenix and San Diego areas in 2000 and 2001.

An FBI report after a search of Bayoumi's residence asserted that an "exhaustive translation of his documents made it clear that . . . he is providing guidance to young Muslims and some of his writings can be interpreted as jihadist." According to an individual interviewed by the FBI, al Bayoumi's salary from his employer, the Saudi Civil Aviation authority, was approved by Hamid al Rashid. Hamid is the father of Saud al Rashid, whose photo was found in a raid of an al Qaeda safehouse in Karachi and who has admitted to being in Afghanistan between May 2000 and May 2001. The FBI noted, however, that there is no direct evidence that the money al Rashid authorized for al Bayoumi was used for terrorist purposes.

In September 1998, the FBI opened a counterterrorism inquiry on al Bayoumi. . . . During the counterterrorism inquiry, the FBI discovered that al Bayoumi had been in contact with several persons who were under FBI investigation. . . .

Despite the fact that he was a student, al Bayoumi had access to seemingly unlimited funding from Saudi Arabia. For example, an FBI source identified al Bayoumi as the person who delivered $400,000 from Saudi Arabia for the Kurdish mosque in San Diego. One of the FBI's best sources in San Diego informed the FBI that he thought that al Bayoumi must be an intelligence officer for Saudi Arabia or another foreign power.

The Bureau closed its inquiry on al Bayoumi in July 1999 for reasons that remain unclear. The responsible FBI agent said that she closed the inquiry because the original complaint . . . turned out to be false and she had developed no other information of such significance as to justify continuing the investigation. . . .

Although the FBI has not developed definitive evidence that Osama Bassnan, another Saudi national living in San Diego, had ties to al Hazmi and al Mihdhar, . . . information obtained by the Joint Inquiry suggests such a connection. Bassnan was a close associate of al Bayoumi. . . . Bassnan also had close ties to a number of other persons connected to the hijackers. . . . Bassnan lived in the apartment complex in San Diego across the street from al Hazmi and al Mihdhar. . . .

The FBI did not investigate Bassnan before September 11, but had been made aware of him on several occasions. In May 1992, the State Department provided the FBI with a box of documents recovered from an abandoned car. The documents were in Arabic, and one, a newsletter to supporters of the Eritrean Islamic Jihad (EIJ) Movement, provided updates on the EIJ's council and was marked "confidential." The box contained letters addressed to Bassnan that discussed plans to import used cars to the United States. The FBI opened a counterterrorism inquiry on the EIJ, but, having failed to develop information that would predicate further investigation, closed the investigation in December 1992. In 1993, the FBI received reports that Bassnan had hosted a party for the "Blind Sheikh" [Omar Abd al Rahman, tied to terrorism in New York] in Washington, D.C. in 1992. However, the FBI did not open an investigation.

The Intelligence Community had information connecting bin Laden to the EIJ as of 1996. . . . In addition, FBI documents note that a high-level member of the EIJ was on bin Laden's Shura Council. A May 2000 FBI document indicates that FBI Headquarters personnel were not handling EIJ matters due to resource constraints.

[The identities of several individuals whose activities are discussed in this report have been deleted by the Joint Inquiry . . . due to the as yet unresolved nature of much of the information regarding their activities.]

After the September 11 attacks, the FBI developed information that al Hazmi and al Mihdhar were closely affiliated with an Imam in San Diego who reportedly served as their spiritual advisor. . . . Several persons informed the FBI after September 11 that this Imam had closed-door meetings in San Diego with al Mihdhar, al Hazmi and another individual, whom al Bayoumi had asked to help the attackers. This Imam moved to Falls Church, Virginia, in 2001. . . . In 2001, hijackers al Hazmi and Hanjour also moved to Falls Church and began to attend the mosque with which the Imam was associated. One of the members of the mosque helped them find an apartment in the area and, after approximately a month, this person drove Hanjour and al Hazmi, along with two other hijackers, to Connecticut and then to Paterson, New Jersey. From the hotel in Connecticut where they stayed for two nights, a total of 75 calls were made to locate apartment, flight schools, and car rental agencies for the hijackers. The hijackers then returned to Paterson on their own. During a search of Ramzi Binalshibh's residence in Germany, police found the phone numbers for the Imam's mosque. The FBI agent responsible for the September 11 investigation informed Joint Inquiry staff that "there's a lot of smoke out there" with regard to the Imam's connection to the hijackers. . . .

The FBI closed its inquiry into the activities of the Imam in March 2000, approximately two months after al Mihdhar and al Hazmi arrived in San Diego. . . . In the case closing memorandum, the agent asserted that the Imam had been "fully identified and does not meet the criterion for [further] investigation." The investigation was closed despite the Imam's contacts with other subjects of counterterrorism investigations and reports concerning the Imam's connection to suspect organizations. The Bureau's written response to the Joint Inquiry asserts that "the Imam was a 'spiritual leader' to many in the community" and that hundreds of Muslims associated with him. . . .

THE HAMBURG TERRORIST CELL

According to the FBI, "much of what took place on September 11, 2001 originated during the mid–1990s when [hijacker pilots]

Mohammed Atta, Marwan al Shehhi, and Ziad Jarrah moved to Germany, eventually settling in Hamburg, and began to associate with Islamic extremists."

An FBI agent asserted in a Joint Inquiry interview that the three future hijackers were not radicals when they came to Germany, but became so during their time there. While in Hamburg, Atta, al Shehhi, and Jarrah attended the al Quds mosque where they met a group of radical Islamists, including Muhammad Heydar Zammar, Mamoun Darkazanli, Zakariya Essabar, Ramzi Binal-shibh, Said Bahaji, and Munir Motassadeq. The hijackers prayed, worked, lived, socialized, and attended university classes with this group, which has become known as the "Hamburg Cell."

Zammar and Darkazanli were known . . . before September 11. Zammar was born in Syria in 1961, moved to Germany, and obtained German citizenship. According to an FBI summary of its September 11 investigation, Zammar is believed to have recruited Atta, al Shehhi, and Jarrah into al Qaeda and encouraged their participation in the September 11 attacks.

Darkazanli is a Syrian national, born in 1958. He entered Germany in 1983 and became a naturalized German citizen in 1990, though he retained his Syrian citizenship. While Darkazanli's relationship to the future hijackers is less clear, he is a close associate of Zammar.

According to the FBI, Binalshibh and Essabar were to have participated in the conspiracies that carried out the September 11 attacks. A martyr video was discovered in Binalshibh's possessions in Afghanistan, and . . . reportedly [there was] information about flight training on Essabar's computer. However, neither was able to obtain a U.S. entry visa. Before the attacks, Binalshibh and Bahaji left for Pakistan where Binalshibh was eventually captured. . . . Motassadeq lived with Atta and signed his will, and also had power of attorney for al Shehhi. . . .

After September 11, the FBI discovered that Darkazanli traveled to Spain in the summer of 2001 at approximately the same time that Atta was there. It is possible that Darkazanli and Atta met with [Edin Barakat] Yarkas, [a suspected al Qaeda leader,] who may have had advance knowledge of the September 11 attacks.

Spanish authorities intercepted a call to Yarkas on August 27, in which he was told, "we have entered the field of aviation and we have even slit the throat of the bird." The FBI speculates that the "bird" represented the bald eagle, symbol of the United States. Yarkas, who was arrested by the Spanish on November 13, 2001, has met at least twice with bin Laden. A Spanish indictment alleges that he had contacts with Mohammed Atta and Ramzi Binalshibh. . . .

According to CIA documents, the U.S. Intelligence Community first became aware of Darkazanli in 1993 when a person arrested in Africa carrying false passports and counterfeit money was found with Darkazanli's telephone number. A CIA report notes that, despite careful scrutiny of Darkazanli and his business dealings, authorities were not able to make a case against him.

The FBI became interested in Darkazanli in 1998 after the arrests of Wadi el Hage and Abu Hajer, operatives in bin Laden's network. According to FBI documents, Darkazanli's fax and telephone numbers were listed in el Hage's address book. El Hage has been convicted for his role in the 1998 Embassy bombings and is in U.S. custody. The FBI also discovered that Darkazanli had power of attorney over a bank account belonging to Hajer, a high-ranking al Qaeda member who has served on its Shura Council. Hajer is currently in U.S. custody. . . .

Zammar had come to the CIA and FBI's attention on numerous occasions before the September 11 attacks. CIA documents refer to Zammar as an Islamic extremist and note that his name has turned up in the possession of several extremists questioned or detained. . . . In mid-1999 . . . Zammar was in direct contact with one of bin Laden's senior operational coordinators.

In March 1999, CIA received intelligence about a person named "Marwan" who had been in contact with Zammar and Darkazanli. Marwan was described as a student who had spent time in Germany. . . . The CIA speculated at the time that this was a bin Laden associate who lived in the United Arab Emirates, but now believes that Marwan was Marwan al Shehhi, one of the presumed hijacker pilots. After September 11, the FBI received information about additional connections before the attacks between Zammar and persons who participated in the attacks.

Considerable pressure was placed on foreign authorities in the years leading up to the September 11 attacks to target Darkazanli, Zammar, and other radicals . . . . A senior U.S. Government officer told the Joint Inquiry that significant information concerning al Qaeda members had been shared with foreign authorities, but that it became apparent only after September 11, 2001 that the foreign authorities had been watching some of those persons before that date. . . .

Significant legal barriers restricted Germany's ability to target Islamic fundamentalism. Before September 11, it was not illegal in Germany to be a member of a foreign terrorist organization, to raise funds for terrorists, or plan a terrorist act outside German territory. This law has since been changed. A legal privilege also dramatically restricted the government's ability to investigate religious groups. In fact, due to the difficulty in investigating terrorist cases, the German government would often attempt to investigate terrorist subjects for money laundering. Unfortunately, laundering laws were difficult to enforce. For example, over the past several years, out of three to four hundred money laundering investigations, only one person has been convicted. . . . The German government apparently did not consider Islamic groups a threat and was unwilling to devote significant investigative resources to this target. . . .

U.S. efforts . . . also provide a window into CIA and FBI coordination and information sharing. Both agencies were interested in radical Islamists. . . . However, on several occasions the FBI and CIA unknowingly operated against the same targets. The FBI legal attaché in Germany did not recall getting information about Darkazanli and Zammar from the German government or the CIA before September 11. He was unaware that Darkazanli and Zammar had been the subject of government investigations before the attacks.

THE HIJACKERS' VISAS

The Joint Inquiry reviewed passport and visa histories of the nineteen hijackers involved in the September 11 attacks to determine whether they entered the United States legally. It also sought to determine whether there were anomalies in the visa process that might have alerted U.S. Government officials to the hijackers in some way.

Over ten million applications for visas to enter the United States are received each year at approximately two hundred fifty consular locations. Consular officers at posts abroad review all applications and interview selected applicants to determine whether they are likely to return to countries of origin in accordance with the visa or are suspected of criminal or terrorist activities. Consular officers must certify in writing that they have checked applicant names against the State Department's watchlist.

Although there were anomalies and mistakes on some of the hijackers' visa applications, consular-affairs experts at the State Department contended in Joint Inquiry interviews that these errors were "routine." By contrast, an October 2002 review by the General Accounting Office (GAO) concluded that the omissions and inconsistencies in the hijacker's applications should have raised concerns about why they wanted visas to come to the United States.

Fifteen of the 19 hijackers were Saudi nationals who received visas in Saudi Arabia. Before September 11, the United States had not established heightened screening for illegal immigration or terrorism by visitors from Saudi Arabia. In a Joint Inquiry hearing, DCI Tenet described a less than rigorous review of visa applicants in Saudi Arabia before September 11:

Most of the young Saudis [hijackers] obtained their U.S. visas in the fall of 2000. The State Department did not have a policy to stringently examine Saudis seeking visas before 11 September because there was virtually no risk that Saudis would attempt to reside or work illegally in the U.S. after their visas expired. U.S. Embassy and consular officials do cursory searches on Saudis who apply for visas, but if they do not appear on criminal or terrorist watchlists they are granted a visa. Thousands of Saudis every year are granted visas, as a routine; the majority are not even interviewed. The vast majority of Saudis study, vacation, or do business in the U.S. and return to the kingdom.

Consistent with this description of the situation, the Joint Inquiry's review confirmed that, prior to September 11, 2001, only a small percentage of visa applicants in Saudi Arabia were interviewed by consular affairs officers; travel agencies were used to deliver visa applications to consular offices in Saudi Arabia; and a relatively low standard was applied in scrutinizing visa applications for accuracy and completeness in Saudi Arabia.

The 19 hijackers received visas at consular offices abroad in accordance with routine procedures. The majority of the hijackers sought new passports shortly before applying for visas. Requests for new passports can stem from theft, loss, or accidental destruction. However, terrorists also often try to hide travel to countries that provide terrorist training by acquiring new passports.

Multiple-entry visas were issued to the hijackers for periods ranging from two to ten years. Eighteen of the nineteen received B–1/B–2 visas for tourist and business purposes. The nineteenth hijacker, Hani Hanjour, was issued a B–1/B–2 visa in error. He should have been issued an F–1 visa for study in the United States because he had expressed a desire to study English here. Recognizing the error, the INS issued Hanjour an F–1 visa when he arrived in the United States.

At their ports-of-entry, the hijackers were issued "stay visas" valid for six months. Some hijackers, Atta, Hanjour, al Shehhi, al Mihdhar, and Jarrah, entered and re-entered the United States for several six-month periods before September 11. They stayed for five or six months, went abroad for weeks or months, re-entered the United States, and received additional six-month stays.

Since the majority of the hijackers were Saudi nationals who received their visas in Saudi Arabia, questions have been raised about the "Visa Express" program, a process in many countries that encourages visa applicants to submit non-immigrant applications to designated travel agencies or other collection points for forwarding to U.S. embassies. In Joint Inquiry interviews, State Department officials described Visa Express as simply an application collection process and not a visa adjudication, issuance, or determination system. Visa Express is merely a way of "dropping the application off." Travel agencies assist by giving applicants correct forms, helping non-English speakers fill out the forms, and collecting fees. Approximately sixty embassies and consulates throughout the world use travel agencies or other businesses in this manner.

The Visa Express program in Saudi Arabia began in May 2001. Five of the 19 hijackers applied for visas in Saudi Arabia in June, so it is likely that they used travel agencies to acquire application forms and deliver them to the embassy. None of the five, including al Mihdhar, was on a watchlist at the time. Thus, when name checks were performed, the system showed no derogatory information. If derogatory information did exist in the system, as was the case with a suspected terrorist who applied for a visa in Saudi Arabia in August 2001 under the Visa Express program, the watchlist system should block issuance of a visa.

State Department officials informed the Joint Inquiry that the Visa Express program was terminated in Saudi Arabia in July 2002 because news reports suggested that the program allowed Saudi applicants to skirt the normal process. According to State Department officials, the program did not affect the number of Saudis interviewed because applicants are selected for interviews when their applications present signs of an intention to immigrate. These officials said that all applications, including those delivered to consular officers under the Visa Express program in Saudi Arabia, were checked against the watchlist.

The Joint Inquiry also received information from the Immigration and Naturalization Service about the 19 hijackers, two of whom, including Nawaf al Hazmi, had overstayed their visas. In addition, Hani Hanjour had been issued an F–1 visa to study English, but did not register for classes and, therefore, became "a non-immigrant status violator." The INS was not aware of these violations until after September 11.

The Rise of Global Terrorism

EDITOR'S NOTE: Not so long ago, terrorism had a recognizable face. Nations like Syria, Libya and Iran sponsored bombers and hijackers to win attention to their national aims. The task of target countries was equally clear: To defeat the terrorists, neutralize their sponsors. But in the last decade a new breed of Islamic terrorist has emerged from the downtrodden societies of the Middle East. Attached to no nation but infiltrating many, their strategy is to inflict mass casualties and their aim is to attack no less than the heart of Western civilization. The preeminent practitioner of modern terrorism is Osama bin Laden, and in the space of a decade he has managed to draw the United States into a declaration of global war. The Joint Inquiry brainstormed the weapons that must be developed to win the war: new tools of counterterrorism, more aggressive strategies and tactics—and an unprecedented focus on the threat of devastating violence in the American homeland.

A NEW BREED

A basic question before the Joint Inquiry was whether the Intelligence Community adequately recognized the threat international terrorist groups posed to the United States. The Inquiry therefore examined the evolution of the terrorist threat to this country, the Community's response since the creation of the Counterterrorist Center (CTC) in 1986, and what the Community has or should have learned from all sources, including previous terrorist attacks, about the threat to the United States.

Understanding the September 11 attacks requires an historical perspective broader than the details of those attacks. Consequently, the Joint Inquiry took note of major acts of terrorism directed against the United States in the 1980s and early 1990s, including:

- The 1983 bombings of the U.S. Embassy and Marine Barracks in Beirut by Islamic Jihad

- The March 1984 kidnapping and murder of William Buckley, a CIA official in Beirut, and the subsequent kidnapping of other U.S. citizens in Lebanon

- The April 1984 bombing of a restaurant frequented by members of the U.S. armed forces near Torrejon Airbase in Spain by the Iranian-backed terrorist group Hizbollah

- The September 1984 bombing of the U.S. Embassy annex in Beirut

- The June 1985 hijacking of TransWorld Airways Flight 847

- The October 1985 hijacking of the cruise ship *Achille Lauro*

- The November 1985 hijacking of an EgyptAir flight from Athens and

- The December 1985 attack on the Rome and Vienna airports by the Abu Nidal organization.

Before the emergence of al Qaeda in the early 1990s, attacks like these shaped the U.S. Government's conception of how terrorist groups behaved. In general, those groups were viewed as instruments of the nation states that sponsored them and they were not interested in mass casualties. The lessons learned at that time were reflected in Joint Inquiry testimony by former National Security Advisor Brent Scowcroft [who served in the first Bush administration]:

[In the late 1980s], terrorism was primarily a phenomenon which was state-sponsored or state-assisted or tolerated. And therefore, it was natural for us to think of deterring or dealing with terrorism primarily through the sponsor than through the terrorist organizations directly where things like deterrence and so on would have some impact. . . . A further point, none of the terrorist organizations at that time so far as we knew had global reach. This meant that while U.S. persons, U.S. interests, and U.S. assets were not immune from terrorist attack, the United States homeland, in effect, was. And that certainly colored how terrorism was viewed. Terrorist organizations appeared to be either regionally or issue related. And even though Hezbollah was thought to be behind many of the terrorist acts that occurred during the Reagan Administration, the acts themselves seemed to be relatively independent and uncoordinated events rather than part of an overall strategy.

Terrorism aimed at the United States began to take on a different set of characteristics in the 1990s as bin Laden and al Qaeda emerged as a threat to the United States. Bin Laden was intent on striking inside the United States, and the Intelligence Community detected numerous signs of a pending terrorist attack by al Qaeda in the spring and summer of 2001.

THE BIN LADEN STYLE

International terrorism struck directly in the United States in February 1993, when a truck bomb exploded in the parking garage of the World Trade Center in New York City. A second alarm sounded in June 1993 when the FBI arrested eight persons for plotting to bomb New York City landmarks, including the United Nations and the Lincoln and Holland tunnels. The central figures in these plots were Ramzi Yousef and Sheikh Omar Abd al Rahman, who was the spiritual leader of both Gama'at al Islamiya and Egyptian Islamic Jihad. Although the Intelligence Community has not established that bin Laden had a role in either plot, both Yousef and Rahman were later determined to have ties to bin Laden. Both 1993 plots featured the deliberate intent to kill thousands of innocents by a group composed of different nationalities without a state sponsor, characteristics previously absent from terrorist schemes.

The new trend in terrorism became more apparent in January 1995 when Philippine National Police discovered Ramzi Yousef's bomb-making laboratory in Manila and arrested his accomplice, Abdul Hakim Murad. Captured material and interrogations of Murad revealed Yousef's plot to kill the Pope, bomb the U.S. and Israeli embassies in Manila, blow up twelve U.S. airliners over the Pacific Ocean, and crash a plane into CIA Headquarters. These plans were known collectively as the "Bojinka Plot." Murad was eventually convicted for his role in the plot and is currently incarcerated in the United States.

It is worth noting that Murad was charged only for his involvement in the scheme to blow up the airliners over the Pacific and not for the other aspects of the Bojinka Plot. Because the plans to crash a plane into CIA Headquarters and to assassinate the Pope were only at the "discussion" stage, prosecutors decided not to include those plots in the indictment. FBI agents who were interviewed by the Joint Inquiry about the Bojinka Plot confirmed this tight focus on the elements of the crime investigated and charged, explaining that the case was about a plan to blow up twelve airliners and, therefore, other aspects of the plot were not relevant to the prosecution. As a result, the Joint Inquiry was able to locate almost no references to the plan to crash a plane into CIA Headquarters in the FBI's investigatory files on the case.

The first World Trade Center bombing, the New York City landmarks plot, and the Bojinka Plot pointed to a new form of terrorism. The plots revealed a growing threat from persons who

ascribed to a radical interpretation of Sunni Islam; they ᵢ...
infliction of mass casualties; and they confirmed that international terrorists were interested in attacking symbolic targets within the United States, such as the World Trade Center.

The increasing development of religious-based terrorist organizations in the 1990s contributed directly to the emergence of this new form. As Bruce Hoffman, a terrorism expert with the RAND Corporation, noted in a statement for the Joint Inquiry record: "[F]or the religious terrorist, violence first and foremost is a sacramental act or a divine duty."

The new breed also focused on America. In testimony before the Joint Inquiry, former National Security Advisor Sandy Berger noted that the new terrorists were "hardened by battle against the Soviets in Afghanistan in the '80s and energized against the United States by the military presence we left in Saudi Arabia after the Gulf War."

The first attack on the World Trade Center in 1993, five years before bin Laden openly called on his followers to bring jihad to America, was a clear signal that Sunni extremists sought to kill Americans on American soil. Seven years later, the arrest of Ahmed Ressam and the seizure of bomb-making materials in his car at the U.S./Canada border should have dispelled all doubt that al Qaeda and its sympathizers sought to operate on U.S. soil, even though most of the terrorist masterminds remained overseas.

Emphasis on mass casualties was another important change from the terrorism the United States witnessed in the 1980s. Although attacks in the 1980s sometimes were intended to kill hundreds of official or military personnel, for example, the bombings of the Marine barracks and the U.S. Embassy in Lebanon, no major terrorist group attempted to kill thousands of civilians. Brian Jenkins, an expert on terrorism, wrote in 1975: "[T]errorists want a lot of people watching and a lot of people listening and not a lot of people dead." Twenty years later, Director of Central Intelligence James Woolsey [who served in the Clinton administration] contended that: "[T]oday's terrorists don't want a seat at the table; they want to destroy the table and everyone sitting at it." The 1999 edition of the FBI's Terrorism in the United States pointed out that the number of terrorist attacks had decreased in the 1990s, but the number of casualties had increased. Terrorism had evolved from a frightening episodic danger that could kill hundreds to an ominous menace that directly threatened the lives of tens of thousands of Americans.

It took some time for the Intelligence Community to recognize the emergence of this new form of terrorism. In Joint Inquiry interviews, FBI personnel who were involved in the investigation of the 1993 World Trade Center bombing suggest that the Intelligence Community was initially confused about the new adversary. This form of terrorism featured Arabs from countries hostile to one another working together without a state sponsor. Counterterrorism experts eventually recognized the shift and incorporated it into their analyses. A July 1995 National Intelligence Estimate, for example, identified a "new breed" of terrorist, who did not have a state sponsor, was loosely organized, favored an Islamic agenda, and had an extreme penchant for violence.

Osama bin Laden's connection to international terrorism first came to the attention of the Intelligence Community in the early 1990s. According to a former CTC Chief in testimony before the Joint Inquiry, bin Laden was first seen as "a rich Saudi supporting Islamic extremist causes." He founded the al Qaeda organization in 1989 and moved to Sudan in 1991 or 1992. During his time in Sudan, bin Laden built a network of international Islamic extremists and allied himself with other Sunni terrorist groups.

Bin Laden drew on a broad network of Islamic radicals fighting in the Balkans, Chechnya, and Kashmir in an attempt—in their eyes—to defend Islam against its persecutors. Fighters from Saudi Arabia, Egypt, Pakistan, and many other countries took up arms to aid their co-religionists, while Muslims from around the world contributed money. Although the specific actions of al Qaeda often did not enjoy widespread support, the causes it championed were viewed as legitimate, indeed laudable, in much of the Muslim world.

In December 1992, as U.S. military forces were deploying to Somalia as part of a United Nations operation to provide humanitarian assistance to a starving population, Islamic extremists attacked a hotel in Aden, Yemen housing U.S. service members supporting that operation. An Intelligence Community paper from April 1993 concluded that "[bin Laden's] group almost certainly played a role" in that attack. An article from an April 1993 National Intelligence Daily also took note that three to four hundred Islamic militants had received training the previous year at military camps in Afghanistan funded by Persian Gulf Arabs. One camp was run by an Egyptian and funded by bin Laden.

In Joint Inquiry testimony, former CTC Chief Cofer Black [head of the CIA's Counterterrorist Center from 1999 to 2002] reported that the CIA learned in 1993 that "bin Laden was channeling funds to Egyptian extremists" and in 1994 that "al Qaeda was financing at least three terrorist training camps in northern Sudan." He also noted bin Laden's connection to the 1995 assassination attempt against Egyptian President [Hosni] Mubarak and explained that "an al Qaeda defector [had] laid out for us bin Laden's role as a head of a global terrorist network."

In November 1995, five Americans were killed when the Office of Program Management at a Saudi National Guard facility in Riyadh was bombed. According to the Intelligence Community, the cumulative body of evidence eventually suggested that bin Laden and a group he supported were responsible. . . .

In May or June 1996, bin Laden moved from Sudan to Afghanistan, where he was treated as an honored guest of the Taliban, then the dominant political and military group. According to [Director of Central Intelligence (DCI) George] Tenet's testimony before the Joint Inquiry, "[O]nce bin Laden found his safe haven in Afghanistan, he defined himself publicly as a threat to the United States. In a series of declarations, he made clear his hatred for Americans and all we represent."

In August 1996, bin Laden issued a public fatwa or religious decree, authorizing attacks by his followers against Western military targets on the Arabian Peninsula. In February 1998, bin Laden and four other extremists issued another public fatwa expanding the 1996 fatwa to include U.S. military and civilian targets anywhere in the world. In a May 1998 press conference, bin Laden publicly discussed "bringing the war home to America."

On August 7, 1998, two truck bombs destroyed U.S. embassies in Nairobi, Kenya and Dar es Salaam, Tanzania. Two hundred twenty-four people, including twelve Americans, were killed in the attacks and 5,000 were injured. The Intelligence Community confirmed very quickly that these attacks had been carried out by bin Laden's terrorist network. The attacks showed that the group was capable of carrying out simultaneous attacks and inflicting mass casualties.

In early December 1999, the Jordanian government arrested members of a terrorist cell that planned to attack religious sites and tourist hotels in connection with the Millennium celebrations. About a week later, in mid-December 1999, Algerian extremist Ahmed Ressam tried to enter the United States from Canada with bomb-making chemicals and detonator equipment. He was arrested after an alert Customs agent asked to search his car and he attempted to flee. Investigation revealed that his target was Los Angeles International Airport and that he was an operative with ties to bin Laden's network.

In describing what the U.S. Government might have done differently before September 11, DCI Tenet testified:

[T]he one thing that strikes me that we all just let pass from the scene after the Millennium threat was this fellow who tried to cross the border from Canada into the United States. There were no attacks. There were no Americans killed. We didn't have any hearings. We didn't talk about failures. We didn't talk about accountability. We just assumed the system would keep working because it prevented the last attack. He tried to cross the border; and I think one of the things that everybody should have done is say, "what does this mean?," more carefully, rather than just moving from this threat to the next. Assuming that it had been disrupted, what does it mean for the homeland? Should we have taken more proactive measures sooner? Hindsight is perfect, but it is the one event that sticks in my mind.

In October 2000, bin Laden operatives carried out an attack by boat on U.S.S. *Cole*, as it was refueling in Aden, Yemen. Seven-

teen U.S. sailors were killed. An investigation reveale
U.S.S. *The Sullivans* had been the original target of the *Cole* attack
in January 2000, but the terrorists' boat had sunk from the weight
of the explosives loaded on it.

As the 1990s progressed, it became clear that bin Laden's terrorist network was unusual, although not unique, in its skill, dedication, and ability to evolve. The 1998 embassy attacks, the
planned attack in Jordan around the Millennium, and the attack
on U.S.S. *Cole* suggested a highly capable adversary. Operations
carried out by bin Laden's network before September 11 suggested several worrisome traits:

- Long-range planning. The 1998 attack on two U.S. embassies
  in East Africa took five years from its inception. The planning
  for the attack on U.S.S. *Cole* took several years.

- Simultaneous operations. The 1998 attack on the two embassies and the Millennium plots demonstrated that al Qaeda was
  able to conduct simultaneous attacks, suggesting sophisticated
  overall planning. In a statement for the Joint Inquiry record,
  RAND's Bruce Hoffman noted that simultaneous terrorist
  attacks are rare, as few groups have enough skilled operators,
  logisticians, and planners to conduct such operations.

- Operational security. Terrorist manuals and training emphasize
  that operations should be kept secret and details compartmented. Communications security is also stressed. Thus, disrupting these operations is difficult, even if low-level foot
  soldiers make mistakes and are arrested. Several attacks carried
  out by bin Laden's operatives occurred with little warning.
  Even the successful disruption of part of a plot, as occurred
  during the Millennium, does not necessarily reveal other
  planned attacks, such as an attack on a U.S. warship planned
  for around the same time.

- Flexible command structure. Bin Laden's network uses at least
  four different operational styles: a top-down approach employ-

ing highly-skilled radicals; training amateurs like Richard Reid, the so-called "shoebomber," to conduct simple, but lethal attacks; helping local groups with their own plans, as with Jordanian plotters during the Millennium; and fostering like-minded insurgencies. Tactics that can stop one type of attack do not necessarily work against others.

- Imagination. Most terrorists are conservative in their methods, relying on small arms or simple explosives. The attack on U.S.S. *Cole*, however, was a clear indication of the bin Laden network's tactical flexibility and willingness to go beyond traditional delivery means and targets.

Size also distinguishes bin Laden's network from many terrorist groups. The recently disrupted Greek radical group, November 17, for example, contained fewer than fifty people. According to Hoffman, the Japanese Red Army and the Red Brigades both had fewer than one hundred dedicated members. Even the Irish Republican Army, one of the most formidable terrorist organizations in the 1970s and 1980s, had no more than four hundred activists. Arresting and prosecuting members of these groups was an effective way to end or lessen the threat they posed.

Although the number of highly skilled and dedicated persons who have sworn fealty to bin Laden was probably in the low hundreds before September 11, the organization as a whole is much larger, with tens of thousands having gone through the training camps in Afghanistan. Its organizational and command structures, which employ many activists who are not formal members of the organization, make it difficult to determine where al Qaeda ends and other radical groups begin. Media reports indicate that al Qaeda has trained thousands of activists in Sudan and Afghanistan, and interviews of intelligence officials indicate that al Qaeda can draw on thousands of supporters when raising funds, planning, and executing attacks.

STORM CLOUDS OVER AMERICA

Central to the September 11 plot was bin Laden's determination to carry out a terrorist operation inside the United States. The Joint Inquiry therefore reviewed information the Intelligence Community held before September 11 that suggested that an attack within the United States was a possibility. Our review confirmed that, shortly after bin Laden's May 1998 press conference, the Community began to acquire intelligence that bin Laden's network intended to strike within the United States. Many of these reports were disseminated throughout the Community and to senior U.S. policymakers.

These intelligence reports should be understood in their proper context. First, they generally did not contain specific information as to where, when, and how a terrorist attack might occur, and, generally, they were not corroborated. Second, these reports represented a small percentage of the threat information that the Intelligence Community obtained during this period, most of which pointed to the possibility of attacks against U.S. interests overseas. Nonetheless, there was a modest, but relatively steady stream of intelligence indicating the possibility of terrorist attacks inside the United States. Third, the credibility of the sources providing this information was sometimes questionable. While one could not, as a result, give too much credence to some of the individual reports, the totality of the information in this body of reporting clearly reiterated a consistent and critically important theme: bin Laden's intent to launch terrorist attacks within the United States.

The Joint Inquiry reviewed many intelligence reports, including:

- In June 1998, the Intelligence Community obtained information from several sources that bin Laden was considering attacks in the United States, including Washington, D.C., and New York. This information was provided to . . . senior government officials in July 1998.

- In August 1998, the Intelligence Community obtained information that a group of unidentified Arabs planned to fly an explosives-laden plane from a foreign country into the World Trade Center. The information was passed to the FBI and the FAA [Federal Aviation Administration]. The latter found the plot to be highly unlikely, given the state of the foreign country's aviation program. Moreover, the agencies believed that a flight originating outside the United States would be detected before it reached its intended target inside the United States. The FBI's New York office took no action on the information, filing the communication in the office's bombing file. The Intelligence Community acquired additional information since then suggesting links between this group and other terrorist groups, including al Qaeda.

- In September 1998, the Community prepared a memorandum detailing al Qaeda infrastructure in the United States, including the use of fronts for terrorist activities. This information was provided to . . . senior government officials in September 1998.

- In September 1998, the Community obtained information that bin Laden's next operation might involve flying an explosives-laden aircraft into a U.S. airport and detonating it. This information was provided to . . . senior government officials in late 1998.

- In October 1998, the Community obtained information that al Qaeda was trying to establish an operative cell within the United States. This information suggested an effort to recruit U.S. citizen Islamists and U.S.-based expatriates from the Middle East and North Africa.

- In the fall of 1998, the Community received information concerning a bin Laden plot involving aircraft in the New York and Washington, D.C. areas.

- In November 1998, the Community obtained information that

a bin Laden terrorist cell was attempting to recruit a group of five to seven men from the United States to travel to the Middle East for training, in conjunction with a plan to strike U.S. domestic targets.

- In November 1998, the Community received information that bin Laden and senior associates had agreed to allocate rewards for the assassination of four "top" intelligence agency officers. The bounty for each assassination was $9 million. The bounty was in response to the U.S. announcement of an increase in the reward for information leading to bin Laden's arrest.

- In the spring of 1999, the Community obtained information about a planned bin Laden attack on a government facility in Washington, D.C.

- In August 1999, the Community obtained information that bin Laden's organization had decided to target the U.S. Secretary of State, Secretary of Defense, and DCI. "Target" was interpreted by Community analysts to mean "assassinate."

- In September 1999, the Community obtained information that bin Laden and others were planning a terrorist act in the United States, possibly against specific landmarks in California and New York City.

- In late 1999, the Community obtained information regarding possible bin Laden network plans to attack targets in Washington, D.C. and New York City during the Millennium celebrations.

- On December 14, 1999, Ahmed Ressam was arrested as he attempted to enter the United States from Canada, and chemicals and detonator materials were found in his car. Ressam's intended target was Los Angeles International Airport. Ressam was later determined to have links to bin Laden's terrorist network.

- In February 2000, the Community obtained information that bin Laden was making plans to assassinate U.S. intelligence officials, including the Director of the FBI.

- In March 2000, the Community obtained information regarding the types of targets that operatives in bin Laden's network might strike. The Statue of Liberty was specifically mentioned, as were skyscrapers, ports, airports, and nuclear power plants.

- In March 2000, the Intelligence Community obtained information suggesting that bin Laden was planning attacks in specific West Coast areas, possibly involving the assassination of several public officials.

- In April 2001, the Community obtained information from a source with terrorist connections who speculated that bin Laden was interested in commercial pilots as potential terrorists. The source warned that the United States should not focus only on embassy bombings, that terrorists sought "spectacular and traumatic" attacks and that the first World Trade Center bombing would be the type of attack that would be appealing. The source did not mention a timeframe for an attack. Because the source was offering personal speculation and not hard information, the information was not disseminated within the Intelligence Community.

The Joint Inquiry did not find any comprehensive Intelligence Community list of bin Laden-related threats to the United States that was prepared and presented to policymakers before September 11. Such a compilation might have highlighted the volume of information the Community had acquired about bin Laden's intention to strike inside the United States.

Nonetheless, the Intelligence Community did not leave unnoticed bin Laden's February 1998 declaration of war and intelligence reports indicating possible terrorist attacks inside the United States. The Community advised senior officials, including . . . the Congress, of the serious nature of the threat. The Joint

Inquiry also reviewed documents, other than intelligence reports, that demonstrate that the Intelligence Community, at least at senior levels, understood the threat bin Laden posed to the domestic United States, for example:

- A December 1998 Intelligence Community assessment that bin Laden "is actively planning against U.S. targets. . . . Multiple reports indicate OBL is keenly interested in striking the U.S. on its own soil. . . . [A]l Qaeda is recruiting operatives for attacks in the U.S. but has not yet identified potential targets."

- The December 1998 declaration of war memorandum from the DCI to his deputies at the CIA:
  We must now enter a new phase in our effort against bin Laden. . . . [W]e all acknowledge that retaliation is inevitable and that its scope may be far larger than we have previously experienced. . . . We are at war. . . . I want no resources or people spared in this effort, either inside CIA or the [Intelligence] Community.

- A document prepared by the CIA and signed by the President in December 1998:
  The Intelligence Community has strong indications that bin Laden intends to conduct or sponsor attacks inside the United States.

- June 1999 testimony to the Senate Select Committee on Intelligence by the CTC Chief and a July 1999 briefing to House Permanent Select Committee on Intelligence staff members describing reports that bin Laden and his associates were planning attacks inside the United States.

- A document prepared by the CIA and signed by the President in July 1999 characterizing bin Laden's February 1998 statement as a "de facto declaration of war" on the United States.

In testimony before the Joint Inquiry, however, former

National Security Advisor Sandy Berger put this information in context:

> The stream of threat information we received continuously from the FBI and CIA pointed overwhelmingly to attacks on U.S. interests abroad. Certainly the potential for attacks in the United States was there.

The Joint Inquiry record confirms that, in the eyes of the Intelligence Community, the world appeared increasingly dangerous for Americans in the spring and summer of 2001. During that period, the Intelligence Community detected a significant increase in information that bin Laden and al Qaeda intended to strike against U.S. interests in the very near future. Some Community officials have suggested that the increase in threat reporting was unprecedented, at least in their own experience. While the reporting repeatedly predicted dire consequences for Americans, it did not provide specific detail that could be acted on.

Between late March and September 2001, the Intelligence Community identified numerous signs of an impending terrorist attack, some of which pointed specifically to the United States as a target:

- In March, an intelligence source claimed that a group of bin Laden operatives was planning to conduct an unspecified attack in the United States in April 2001. One of the operatives allegedly resided in the United States.

- In April, the Intelligence Community obtained information that unspecified terrorist operatives in California and New York State were planning a terrorist attack in those states for April.

- Between May and July, the National Security Agency reported at least thirty-three communications suggesting a possibly imminent terrorist attack. The Intelligence Community thought at the time that one of them might have constituted a signal to proceed with terrorist operations. While none of these reports provided specific information on the attack, and it was not clear that any persons involved in the intercepted communications had first-hand knowledge of where, when, or how an attack might occur, they were widely disseminated within the Intelligence Community.

- In May, the Intelligence Community obtained a report that bin Laden supporters were planning to infiltrate the United States by way of Canada to carry out a terrorist operation using high explosives. This report mentioned without specifics an attack within the United States. In July, this information was shared with the FBI, the Immigration and Naturalization Service, the Customs Service, and the State Department and was included in an intelligence report for senior government officials in August.

- In May, the Department of Defense acquired and shared with other elements of the Intelligence Community information suggesting that seven persons associated with bin Laden had departed various locations for Canada, the United Kingdom, and the United States.

- In June, CTC obtained information that key operatives in bin Laden's organization were disappearing, while others were preparing for martyrdom.

- In July, the CTC became aware of a person who had recently been in Afghanistan who reported, "Everyone is talking about an impending attack." The Intelligence Community was also aware that bin Laden had stepped up his propaganda efforts in the preceding months.

- On August 16, the INS detained Zacarias Moussaoui in Minneapolis, Minnesota. His conduct had aroused suspicions about why he was learning to fly large commercial aircraft and had prompted the flight school he was attending to contact the local FBI field office. FBI agents believed that Moussaoui might have intended to carry out a terrorist act.

- On August 23, CIA requested that [Khalid] al Mihdhar and [Nawaf] al Hazmi, who had first come to the attention of the CIA and NSA in 1999 as possible associates of bin Laden's network, be added to the Department of State watchlist for denying entry to the United States.

- In late summer, the Intelligence Community obtained information that a person associated with al Qaeda was considering terrorist operations in the United States. There was no information as to the timing or possible targets.

- On September 10, NSA intercepted two communications . . . suggesting imminent terrorist activity. These communications were not translated into English and disseminated until September 12. They were not specific, and it is unclear whether they referred to the September 11 attacks.

During the summer of 2001, the Intelligence Community also disseminated information to a wide range of senior government officials at all federal agencies and military commands about the potential for imminent terrorist attacks. For example:

- On June 25, the Intelligence Community issued a terrorist threat advisory warning government agencies that there was a high probability of an imminent "spectacular" terrorist attack resulting in numerous casualties against U.S. interests abroad by Sunni extremists associated with al Qaeda.

- Subsequently, intelligence information provided to . . . senior government leaders on June 30 indicated that bin Laden's organization expected near-term attacks to have dramatic consequences on governments or cause major casualties.

- A briefing prepared for senior government officials at the beginning of July asserted: "Based on a review of all-source reporting over the last five months, we believe that OBL will launch a significant terrorist attack against U.S. and/or Israeli interests in the coming weeks. The attack will be spectacular and designed to inflict mass casualties against U.S. facilities or interests. Attack preparations have been made. Attack will occur with little or no warning."

• Later, on July 9, intelligence information provided to . . . senior government leaders indicated that members of bin Laden's organization continued to expect imminent attacks on U.S. interests.

Of particular interest to the Joint Inquiry was whether and to what extent the President received threat-specific warnings during this period. Access to this information was denied the Joint Inquiry by the White House. However, the Joint Inquiry was told by a representative of the Intelligence Community that, in August 2001, a closely held intelligence report for . . . senior government officials included information that bin Laden had wanted to conduct attacks in the United States since 1997. [In April 2004 the Bush Administration declassified the report, a Presidential Daily Brief delivered by the CIA on August 6, 2001. The briefing, entitled "Bin Laden Determined to Strike in U.S.," is reproduced in the appendix to this book.]

The Joint Inquiry was also interested in the nature and scope of the intelligence that was being provided to senior policymakers regarding the terrorist threat. In addition to the Presidential Daily Brief, the Intelligence Community produces a Senior Executive Intelligence Brief (SEIB) each day, a series of short articles that summarize political, military, economic, and diplomatic developments around the world of particular interest to senior government executives. The Joint Inquiry reviewed SEIBs distributed by the Intelligence Community in the spring and summer of 2001 and confirmed a rise in reporting on bin Laden between March and June. This increase was still only a relatively small portion of the array of intelligence subjects that the SEIBs brought to the attention of policymakers. For example, the peak in bin Laden-related reporting came in June 2001 when Islamic extremists, including bin Laden and al Qaeda, were referred to in eighteen of the 298 articles that appeared in the SEIBs that month.

The rise in threat reporting concerning bin Laden in 2001, though lacking in detail, did generate government terrorist advisories and warnings, including:

- An FAA Circular on June 22, 2001, referring to a possible hijacking plot by Islamic terrorists to secure the release of fourteen persons incarcerated in the United States in connection with the 1996 bombing of Khobar Towers [in Saudi Arabia].

- A public, worldwide caution issued by the State Department on June 22, warning Americans traveling abroad of the increased risk of a terrorist action.

- Four terrorism warning reports or warning report extensions issued by the Department of Defense on June 22 and 26, and July 6 and 20, primarily to alert U.S. military forces and the Department of Defense to signs that bin Laden's network was planning a near-term, anti-U.S. terrorist operation.

- A State Department démarche to Taliban representatives in Pakistan on June 26, 2001, declaring that the Taliban would be held responsible for terrorist attacks carried out by bin Laden or al Qaeda.

- An FBI communication on July 2, advising federal, state, and local law enforcement agencies of increased threat reporting about groups aligned with or sympathetic to bin Laden. The communication noted that the majority of the reports suggested a potential for attacks against U.S. targets abroad and that the FBI had no information suggesting a credible threat of terrorist attack in the United States, although the possibility could not be discounted.

Deputy Secretary of State Richard Armitage described the situation to the Joint Inquiry:

In fact, [the intelligence] was good enough for us to take several steps. We issued between January and September nine warnings, five of them global, because of the threat information we were receiving from the intelligence agencies in the summer, when George Tenet was around town literally pounding on desks saying, something is happening, this is an unprecedented level of threat information. He didn't know where it was going to happen, but he knew that it was coming.

Interviews conducted during the Joint Inquiry show that the general view within the Intelligence Community in the spring and summer of 2001 was that an attack on U.S. interests was more likely to occur overseas, possibly in Saudi Arabia and Israel. Intelligence information, the arrest of suspected terrorists in the Middle East and Europe, and a credible report of a plan to attack a U.S. embassy in the Middle East shaped the Community's thinking about where an attack was likely to occur. In fact, FBI agents working in Yemen on the *Cole* investigation were told to leave the country because of concern about a possible attack.

The belief that an attack was likely to occur overseas was also reflected in numerous statements and data the Joint Inquiry reviewed, for example:

- In a May 16, 2002 press briefing, National Security Advisor Condoleezza Rice said: "I want to reiterate that during this time, the overwhelming bulk of the evidence was that this was an attack that was likely to take place overseas."

- The FBI's Assistant Director for Counterterrorism at the time said that the intelligence he was seeing led him to believe with a high probability—"98 percent"—that an attack would occur overseas.

- At a Joint Inquiry hearing, Deputy Secretary of State Richard Armitage testified: "I, in general, perceived the threat to be at our interests overseas, primarily in the Gulf, some in Southeast

Asia, and most definitely in Israel. That is from my point of view and the Department of State."

- At the same hearing, Deputy Secretary of Defense Paul Wolfowitz testified: "I would say near-term we perceived the threat to be overseas, as Secretary Armitage says. In the mid- to longer-term, we perceived the threat to be mass casualties in the United States as a result of chemical or biological or conceivably nuclear attack. . . . "

- Deputy National Security Advisor Steve Hadley asserted in a written response to Joint Inquiry questions:
  The specific warning the Administration did have pointed to operations against U.S. interests abroad. . . . The threat warnings, in the spring and summer of 2001, did not, to my knowledge, include any specific warning information to indicate plans for terrorist attacks inside the United States. . . . During this period of increased threat reporting, information from [Intelligence Community] agencies focused specifically on potential attacks in Europe, the Middle East, and the Arabian Peninsula. . . . [Intelligence Community] officials, however, did not discount the possibility of domestic attacks by al Qaeda and other groups.

Bin Laden-related threat reporting began to decline in July 2001. The Intelligence Community did, however, continue to follow up on some of the information in its possession.

THE TERRORIST THREAT FROM THE AIR

Central to the September 11 attacks was the terrorists' use of airplanes as weapons, which National Security Advisor Condoleezza Rice addressed in a May 2002 press briefing:

I don't think anybody could have predicted that these same people would take an airplane and slam it into the World Trade Center, taken another one and slam it into the Pentagon; that they would try to use an airplane as a missile, a hijacked airplane as a missile. All of this reporting about hijacking was about traditional hijacking. You take a plane—people were worried they might blow one up, but they were most worried that they might try to take a plane and use it for release of the blind Sheikh or some of their own people.

The Joint Inquiry confirmed that, before September 11, the Intelligence Community produced at least twelve reports over a seven-year period suggesting that terrorists might use airplanes as weapons. As with the intelligence reports indicating bin Laden's intentions to strike inside the United States, the credibility of sources was sometimes questionable and information often sketchy. The reports reviewed by the Joint Inquiry included:

- In December 1994, Algerian Armed Islamic Group terrorists hijacked an Air France flight in Algiers and threatened to crash it into the Eiffel Tower. French authorities deceived the terrorists into thinking the plane did not have enough fuel to reach Paris and diverted it to Marseilles. A French anti-terrorist force stormed the plane and killed all four terrorists.

- In January 1995, a Philippine National Police raid turned up material in a Manila apartment suggesting that Ramzi Yousef, Abdul Murad, and Khalid Sheikh Mohammed planned, among other things, to crash an airplane into CIA Headquarters. The police said that the same group was responsible for the bombing of a Philippine airliner on December 12, 1994. Information on the threat was passed to the FAA, which briefed U.S. and major foreign carriers.

- In January 1996, the Intelligence Community obtained information concerning a planned suicide attack by persons associated with Sheikh al Rahman and a key al Qaeda operative to fly to the United States from Afghanistan and attack the White House.

- In October 1996, the Intelligence Community obtained information regarding an Iranian plot to hijack a Japanese plane over Israel and crash it into Tel Aviv. A passenger would board the plane in the Far East, commandeer the aircraft, order it to fly over Tel Aviv, and crash the plane into the city.

- In 1997, an FBI Headquarters unit became concerned about the possibility that an unmanned aerial vehicle (UAV) would be used in terrorist attacks. The FBI and CIA became aware of reports that a group had purchased a UAV and concluded that the group might use the plane for reconnaissance or attack. The possibility of an attack outside the United States was thought to be more likely, for example, by flying a UAV into a U.S. embassy or a U.S. delegation.

- In August 1998, the Intelligence Community obtained information that a group, since linked to al Qaeda, planned to fly an explosives-laden plane from a foreign country into the World Trade Center. As explained earlier, the FAA found the plot to be highly unlikely given the state of the foreign country's aviation program. Moreover, the agencies concluded that a flight originating outside the United States would be detected before it reached its target. The FBI's New York office took no action on the information.

- In September 1998, the Intelligence Community obtained information that bin Laden's next operation might involve flying an explosives-laden aircraft into a U.S. airport and detonating it. This information was provided to senior government officials in late 1998.

- In November 1998, the Intelligence Community obtained information that the Turkish Kaplancilar, an Islamic extremist group, had planned a suicide attack to coincide with celebrations marking the death of Ataturk, the founder of modern Turkey. The conspirators, who were arrested, planned to crash an airplane packed with explosives into Ataturk's tomb during a ceremony. The Turkish press said the group had cooperated with bin Laden, and the FBI's New York office included this incident in a bin Laden database.

- In February 1999, the Intelligence Community obtained information that Iraq had formed a suicide pilot unit that it planned to use against British and U.S. forces in the Persian Gulf. The CIA commented that this was highly unlikely and probably disinformation.

- In March 1999, the Intelligence Community obtained information regarding plans by an al Qaeda member, who was a U.S. citizen, to fly a hang glider into the Egyptian Presidential Palace and detonate explosives. The person, who received hang glider training in the United States, brought a hang glider to Afghanistan. However, various problems arose during the testing of the glider. He was subsequently arrested and is in custody abroad.

- In April 2000, the Intelligence Community obtained information regarding an alleged bin Laden plot to hijack a Boeing 747. The source, a "walk-in" to the FBI's Newark office, claimed that he had learned hijacking techniques and received arms training in a Pakistani camp. He also claimed that he was to meet five or six persons in the United States. Some of these persons would be pilots who had been instructed to take over a plane, fly to Afghanistan, or, if they could not make it there, blow the plane up. Although the source passed a polygraph, the Bureau was unable to verify any aspect of his story or identify his contacts in the United States.

- In August 2001, the Intelligence Community obtained information about a plot to bomb the U.S. embassy in Nairobi from an airplane or crash the airplane into it. The Intelligence Community learned that two people who were reportedly acting on instructions from bin Laden met in October 2000 to discuss this plot.

The CIA disseminated several of these reports to the FBI and to agencies responsible for preventive actions. These included the FAA, which is responsible for issuing security directives, alerting domestic and international airports and airlines of threats the Intelligence Community has identified.

In testimony before the Joint Inquiry, DCI Tenet mentioned additional evidence developed since September 11 concerning al Qaeda's intention of to use airplanes as weapons:

> After 11 September, we learned from a foreign government service that in 1996, bin Laden's second-in-command, Muhammad Atif, drew up a study on the feasibility of hijacking US planes and destroying them in flight, possibly influenced by Yousef's and Mukhtar's [an alias of Khalid Sheikh Mohammed] unrealized plans [the Bojinka Plot]. . . . Bin Laden's determination to strike America at home increased with the issuance of the February 1998 *fatwa* targeting all Americans, both military and civilian. The ideas about destroying commercial airliners that had been circulating in al Qaeda leadership circles for several years appear to have been revived after that *fatwa*, in the early planning stages of the 9/11 plot. We believe that outside events also shaped al Qaeda leaders' thinking about an airliner attack. . . . [T]he October 1999 crash of Egypt Air Flight 990, attributed in the media to a suicidal pilot, may have encouraged al Qaeda's growing impression that air travel was a vulnerability for the United States.

Despite these reports, the Intelligence Community did not produce any specific assessments of the likelihood that terrorists would use airplanes as weapons, and U.S. policymakers apparently remained unaware of this kind of potential threat. Former National Security Advisor Sandy Berger testified before the Joint Inquiry: "We heard of the idea of airplanes as weapons, but I don't recall being presented with any specific threat information about an attack of this nature or any alert highlighting this threat or indicating it was any more likely than any other." In response to written Joint Inquiry questions, Deputy National Security Advisor Steve Hadley asserted:

Before September 11, I do not recall receiving any information concerning al Qaeda using aircraft as weapons for attacks within the United States. One CIA analysis stated that al Qaeda was interested in possible hijackings in order to win the release of imprisoned al Qaeda members, but did not mention the possibility of using aircraft themselves as weapons.

The failure to consider seriously the use of aircraft as weapons may be the result of insufficient resources directed to intelligence analysis. Before September 11, CTC had forty analysts to analyze terrorism issues worldwide, with only one of its five analytic branches focused on terrorist tactics. As a result, the only terrorist tactic on which CTC had performed strategic analysis was the use of chemical, biological, radiological and nuclear weapons because of the obvious potential for mass casualties.

Aviation-related terrorism was included in some broader terrorist threat assessments, such as the National Intelligence Estimate (NIE) on terrorism. For example, a 1995 NIE mentioned the plot to blow up twelve U.S. airliners and cited the consideration the Bojinka conspirators gave to attacking CIA Headquarters with an aircraft laden with explosives. The FAA worked with the Intelligence Community on this analysis and drafted the section addressing the threat to civil aviation, which said:

Our review of the evidence . . . suggests the conspirators were guided in their selection of the method and venue of attack by carefully studying security procedures in place in the region. If terrorists operating in [the United States] are similarly methodical, they will identify serious vulnerabilities in the security system for domestic flights.

A 1997 update to the 1995 NIE concluded:

Civil aviation remains a particularly attractive target in light of the fear and publicity the downing of an airliner would evoke and the revelations last summer of the U.S. air transport sectors' vulnerabilities.

As a result of the increasing threats to aviation, Congress required the FAA and FBI to conduct joint threat and vulnerability assessments of security at select "high risk" U.S. airports and to provide annual reports to Congress. A classified portion of the December 2000 report downplayed the threat to domestic aviation:

> FBI investigations confirm domestic and international terrorist groups operating within the U.S. but do not suggest evidence of plans to target domestic civil aviation. Terrorist activity within the U.S. has focused primarily on fundraising, recruiting new members, and disseminating propaganda. While international terrorists have conducted attacks on U.S. soil, these acts represent anomalies in their traditional targeting which focuses on U.S. interests overseas.

Thus, less than a year before the September 11 attacks, and notwithstanding intelligence information to the contrary, the FBI and FAA assessed the prospects of a terrorist incident targeting domestic civil aviation in the United States as relatively low.

After September 11, the CIA acknowledged some of the information that was available regarding the use of airplanes as weapons. A draft analysis dated November 19, 2001, "The 11 September Attacks: A Preliminary Assessment," explains:

> We do not know the process by which bin Laden and his lieutenants decided to hijack planes with the idea of flying them into buildings in the United States, but the idea of hijacking planes for suicide attacks had long been current in jihadist circles. For example, GIA terrorists from Algeria had planned to crash an Air France jet into the Eiffel Tower in December 1994, and Ramzi Yousef—a participant in the 1993 World Trade Center bombing—planned to explode 12 U.S. jetliners in mid-air over the Pacific in the mid-1990s. Likewise the World Trade Center had long been a target of terrorist bombers.

Despite that intelligence, the Joint Inquiry found no evidence that, before September 11, analysts in the Intelligence Community were:

- cataloguing information regarding the use of airplanes as weapons as a terrorist tactic;

- sending requirements to collectors to look for additional information on this threat; or

- considering the likelihood that bin Laden, al Qaeda, or any other terrorist group would attack the United States or U.S. interests in this way.

The CTC's Deputy Director acknowledged that the CIA had not performed strategic analysis on airplanes as weapons before September 11. He also explained ways in which CTC has sought to improve its analytic capabilities since then:

> We have a couple of approaches to strategic analysis in CTC now. . . . We have spent a fair amount of analytic time looking at intelligence reporting that [al Qaeda is] going to use a particular type of tactic or go after a particular type of target, other intelligence reporting . . . that shows that they have actually trained at that tactic or trained for that type of target. . . . When you get all . . . of those ingredients, that's pretty sobering. What is most alarming to us is the number of tactics that we've gotten that kind of a case on[:] . . . on surface-to-air missiles . . . use of truck bombs and car bombs . . . the use of aircraft, both aircraft hijackings and aircraft as weapons . . . the use of improvised explosive devices like Mr. Reid put in his shoes several months ago . . . the use of poisons and toxins. Put it all together and you can say that al Qaeda has built a handful of cards, any of which it could be playing, all of which it intends at some point and with some opportunity to play. Its choices are very broad and very frightening.

Even if enough analysis is done to provide better analysis to policymakers regarding strategic threats, there remains the issue of how much influence that information will have in warning other federal entities and the private sector. In discussing what could have been done better before September 11, the DCI told the Joint Inquiry that the failure to focus on the use of airplanes as weapons was just one area that should have been part of a "systematic thought process to think about how you play defense":

> You can disseminate all of the threat reportings you want. You can do the strategic analysis about airplanes. You can do the strategic analysis about car bombs, truck bombs, assassination attempts, fast boats and everything else. You can put all of that out there to people. Unless somebody is thinking about the homeland from the perspective of buttoning it down to basically create a deterrence that may work, your assumption will be that the FBI and the CIA are going to be one-hundred percent flawless all of the time. And it will never happen.

Rethinking America's War against Terror

EDITOR'S NOTE: The Clinton and Bush administrations both recognized the menace of bin Laden and declared war against the lethal new transnational enemy that al Qaeda represented. Both presidents ordered the nation's array of intelligence agencies to take the battle to the terrorists. But neither administration managed to put much pressure on the enemy. Before September 11, al Qaeda ranked high on the intelligence community's priority list, but so did Balkan strife, Indian-Pakistani nuclear tensions and a showdown with China, among other crises. More important, America's intelligence agencies—feuding, turf-conscious, and divided between domestic and international mandates—were in no shape to defeat hijackers who could be recruited in Germany, financed by Gulf money, indoctrinated in Afghanistan, briefed in Malaysia and trained in Florida. The Joint Inquiry examined the many cracks in America's counterterrorism defenses.

THE POST-COLD-WAR THAW

As the threat from al Qaeda increased in the 1990s, concern grew about the danger to America. The Clinton Administration steadily increased its attention to terrorism, which became a top priority after the August 1998 attacks on U.S. embassies in Kenya and Tanzania. The Bush Administration also devoted considerable attention to the al Qaeda threat as it conducted a policy review in the months before September 11.

Despite sharpened focus in the years before September 11, terrorism remained only one concern of many. . . . The process for setting intelligence priorities was also vague and confusing, and neither the Clinton nor the Bush Administration developed an integrated counterterrorism strategy that drew on all elements of national power before September 11.

Counterterrorism was not a top intelligence priority in the immediate aftermath of the Cold War. Former National Security Advisor Brent Scowcroft testified that the first Bush Administration focused primarily on the former Soviet Union. Moreover, the sense of immediacy diminished because the incidence and severity of terrorism had declined since the Reagan Administration. Mr. Scowcroft noted that the focus of discussions on terrorism was state-sponsored attacks, from which the U.S. homeland was thought to be immune.

As a result, neither the first Bush administration nor the Intelligence Community devoted considerable attention to terrorism at the time. Former National Coordinator for Counterterrorism Richard Clarke [who served both the Clinton and Bush administrations] noted that the first Bush Administration approved only one "narrow document" related to terrorism, suggesting that the subject was not a high priority. Thus, as former National Security Advisor Sandy Berger testified:

> When President Clinton began his first term in 1993, the Intelligence Community was primarily focused on the agenda created by the Soviet Union's collapse, the Cold War's end, and our Gulf War victory. . . . The CIA maintained no significant assets in Afghanistan after our withdrawal from the region in 1989. Little was known about Osama bin Laden except that he was one of many financiers of terrorist groups.

THE CLINTON RECORD

Mr. Clarke has testified that, when the Clinton Administration came into office, "the furthest thing from [its] mind in terms of the policy agenda was terrorism." This quickly ended with Mir Amal Kansi's murder of two CIA employees outside agency Headquarters shortly after President Clinton's inauguration. That event, plus the Iraqi attempt to assassinate former President Bush in 1993 and the February 1993 bombing of the World Trade Center, "catapulted" terrorism onto the Administration's agenda, according to Mr. Berger. He also noted that these events led to the President becoming personally focused on terrorism.

The Clinton Administration issued several documents that many witnesses saw as reflecting the growing importance of terrorism:

- In 1995, the Clinton Administration issued Presidential Decision Directive (PDD) 35, which former National Security Advisor Anthony Lake described as "formally establish[ing] our top intelligence priorities and plac[ing] terrorism among them, led only by intelligence support for our troops in the field and a small number of states that posed an immediate or potential serious threat to the United States."

- Several months later in 1995, the President issued PDD 39, the first PDD issued explicitly on terrorism since the Reagan administration. Mr. Lake noted that PDD 39 "mandated increased efforts to capture terrorists abroad; high priority for detecting and preventing attacks with weapons of mass destruction; and the exchange between the FBI and CIA of high-level anti-terrorism officials."

- In 1998, Presidential Decision Directives 62 and 63 were issued to raise the importance of counterterrorism within the interagency process and to clarify responsibilities for reacting to an attack. According to Mr. Clarke, these directives established an interagency coordination process, to include regular meetings to evaluate threats, discuss resources, and treat counterterrorism as a continuous, rather than *ad hoc* concern.

Al Qaeda emerged as a leading adversary during the second term of the Clinton Administration. Mr. Berger told the Joint Inquiry that bin Laden was portrayed as a financier as late as 1996, but that U.S. knowledge of his activities and concern about the threat his organization posed began to grow rapidly. After the August 1998 attack on U.S. embassies in Kenya and Tanzania, bin Laden dominated U.S. counterterrorism concerns. As Mr. Berger testified, "In 1996 he was on the radar screen; in 1998 he was the radar screen."

Senior level officials met frequently on terrorism. In the months before the Millennium celebrations, according to Mr. Berger, there were constant Principals Meetings and much senior level attention to the risk of an al Qaeda attack. According to Deputy National Security Advisor Steve Hadley, Mr. Berger and Mr. Clarke both emphasized the importance of terrorism during the transition from the Clinton to the Bush Administration.

THE BUSH RECORD

Transitions between administrations always take considerable time. For some high level positions, such as National Coordinator for Counterterrorism, it is difficult if not impossible to maintain continuity or an intense daily focus on an issue, if the status of the person holding the position is unclear. Mr. Berger explained that the Clinton Administration did not respond to the October 2000 attack on U.S.S. *Cole*, in part, because it believed that the incoming Bush Administration should handle the matter. However, Bush Administration officials testified that they did not begin their major counterterrorism policy review until April 2001. Thus, it appears that significant slippage in counterterrorism policy may have taken place in late 2000 and early 2001. At least part of this was due to the unresolved status of Mr. Clarke as National Coordinator for Counterterrorism and his uncertain mandate to coordinate Bush Administration policy on terrorism and specifically on bin Laden.

Al Qaeda remained an intelligence priority under the Bush administration. . . . As Deputy Secretary of State Richard Armitage testified to the Joint Inquiry on September 19, 2002:

> The National Security Council . . . called for new proposals [in March 2001] on a strategy that would be more aggressive against al Qaeda. The first deputies meeting, which is the first decision making body in the administration, met on the 30th of April and set off on a trail of initiatives to include financing, getting at financing, to get at increased authorities for the Central Intelligence Agency, sharp end things that the military was asked to do. . . . So, from March through about August, we were preparing a national security Presidential directive, and it was distributed on August 13 to the principals for their final comments. And then, of course, we had the events of September 11. . . .

That policy review reportedly involved drafting new covert action authorities, several senior level meetings to discuss policy alternatives, and exploration of other initiatives. The review was nearing completion in the days before September 11.

COMPETING AGENDAS

Counterterrorism was only one of many priorities for both the Clinton and Bush Administrations. Although a complete review of their policy priorities is beyond the scope of this inquiry, several senior officials have suggested the wide range of concerns that faced both administrations:

- Intelligence Community officials with responsibility for resource management noted that a range of regional and global issues were important concerns that policymakers emphasized in allocating resources.

- Mr. Clarke explained that he faced resistance to using military force in Afghanistan, in part because the United States was already bombing Iraq and Serbia.

- Former Clinton Assistant Secretary of State for South Asia Karl Inderfurth noted in an interview that the East Africa embassy bombings made counterterrorism the top U.S. priority in its dealings with the Taliban regime in Afghanistan. Before then, ending the civil war, advancing women's rights, and establishing a broad-based government were U.S. priorities for that country.

- Mr. Inderfurth also noted that concerns about an Indian-Pakistani conflict, or even nuclear confrontation, competed with efforts to press Pakistan on terrorism.

- Mr. Hadley noted that Bush Administration concerns before September 11 included the P–3 aircraft incident with China and the June 2001 G–8 Summit.

Even those involved directly in counterterrorism efforts focused much of their attention on groups other than al Qaeda and its affiliates. Mr. Clarke told the Joint Inquiry that Iran and the Lebanese Hizbollah were the most important terrorist concerns during the first Clinton Administration. This was corroborated by Mr. Lake, who noted that the Administration's "primary preoccupation was on state sponsors of terrorism and such organizations as Hizbollah." The Iranian supported attack on the U.S. military at Khobar Towers in 1996 reinforced this concern, according to Mr. Clarke.

Several agencies also focused their counterterrorism efforts on force protection. After the embassy bombings, the State Department tried to augment security in its facilities worldwide. Similarly, the attacks on Khobar Towers and U.S.S. *Cole* led to increased Defense Department and military efforts to protect U.S. military facilities and assets abroad.

Moreover, the process of setting intelligence priorities was often confusing. Mr. Clarke noted that the White House "never really gave good systematic, timely guidance to the Intelligence Community about what the priorities were at the national level." Mr. Hadley stated that Bush Administration officials were told during the transition that "this priority-setting process [PDD-35] . . . was not effective for communicating changing priorities over time." Joint Inquiry interviews with Intelligence Community officials suggest that many felt that the prioritization process was so broad as to be meaningless.

There was also bureaucratic confusion about responsibility for counterterrorism. Despite efforts by the NSC's [National Security Council] Counterterrorism Security Group to streamline the process, agencies often did not coordinate their counterterrorism efforts. Mr. Inderfurth noted that the State Department had different elements working on counterterrorism in regard to Afghanistan, Saudi Arabia, embassy security, and other matters. Former Deputy Secretary of Defense John Hamre noted in an interview that several different components of the Defense Department were involved in counterterrorism, often with little coordination.

NEW POLICIES

In accordance with the growing importance of terrorism, Clinton Administration officials took several steps to strengthen U.S. counterterrorism efforts. During the late 1990s, the CIA initiated a campaign, working with foreign liaison services to disrupt and "take down" al Qaeda and other terrorist cells around the world. Mr. Clarke told the Joint Inquiry that "'disrupt' means 'arrest,' if possible, have the host country arrest, or if there is any reason to bring them back to the United States, to arrest them and bring them back here." The Clinton Administration strongly backed this campaign, according to Mr. Berger, who pointed out that terrorist cells were dismantled and disrupted in more than twenty countries as a result.

The Clinton Administration used military force, albeit in a limited manner as is discussed in detail in a separate chapter. Mr.

Clarke noted that the retaliatory strike on Iraq in 1993 for its attempted assassination of former President Bush was the first time the U.S. had used military force to punish a state for terrorism since 1986. According to Mr. Berger, the 1998 cruise missile strikes on terrorism-linked facilities in Afghanistan and Sudan were meant to demonstrate the Clinton Administration's seriousness, as well as to disrupt al Qaeda's infrastructure. The Clinton Administration also initiated an increasingly aggressive covert action policy. . . .

Mr. Berger, Mr. Clarke, and Mr. Lake noted several other measures the Clinton Administration initiated:

- Increasing intelligence funding after 1995

- More than doubling the number of FBI agents devoted to, and more than tripling the FBI budget for, counterterrorism

- Expanding the size of the CTC and otherwise increasing CIA efforts against terrorism

- Passing the Anti-Terrorism and Effective Death Penalty Act in 1996 and legislation to track foreign student visas

- Pressing CIA to establish an operational unit focused on tracking bin Laden and terrorist financing (Intelligence Community and Clinton Administration officials differ as to who deserves credit for this effort)

- Encouraging CIA and the FBI to improve cooperation on terrorism, including exchanging senior officials (officials in the FBI, CIA, and Clinton Administration also differ as to who deserves credit for this effort)

- Increasing diplomatic pressure on the Taliban through bilateral discussions, U.N. sanctions, and freezing of assets.

Policymakers report to the Joint Inquiry that they had limited flexibility with regard to Afghanistan. Mr. Berger testified that neither Congress, the media, nor the international community supported invading Afghanistan before September 11. During the Bush Administration, the United States issued a démarche to the Taliban in June 2001, noting that it would be held accountable for al Qaeda attacks on the United States.

Neither the Clinton nor Bush Administration aggressively tried to disrupt al Qaeda financing. A former Intelligence Community official testified that in 1996 or 1997 the Intelligence Community had plans . . . the Treasury Department blocked. . . . Because of Treasury's concerns, the Intelligence Community, according to the former official, was limited before September 11. . . . Mr. Clarke noted that counterterrorism officials hoped to appeal Treasury's initial position by presenting concrete information on terrorism fundraising. The Intelligence Community, however, was not able to provide the information.

THE LAW ENFORCEMENT APPROACH

Some policymakers recognized that countering al Qaeda required the application of all aspects of U.S. power. According to testimony from Deputy Secretary of Defense Paul Wolfowitz, the effort against al Qaeda:

> . . . is not just something for the Intelligence Community alone; . . . you can't go to war against al Qaeda without recognizing the role that the Government of Afghanistan is playing. You can't go after the Government of Afghanistan without recognizing the problems in your relationship particularly with Pakistan, but with other neighboring countries, and you can't get serious about this without looking at military options.

Before September 11, however, neither the Clinton nor Bush Administration developed a plan to disrupt al Qaeda that integrated U.S. diplomatic, economic, intelligence, and military assets. Deputy Secretary of State Richard Armitage testified that the Bush Administration received briefings on the urgency of the al Qaeda threat, but "we were never given a plan," a contention Mr. Berger echoed. Mr. Wolfowitz testified that even contingency planning for using the military for counterterrorism "was in the very most primitive stages." General Hugh Shelton, former Chairman of the Joint Chiefs of Staff, told the Joint Inquiry that he did not believe that policymakers had any serious plans to use the military in a significant way against the Taliban before September 11.

In the absence of a more comprehensive strategy, the United States defaulted to relying on law enforcement, at home and abroad, as the leading instrument in the fight against al Qaeda. The perpetrators of the 1993 World Trade Center bombing and the plot against New York City landmarks, several conspirators in the 1998 embassy bombings, and several members of a group that planned Millennium attacks were all prosecuted. This emphasis on prosecution continued a trend begun in the 1980s when Congress and President Reagan gave the FBI an important role in countering international terrorism, including attacks overseas.

Government officials apparently never intended to rely exclusively on law enforcement to fight terrorism. Senior Department of Justice officials testified that they saw their efforts as an adjunct to other means of fighting terrorism. Mary Jo White, who as U.S. Attorney for the Southern District of New York prosecuted many of the most important cases against al Qaeda, testified before the Joint Inquiry that "no one considered prosecutions to be the country's counterterrorism strategy or even a particularly major part of it." Mr. Wolfowitz testified that terrorism "is not a law enforcement problem, and it can't be dealt with simply by retaliating against individual acts of terrorism." However, covert action and military force had little impact before September 11.

Prosecutions do have several advantages in the fight against terrorism. As Ms. White noted in her testimony and in an interview, prosecutions take terrorists off the street. She acknowledged that this does not shut down an entire group, but some bombs, she said, do not go off as a result of arrests. In addition, she pointed out that critical intelligence often comes from the investigative process, as individual terrorists confess or reveal associates through their personal effects and communications. As former FBI Director Louis Freeh asserted in an interview, "You can't divorce arrest from prevention." Ms. White contended that the prosecutions might deter some, though not all individuals from violence. Finally, the threat of a jail sentence often induces terrorists to cooperate with investigators and provide information.

Heavy reliance on law enforcement, however, has costs. National Intelligence Officer for the Near East and South Asia Paul Pillar noted in Joint Inquiry testimony that it is easier to arrest terrorist underlings than masterminds. Those who organize and plan attacks, particularly the ultimate decisionmakers who authorize them, are often thousands of miles away when an attack is carried out. In addition, the deterrent effect of imprisonment is often minimal for highly motivated terrorists such as those in al Qaeda.

Moreover, law enforcement is time-consuming. The CIA and the FBI expended considerable resources supporting investigations in Africa and in Yemen into the embassy and U.S.S. *Cole* attacks, a drain on scarce resources that could have been used to gather information and disrupt future attacks. Finally, law enforcement standards of evidence are high, and establishing a legal case that meets these standards often requires unattainable intelligence and threatens to compromise sensitive sources or methods.

At times, law enforcement and intelligence have competing interests. The former head of the FBI's International Terrorism Section noted that Attorney General Reno leaned toward closing down surveillances under the Foreign Intelligence Surveillance Act if they hindered criminal cases. In addition, convictions that help disrupt terrorists are often based on lesser charges (such as immigration violations), and this may not always convince FBI field personnel that the effort is worthwhile compared with other cases that put criminals in jail for many years. As former FBI Assistant Director for Counterterrorism Dale Watson explained, Special Agents in Charge of FBI field offices focused more on convicting than on disrupting.

Reliance on law enforcement when individuals have fled to a hostile country, such as Iran or the Taliban's Afghanistan, appears particularly ineffective, as the masterminds are often beyond the reach of justice. One FBI agent scorned the idea of using the Bureau to take the lead in countering al Qaeda, noting that all the FBI can do is arrest and prosecute. They cannot shut down training camps in hostile countries. He noted that the strategy is "like telling the FBI after Pearl Harbor, 'Go to Tokyo and arrest the Emperor.'" In his opinion, a military solution was necessary because "[t]he Southern District doesn't have any cruise missiles."

DISRUPTIONS AND RENDITIONS

Disruptions and renditions are important tools in the fight against terrorism, and terrorist activity can be disrupted in many ways. Examples include watchlists to deny entry into the United States, liaison relationships with foreign intelligence and law-enforcement services willing to arrest and detain radicals, raids on terrorist facilities, and criminal investigations and prosecutions.

In testimony to the Joint Inquiry, the DCI summed up the ultimate disruption of al Qaeda operations—destruction of the Afghani sanctuary:

> In this struggle, we must play offense as well as defense. The move into the Afghanistan sanctuary was essential. We have disrupted the terrorists' plans, denied them the comfort of their bases and training facilities and the confidence that they can mount and remount attacks without fear of serious retribution.

Disruption became increasingly important in the years before September 11. Following the arrest of Ahmed Ressam with explosives at the U.S./Canada border and the discovery of plots in Jordan during the Millennium celebrations, a worldwide effort was launched to thwart other attacks. The effort involved dozens of foreign intelligence services, which detained suspected radicals, minimally to keep them off the streets, but also in the hope of gaining confessions or intimidating them into aborting planned attacks. Former National Security Advisor Sandy Berger gave some idea of the scope of these disruption efforts when he testified that the Intelligence Community had worked around the world since 1997 to dismantle al Qaeda cells in about twenty countries.

A rendition is the arrest and detention of terrorist operatives for return to the United States or another country for prosecution. Renditions often lead to confessions, and they disrupt terrorist plots by shattering cells and removing key individuals. In practice, almost all renditions entail disruptions.

Working with a wide array of foreign governments, CIA and FBI have helped deliver dozens of suspected terrorists to justice. CTC officers responsible for the renditions program told the Joint Inquiry that, from 1987 to September 11, 2001, CTC was involved in the rendition of several dozen terrorists, a number that increased substantially after September 11. Former National Counterterrorism Coordinator Richard Clarke described for the Joint Inquiry a particularly successful program, through which "we were able to identify al Qaeda members throughout the world. . . ."

The emphasis on renditions and disruptions increased as the Intelligence Community received more frequent reports of impending al Qaeda attacks in the spring and summer of 2001. As DCI Tenet testified:

Starting in the spring and continuing through the summer of 2001 we saw a significant increase in the level of threat reporting. Again, working with the FBI and foreign liaison services, we thwarted attacks on the U.S. Embassy in Paris, our Embassy in Yemen, U.S. facilities in Saudi Arabia and operations to kidnap U.S. citizens. We approached twenty countries with specific targets for disruption, prompting arrests. . . .

AFGHANISTAN: THE TERRORIST SANCTUARY

Between 1996 and September 2001, the United States worked with dozens of foreign governments to disrupt al Qaeda, arrest and interrogate its operatives, and prevent terrorist attacks. Throughout that period, Afghanistan was a terrorist safe haven, in which al Qaeda built a network for planning attacks, training and vetting recruits, and indoctrinating potential radicals. In essence, al Qaeda created a terrorist army in Afghanistan with little interference. As DCI George Tenet explained in testimony before the Joint Inquiry:

> The terrorist plotting, planning, recruiting, and training in the late 1990s were aided immeasurably by the sanctuary the Taliban provided.
>
> - Afghanistan had served as a place of refuge for international terrorists since the 1980s. The Taliban actively aided bin Laden by assigning him guards for security, permitting him to build and maintain terrorist camps, and refusing to cooperate with efforts by the international community to extradite him.
>
> - In return, bin Laden invested vast amounts of money in Taliban projects and provided hundreds of well-trained fighters to help the Taliban consolidate and expand their control of the country.
>
> - While we often talk of two trends in terrorism—state supported and independent—in bin Laden's case with the Taliban what we had was something completely new: a *terrorist* sponsoring a *state*. (Emphasis in original.)

Some CIA analysts and operators told Joint Inquiry staff that they recognized as early as 1997 that bin Laden's terrorist organization would continue to train cadres of Islamic extremists and generate numerous terrorist operations, as long as the Taliban granted al Qaeda sanctuary in Afghanistan.

Failure to eliminate Afghanistan as a terrorist sanctuary had practical operational consequences. In describing to the Joint Inquiry the CIA's 1999 plan to capture and bring bin Laden and his principal lieutenants to justice, DCI Tenet explained that, because "U.S. policy stopped short of replacing the Taliban regime, . . . the ability of the U.S. Government to exert pressure on bin Laden" was seriously limited. Because our government had "no official presence in Afghanistan, and relations with the Taliban were seriously strained," the DCI asserted, it became much "more difficult to gain access to bin Laden and al Qaeda personnel."

Between 1999 and 2001, the government did undertake some efforts to address the problem of Afghanistan as a terrorist sanctuary. In 1999, senior CIA and State Department officials began to focus on the Taliban as an integral part of the terrorist problem. In 1999 and 2000, the State Department worked with the United Nations Security Council to obtain resolutions rebuking the Taliban for harboring bin Laden and allowing terrorist training. The Defense Department began to focus on this issue in late 2000 after the *Cole* bombing and formulated military options for dealing with the Taliban.

According to Steve Hadley, President Bush's Deputy National Security Advisor, the Bush Administration initiated shortly after taking office a senior-level review of al Qaeda policy. In the summer of 2001, the State Department sent a démarche to Taliban representatives in Pakistan, which noted threats to Americans emanating from Afghanistan and declared that the United States would hold the regime responsible for actions by terrorists the Taliban harbored. None of these actions appears to have restrained terrorist training or al Qaeda's ability to operate in Afghanistan.

Despite the Intelligence Community's growing recognition that Afghanistan was churning out thousands of radicals, the Joint Inquiry found little effort to integrate the instruments of national power—diplomatic, intelligence, economic, and military—to address the problem effectively. . . . Little effort was made to use the full force of the U.S. military before September 11, with the exception of August 1998 cruise missile strikes. Former National Security Advisor Sandy Berger testified that there was little public or Congressional support for an invasion of Afghanistan before September 11.

Permitting the sanctuary in Afghanistan to exist allowed bin Laden's key operatives to meet, plan, train recruits, and ensure that al Qaeda's masterminds remained beyond the reach of international justice. In testimony before the Joint Inquiry, the DCI explained:

> Nothing did more for our ability to combat terrorism than the President's decision to send us into the terrorists' sanctuary. By going in massively, we were able to change the rules for the terrorists. Now they are the hunted. Now they have to spend most of their time worrying about their survival. Al Qaeda must never again acquire a sanctuary.

THE INTELLIGENCE COMMUNITY

The nation's experience with international terrorism in the 1980s began with the bombings of the U.S. Embassy in Beirut in April 1983 and a U.S. Marine barracks in Beirut in October. The Islamic Jihad claimed responsibility for both attacks, which were followed by the March 1984 kidnapping and murder of William Buckley, a CIA official in Beirut. Over the next two years, terrorist groups kidnapped other American citizens in Lebanon who were not connected to the U.S. Government.

In April 1984, the Iranian backed terrorist group Hizbollah claimed responsibility for the bombing of a restaurant frequented by U.S. service members near Torrejon Airbase in Spain. In September 1984, the U.S. Embassy annex in Beirut was bombed. 1985 brought a flurry of terrorist activity against U.S. citizens and interests, including the June 1985 hijacking of TransWorld Airways Flight 847, the October 1985 hijacking of the cruise ship *Achille Lauro*, and the November 1985 hijacking of an EgyptAir flight from Athens to Malta. In December 1985, terrorists from the Abu Nidal organization attacked the Rome and Vienna airports.

Certain responses by the U.S. Government to the emerging

threat were of particular interest to the Joint Inquiry because they became the foundation of our policy toward international terrorism before the September 11 attacks. A task force led by Vice President George H. W. Bush made a series of recommendations in a December 1985 report on combating terrorism, some of which were quickly implemented:

- President Reagan signed National Security Decision Directive 207 in January 1986, outlining our nation's policy with respect to international terrorism and assigning counterterrorist functions to government components.

- The Director of Central Intelligence's Counterterrorist Center was established in February 1986 as the focal point for counterterrorism.

- A directive signed in the spring of 1986 authorized the CIA to conduct certain counterterrorist activities.

As is explained in more detail in other sections of this report, America first faced major international terrorist attacks within the United States in February 1993 when a bomb was detonated in the World Trade Center and in June 1993 when the FBI arrested eight persons for plotting to bomb New York City landmarks. In 1996, as bin Laden's involvement in directing terrorist acts became more evident, the Counterterrorist Center created a special unit with ten to fifteen members to focus on him. Since 1996, the Community has been actively engaged in operations with mixed success to collect intelligence on bin Laden and disrupt his network. On September 10, 2001, thirty-five to forty people were assigned to the CTC's bin Laden unit. In 1999, the FBI also created a bin Laden unit at Headquarters. Approximately nineteen persons were working in that unit on September 10.

In August 1998 after the two embassy bombings in Africa, the Intelligence Community quickly confirmed that the attacks had been carried out by bin Laden's network. The DCI made combating the threat bin Laden posed one of the Intelligence Community's highest priorities, establishing it as a "Tier [Zero] priority."

THE DECLARATION OF WAR

Whether and when the Intelligence Community as a whole recognized that bin Laden was waging war on the United States and that it was necessary to respond in kind is an important factor in assessing the Community's response to the threat bin Laden's network posed. In interviews, many persons on the National Security Council staff and at CTC pointed to the August 1998 bombings of two U.S. embassies in East Africa as the moment when they recognized that bin Laden was waging war against the United States. That judgment was reflected in two statements by President Clinton in the immediate aftermath of the bombings:

- On August 20, 1998, in an address to the nation on military action against terrorist sites in Afghanistan and Sudan, President Clinton declared: "A few months ago, and again this week, bin Laden publicly vowed to wage a terrorist war against America."

- On August 22, 1998, in a radio address to the nation, President Clinton declared: "Our efforts against terrorism cannot and will not end with this strike. We should have realistic expectations about what a single action can achieve, and we must be prepared for a long battle."

In December 1998, Director of Central Intelligence George Tenet elaborated on the President's statements in a memorandum to senior CIA managers, the Deputy DCI for Community Management, and the Assistant DCI for Military Support, declaring war on bin Laden:

We must now enter a new phase in our effort against bin Laden. . . . We are at war. . . . I want no resources or people spared in this effort, either inside [the] CIA or the Community.

"THE PLAN"

The DCI stated to the Joint Inquiry that in early 1999, following his declaration, he ordered a baseline review of CIA's operational strategy against bin Laden. According to the DCI's testimony before the Joint Inquiry, the CIA "produced a new comprehensive operational plan of attack against the bin Laden/al Qaeda target inside and outside Afghanistan," a plan of attack that in subsequent testimony the DCI simply called "The Plan":

> The Plan included a strong and focused intelligence collection program to track—and then act against—bin Laden and his associates in terrorist sanctuaries. It was a blend of aggressive human source collection—both unilateral and with foreign partners—and enhanced technical collection. . . . To execute the Plan, CTC developed a program to select and train the right officers and put them in the right places. We moved talented and experienced operations officers into the [CTC]. We also initiated a nationwide program to identify, vet and hire qualified personnel for counterterrorist assignments in hostile environments. We sought native fluency in the languages of the Middle East and South Asia, combined with policy, military, business, technical, or academic experience. In addition, we established an eight-week Counterterrorist Operations Course to share the tradecraft we had developed and refined over the years.

According to documents reviewed by the Joint Inquiry, "The Plan" included covert action and technical collection aimed at capturing bin Laden and his principal lieutenants. . . . The Plan was the Intelligence Community's strongest response before September 11, 2001 to the bin Laden threat and the DCI's declaration. . . .

SHORTCOMINGS IN
THE INTELLIGENCE RESPONSE

The Joint Inquiry has determined that the Intelligence Community as a whole was not on a war footing before September 11. For example, knowledge of the DCI's declaration appears to have been limited. Some senior managers at NSA and DIA [Defense Intelligence Agency] were aware of the statement, but many in the FBI had not heard of it. For example, the Assistant Director of the FBI's Counterterrorism Division testified to the Joint Inquiry that he "was not specifically aware of that declaration of war." Senior officers in other components of the government, including the Defense Department and the U.S. military, apparently were also unaware of the declaration. When asked whether he knew that the United States had been at war with bin Laden, Deputy Secretary of State Richard Armitage responded:

> I was briefed in January and February [2001], leading to my hearings in March before the U.S. Senate. The term "at war" was, to my knowledge, not used. There was no question, though, that we were in a struggle with al Qaeda, and al Qaeda was the very first thing that the administration took on at the deputies level.

The Joint Inquiry also reviewed whether the DCI's declaration of war had any real effect in the covert action area prior to September 11, 2001. Cofer Black, former CTC Chief, explained in a statement to the Joint Inquiry: "[A]fter 9/11, the gloves came off."

Resources dedicated to counterterrorism generally increased during the 1990s. Notwithstanding the DCI's December 1998 exhortation to spare no resources, however, counterterrorism had to compete with other intelligence priorities. Senior CIA officers pointed to, for example, a variety of regional and global issues as intelligence priorities that required resource allocations. In testimony before the Joint Inquiry, the DCI took note of those competing intelligence requirements:

> As I "declared war" against al Qaeda in 1998—in the aftermath of

the East Africa embassy bombings—we were in our fifth year of round-the-clock support to Operation Southern Watch in Iraq. Just three months earlier, we were embroiled in answering questions on the India and Pakistan nuclear tests and trying to determine how we could surge more people to understanding and countering weapons of mass destruction proliferation. In early 1999, we surged more than 800 analysts and redirected collection assets from across the Intelligence Community to support the NATO bombing campaign against the Federal Republic of Yugoslavia.

The only substantial infusion of personnel to counterterrorism occurred after September 11, 2001, when the number of CIA personnel assigned to CTC nearly doubled—from approximately 400 to approximately 800—and additional contractors were hired in support of CTC. No comparable shift of resources occurred in December 1998 after the DCI's declaration of war, in December 1999 during the Millennium crisis, or in October 2000 after the attack on U.S.S. *Cole*.

NSA Director [Michael] Hayden described a similar situation before September 11:

We, like everyone else at the table, were stretched thin in September. The war against terrorism was our number one priority. We had about five number one priorities. And we had to balance what we were doing against all of them.

General Hayden asserted that he knew what NSA had to do to target bin Laden effectively before September 11, but was unable to obtain Intelligence Community support and resources for that purpose:

Given all the other intelligence priorities, it would have been difficult at that time within the [Intelligence Community] or the Department of Defense to accept the kind of resource decisions that would have been necessary to make our effort against the target more robust. NSA was focused heavily on [a range of regional and global issues]. Our resources, both human and financial, were in decline. Our efforts in 2000 to churn money internally were not accepted by the Community; its reliance on [signals intelligence] had made it reluctant to give it up.

The Joint Inquiry also learned that, even after the DCI's declaration of war, there was considerable variation in the degree to which FBI-organized Joint Terrorism Task Forces prioritized and coordinated efforts targeting bin Laden and al Qaeda in the United States. While the Bureau's New York office took the lead in the vast majority of counterterrorism investigations concerning bin Laden, many other FBI offices around the country were unaware of the magnitude of the threat. In an interview, former National Coordinator for Counterterrorism Richard Clarke contended that FBI field offices, except New York, were "clueless" about counterterrorism and al Qaeda and did not make them priorities. Former National Security Advisor Berger testified before the Joint Inquiry: "What we have learned since 9/11 makes clear that the FBI, as an organization, was not as focused [on the counterterrorism mission]."

THE RESPONSIBILITY OF THE PRESIDENT AND HIS POLICYMAKERS

The DCI's December 1998 declaration was remarkable for its foresight and aggressiveness. But it could only have effect within a limited sphere because coordinating the U.S. Government's response to the bin Laden threat was not the responsibility of the DCI or the Intelligence Community, but of the President and the National Security Council.

In a Joint Inquiry briefing, Mr. Clarke touched on this issue when he discussed Presidential Decision Directive 62, "Protection Against Unconventional Threat to the Homeland and Americans Overseas." That PDD was signed by President Clinton in May 1998, before the bombings of the two U.S. Embassies in Africa and before the DCI's declaration of war. According to

Mr. Clarke, the PDD created a ten-program counterterrorism initiative and assigned counterterrorist responsibilities to specific agencies:

- Apprehension, extradition, rendition, and prosecution (Department of Justice);

- Disruption (CIA);

- International cooperation (State);

- Preventing terrorist acquisition of weapons of mass destruction (National Security Council);

- Consequence management (Department of Justice/Federal Emergency Management Agency);

- Transportation security (Department of Transportation);

- Protection of critical infrastructure and cyber systems (National Security Council);

- Continuity of operations (National Security Council);

- Countering the foreign terrorist threat in the United States (Department of Justice); and

- Protection of Americans overseas (Departments of State and Defense).

Within that effort were the seeds of an integrated, comprehensive government-wide strategy for countering the bin Laden threat that could have put the nation on a war footing before September 11. The initiative is perhaps the closest that President Clinton and the National Security Council came between 1998 and the Administration's departure from office in January 2001 to a coordinated response to the threat. However, the PDD does not appear to have had much impact. It is clearly not as straight-forward as the DCI's declaration and, beyond Mr. Clarke's reference to it in his testimony, no other Joint Inquiry witness pointed to PDD–62 as the policy guiding the government's response to the growing al Qaeda threat.

Shortly after the Bush Administration took office in January 2001, the National Security Council undertook a review of existing policy for dealing with al Qaeda. In response to written Joint Inquiry questions, Deputy National Security Advisor Steve Hadley explained:

> The Administration took the al Qaeda threat seriously and, from the outset, began considering a major shift in United States counterterrorism policy. From the first days of the Bush Administration through September 2001, it conducted a senior level review of policy for dealing with al Qaeda. The goal was to move beyond the policy of containment, criminal prosecution, and limited retaliation for specific attacks, toward attempting to "roll back" al Qaeda. The new goal was to eliminate completely the ability of al Qaeda and other terrorist groups of global reach to conduct terrorist attacks against the United States. . . . Between May and the end of July 2001, four Deputies Committee meetings were held directly related to the regional issues which had to be resolved in order to adopt a more aggressive strategy for dealing with al Qaeda. . . .

This new policy might have produced a coordinated government response to the bin Laden threat or put the nation on more of a war footing with al Qaeda before September 11. However, as Mr. Hadley noted, "[t]he Administration finalized its review of policy on al Qaeda at an NSC Principals Committee meeting on September 4, 2001." President Bush had not reviewed the draft policy before September 11.

In short, the DCI and other Intelligence Community officials recognized the bin Laden threat. Notwithstanding the DCI's declaration, President Clinton's August 1998 statements, and intelligence reports to policymakers over many years indicating that bin Laden was waging war on the United States, neither President Clinton nor President Bush nor their National Security Councils put the government or the Intelligence Community on a war footing before September 11.

LACK OF AN INTEGRATED RESPONSE

As Osama bin Laden's direct involvement in planning and directing terrorism became more evident, CTC created a unit to focus specifically on bin Laden and the threat he posed to U.S. interests. CTC personnel recognized as early as 1996 that bin Laden posed a grave danger to the United States.

Following the August 1998 bombings of two U.S. embassies, the DCI placed bin Laden's terrorist network among the Intelligence Community's highest priorities. . . . Evidence of a fragmented Intelligence Community can be found in the limited distribution of the DCI's declaration. The Community as a whole had only a limited awareness of the statement. For example, although some senior NSA and DIA managers were aware of it, few FBI personnel were. The Assistant Director of the FBI's Counterterrorism Division told the Joint Inquiry that he "was not specifically aware of that declaration of war." Equally disturbing, Joint Inquiry interviews of FBI field personnel showed that they did not know of the DCI's declaration, and some had only passing familiarity with bin Laden and al Qaeda before September 11. Senior U.S. military officers were also unaware of the DCI's declaration.

A former chief of the unit in the DCI's Counterterrorist Center formed to focus on bin Laden put it succinctly:

In my experience between 1996 and 1999, CIA's Directorate of Operations was the only component of the Intelligence Community that could be said to have been waging the war that bin Laden declared against the United States in August of 1996. The rest of the CIA and the Intelligence Community looked on our efforts as eccentric and, at times, fanatic.

Additional evidence of the absence of a comprehensive coun-terterrorist strategy and authoritative leadership can be found in "The Plan" the DCI described in testimony before the Joint Inquiry:

> In spring of 1999, we produced a new comprehensive opera-tional plan of attack against [bin Laden] and al Qaeda inside and outside of Afghanistan. The strategy was previewed to senior CIA management by the end of July of 1999. By mid-September, it had been briefed to the CIA operational level personnel, to NSA, to the FBI, and other partners. The CIA began to put in place the elements of this operational strategy which structured the agency's counterterrorism activity until September 11 of 2001.

> According to documents reviewed by the Joint Inquiry, in 1999 . . . "The Plan" focused principally on CIA covert action and technical collection aimed at capturing bin Laden. "The Plan" was also significant for what it did not include:

- A Community estimate of the threat bin Laden's network posed to the United States and to U.S. interests overseas;

- Significant participation by elements of the Intelligence Com-munity other than the CIA;

- Delineation of the resources required to execute the plan;

- Decisions to downgrade other Community priorities to accommodate the priorities of the plan;

- Attention to the threat to and vulnerabilities of the U.S. home-land; and

- Discussion of FBI involvement in the plan.

The Assistant Director of the FBI's Counterterrorism Division testified to the Joint Inquiry that the FBI had no war plan against

bin Laden: "Absolutely, we did not [have a plan] at that time."
When asked how the FBI's counterterrorism program fit into the
overall Community program, the Assistant Director replied:

> I am not sure if I know the answer to that. I talked to [the DCI]
> briefly about this. I have talked to [the CTC Chief] before—the
> answer to your question is, I don't know the answer.

The lack of involvement by agencies other than the CIA is particularly troubling, given gaps in efforts by those agencies to
address the threat. For example, while the CIA devoted resources
to bin Laden, covert action, and Afghanistan, the FBI focused on
investigating funding for terrorist groups other than al Qaeda,
even though FBI leadership recognized after the embassy bombings in August 1998 that al Qaeda posed an increasing threat. In
some FBI field offices, there was little appreciation for bin Laden
and al Qaeda, including the San Diego office where FBI agents
would discover after September 11 connections between terrorist
sympathizers and at least two hijackers.

Consistent with this evidence of the absence of a comprehensive strategy is a recent finding by the Inspector General for the
Department of Justice that "[t]he FBI has never performed a
comprehensive written assessment of the risk of the terrorist
threat facing the United States":

> Such an assessment would be useful not only to define the nature,
> likelihood, and severity of the threat but also [to] identify intelli-
> gence gaps that need to be addressed. Moreover, . . . comprehen-
> sive threat and risk assessments would be useful in determining
> where to allocate attention and resources . . . on programs and ini-
> tiatives to combat terrorism.

This assessment still had not been completed as recently as
FBI Director [Robert] Mueller's Joint Inquiry testimony on
October 17, 2002. Likewise, the DCI's National Intelligence
Council never produced a National Intelligence Estimate on the
threat al Qaeda and bin Laden posed to the United States.

Absent a comprehensive strategy for combating the threat bin

Laden posed, the DCI could not be assured that the entire Intelligence Community would focus on the "war." The record of the Joint Inquiry also establishes that the DCI was unable or unwilling to enforce priorities and marshal resources in accordance with his declaration that the Intelligence Community was "at war." Despite the DCI's declaration, the Joint Inquiry heard repeatedly about CIA intelligence priorities that competed with bin Laden for personnel and funds, including other high priority intelligence targets worldwide. . . .

The Joint Inquiry record establishes that, even within the CIA, the DCI did not enforce priorities or marshal resources effectively against the al Qaeda threat. Despite the DCI's declaration of war against bin Laden, there is substantial evidence that the CIA's Counterterrorist Center had insufficient personnel before September 11, which had a substantial impact on its ability to detect and monitor al Qaeda. For example, a former CTC Chief testified before the Joint Inquiry that he did not have the resources to counter the threat bin Laden posed:

> The three concepts I would like to leave you with are people, the finances, and operational approvals or political authorities. We didn't have enough of any of these before 9/11.

When asked why personnel were not marshaled to CTC to fight bin Laden's network, the former Chief recalled the CIA's Deputy Director of Operations explaining that there were not enough personnel to go around and that CTC was already well supplied with staff compared to other CIA divisions.

A former Chief of the CTC unit dedicated to bin Laden also told us, in a judgment confirmed by his successor:

> We never had enough officers from the Directorate of Operations. The officers we had were greatly overworked. . . . We also received marginal analytic support from the Directorate of Intelligence. . . .

In particular, a CIA officer commented on the reasons for the

CIA's failure to follow through on information about two September 11 hijackers who came to the attention of the Intelligence Community in January 2000:

> How could these misses have occurred? . . . The CIA operators focused on the Malaysia meeting [the hijackers attended]; when it was over, they focused on other, more urgent operations against threats real or assessed. Of the many people involved, no one detected that the data generated by this operation crossed a reporting threshold, or, if they did, they assumed that the reporting requirement had been met elsewhere. . . . They are the kinds of misses that happen when people—even very competent, dedicated people such as the CIA officers and FBI agents and analysts involved in all aspects of this story—are simply overwhelmed.

On September 12, 2002, there was a substantial infusion of personnel into the CTC. No comparable shift of resources occurred in December 1998 after the DCI's declaration of war, in December 1999 during the Millennium crisis, or in October 2000 after the attack on U.S.S. *Cole*. In testimony before the Joint Inquiry, DCI George Tenet asserted, "In hindsight, I wish I had said, 'Let's take the whole enterprise down,' and put 500 more people there sooner." It is noteworthy that the DCI's comments were limited to the CIA and did not encompass the resources of other agencies within the Intelligence Community.

In response to questions about efforts to obtain additional counterterrorism resources, DCI Tenet described to the Joint Inquiry his inability, before September 11, to generate necessary support within the Executive Branch:

> [I would ask every] year in [the] budget submission. . . . I'm not talking about the Committee. I'm talking about the front end at OMB [the White House Office of Management and Budget] and the hurdle you have to get through to fully fund what we thought we needed to do the job. Senator [Jon] Kyl once asked me, "How much money are you short?" "I'm short $900 million to $1 billion every year for the next five years," is what I answered. And we told

that to everybody downtown for as long as anybody would listen and never got to first base. So you get what you pay for in terms of our ability to be as big and robust as people—and when I became Director, we had . . . case officers around the world. Now we're up to about and the President's given us the ability to grow that by another. And everybody wonders why you can't do all the things people say you need to do. Well, if you don't pay at the front end, it ain't going to be there at the back end.

The inability to realign Intelligence Community resources to combat the threat bin Laden posed is in part a direct consequence of the limited authority the DCI enjoys over major portions of the Intelligence Community. . . . While the DCI has statutory responsibility spanning the Intelligence Community, his actual authority is limited to budgets and personnel over which he exercises direct control: the CIA, the Office of the DCI, and the Community Management Staff. As former House Intelligence Committee Chairman Lee Hamilton told the Joint Inquiry:

Currently, the Director of Central Intelligence, the leading intelligence figure, . . . control[s] but a small portion of his budget. The DCI has, as I understand it, enhanced authority after 1997, and that permits him to consolidate the national intelligence budget, to make some trade-offs, but given the overwhelming weight of the Defense Department in the process, that is of limited value. . . . [T]he thing that puzzles me here is why we reject for the Intelligence Community the model of organization that we follow in every other enterprise in this country. We have someone at the head who has responsibility and accountability. We accept that. But for some reason, we reject it when it comes to the Intelligence Community.

In sum, the Joint Inquiry found leadership and structural failings in the Intelligence Community's response to the bin Laden threat. Proposals to restructure the Community are examined in another section of this report.

THE INTELLIGENCE COMMUNITY'S
DOMESTIC FAILURE

Throughout the 1990s, the desire and capacity of international terrorist groups, particularly Islamic radicals, to strike the United States at home increased dramatically. Several terrorist attacks and disrupted plots in the 1990s underscored the reality of this danger. Recognizing the threat, the Intelligence Community warned regularly and repeatedly that al Qaeda and affiliated radicals sought to kill Americans on U.S. soil.

The FBI increased its focus on terrorism in the 1990s, but critics charge that it neither focused sufficiently on radical Islamist activities in the United States nor properly aligned itself to counter the growing danger of terrorism domestically. As a result, the critics say, radical Islamists were able to exploit our freedoms and operate undetected within the United States. Several senior FBI officials, however, contend that countering terrorism at home was a top priority and that Islamic radicals simply did not present opportunities for the FBI to disrupt their activities.

Other Intelligence Community members made only limited contributions to preventing attacks at home and refrained from activities that could be construed as monitoring American citizens. The CIA provided general assessments, noting the risk to the United States. NSA offered some leads related to possible radical activity in the United States, but chose not to intercept communications between individuals in the United States and foreign countries. In general, the Community as a whole did not come together to close gaps in coverage of international terrorist activity in the United States.

As is explained in other sections of this report, in the 1990s, it became clear that al Qaeda was a deadly adversary operating in America and able to levy attacks on U.S. soil. The relative immunity from international terrorism that America had enjoyed for many years was gone. Al Qaeda was also unusual in its dedication, size, organizational structure, and mission. As former CTC Chief Cofer Black testified, al Qaeda became more skilled and attracted more adherents throughout the 1990s, becoming in essence a small army by the end of the decade.

The Intelligence Community repeatedly warned that al Qaeda had both the capability and the intention to threaten the lives of thousands of Americans and that it wanted to strike within the United States. This information was conveyed in intelligence reports, broader intelligence assessments, counterterrorism policy documents, and classified Congressional testimony. Policymakers from the Clinton and Bush administrations have testified that the Intelligence Community repeatedly warned them of the danger al Qaeda posed and the urgency of the threat.

STEPS TAKEN TO FIGHT INTERNATIONAL TERRORISM AT HOME

The FBI increased its focus on terrorism throughout the 1990s and helped prevent several major attacks that would have killed many innocent people. According to Director Mueller, these schemes included a 1993 plot to attack New York City landmarks; a 1995 plot to bomb U.S. commercial aircraft; a 1997 plot to place pipe bombs in New York City subways; and a plot to bomb the Los Angeles airport in December 1999.

The FBI took several important measures to improve its ability to fight international terrorism in the United States. Former Director Freeh testified that, during the 1990s, the FBI more than doubled the number of personnel working counterterrorism, and its counterterrorism budget more than tripled. In 1998, former Assistant Director for Counterterrorism Dale Watson and other FBI leaders recognized that the Bureau was reacting to terrorist attacks rather than preventing them. They initiated the "MAXCAP05" program to improve the FBI's ability to counter terrorism. In 1999, the FBI made counterterrorism a separate Headquarters division, elevating its importance within the Bureau, and created a separate operational unit focused on bin Laden.

Several current and past senior FBI officials have also testified about Bureau initiated personnel exchanges with the CIA and the expansion of its Legal Attaché program (stationing FBI representatives in U.S. Embassies), both of which deepened the FBI's ability to link domestic and international threats. Finally, former Director Freeh has testified that Joint Terrorism Task Forces (JTTFs) were given increasing prominence throughout the 1990s. The JTTF model, originally created to improve coordination between the FBI and the New York City Police Department, was expanded to other cities after the first World Trade Center attack. Over time, the number of JTTFs increased, improving coordination with state and local officials and even other elements of the Intelligence Community, as CIA officers joined several task forces.

STEPS NOT TAKEN

In spite of these steps, several critics contend that the Intelligence Community did not pay sufficient attention to the risk of an attack at home, and that, as a result, the United States became a sanctuary for radical terrorists:

- Former National Security Advisor Brent Scowcroft testified that as a result of American freedoms and civil liberties, "the safest place in the world for a terrorist to be is inside the United States. . . . As long as [terrorists] don't do something that trips them up against our laws, they can do pretty much all they want."

- Richard Clarke, former NSC Special Coordinator for Counterterrorism, contends that, with the exception of the New York office, FBI field offices around the country were "clueless" about counterterrorism and al Qaeda and did not make these targets priorities. Former National Security Advisor Berger testified that the FBI was not sufficiently focused on counterterrorism before September 11.

- As the Joint Inquiry record confirms, FBI officials working on terrorism faced competing priorities and the ranks of those focusing on al Qaeda were not sufficiently augmented. Only one FBI strategic analyst focused exclusively on al Qaeda before September 11. The former Chief of the FBI's International Terrorism Section stated that he had more than one hundred fewer Special Agents working on international terrorism on September 11 than he did in August 1998.

• Interviews of FBI New York field office and FBI Headquarters personnel suggest that the New York Field Office, the office of origin for all major bin Laden related investigations, focused primarily on investigating overseas attacks.

• The terrorist threat was viewed through a narrow lens because of the FBI's case-based approach. Interviews of FBI personnel show that analysts were sent to operational units to assist in case work rather than assess data gathered by the various field offices.

• According to FBI agents, FBI counterterrorism training was extremely limited before September 11.

• Former U.S. Attorney Mary Jo White testified that the FBI often lacked linguists competent in the languages and dialects spoken by radicals linked to al Qaeda.

• An FBI agent with considerable counterterrorism experience noted that foreign governments often knew more about radical Islamist activity in the United States than did the U.S. Government because they saw this activity as a threat to their own existence.

As is discussed in other sections of this report, the Joint Inquiry record confirms that the FBI's decentralized structure and inadequate information technology made the Bureau unable to correlate the knowledge possessed by its components. The FBI did not gather intelligence from all its many cases nation-wide to produce an overall assessment of al Qaeda's presence in the

United States. The Joint Inquiry has also found that many FBI field offices had not made counterterrorism a top priority and they knew little about al Qaeda before September 11.

The FBI also did not inform policymakers of the extent of terrorist activity in the United States, although former Director Freeh stated that he met regularly with senior U.S. Government officials to discuss counterterrorism. Former National Security Advisor Berger has testified that the FBI assured him that there was little radical activity in the United States and that this activity was "covered." Although the FBI conducted many investigations, these pieces were not fitted into a larger picture.

FBI officials argue that al Qaeda and its sympathizers proved a difficult target in the United States. Director Mueller contends that the hijackers did little to arouse suspicion in the United States, staying away from known terrorist sympathizers:

They gave no hint to those around what they were about. They came lawfully. They lived lawfully. They trained lawfully.

This judgment is corroborated by several senior FBI investigators who point out that, although "international radical fundamentalists" operate in the United States, "real al Qaeda members," those involved in planning or carrying out attacks, avoid other radicals and radical mosques as part of their tradecraft. As is discussed elsewhere in this report, that judgment is open to some question, based on what is now known about the activities of the hijackers in the United States.

Former FBI Director Freeh also noted in an interview that al Qaeda operations were small and were not connected to real "cells," and the former Assistant Director for the FBI's Counterterrorism Division contended that many of the "red flags" now apparent are visible only in hindsight. Other FBI officials noted in testimony that U.S. protection of civil liberties precluded the use of intrusive investigative techniques, and Mr. Freeh criticized the idea of using the FBI preventively by being much more aggressive as a potential risk to a democratic and open society.

Finally, FBI officials contend that resources were limited,

while requirements kept increasing. Former Director Freeh and the Assistant Director for the Counterterrorism Division testified that the FBI provided security against terrorism at trials, at special events such as the Olympics, and for meetings of world leaders, all of which demanded considerable resources. In addition, cyber threats and weapons of mass destruction demanded FBI attention. Mr. Freeh testified that, by the end of the decade, "the allocations were insufficient to maintain the critical growth and priority of the FBI's counterterrorism program."

The Joint Inquiry received mixed reports regarding the FBI's aggressiveness in penetrating radical Islamic groups in the United States. Former U.S. Attorney Mary Jo White testified that FBI sources proved invaluable in the successful prevention of the 1993 attack on New York landmarks and the prosecution of the first World Trade Center attack that same year. In addition, the FBI had numerous wiretaps and several human informants in its effort to target various radical Islamist organizations.

However, an FBI official involved in the investigations of the first World Trade Center attack and other terrorist plots argued that the FBI made it exceptionally difficult to handle sources and that this difficulty increased in the 1990s. The agent contended that the FBI did not want to be associated with persons engaged in questionable activities, even though they can provide useful information. In addition, he asserted that agent performance ratings downgraded the importance of developing informants. Director Mueller, however, testified that many constraints and restrictions had decreased since the 1970s, enabling FBI agents to recruit sources with few impediments.

THE COUNTERTERRORISM GAP

The criticisms regarding the FBI's limited attention to the danger at home reflects a large gap in the nation's counterterrorism structure, a failure to focus on how an international terrorist group might target the United States itself. No agency appears to have been responsible for regularly assessing the threat to the homeland. In his testimony before the Joint Inquiry, Deputy Secretary of Defense Wolfowitz asserted that an attack on the United States fell between the cracks in the U.S. Intelligence Community's division of labor. He noted that there is "a problem of where responsibility is assigned."

The CIA and NSA followed events overseas, and their employees saw their job as passing relevant threat information to the FBI. Both the CIA and NSA are leery of activity that suggests they are monitoring U.S. citizens or conducting assessments linked to the activities of persons in the United States, a task that officials interviewed at these agencies believed belongs exclusively to the FBI. The FBI, on the other hand, does not have the analytic capacity to prepare assessments of U.S. vulnerability and relies heavily on the CIA for much of its analysis.

At times, the CIA ignored threat activity linked to the United States, focusing instead on radical activity overseas. For instance, one CIA officer told the Joint Inquiry in an interview that the travel of two hijackers to Los Angeles was not important and that he was interested only in their connection to Yemen.

A particular failure by NSA and the FBI to coordinate the interception of communications by al Qaeda operatives before September 11 illustrates the gaps between programs implemented by the members of the Intelligence Community. Both the FBI and NSA had programs in place to collect al Qaeda communications. . . . The FBI had not identified a significant number of al Qaeda cells in the United States and, thus, had fewer opportunities to use electronic surveillance against these targets.

While each agency pursued its own collection strategy, neither exerted any effort to develop a coordinated plan to intercept international communications, particularly those between the United States and foreign countries. We now know that several hijackers communicated extensively abroad after arriving in the United States and that at least two entered, left, and returned to this country. Effective coordination among the Intelligence Community agencies could have provided potentially important information about hijacker activities and associations before September 11.

NSA analyzed several communications from early 2000 involving hijacker Khalid al Mihdhar and a suspected terrorist facility in the Middle East that was associated with al Qaeda's activities directed against United States' interests. . . . The Intelligence Community did not determine until after September 11, 2001 that these contacts occurred while al Mihdhar was in the United States. . . . Knowledge of al Mihdhar's presence in the United States could have proven crucial to launching an investigation that might have revealed information about him and his roommate, hijacker Nawaf al Hazmi, who came into contact with Hani Hanjour and other hijackers at various times in 2001.

Better coordination between NSA and the FBI might have improved prospects for determining that al Mihdhar was in this country in early 2000; led to the collection of information concerning international communications by other hijackers; identified radical suspects; and created leads for the FBI. Both NSA and FBI are authorized to access international communications between the United States and foreign countries. . . .

Both agencies had independently learned of the suspected terrorist facility in the Middle East and knew that it was linked to al Qaeda activities directed against United States interests. The FBI informed NSA when it learned of the suspected terrorist facility in August 1998. NSA disseminated several reports of communications involving the suspected terrorist facility in the Middle East to the FBI. . . . However, NSA and the FBI did not fully coordinate their efforts, and, as a result, the opportunity to determine al Mihdhar's presence in the United States was lost.

. . . NSA Director Hayden testified before the Joint Inquiry that the collection of communications between the United States and foreign countries will most likely contain information about . . . domestic activities and, thus, . . . is the responsibility of the FBI, not NSA. General Hayden contrasted the foreign intelligence value of such intercepts and their domestic security value. If the former is at stake, he asserted, NSA should intercept the communications; if the latter, the FBI.

General Hayden, senior NSA managers, NSA legal staff, and NSA analysts made clear in Joint Inquiry testimony and interviews that they do not want to be perceived as focusing NSA capabilities against "U.S. persons" in the United States. The Director and his staff were unanimous that lessons NSA learned as a result of Congressional investigations during the 1970s should not be forgotten.

Whatever the merits of this position, it was incumbent on NSA and the FBI to coordinate so that the full range of intelligence collection weapons in the arsenal of the Intelligence Community could have been deployed against the terrorist threat. . . .

[That was just one aspect of a larger problem.] Before September 11, 2001, the Intelligence Community had not melded into an effective team to prevent terrorist attacks within the United States. Efforts had been taken to improve cooperation between the CIA and FBI. After the DCI created the CTC in 1986, for instance, CIA and FBI cross-detailed personnel to each other's counterterrorism units, but this did not lead to a plan between those two agencies or across the Community to integrate intelligence collection and analysis. In the absence of a plan, agencies tended to operate independently.

Prior to September 11, information was inadequately shared not only within the Intelligence Community, but also between the Community, other federal agencies, and state and local authorities. In sum, the Joint Inquiry discovered significant problems in how intelligence agencies shared information among themselves and with entities that need information to protect the nation against terrorist attack.

Findings

FACTUAL FINDINGS: CONCLUSION

[F]or a variety of reasons, the Intelligence Community failed to capitalize on both the individual and collective significance of available information that appears relevant to the events of September 11. As a result, the Community missed opportunities to disrupt the September 11 plot by denying entry to or detaining would-be hijackers; to at least try to unravel the plot through surveillance and other investigative work within the United States; and, finally, to generate a heightened state of alert and thus harden the homeland against attack.

No one will ever know what might have happened had more connections been drawn between these disparate pieces of information. We will never definitively know to what extent the Community would have been able and willing to exploit fully all the opportunities that may have emerged. The important point is that the Intelligence Community, for a variety of reasons, did not bring together and fully appreciate a range of information that could have greatly enhanced its chances of uncovering and preventing Osama bin Laden's plan to attack the United States on September 11, 2001.

SYSTEMIC FINDINGS

Our review of the events surrounding September 11 has revealed a number of systemic weaknesses that hindered the Intelligence Community's counterterrorism efforts before September 11. If not addressed, these weaknesses will continue to undercut U.S. counterterrorist efforts. In order to minimize the possibility of attacks like September 11 in the future, effective solutions to those problems need to be developed and fully implemented as soon as possible.

1. Finding

Prior to September 11, the Intelligence Community was neither well organized nor equipped, and did not adequately adapt to meet the challenge posed by global terrorists focused on targets within the domestic United States. Serious gaps existed between the collection coverage provided by U.S. foreign and U.S. domestic intelligence capabilities. The U.S. foreign intelligence agencies paid inadequate attention to the potential for a domestic attack. The CIA's failure to watchlist suspected terrorists aggressively reflected a lack of emphasis on a process designed to protect the homeland from the terrorist threat. As a result, CIA employees failed to [warn the State Department and FBI about two terrorists who had traveled from Asia to California]. At home, the counterterrorism effort suffered from the lack of an effective domestic intelligence capability. The FBI was unable to identify and monitor effectively the extent of activity by al Qaeda and other international terrorist groups operating in the United States. Taken together, these problems greatly exacerbated the nation's vulnerability to an increasingly dangerous and immediate international terrorist threat inside the United States.

•

Prior to September 11, CIA and NSA [National Security Agency] continued to focus the bulk of their efforts on the foreign operations of terrorists. While intelligence reporting indicated that al Qaeda intended to strike in the United States, these agencies believed that defending against this threat was primarily the responsibility of the FBI. This Joint Inquiry found that both agencies routinely passed a large volume of intelligence to the FBI, but that neither agency followed up to determine what the FBI learned from or did with that information. Neither did the FBI keep NSA and CIA adequately informed of developments within its areas of responsibility. . . .

The CIA's inconsistent performance regarding the watchlisting of suspected terrorists prior to September 11 also suggests a lack of attention to the domestic threat. Watchlists are a vital link in denying entry to the United States by terrorists and others who threaten the national security, and CTC [Counterterrorist Center] had reminded personnel of the importance of watchlisting in December 1999. Yet, some CIA officers in CTC indicated they did not put much emphasis on watchlists. The Joint Inquiry confirmed that there was no formal process in place at the CTC prior to September 11 for watchlisting suspected terrorists. . . .

There were also gaps between NSA's coverage of foreign communications and the FBI's coverage of domestic communications that suggest a lack of sufficient attention to the domestic threat. Prior to September 11, neither agency focused on the importance of identifying and then ensuring coverage of communications between the United States and suspected terrorist-associated facilities abroad. Consistent with its focus on communications abroad, NSA adopted a policy that avoided intercepting the communications between individuals in the United States and foreign countries. . . .

While the FBI's counterterrorist program had produced successful investigations and major prosecutions of both domestic and international terrorists, numerous witnesses told the Joint Inquiry that the program was, at least prior to September 11, incapable of producing significant intelligence products. The FBI's traditional reliance on an aggressive, case-oriented, law enforcement approach did not encourage the broader collection and analysis efforts that are critical to the intelligence mission. Lacking appropriate personnel, training, and information systems, the FBI primarily gathered intelligence to support specific investigations, not to conduct all-source analysis for dissemination to other intelligence agencies.

2. Finding

Prior to September 11, 2001, neither the U.S. Government as a whole nor the Intelligence Community had a comprehensive counterterrorist strategy for combating the threat posed by Osama bin Laden. Furthermore, the Director of Central Intelligence (DCI) was either unwilling or unable to marshal the full range of Intelligence Community resources necessary to combat the growing threat to the United States.

•

The record of this Joint Inquiry indicates that the DCI *did not* marshal resources effectively even within CIA against the threat posed by al Qaeda. Despite the DCI's declaration to CIA officials that the Agency was at war with bin Laden, there is substantial evidence that the DCI's Counterterrorist Center needed additional personnel prior to September 11, and that the lack of resources had a substantial impact on its ability to detect and monitor al Qaeda's activities. . . .

The inability to realign Intelligence Community resources to combat the threat posed by Osama bin Laden is a relatively direct consequence of the limited authority of the DCI over major portions of the Intelligence Community. As former Senator Warren Rudman noted on October 8, 2002 in his testimony before the Joint Inquiry: "You have a Director of Central Intelligence who is also the Director of CIA; eighty-five percent of [the Intelligence Community's budget] is controlled by the Department of Defense."

3. Finding

Between the end of the Cold War and September 11, 2001, overall Intelligence Community funding fell or remained even in constant dollars, while funding for the Community's counterterrorism efforts increased considerably. Despite those increases, the

accumulation of intelligence priorities, a burdensome requirements process, the overall decline in Intelligence Community
funding, and reliance on supplemental appropriations made it
difficult to allocate Community resources effectively against an
evolving terrorist threat. Inefficiencies in the resource and
requirements process were compounded by problems in Intelligence Community budgeting practices and procedures.

•

The growing inadequacy of the [Clinton administration's 1995
intelligence directive] fueled an overburdened and increasingly
ineffective requirements system within the Intelligence Community. At NSA, for example, an official described the [1995]
requirements system as "cumbersome." NSA analysts acknowledged that they had far too many broad requirements—some
1500 formal requirements by September 11—that covered virtually every situation and target. Working from these 1500 formal
requirements, NSA had developed almost 200,000 "Essential
Elements of Information" that were desired by its customers.
While they understood the gross priorities and worked on the
requirements that were practicable on any given day, several NSA
analysts acknowledged that the priority demands sometimes precluded them from delving as deeply into certain areas as they
would have liked. . . .

CIA officials said that, because overall resources were finite,
any increased focus on counterterrorism meant that other issues
would have to receive less attention. At the FBI, where overall
funding had increased, officials said that substantial efforts
focused on investigating terrorist cases overseas, critical infrastructure protection programs, and other priorities not directly
related to strategic intelligence or al Qaeda activity within the
United States. . . .

Even within the CTC, the staff and resources dedicated to
counterterrorism could not keep pace with the amount and scope
of incoming intelligence reporting.

4. Finding

While technology remains one of this nation's greatest advantages, it has not been fully and most effectively applied in support of U.S. counterterrorism efforts. Persistent problems in this area included a lack of collaboration between Intelligence Community agencies, a reluctance to develop and implement new technical capabilities aggressively, the FBI's reliance on outdated and insufficient technical systems, and the absence of a central counterterrorism database.

•

In Joint Inquiry interviews, agency personnel stated that, while individual relationships and cooperation between CIA and NSA at the working level had often been very good, relationships at the mid- and upper-management levels of those agencies were often strained. CIA perceived NSA as wanting to control technology use and development, while NSA was concerned that CIA was engaged in operations that were NSA's responsibility. As a result, significant agency resources were devoted to documenting authorities and responsibilities. For example, no less than seven executive-level memoranda (including one from the President) have been necessary to reach agreement and define the responsibilities and authorities of CIA and NSA in one counterterrorism effort. The agencies also established a Senior Partnership Advisory Group to continue to deal with these issues and CIA assigned several officers to NSA to enhance technology development.

Prior to September 11, the Director of NSA publicly acknowledged the challenge posed by Osama bin Laden's access to the modern communications technology developed by a three trillion dollar industry. Despite this recognition, NSA failed to focus its efforts against al Qaeda's use of certain forms of this technology. . . . NSA also had not adapted technology fully to the challenge of transnational threats such as terrorism. These present much different challenges than those posed by state actors, such as the former Soviet Union, that were NSA's primary targets in the 1980s. . . .

Similarly, NSA could not demonstrate its current analytic tools to the Joint Inquiry and could not identify upgrades that will assist NSA analysts in identifying critical intelligence amidst the large volumes of information it collects. In the absence of such tools, NSA language analysts must still conduct the bulk of their work with pencil and paper. Many develop their own personal "databases" on index cards that cannot be made readily available to counterterrorism analysts at other agencies. NSA's highly publicized TRAILBLAZER program was often cited by NSA officials as the solution to many of these problems, but the implementation of those solutions is three to five years away and confusion still exists at NSA as to what will actually be provided by that program. . . .

The FBI deployed its Automated Case System (ACS) in 1995 to replace a system of written reports and indices. The ACS was supposed to enable agents to send leads to other FBI offices and units and to have access to a vast array of data electronically. However, study after study has concluded that ACS is limited in its search capacity, difficult to use, and unreliable. The Chief of the FBI's Radical Fundamentalist Unit (RFU) testified that ACS remains unfriendly, unreliable and unworkable, and that, instead of using ACS to manage cases, many agents rely on e-mail and paper copies to transmit important data.

5. Finding

Prior to September 11, the Intelligence Community's understanding of al Qaeda was hampered by insufficient analytic focus and quality, particularly in terms of strategic analysis. Analysis and analysts were not always used effectively because of the perception in some quarters of the Intelligence Community that they were less important to agency counterterrorism missions than were operations personnel. The quality of counterterrorism analysis was inconsistent, and many analysts were inexperienced, unqualified, under-trained, and without access to critical information. As a result, there was a dearth of creative, aggressive analysis targeting bin Laden and a persistent inability to comprehend the collective significance of individual pieces of intelligence. These analytic deficiencies seriously undercut the ability of U.S. policymakers to understand the full nature of the threat, and to make fully informed decisions.

•

In terms of "work years," the equivalent of nine analyst work years was expended on al Qaeda within CTC's Assessments and Information Group in September 1998. According to CIA, nine CTC analysts and eight analysts in the Directorate of Intelligence were assigned to [Osama bin Laden] in 1999. This was only a fraction of the analytic effort that was to be devoted to al Qaeda in July 2002. . . .

At the FBI, there were fewer than ten tactical analysts and only one strategic analyst assigned to al Qaeda prior to September 11, 2001. The NSA had only a limited number of Arabic linguists, on whom analysis depends, and, prior to September 11, few were dedicated full-time to targeting al Qaeda. At the time, NSA's Arabic linguists were also being used to support other high priority targets in the region and to translate intelligence originating in the region and elsewhere. . . .

The other two primary all-source analysis centers, [the Defense Intelligence Agency's] Joint Intelligence Task Force Combating Terrorism, and State Department's Bureau of Intelligence Research (INR), focused on anti-terrorism and force protection analysis to protect overseas equities. INR dedicated one analyst solely to al Qaeda, and, at Secretary of State direction, provided a daily summary of intelligence relating to Osama bin Laden and his activities. [Defense intelligence] devoted 30 analysts to Sunni Extremism and, on any given day, several of them— augmented by Reservists—would be involved with Osama bin Laden-related issues. . . .

The Intelligence Community's focus was also far more oriented toward tactical analysis of al Qaeda in support of operations than on the strategic analysis needed to develop a broader understanding of the threat and the organization. For example, as mentioned earlier, the DCI's National Intelligence Council never produced a National Intelligence Estimate (NIE) on the threat to the United States posed by al Qaeda and Osama bin Laden.

Active analytic efforts to identify the scope and nature of the threat, particularly in the domestic United States, were clearly inadequate. . . .

There also was, and apparently continues to be, a reluctance at CIA to provide raw data to analysts outside the Agency. DCI [George] Tenet testified that even analysts at the Department of Homeland Security will not be allowed access to CIA raw data.

6. Finding

Prior to September 11, the Intelligence Community was not prepared to handle the challenge it faced in translating the volumes of foreign language counterterrorism intelligence it collected. Agencies within the Intelligence Community experienced backlogs in material awaiting translation, a shortage of language specialists and language-qualified field officers, and a readiness level of only 30% in the most critical terrorism-related languages.

•

The NSA Senior Language Authority explained to the Joint Inquiry that the Language Readiness Index for NSA language personnel working in the counterterrorism "campaign languages" is currently around 30%. This Index is based on the percentage of the mission that is being performed by qualified language analysts. The current low level of the Index is due in part to the fact that NSA has moved roughly [deleted] language personnel since September 11 from areas in which they were performing quite well to counterterrorism, where they must gain experience and expertise before their performance can improve.

According to the Chief of the FBI's Language Services Division, prior to September 11, the Bureau employed [deleted] Arabic speakers and was experiencing a translation backlog. As a result, 35% of Arabic language materials derived from Foreign Intelligence Surveillance Act (FISA) collection were not reviewed or translated. If the number of Arabic speakers was to remain at [deleted], the projected backlog would rise to 41% in 2003.

The Director of the CIA Language School testified that, given the CIA's language requirements, the CIA Directorate of Operations is not fully prepared to fight a worldwide war on terrorism and at the same time carry out its traditional agent recruitment and intelligence collection mission.

7. Finding

Prior to September 11, the Intelligence Community's ability to produce significant and timely signals intelligence on counterterrorism was limited by NSA's failure to address modern communications technology aggressively, continuing conflict between Intelligence Community agencies, NSA's cautious approach to any collection of intelligence relating to activities in the United States, and insufficient collaboration between NSA and the FBI regarding the potential for terrorist attacks within the United States.

•

Before September 11, it was NSA policy not to target terrorists in the United States, even though it could have obtained a Foreign Intelligence Surveillance Court order authorizing such collection. [The NSA Director] testified that it was more appropriate for the FBI to conduct such surveillance because NSA does not want to be perceived as targeting individuals in this country and because the intelligence produced about communicants in the United States is likely to be about their domestic activities.

As a result, NSA regularly provided information about these targets to the FBI—both in its regular reporting and in response to specific requests from the FBI— . . . that NSA acquired in the course of its collection operations. The FBI used this information in its investigations and obtained FISA Court authorization for electronic surveillance . . . when FBI officials determined that such surveillance was necessary to assist one of its intelligence or law enforcement investigations.

8. Finding

The continuing erosion of NSA's program management expertise and experience has hindered its contribution to the fight against terrorism. NSA continues to have mixed results in providing timely technical solutions to modern intelligence collection, analysis, and information sharing problems.

•

One of the side effects of NSA's downsizing, outsourcing, and transformation has been the loss of critical program management expertise, systems engineering, and requirements definition skills. These skills were devalued by NSA during the 1990s when most technical development was done within the agency. . . . The impact of this lack of program management was evident during interviews with analysts who expressed frustration regarding their current working environment. For example, they must now write three versions of reports in order to accommodate the demands of various customers and uses.

9. Finding

The U.S. Government does not presently bring together in one place all terrorism-related information from all sources. While CTC does manage overseas operations and has access to most Intelligence Community information, it does not collect terrorism-related information from all sources, domestic and foreign. Within the Intelligence Community, agencies did not adequately share relevant counterterrorism information prior to September 11. This breakdown in communications was the result of a number of factors, including differences in the agencies' missions, legal authorities and cultures. Information was not sufficiently shared, not only between different Intelligence Community agencies, but also within individual agencies, and between the intelligence and the law enforcement agencies.

•

[T]he FBI typically used information obtained through the Foreign Intelligence Surveillance Act (FISA) only in connection with the cases in which it was obtained and would not routinely disseminate it within the FBI or to other members of the Intelligence Community. . . .

Culture and policy issues also limited the extent to which CIA shared counterterrorism information within the Intelligence Community. . . . For example, the DCI acknowledged in his testimony that CIA was not sufficiently focused on advising the State Department to watchlist all terrorist operatives who might be traveling to the United States, even though this would provide valuable information to domestic agencies in targeting these persons at ports of entry. . . .

The Joint Inquiry also heard from many different agencies within the Intelligence Community, most notably the Defense Intelligence Agency (DIA), that the perception that collecting agencies have "ownership" of the intelligence they acquire impedes the free flow of information. In a Joint Inquiry interview, one DIA official complained that analysts were often denied access to critical intelligence held in other Intelligence Community agencies.

10. Finding

Serious problems in information sharing also persisted, prior to September 11, between the Intelligence Community and relevant non-Intelligence Community agencies. This included other federal agencies as well as state and local authorities. This lack of communication and collaboration deprived those other entities, as well as the Intelligence Community, of access to potentially valuable information in the "war" against bin Laden. The Inquiry's focus on the Intelligence Community limited the extent to which it explored these issues, and this is an area that should be reviewed further.

•

Officials in the Departments of Treasury, Transportation, and State told the Joint Inquiry that, although they receive threat information from the Intelligence Community, they do not always receive the information that adds context to the threat warnings. In many instances, officials told the Joint Inquiry, this lack of context prevents them from properly estimating the value of the threat information and taking preventive actions. The Joint Inquiry was also told that not all threat information in the possession of the Intelligence Community is shared with non-Intelligence Community entities that need it the most in order to counter the threats.

For example, DCI Tenet testified that: "The documents we've provided show some 12 reports spread over seven years which pertain to possible use of aircraft as terrorist weapons. We disseminated those reports to the appropriate agencies, such as the FAA [Federal Aviation Administration], the Department of Transportation and the FBI as they came in." Subsequently, the Transportation Security Intelligence Service (TSIS)—which formerly was the Intelligence Office at FAA—researched the 12 reports mentioned by DCI Tenet to determine what actions had been taken as a result. TSIS reported to the Joint Inquiry that it had no record of having received three of those reports, two others had been derived from State Department cables, and one report was not received at all by FAA until after September 11, 2001.

11. Finding

Prior to September 11, 2001, the Intelligence Community did not effectively develop and use human sources to penetrate the al Qaeda inner circle. This lack of reliable and knowledgeable human sources significantly limited the Community's ability to acquire intelligence that could be acted upon before the September 11 attacks. In part, at least, the lack of unilateral (i.e., U.S.-recruited) counterterrorism sources was a product of an excessive reliance on foreign liaison services.

•

According to senior CTC officials, CIA had no penetrations of al Qaeda's leadership and never obtained intelligence that was sufficient for action against Osama bin Laden from anyone. A large number of current and former CTC officers indicated that

CTC had numerous unilateral sources outside the leadership who were reporting on al Qaeda, and a larger number who were being developed for recruitment, prior to September 11. The best source was handled jointly by CIA and the FBI. In addition, CIA managed a network . . . in Afghanistan that often reported information regarding bin Laden issues and relations with the Taliban. They occasionally provided threat information as well, but had no access to al Qaeda's leadership.

12. Finding

During the summer of 2001, when the Intelligence Community was bracing for an imminent al Qaeda attack, difficulties with FBI applications for Foreign Intelligence Surveillance Act (FISA) surveillance and the FISA process led to a diminished level of coverage of suspected al Qaeda operatives in the United States. The effect of these difficulties was compounded by the perception that spread among FBI personnel at Headquarters and the field offices that the FISA process was lengthy and fraught with peril.

•

Most of the FISA orders targeting al Qaeda that expired after March 2001 were not renewed before September 11. The Joint Inquiry received inconsistent figures regarding the specific number of FISA orders that were allowed to expire during the summer of 2001. One FBI manager stated that no FISA orders targeted against al Qaeda existed in 2001, others interviewed said there were up to [deleted] al Qaeda orders at that time, and an OIPR [Office of Intelligence, Policy and Review in the Justice Department] official explained that approximately two-thirds of the number of FISA orders targeted against al Qaeda had expired in 2001.

13. Finding

[Deleted]

14. Finding

Senior U.S. military officials were reluctant to use U.S. military assets to conduct offensive counterterrorism efforts in Afghanistan, or to support or participate in CIA operations directed against al Qaeda prior to September 11. At least part of this reluctance was driven by the military's view that the Intelligence Community was unable to provide the intelligence needed to support military operations. Although the U.S. military did participate in . . . counterterrorism efforts to counter Osama bin Laden's terrorist network prior to September 11, 2001, most of the military's focus was on force protection.

•

Lower-level military officers appeared to be more enthusiastic than senior military officials about active military participation in counterterrorism efforts. Senior CIA officers, CIA documents, and at least one former special operations forces commander indicated, in interviews and testimony, that military operators were both capable and interested in conducting a special operations mission against bin Laden in Afghanistan prior to September 11. A former JSOC [Joint Special Operations Command] commander told the Joint Inquiry that his units did have the ability to put small teams into Afghanistan. A CIA document commenting on the prospects of Joint Special Operations Command units participating in an operation to capture bin Laden said: "lots of desire at the [military] working level," but there was "reluctance at the political level." . . .

In general, however, the CIA and U.S. military did not engage in joint operations, pool their assets, or develop joint plans against Osama bin Laden in Afghanistan prior to September 11, 2001— despite interest in such joint operations at the CIA.

15. Finding

The Intelligence Community depended heavily on foreign intelligence and law enforcement services for the collection of counterterrorism intelligence and the conduct of other counter-terrorism activities. The results were mixed in terms of productive intelligence, reflecting vast differences in the ability and willingness of the various foreign services to target the bin Laden and al Qaeda network. Intelligence Community agencies sometimes failed to coordinate their relationships with foreign services adequately, either within the Intelligence Community or with broader U.S. Government liaison and foreign policy efforts. This reliance on foreign liaison services also resulted in a lack of focus on the development of unilateral human sources.

•

Regarding Saudi Arabia, former FBI Director Louis Freeh testified that, following the 1996 Khobar Towers bombing, the FBI "was able to forge an effective working relationship with the Saudi police and Interior Ministry." A considerable amount of personal effort by Director Freeh helped to secure what he described as "unprecedented and invaluable" assistance in the Khobar Towers bombing investigation from the Saudi Ambassador to the United States and the Saudi Interior Minister.

By contrast, the Committees heard testimony from U.S. Government personnel that Saudi officials had been uncooperative and often did not act on information implicating Saudi nationals. According to a U. S. Government official, it was clear from about 1996 that the Saudi Government would not cooperate with the United States on matters relating to Osama bin Laden. . . . A number of U. S. Government officials complained to the Joint Inquiry about a lack of Saudi cooperation in terrorism investigations both before and after the September 11 attacks. . . .

Several other Arab governments hesitated to share information gleaned from arrests of suspects in the U.S.S. *Cole* bombing and other attacks. Even several European governments were described to the Joint Inquiry as indifferent to the threat al Qaeda posed prior to September 11, while others faced legal restrictions that impeded their ability to share intelligence with the United States or to disrupt terrorist cells.

16. Finding

The activities of the September 11 hijackers in the United States appear to have been financed, in large part, from monies sent to them from abroad and also brought in on their persons. Prior to September 11, there was no coordinated U.S. Government-wide strategy to track terrorist funding and close down their financial support networks. There was also a reluctance in some parts of the U.S. Government to track terrorist funding and close down their financial support networks. As a result, the U.S. Government was unable to disrupt financial support for Osama bin Laden's terrorist activities effectively.

•

Prior to September 11, 2001, no single U.S. Government agency was responsible for tracking terrorist funds, prioritizing and coordinating government-wide efforts, and seeking international collaboration in that effort. Some tracking of terrorist funds was undertaken before September 11. For the most part, however, these efforts were unorganized and ad-hoc, and there was a reluctance to take actions such as seizures of assets and bank accounts and arrests of those involved in the funding. A U.S. Government official testified before the Joint Inquiry, for example, that this reluctance hindered counterterrorist efforts against bin Laden: "Treasury was concerned about any activity that could adversely affect the international financial system. . . ."

On September 24, 2001, President Bush gave a new priority to the tracking of terrorist funds when he stated: "We will direct every resource at our command to win the war against terrorists, every means of diplomacy, every tool of intelligence, every instrument of law enforcement, *every financial influence. We will starve the terrorists of funding.*" (Emphasis added.) The President made this statement four days after signing an executive order to block the funds of terrorists and their associates. Substantial actions have been taken by the U.S. Government in this area since September 11, including blocking terrorist-related assets; seizing assets and smuggled bulk cash; arresting terrorist financiers and indicting them; and shutting down front companies, charities, banks, and hawala conglomerates that served as financial support networks for al Qaeda and bin Laden.

RELATED FINDINGS

17. Finding

Despite intelligence reporting from 1998 through the summer of 2001 indicating that Osama bin Laden's terrorist network intended to strike inside the United States, the United States Government did not undertake a comprehensive effort to implement defensive measures in the United States.

•

The intelligence that was acquired and shared by the Intelligence Community was not specific as to time and place, but should have been sufficient to prompt action to insure a heightened sense of alert and implementation of additional defensive measures. Such actions could have included: strengthened civil aviation security measures; increased attention to watchlisting suspected terrorists so as to keep them out of the United States; greater collaboration with state and local law enforcement authorities concerning the scope and nature of the potential threat; a sustained national effort to inform and alert the American public to the growing danger; and improved capabilities to deal with the consequences of attacks involving mass destruction and casualties. The U.S. Government did take some steps in regard to detecting and preventing the use of weapons of mass destruction, but did not pursue a broad program of additional domestic defensive measures or public awareness.

18. Finding

Between 1996 and September 2001, the counterterrorism strategy adopted by the U. S. Government did not succeed in eliminating Afghanistan as a sanctuary and training ground for Osama bin Laden's terrorist network. A range of instruments was used to

counter al Qaeda, with law enforcement often emerging as a leading tool because other means were deemed not to be feasible or
failed to produce results. Although numerous successful prosecutions were generated, law enforcement efforts were not adequate
by themselves to target or eliminate bin Laden's sanctuary. While
the United States persisted in observing the rule of law and
accepted norms of international behavior, bin Laden and al
Qaeda recognized no rules and thrived in the safe haven provided
by Afghanistan.

•

Permitting the sanctuary in Afghanistan to exist for as long as
it did allowed bin Laden's key operatives to meet, plan operations, train recruits, identify particularly capable recruits or those
with specialized skills, and ensure that al Qaeda's masterminds
remained beyond the reach of international justice. In his testimony before the Joint Committee on October 17, 2002, the DCI
responded to a question about what he would do differently prior to
September 11, 2001, saying: "[H]indsight is perfect, we should
have taken down that sanctuary a lot sooner. The circumstances
at the time may have not warranted, the regional situation may
have been different, and after [September] 11 all I can tell you is
we let a sanctuary fester, we let him build capability."

19. Finding

Prior to September 11, the Intelligence Community and the U.S.
Government labored to prevent attacks by Osama bin Laden and
his terrorist network against the United States, but largely without the benefit of an alert, mobilized and committed American
public. Despite intelligence information on the immediacy of the
threat level in the spring and summer of 2001, the assumption
prevailed in the U.S. Government that attacks of the magnitude
of September 11 could not happen here. As a result, there was
insufficient effort to alert the American public to the reality and
gravity of the threat.

•

Clearly, there were Presidential remarks regarding terrorism in the years before September 11, 2001, including references to the threat that bin Laden's network posed to the interests of the United States. There were also periodic statements and references to the threat from terrorism and bin Laden in Congressional testimony and elsewhere by both the DCI and the FBI Director. . . . These efforts were, however, largely sporadic and, given the classified nature of intelligence, limited in terms of the specifics that could be shared with the public about the immediacy and gravity of the threat. They were not sufficient to mobilize and sustain heightened public awareness about the danger of a domestic attack.

20. Finding

Through its investigation, the Joint Inquiry developed information suggesting specific sources of foreign support for some of the September 11 hijackers while they were in the United States. The Joint Inquiry's review confirmed that the Intelligence Community also has information, much of which has yet to be independently verified, concerning these potential sources of support. In their testimony, neither CIA nor FBI officials were able to address definitively the extent of such support for the hijackers globally or within the United States or the extent to which such support, if it exists, is knowing or inadvertent in nature. Only recently, and at least in part due to the Joint Inquiry's focus on this issue, did the FBI and CIA strengthen their efforts to address these issues. In the view of the Joint Inquiry, this gap in U.S intelligence coverage is unacceptable, given the magnitude and immediacy of the potential risk to U.S. national security. The Intelligence Community needs to address this area of concern as aggressively and quickly as possible.

Recommendations

Since the National Security Act's establishment of the Director of Central Intelligence and the Central Intelligence Agency in 1947, numerous independent commissions, experts, and legislative initiatives have examined the growth and performance of the U.S. Intelligence Community. While those efforts generated numerous proposals for reform over the years, some of the most significant proposals have not been implemented, particularly in the areas of organization and structure. These Committees believe that the cataclysmic events of September 11, 2001 provide a unique and compelling mandate for strong leadership and constructive change throughout the Intelligence Community. With that in mind, and based on the work of this Joint Inquiry, the Committees recommend the following:

---

1. Congress should amend the National Security Act of 1947 to create and sufficiently staff a statutory Director of National Intelligence* who shall be the President's principal advisor on intelli-

*All references to the Director of National Intelligence in other recommendations assume recommendation #1 is adopted. In the event there is no Director of National Intelligence created, the Director of Central Intelligence should be substituted for the Director of National Intelligence.

gence and shall have the full range of management, budgetary and personnel responsibilities needed to make the entire U.S. Intelligence Community operate as a coherent whole. These responsibilities should include:

- establishment and enforcement of consistent priorities for the collection, analysis, and dissemination of intelligence throughout the Intelligence Community;

- setting of policy and the ability to move personnel between elements of the Intelligence Community;

- review, approval, modification, and primary management and oversight of the execution of Intelligence Community budgets;

- review, approval, modification, and primary management and oversight of the execution of Intelligence Community personnel and resource allocations;

- review, approval, modification, and primary management and oversight of the execution of Intelligence Community research and development efforts;

- review, approval, and coordination of relationships between the Intelligence Community agencies and foreign intelligence and law enforcement services; and

- exercise of statutory authority to insure that Intelligence Community agencies and components fully comply with Community-wide policy, management, spending, and administrative guidance and priorities.

The Director of National Intelligence should be a Cabinet level position, appointed by the President and subject to Senate confirmation. Congress and the President should also work to insure that the Director of National Intelligence effectively exercises these authorities.

To insure focused and consistent Intelligence Community

leadership, Congress should require that no person may simultaneously serve as both the Director of National Intelligence and the Director of the Central Intelligence Agency, or as the director of any other specific intelligence agency.

---

2. Current efforts by the National Security Council to examine and revamp existing intelligence priorities should be expedited, given the immediate need for clear guidance in intelligence and counterterrorism efforts. The President should take action to ensure that clear, consistent, and current priorities are established and enforced throughout the Intelligence Community. Once established, these priorities should be reviewed and updated on at least an annual basis to ensure that the allocation of Intelligence Community resources reflects and effectively addresses the continually evolving threat environment. Finally, the establishment of Intelligence Community priorities, and the justification for such priorities, should be reported to both the House and Senate Intelligence Committees on an annual basis.

---

3. The National Security Council, in conjunction with the Director of National Intelligence, and in consultation with the Secretary of the Department of Homeland Security, the Secretary of State and Secretary of Defense, should prepare, for the President's approval, a U.S. government-wide strategy for combating terrorism, both at home and abroad, including the growing terrorism threat posed by the proliferation of weapons of mass destruction and associated technologies. This strategy should identify and fully engage those foreign policy, economic, military, intelligence, and law enforcement elements that are critical to a comprehensive blueprint for success in the war against terrorism.

As part of that effort, the Director of National Intelligence shall develop the Intelligence Community component of the strategy, identifying specific programs and budgets and including plans to address the threats posed by Osama bin Laden and al Qaeda, Hezbollah, Hamas, and other significant terrorist groups. Consistent with applicable law, the strategy should effectively employ and integrate all capabilities available to the Intelligence Community against those threats and should encompass specific efforts to:

- develop human sources to penetrate terrorist organizations and networks both overseas and within the United States;

- fully utilize existing and future technologies to better exploit terrorist communications; to improve and expand the use of data mining and other cutting edge analytical tools; and to develop a multi-level security capability to facilitate the timely and complete sharing of relevant intelligence information both within the Intelligence Community and with other appropriate federal, state, and local authorities;

- enhance the depth and quality of domestic intelligence collection and analysis by, for example, modernizing current intelligence reporting formats through the use of existing information technology to emphasize the existence and the significance of links between new and previously acquired information;

- maximize the effective use of covert action in counterterrorist efforts;

- develop programs to deal with financial support for international terrorism; and

- facilitate the ability of CIA paramilitary units and military special operations forces to conduct joint operations against terrorist targets.

---

4. The position of National Intelligence Officer for Terrorism should be created on the National Intelligence Council and a

highly qualified individual appointed to prepare intelligence estimates on terrorism for the use of Congress and policymakers in the Executive Branch and to assist the Intelligence Community in developing a program for strategic analysis and assessments.

---

5. Congress and the Administration should ensure the full development within the Department of Homeland Security of an effective all-source terrorism information fusion center that will dramatically improve the focus and quality of counterterrorism analysis and facilitate the timely dissemination of relevant intelligence information, both within and beyond the boundaries of the Intelligence Community. Congress and the Administration should ensure that this fusion center has all the authority and the resources needed to:

- have full and timely access to all counterterrorism-related intelligence information, including "raw" supporting data as needed;

- have the ability to participate fully in the existing requirements process for tasking the Intelligence Community to gather information on foreign individuals, entities and threats;

- integrate such information in order to identify and assess the nature and scope of terrorist threats to the United States in light of actual and potential vulnerabilities;

- implement and fully utilize data mining and other advanced analytical tools, consistent with applicable law;

- retain a permanent staff of experienced and highly skilled analysts, supplemented on a regular basis by personnel on "joint tours" from the various Intelligence Community agencies;

- institute a reporting mechanism that enables analysts at all the intelligence and law enforcement agencies to post lead information for use by analysts at other agencies without waiting for dissemination of a formal report;

- maintain excellence and creativity in staff analytic skills through regular use of analysis and language training programs; and

- establish and sustain effective channels for the exchange of counterterrorism-related information with federal agencies outside the Intelligence Community as well as with state and local authorities.

---

6. Given the FBI's history of repeated shortcomings within its current responsibility for domestic intelligence, and in the face of grave and immediate threats to our homeland, the FBI should strengthen and improve its domestic capability as fully and expeditiously as possible by immediately instituting measures to:

- strengthen counterterrorism as a national FBI program by clearly designating national counterterrorism priorities and enforcing field office adherence to those priorities;

- establish and sustain independent career tracks within the FBI that recognize and provide incentives for demonstrated skills and performance of counterterrorism agents and analysts;

- significantly improve strategic analytical capabilities by assuring the qualification, training, and independence of analysts, coupled with sufficient access to necessary information and resources;

- establish a strong reports officer cadre at FBI Headquarters and field offices to facilitate timely dissemination of intelligence from agents to analysts within the FBI and other agencies within the Intelligence Community;

- implement training for agents in the effective use of analysts and analysis in their work;

- expand and sustain the recruitment of agents and analysts with the linguistic skills needed in counterterrorism efforts;

- increase substantially efforts to penetrate terrorist organizations operating in the United States through all available means of collection;

- improve the national security law training of FBI personnel;

- implement mechanisms to maximize the exchange of counter-terrorism- related information between the FBI and other federal, state and local agencies; and

- finally solve the FBI's persistent and incapacitating information technology problems.

---

7. Congress and the Administration should carefully consider how best to structure and manage U.S. domestic intelligence responsibilities. Congress should review the scope of domestic intelligence authorities to determine their adequacy in pursuing counterterrorism at home and ensuring the protection of privacy and other rights guaranteed under the Constitution. This review should include, for example, such questions as whether the range of persons subject to searches and surveillances authorized under the Foreign Intelligence Surveillance Act (FISA) should be expanded.

Based on their oversight responsibilities, the Intelligence and Judiciary Committees of the Congress, as appropriate, should consider promptly, in consultation with the Administration, whether the FBI should continue to perform the domestic intelligence functions of the United States Government or whether legislation is necessary to remedy this problem, including the possibility of creating a new agency to perform those functions.

Congress should require that the new Director of National Intelligence, the Attorney General, and the Secretary of the Department of Homeland Security report to the President and the Congress on a certain date concerning:

- the FBI's progress since September 11, 2001 in implementing the reforms required to conduct an effective domestic intelligence program, including the measures recommended above;

- the experience of other democratic nations in organizing the conduct of domestic intelligence;

- the specific manner in which a new domestic intelligence service could be established in the United States, recognizing the need to enhance national security while fully protecting civil liberties; and

- their recommendations on how to best fulfill the nation's need for an effective domestic intelligence capability, including necessary legislation.

---

8. The Attorney General and the Director of the FBI should take action necessary to ensure that:

- the Office of Intelligence Policy and Review and other Department of Justice components provide in-depth training to the FBI and other members of the Intelligence Community regarding the use of the Foreign Intelligence Surveillance Act (FISA) to address terrorist threats to the United States;

- the FBI disseminates results of searches and surveillances authorized under FISA to appropriate personnel within the FBI and the Intelligence Community on a timely basis so they may be used for analysis and operations that address terrorist threats to the United States; and

- the FBI develops and implements a plan to use authorities provided by FISA to assess the threat of international terrorist groups within the United States fully, including the extent to which such groups are funded or otherwise supported by foreign governments.

---

9. The House and Senate Intelligence and Judiciary Committees should continue to examine the Foreign Intelligence Surveillance Act and its implementation thoroughly, particularly with respect to changes made as a result of the USA PATRIOT Act and the subsequent decision of the United States Foreign Intelligence Court of Review, to determine whether its provisions adequately address present and emerging terrorist threats to the United States. Legislation should be proposed by those Committees to remedy any deficiencies identified as a result of that review.

---

10. The Director of the National Security Agency should present to the Director of National Intelligence and the Secretary of Defense by June 30, 2003, and report to the House and Senate Intelligence Committees, a detailed plan that:

- describes solutions for the technological challenges for signals intelligence;

- requires a review, on a quarterly basis, of the goals, products to be delivered, funding levels and schedules for every technology development program;

- ensures strict accounting for program expenditures;

- within their jurisdiction as established by current law, makes NSA a full collaborating partner with the Central Intelligence

Agency and the Federal Bureau of Investigation in the war on terrorism, including fully integrating the collection and analytic capabilities of NSA, CIA, and the FBI; and

- makes recommendations for legislation needed to facilitate these goals.

In evaluating the plan, the Committees should also consider issues pertaining to whether civilians should be appointed to the position of Director of the National Security Agency and whether the term of service for the position should be longer than it has been in the recent past.

---

11. Recognizing that the Intelligence Community's employees remain its greatest resource, the Director of National Intelligence should require that measures be implemented to greatly enhance the recruitment and development of a workforce with the intelligence skills and expertise needed for success in counterterrorist efforts, including:

- the agencies of the Intelligence Community should act promptly to expand and improve counterterrorism training programs within the Community, insuring coverage of such critical areas as information sharing among law enforcement and intelligence personnel; language capabilities; the use of the Foreign Intelligence Surveillance Act; and watchlisting;

- the Intelligence Community should build on the provisions of the Intelligence Authorization Act for Fiscal Year 2003 regarding the development of language capabilities, including the Act's requirement for a report on the feasibility of establishing a Civilian Linguist Reserve Corps, and implement expeditiously measures to identify and recruit linguists outside the Community whose abilities are relevant to the needs of counterterrorism;

- the existing Intelligence Community Reserve Corps should be expanded to ensure the use of relevant personnel and expertise from outside the Community as special needs arise;

- Congress should consider enacting legislation, modeled on the Goldwater-Nichols Act of 1986, to instill the concept of "jointness" throughout the Intelligence Community. By emphasizing such things as joint education, a joint career specialty, increased authority for regional commanders, and joint exercises, that Act greatly enhanced the joint warfighting capabilities of the individual military services. Legislation to instill similar concepts throughout the Intelligence Community could help improve management of Community resources and priorities and insure a far more effective "team" effort by all the intelligence agencies. The Director of National Intelligence should require more extensive use of "joint tours" for intelligence and appropriate law enforcement personnel to broaden their experience and help bridge existing organizational and cultural divides through service in other agencies. These joint tours should include not only service at Intelligence Community agencies, but also service in those agencies that are users or consumers of intelligence products. Serious incentives for joint service should be established throughout the Intelligence Community and personnel should be rewarded for joint service with career advancement credit at individual agencies. The Director of National Intelligence should also require Intelligence Community agencies to participate in joint exercises;

- Congress should expand and improve existing educational grant programs focused on intelligence-related fields, similar to military scholarship programs and others that provide financial assistance in return for a commitment to serve in the Intelligence Community; and

- the Intelligence Community should enhance recruitment of a more ethnically and culturally diverse workforce and devise a strategy to capitalize upon the unique cultural and linguistic capabilities of first-generation Americans, a strategy designed to utilize their skills to the greatest practical effect while recognizing the potential counterintelligence challenges such hiring decisions might pose.

---

12. Steps should be taken to increase and ensure the greatest return on this nation's substantial investment in intelligence, including:

- the President should submit budget recommendations, and Congress should enact budget authority, for sustained, long-term investment in counterterrorism capabilities that avoid dependence on repeated stop-gap supplemental appropriations;

- in making such budget recommendations, the President should provide for the consideration of a separate classified Intelligence Community budget;

- long-term counterterrorism investment should be accompanied by sufficient flexibility, subject to congressional oversight, to enable the Intelligence Community to rapidly respond to altered or unanticipated needs;

- the Director of National Intelligence should insure that Intelligence Community budgeting practices and procedures are revised to better identify the levels and nature of counterterrorism funding within the Community;

- counterterrorism funding should be allocated in accordance with the program requirements of the national counterterrorism strategy; and

- due consideration should be given to directing an outside agency or entity to conduct a thorough and rigorous cost-benefit analysis of the resources spent on intelligence.

———

13. The State Department, in consultation with the Department of Justice, should review and report to the President and the Congress by June 30, 2003 on the extent to which revisions in bilateral and multilateral agreements, including extradition and mutual assistance treaties, would strengthen U.S. counterterrorism efforts. The review should address the degree to which current categories of extraditable offenses should be expanded to cover offenses, such as visa and immigration fraud, which may be particularly useful against terrorists and those who support them.

———

14. Recognizing the importance of intelligence in this nation's struggle against terrorism, Congress should maintain vigorous, informed, and constructive oversight of the Intelligence Community. To best achieve that goal, the National Commission on Terrorist Attacks Upon the United States should study and make recommendations concerning how Congress may improve its oversight of the Intelligence Community, including consideration of such areas as:

- changes in the budgetary process;

- changes in the rules regarding membership on the oversight committees;

- whether oversight responsibility should be vested in a joint House-Senate Committee or, as currently exists, in separate Committees in each house;

- the extent to which classification decisions impair congressional oversight; and

- how Congressional oversight can best contribute to the continuing need of the Intelligence Community to evolve and

adapt to changes in the subject matter of intellige
needs of policymakers.

––––––––

15. The President should review and consider amendments to the Executive Orders, policies and procedures that govern the national security classification of intelligence information, in an effort to expand access to relevant information for federal agencies outside the Intelligence Community, for state and local authorities, which are critical to the fight against terrorism, and for the American public. In addition, the President and the heads of federal agencies should ensure that the policies and procedures to protect against the unauthorized disclosure of classified intelligence information are well understood, fully implemented and vigorously enforced.

Congress should also review the statutes, policies and procedures that govern the national security classification of intelligence information and its protection from unauthorized disclosure. Among other matters, Congress should consider the degree to which excessive classification has been used in the past and the extent to which the emerging threat environment has greatly increased the need for real time sharing of sensitive information. The Director of National Intelligence, in consultation with the Secretary of Defense, the Secretary of State, the Secretary of Homeland Security, and the Attorney General, should review and report to the House and Senate Intelligence Committees on proposals for a new and more realistic approach to the processes and structures that have governed the designation of sensitive and classified information. The report should include proposals to protect against the use of the classification process as a shield to protect agency self-interest.

––––––––

16. Assured standards of accountability are critical to developing the personal responsibility, urgency, and diligence which our

counterterrorism responsibility requires. Given the absence of any substantial efforts within the Intelligence Community to impose accountability in relation to the events of September 11, 2001, the Director of Central Intelligence and the heads of Intelligence Community agencies should require that measures designed to ensure accountability are implemented throughout the Community. To underscore the need for accountability:

- The Director of Central Intelligence should report to the House and Senate Intelligence Committees no later than June 30, 2003 as to the steps taken to implement a system of accountability throughout the Intelligence Community, to include processes for identifying poor performance and affixing responsibility for it, and for recognizing and rewarding excellence in performance;

- as part of the confirmation process for Intelligence Community officials, Congress should require from those officials an affirmative commitment to the implementation and use of strong accountability mechanisms throughout the Intelligence Community; and

- the Inspectors General at the Central Intelligence Agency, the Department of Defense, the Department of Justice, and the Department of State should review the factual findings and the record of this Inquiry and conduct investigations and reviews as necessary to determine whether and to what extent personnel at all levels should be held accountable for any omission, commission, or failure to meet professional standards in regard to the identification, prevention, or disruption of terrorist attacks, including the events of September 11, 2001. These reviews should also address those individuals who performed in a stellar or exceptional manner, and the degree to which the quality of their performance was rewarded or otherwise impacted their careers. Based on those investigations and reviews, agency heads should take appropriate disciplinary and other action and the President and the House and Senate Intelligence Committees should be advised of such action.

17. The Administration should review and report to the House and Senate Intelligence Committees by June 30, 2003 regarding what progress has been made in reducing the inappropriate and obsolete barriers among intelligence and law enforcement agencies engaged in counterterrorism, what remains to be done to reduce those barriers, and what legislative actions may be advisable in that regard. In particular, this report should address what steps are being taken to insure that perceptions within the Intelligence Community about the scope and limits of current law and policy with respect to restrictions on collection and information sharing are, in fact, accurate and well-founded.

18. Congress and the Administration should ensure the full development of a national watchlist center that will be responsible for coordinating and integrating all terrorist-related watchlist systems; promoting awareness and use of the center by all relevant government agencies and elements of the private sector; and ensuring a consistent and comprehensive flow of terrorist names into the center from all relevant points of collection.

19. The Intelligence Community, and particularly the FBI and the CIA, should aggressively address the possibility that foreign governments are providing support to or are involved in terrorist activity targeting the United States and U.S. interests. State-sponsored terrorism substantially increases the likelihood of successful and more lethal attacks within the United States. This issue must be addressed from a national standpoint and should not be limited in focus by the geographical and factual boundaries of individual cases. The FBI and CIA should aggressively and thoroughly pursue related matters developed through this Joint Inquiry that have been referred to them for further investigation by these Committees.

The Intelligence Community should fully inform the House and Senate Intelligence Committees of significant developments in these efforts, through regular reports and additional communications as necessary, and the Committees should, in turn, exercise vigorous and continuing oversight of the Community's work in this critically important area.

Appendixes

Appendix A

Glossary

KEY NAMES

ALI ABDUL AZIZ ALI: Wired money to the 9/11 hijackers from the United Arab Emirates

MOHAMED YOUSEF MOHAMED ALQUSAIDI: Wired money to the 9/11 hijackers from the United Arab Emirates; believed to be the brother of hijacker pilot Marwan al Shehhi

MUHAMMAD ATIF: Osama bin Laden's top military commander, reportedly killed by U.S. forces in Afghanistan

MOHAMMED ATTA: Hijacker pilot and ringleader educated in Germany, taught to fly in Florida

KHALLAD BIN ATTASH: Al Qaeda trainer and attack planner; linked to the U.S.S. *Cole* bombing and 9/11 hijackers

OMAR AL BAYOUMI: Saudi U.S. resident who helped two hijackers settle in San Diego

RAMZI BINALSHIBH: Friend of the hijackers based in Germany; tried but failed on several occasions to obtain a U.S. visa; arrested in Pakistan and now in U.S. custody

HANI HANJOUR: Hijacker pilot who spent most of a decade living and training in the United States; taught to fly in Arizona

NAWAF AL HAZMI: Hijacker under CIA surveillance in Malaysia before traveling to the United States

SALEM AL HAZMI: Hijacker, brother of Nawaf

ZIAD JARRAH: Hijacker pilot educated in Germany, taught to fly in Florida

OSAMA BIN LADEN: Al Qaeda leader; first declared war against the United States in 1996

AHMED SHAH MASSOUD: Northern Alliance leader and bin Laden foe in Afghanistan; assassinated two days before 9/11

KHALID AL MIHDHAR: Hijacker who was under CIA surveillance in Malaysia before traveling to the United States

KHALID SHEIKH MOHAMMED: Bin Laden lieutenant (AKA Mukhtar, or "the Brain") believed to be the mastermind of the 9/11 attacks; arrested in Pakistan and now in U.S. custody

MUNIR EL MOTASSADEQ: Convicted and imprisoned in a 2003 German trial for aiding the 9/11 hijackers, but subsequently released pending a new trial

ZACARIAS MOUSSAOUI: French citizen arrested at a Minnesota flight school in August 2001 and charged as a conspirator in the 9/11 attacks

ABDUL HAKIM MURAD: Arrested in the Philippines, convicted of complicity in the "Bojinka" plot to blow up U.S. airliners over the Pacific

AL QAEDA: "The Base," Osama bin Laden's terrorist organization

SHEIKH OMAR ABD AL RAHMAN: The "Blind Sheikh" convicted as an organizer of the aborted 1993 attacks on New York bridges, tunnels and landmarks

AHMED RESSAM: Terrorist arrested at the U.S./Canada border with bomb-making materials; confessed to a plan to bomb the Los Angeles airport

MARWAN AL SHEHHI: Hijacker pilot educated in Germany, taught to fly in Florida

YAZID SUFAAT: Hosted the al Qaeda terrorists meeting in Malaysia; later arrested for procuring bomb materials for a terrorist cell in Indonesia

RAMZI YOUSEF: Alias of Abdul Basit Mahmoud Abdul Karim; mastermind of the 1993 World Trade Center bombing and the 1995 "Bojinka" plot to blow up U.S. airliners over the Pacific; now incarcerated in Colorado's Supermax prison

MUHAMMAD HEYDAR ZAMMAR: Acquaintance of the hijackers in Germany; helped recruit them into al Qaeda and send them for training in Afghanistan; arrested by Morocco in October 2001

ABU ZUBAYDAH: Al Qaeda recruiter and strategist; encouraged the plot to attack the Los Angeles airport, according to the Presidential Daily Brief of August 6, 2001

TERMS

U.S. Government Organizations and Officials

CENTCOM: Central Command, U.S. Armed Forces; its area of responsibility stretches from the Horn of Africa to Central Asia, including Afghanistan

CIA: Central Intelligence Agency; coordinates several executive-branch intelligence agencies; collects, produces and disseminates foreign intelligence and counterintelligence; responsible for counterintelligence activities abroad; conducts special activities approved by the president

CSG: Counterterrorism Security Group, NSC, White House; coordinates governmental responses to terror threats; manages terror crises

CTC: Counterterrorist Center, CIA; charged with pre-empting, disrupting and defeating foreign terrorists; coordinates intelligence response to terrorism

DCI: Director of Central Intelligence; heads the CIA; advises the president on foreign intelligence; leads the federation of other executive-branch intelligence organizations

Deputies Committee: Sub-Cabinet-level advisory group of the NSC charged with implementing, monitoring and reviewing national-security policy

DIA: Defense Intelligence Agency, Pentagon; combat support organization that provides foreign military intelligence

DOD: Department of Defense

FAA: Federal Aviation Administration; regulates the civil aviation industry

FBI: Federal Bureau of Investigation, Department of Justice; principal law enforcement investigative arm of the U.S. government and the lead agency responsible for counterterrorism in the United States

GAO: General Accounting Office, Congress; nonpartisan watchdog organization that studies the federal government's spending and programs

INR: Bureau of Intelligence and Research, State Department; harnesses all-source intelligence in the service of U.S. diplomacy

INS: Immigration and Naturalization Service; reorganized after 9/11; immigration enforcement absorbed by the Directorate of Border and Transportation Security; immigration services absorbed by U.S. Citizenship and Immigration Services

IOS: Intelligence Operations Specialist, FBI; examines and interprets national-security or criminal intelligence, assisting agents in their cases

JCS: Joint Chiefs of Staff, Pentagon; top officers of the armed services—Army, Navy, Marines and Air Force; the chairman is the president's top military adviser

JSOC: Joint Special Operations Command; develops special-operations tactics for military units, conducts exercises and training

JTTF: Joint Terrorism Task Force; composed of FBI agents and local police

NSA: National Security Agency, Pentagon; coordinates, directs, and performs all cryptologic functions for the U.S. government; collects, processes and disseminates signals intelligence; serves as the national executive agent for classified communications and computer security

NSC: National Security Council, White House; chaired by the president; includes the vice-president, secretary of state, secretary of the treasury, secretary of defense, chairman of the joint chiefs of staff and others; serves as the president's principal forum for considering national-security and foreign-policy issues

NSLU: National Security Law Unit, FBI; charged with keeping agents compliant with the Foreign Intelligence Surveillance Act and other laws

OIPR: Office of Intelligence Policy and Review, Justice Department; files applications for electronic surveillance and physical searches under the Foreign Intelligence Surveillance Act; advises the attorney general and government agencies—including the FBI and CIA—on national-security law and policy

OMB: Office of Management and Budget, White House; helps the president prepare the federal budget and supervise its administration

Principals Committee: Cabinet-level NSC advisory group; functions as the senior interagency forum for considering national-security policy issues

RFU: Radical Fundamentalist Unit, FBI; clearinghouse for information on terrorists

SOLIC: Special Operations and Low Intensity Conflict office, Pentagon; responsible for counterterrorism policymaking in the Defense Department

TTIC: Terrorist Threat Integration Center, Homeland Security Department; collects, assesses and disseminates intelligence from an all-source database

U.S. Laws and Other Anti-Terror Tools

ACS: Automated Case System, FBI; record system now considered outmoded; new system is intended to be less mistake-prone, more user-friendly

FISA: Foreign Intelligence Surveillance Act; establishes a legal regime for collecting foreign intelligence through surveillance in the United States

NIE: National Intelligence Estimate, produced by the DCI; (1) an assessment of a foreign issue that affects U.S. national security;

(2) a strategic estimate of national capabilities and vulnerabilities

NSPD: National Security Presidential Directive; Bush administration instrument for communicating presidential decisions about the national-security policies of the United States

PDB: Presidential Daily Brief, produced by the DCI; digest of intelligence highlights often delivered to the president and a small group of senior leaders by the DCI personally

PDD: Presidential Decision Directive; Clinton administration document for promulgating presidential decisions on national security

SEIB: Senior Executive Intelligence Brief, produced by the DCI; a version of the PDB delivered to a wider circle of top officials

Other Terms

ISID: Interservices Intelligence Directorate, Pakistan; the country's primary intelligence organization

MI–5: Britain's internal security service

OBL: Osama bin Laden

UAE: United Arab Emirates

UAV: Unmanned Aerial Vehicle

WMD: Weapons of Mass Destruction, including nuclear, biological and chemical

Appendix B

The 9/11 Hijackers

American Airlines Flight 11 departed Boston for Los Angeles at 7:59 A.M. and crashed into the north tower of the World Trade Center at 8:45 A.M.

Mohammed Atta (Pilot)
Abdul Aziz al Omari
Wail al Shehri
Walid al Shehri
Satam al Suqami

United Airlines Flight 175 departed Boston for Los Angeles at 7:58 A.M. and crashed into the south tower of the World Trade Center at 9:05 A.M.

Marwan al Shehhi (Pilot)
Ahmed al Ghamdi
Hamza al Ghamdi
Fayez Ahmed
Mohand al Shehri

American Airlines Flight 77 departed Washington for Los Angeles at 8:20 A.M. and crashed into the Pentagon at 9:39 A.M.

Hani Hanjour (Pilot)
Khalid al Mihdhar
Majed Moqed
Nawaf al Hazmi
Salem al Hazmi

———

United Airlines Flight 93 departed Newark for San Francisco at 8:42 A.M. and crashed in a field in Pennsylvania at 10:03 A.M.

Ziad Jarrah (Pilot)
Ahmad al Nami
Ahmad al Haznawi
Saeed al Ghamdi

Appendix C

Selected Events in the Chronology of Terrorism, 1983–2004

April 18, 1983

Bombing of U.S. Embassy, Beirut. 63 people were killed and 120 were injured by a 400-pound suicide truck-bomb attack. The Islamic Jihad claimed responsibility.

October 23, 1983

Bombing of U.S. Marine barracks and French Embassy, Beirut. Simultaneous suicide truck-bomb attacks were made on American and French compounds. A 12,000-pound bomb destroyed the U.S. compound, killing 242 Americans, while 58 French troops were killed at the French base. Islamic Jihad claimed responsibility.

March 16, 1984

Kidnapping of U.S. Embassy official William Buckley by the Islamic Jihad, Beirut. Buckley was later murdered.

April 12, 1984

Restaurant bombing near Torrejon Airbase, Spain. 18 U.S. servicemen were killed and 83 people were injured. The Iranian-backed terrorist group Hezbollah claimed responsibility.

September 20, 1984

Bombing of U.S. Embassy annex, Beirut. Islamic Jihad claimed responsibility for a truck bomb that killed more than 20 people, two of whom were U.S. military personnel.

June 14, 1985

Hijacking of TWA 847. The Trans-World Airlines flight was hijacked en route to Rome from Athens by two Lebanese Hezbollah terrorists and forced to fly to Beirut. The eight crew members and 145 passengers were held for 17 days, during which one American hostage, a U.S. Navy sailor, was murdered.

October 7, 1985

Hijacking of *Achille Lauro*. Four Palestinian Liberation Front terrorists seized the Italian cruise liner in the eastern Mediterranean Sea, taking more than 700 hostages. One U.S. passenger was murdered before the Egyptian government offered the terrorists safe haven in return for the hostages' freedom.

November 23, 1985

Hijacking of EgyptAir 648. The airplane bound from Athens was taken over by the Abu Nidal group and forced to land in Malta. Egyptian commandos stormed the plane, leaving 60 dead.

December 27, 1985

Attack on Rome/Vienna airports by the Abu Nidal organization. In Rome 13 people were killed and 75 were wounded. In Vienna gunmen killed three people and wounded 30.

March 30, 1986

Aircraft bombing in Greece. A Palestinian splinter group detonated a bomb as TWA Flight 840 approached Athens airport, killing four U.S. citizens.

April 5, 1986

LaBelle Disco bombing, Germany. Two U.S. soldiers were killed and 79 American servicemen were injured in a Libyan bomb attack on a nightclub in West Berlin.

December 21, 1988

Aircraft bombing, Lockerbie, Scotland. Pan American Airlines Flight 103 was blown up by a bomb placed on the aircraft by Libyan terrorists in Frankfurt. All 259 people on board were killed.

February 26, 1993

Bombing of World Trade Center, New York City. A bomb hidden in a van planted by Islamic terrorists exploded in an underground garage, leaving six people dead and 1,000 injured. The men carrying out the attack were followers of Omar Abd al Rahman, an Egyptian cleric.

April 14, 1993

Attempted assassination of President Bush by Iraqi agents. The Iraqi intelligence service attempted to assassinate former U.S. President George Bush during a visit to Kuwait.

December 24, 1994

Hijacking of Air France flight by members of the Armed Islamic Group. Four terrorists threatened to crash the plane into the Eiffel Tower. They were killed during a rescue effort.

November 13, 1995

Five Americans killed in bombing of Saudi Arabia National Guard facility, Riyadh, Saudi Arabia. The Islamic Movement of Change planted a bomb in the military compound, killing one U.S. citizen, several foreign national employees of the U.S. government and more than 40 others.

June 25, 1996

Bombing of Khobar Towers, Saudi Arabia. A fuel truck carrying a bomb exploded outside the U.S. military's housing facility in Dhahran, killing 19 U.S. military personnel and wounding 515 people, including 240 U.S. personnel. Several groups claimed responsibility for the attack.

August 23, 1996

Bin Laden issued a *fatwa* authorizing attacks on Western military targets in the Arabian Peninsula.

February 23, 1998

Bin Laden publicly called for jihad against U.S. civilians and military personnel anywhere in the world.

August 7, 1998

Bombing of U.S. embassies in East Africa. A bomb exploded at the U.S. Embassy in Nairobi, Kenya, killing 12 U.S. citizens, 32 Foreign Service Nationals (FSNs), and 247 Kenyan citizens. Approximately 5,000 Kenyans, 6 U.S. citizens, and 13 FSNs were injured. Almost simultaneously, a bomb detonated outside the U.S. Embassy in Dar es Salaam, Tanzania, killing 7 FSNs and 3 Tanzanian citizens, and injuring 1 U.S. citizen and 76 Tanzanians. The U.S. Government held Osama bin Laden responsible.

October 12, 2000

Bombing of U.S.S. *Cole*, Aden, Yemen. A small dingy carrying explosives rammed the destroyer, killing 17 sailors and injuring 39 others. Supporters of Osama bin Laden were accused.

September 11, 2001

Terrorist attacks on U.S. homeland. Two hijacked airliners crashed into the twin towers of the World Trade Center. Soon thereafter, the Pentagon was struck by a third hijacked plane. A fourth hijacked plane, suspected to be bound for a high-profile target in Washington, crashed into a field in southern Pennsylvania. The attacks killed nearly 3,000 U.S. citizens and other nationals. Osama bin Laden was the prime suspect.

October 12, 2002

Car bomb explosion in Bali. A car bomb exploded outside the Sari Club Discotheque in Denpasar, Bali, Indonesia, killing 202 people and wounding 300 more. Most of the casualties, including 88 of the dead, were Australian tourists. Seven Americans were among the dead. Al Qaeda claimed responsibility.

May 12, 2003

Truck bomb attacks in Saudi Arabia. Suicide bombers attacked three residential compounds for foreign workers in Riyadh. The 34 dead included 9 attackers, 7 other Saudis, 9 U.S. citizens, and one citizen each from the United Kingdom, Ireland, and the Philippines. Another American died on June 1.

May 16, 2003

Suicide bomb Attacks in Morocco. A team of 12 suicide bombers attacked five targets in Casablanca, killing 43 people and wounding 100. The targets were a Spanish restaurant, a Jewish community center, a Jewish cemetery, a hotel, and the Belgian Consulate. The Moroccan government blamed the Islamist al-Assirat al-Moustaquim (The Righteous Path), but foreign commentators suspected an al Qaeda connection.

August 5, 2003

Hotel bombing in Indonesia. A car bomb exploded outside the Marriott Hotel in Jakarta, killing 10 people and wounding 150. Indonesian authorities suspected the Jemaah Islamiah.

August 19, 2003

Bombing of the UN Headquarters in Baghdad. A truck exploded outside the United Nations Headquarters in Baghdad's Canal Hotel. The 23 dead included UN Special Representative Sergio Viera de Mello. More than 100 people were wounded. It was not clear whether the bomber was a Baath Party loyalist or a foreign Islamic militant. An al Qaeda branch known as the Brigades of the Martyr Abu Hafz al-Masri later claimed responsibility.

November 15, 2003

Synagogue bombings in Istanbul. Two suicide truck bombs exploded outside the Neve Shalom and Beth Israel synagogues in Istanbul, killing 25 people and wounding at least 300 more. The initial claim of responsibility came from a Turkish militant group, the Great Eastern Islamic Raiders' Front, but the next day, the Brigades of the Martyr Abu Hafz al-Masri claimed responsibility.

November 20, 2003

More suicide truck bombings in Istanbul. Two more suicide truck bombings devastated the British HSBC Bank and the British Consulate General in Istanbul, killing 27 people and wounding at least 450. U.S., British, and Turkish officials suspected al Qaeda.

March 11, 2004

Railway bombings, Madrid. The blasts killed 191 people and wounded more than 1,800. Spanish government officials initially suspected the Basque separatist group ETA, but subsequent investigations focused on the Moroccan Islamic Combatant Group.

Appendix D

The Presidential Daily Brief,
August 6, 2001

Bin Ladin Determined To Strike in US

Clandestine, foreign government, and media reports indicate Bin Ladin since 1997 has wanted to conduct terrorist attacks in the US. Bin Ladin implied in US television interviews in 1997 and 1998 that his followers would follow the example of World Trade Center bomber Ramzi Yousef and "bring the fighting to America."

>After US missile strikes on his base in Afghanistan in 1998, Bin Ladin told followers he wanted to retaliate in Washington, according to a ▆▆▆▆▆▆▆▆ service.

>An Egyptian Islamic Jihad (EIJ) operative told an ▆▆▆▆ service at the same time that Bin Ladin was planning to exploit the operative's access to the US to mount a terrorist strike.

The millennium plotting in Canada in 1999 may have been part of Bin Ladin's first serious attempt to implement a terrorist strike in the US. Convicted plotter Ahmed Ressam has told the FBI that he conceived the idea to attack Los Angeles International Airport himself, but that Bin Ladin lieutenant Abu Zubaydah encouraged him and helped facilitate the operation. Ressam also said that in 1998 Abu Zubaydah was planning his own US attack.

>Ressam says Bin Ladin was aware of the Los Angeles operation.

Although Bin Ladin has not succeeded, his attacks against the US Embassies in Kenya and Tanzania in 1998 demonstrate that he prepares operations years in advance and is not deterred by setbacks. Bin Ladin associates surveilled our Embassies in Nairobi and Dar es Salaam as early as 1993, and some members of the Nairobi cell planning the bombings were arrested and deported in 1997.

Al-Qa'ida members—including some who are US citizens—have resided in or traveled to the US for years, and the group apparently maintains a support structure that could aid attacks. Two al-Qa'ida members found guilty in the conspiracy to bomb our Embassies in East Africa were US citizens, and a senior EIJ member lived in California in the mid-1990s.

>A clandestine source said in 1998 that a Bin Ladin cell in New York was recruiting Muslim-American youth for attacks.

We have not been able to corroborate some of the more sensational threat reporting, such as that from a ▆▆▆▆▆▆▆▆▆ service in 1998 saying that Bin Ladin wanted to hijack a US aircraft to gain the release of "Blind Shaykh" 'Umar 'Abd al-Rahman and other US-held extremists.

continued

Declassified and Approved
for Release, 10 April 2004

— Nevertheless, FBI information since that time indicates patterns of
suspicious activity in this country consistent with preparations for
hijackings or other types of attacks, including recent surveillance of
federal buildings in New York.

The FBI is conducting approximately 70 full field investigations
throughout the US that it considers Bin Ladin–related. CIA and the
FBI are investigating a call to our Embassy in the UAE in May saying
that a group of Bin Ladin supporters was in the US planning attacks
with explosives.

Declassified and Approved
for Release, 10 April 2004

Appendix E
The "Phoenix Memo"

SECRET

FEDERAL BUREAU OF INVESTIGATION

Precedence: ROUTINE   Date: 07/10/2001

To: Counterterrorism   Attn: RFU
                                       SSA
                                       IRS

    New York

From: Phoenix
        Contact: SA

Approved By:

Drafted By:

Case ID #: (S)   (Pending)

Title: (S)   ZAKARIA MUSTAPHA SOUBRA;
              IT-OTHER

Synopsis: (S) UBL   supporters attending civil
aviation universities/colleges in the State of Arizona.

              (S)   Derived From   G-3
                     Declassify On: X1

(S) Full Field Investigation Instituted: 04/17/2000 (NONUSPER)

Details: (S) [The purpose of this communication is to advise the
Bureau and New York of the possibility of a coordinated effort by
USAMA BIN LADEN (UBL) to send students to the United States to
attend civil aviation universities and colleges. Phoenix has
observed an inordinate number of individuals of investigative
interest who are attending or who have attended civil aviation
universities and colleges in the State of Arizona. The inordinate
number of these individuals attending these type of schools and
fatwas

SECRET

SE⊗RET

To: Counterterrorism   From: Phoenix
Re: ████████████████   07/10/2001

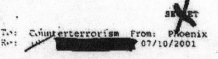

(s) ██ gives reason to
believe that a coordinated effort is underway to establish a
cadre of individuals who will one day be working in the civil
aviation community around the world. These individuals will be in
a position in the future to conduct terror activity against civil
aviation targets.

(S) Phoenix believes that the FBI should accumulate a
listing of civil aviation universities/colleges around the
country. FBI field offices with these types of schools in their
area should establish appropriate liaison: FBIHQ should discuss
this matter with other elements of the U.S. intelligence
community and task the community for any information that
supports Phoenix's suspicions. FBIHQ should consider seeking the
necessary authority to obtain visa information from the USDOS on
individuals obtaining visas to attend these types of schools and
notify the appropriate FBI field office when these individuals
are scheduled to arrive in their area of responsibility.

(S) Phoenix has drawn the above conclusion from
several Phoenix investigations to include captioned investigation
and the following investigations: ████████████████████████████
████████, a Saudi Arabian national and two Algerian Islamic
extremists ██
██████████

(S) Investigation of ZAKARIA MUSTAPHA SOUBRA was
initiated as the result of information provided by ████████████ a
source who has provided reliable information in the past. The
source reported during April 2000 that SOUBRA was a supporter of
UBL and ████████████████████████. SOUBRA arrived in
Arizona from London, England on 08/27/1999 on an F-1 student visa
to attend EMBRY RIDDLE UNIVERSITY (ERU), Prescott, Arizona. ERU
only teaches courses related to the field of aviation. SOUBRA is
an Aeronautical Engineering student at ERU and has been taking
courses in "international security" relating to aviation. SOUBRA,
within weeks of his arrival at Prescott, Arizona, ████████████████
████████████████████████ supporting UBL, at Mosques
located throughout Arizona. SOUBRA has also organized anti United
States and Israeli demonstrations in the area of ARIZONA STATE
UNIVERSITY (ASU), Tempe, Arizona. He has also established and
organized an Islamic student association on the ERU campus
organizing the Muslim student population on the ERU campus.

(S) Phoenix has identified several associates of SOUBRA
at ERU who arrived at the university around the same time that he

SE⊗RET

2

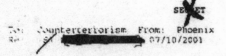

did. These individuals are Sunni Muslims who have the same
radical fundamentalists views as SOUBRA. They come from Kenya,
Pakistan, United Arab Emirates, India, Saudi Arabia and Jordan.
SOUBRA's associates are (S)

(S) The above individuals are involved with SOUBRA and
regularly participate in meetings with him in Prescott, Arizona.

(S) FBIHQ, IRS _____ RFU, wrote an
analytical paper on the _____ dated 11/09/1999, in
support of FBINY investigation captioned: _____

_____ research paper can be found in _____
The following information was gleaned from IRS
research paper.

SECRET

3

(S) " The Fatwa is jihad against the U.S. and British
government, armies, interests, airports (emphasis added by FBI
Phoenix), and instructions and it has been given because of the
U.S. and British aggression against Muslims and the Muslim land
of Iraq...we...confirm that the only Islamic Fatwa against this
explicit aggression is Jihad. Therefore the message for the
British governments or any other government of non-Muslim
countries is to stay away from Iraq, Palestine, Pakistan, Arabia,
etc...or face full scale war of Jihad which it is the
responsibility and the duty of every Muslim around the world to
participate in...We...call upon...Muslims around the world
including Muslims in the USA and in Britian to confront by all
means whether verbally, financially, politically or militarily
the U.S. and British aggression and do their Islamic duty in
relieving the Iraqi people from the unjust sanctions."

(S)   SOUBRA was interviewed by FBI Phoenix on
04/07/2000 and 05/11/2000 at his residence. On 04/07/2000,
interviewing Agents observed photocopied photographs of UBL, IBN
KHATTAB and wounded Chechnyan Mujahadin tacked to his livingroom
wall. SOUBRA admitted to ███████████████████
in the State of Arizona. SOUBRA stated that he considers the
United States Government and U.S. Military forces in the Gulf as
"legitimate military targets of Islam." He also stated that the
targeting of the U.S. Embassies in Africa was "legitimate."
SOUBRA denied having received any military training. However,
Phoenix believes that SOUBRA was being less than truthful in this

regard, SOUBRA was defiant towards interviewing Agents and it was
clear that he was not intimidated by the FBI presence. It is
obvious that he is a hardcore Islamic extremist who views the
U.S. as an enemy of Islam. Investigation of SOUBRA is continuing

To: Counterterrorism From: Phoenix
Re: 07/10/2001

(S) Phoenix believes that it is more than a coincidence
that subjects who are supporters of UBL are attending civil
aviation universities/colleges in the State of Arizona. As
receiving offices are aware, Phoenix has had significant UBL
associates/operatives living in the State of Arizona and
conducting activity in support of UBL [WADIH EL-HAGE, a UBL
lieutenant recently convicted for his role in the 1998 bombings
of U.S. Embassies in Africa, lived in Tucson, Arizona for several
years during the 1980s.

SECRET

To: Counterterrorism From: Phoenix
Re: (S)   07/10/2001

(S) This information is being provided to receiving offices for information , analysis and comments.

To: Counterterrorism   From: Phoenix
Re: 07/10/2001

LEAD(s):

Set Lead 1:

COUNTERTERRORISM

AT WASHINGTON, DC

(S) The RFU/UBLU is requested to consider implementing the suggested actions put forth by Phoenix at the beginning of this communication.

Set Lead 2:

NEW YORK

AT NEW YORK, NEW YORK

(S) Read and Clear

♦♦

8

Index

PUBLICAFFAIRS is a publishing house founded in 1997. It is a tribute to the standards, values, and flair of three persons who have served as mentors to countless reporters, writers, editors, and book people of all kinds, including me.

I. F. STONE, proprietor of *I. F. Stone's Weekly,* combined a commitment to the First Amendment with entrepreneurial zeal and reporting skill and became one of the great independent journalists in American history. At the age of eighty, Izzy published *The Trial of Socrates,* which was a national bestseller. He wrote the book after he taught himself ancient Greek.

BENJAMIN C. BRADLEE was for nearly thirty years the charismatic editorial leader of *The Washington Post.* It was Ben who gave the Post the range and courage to pursue such historic issues as Watergate. He supported his reporters with a tenacity that made them fearless, and it is no accident that so many became authors of influential, best-selling books.

ROBERT L. BERNSTEIN, the chief executive of Random House for more than a quarter century, guided one of the nation's premier publishing houses. Bob was personally responsible for many books of political dissent and argument that challenged tyranny around the globe. He is also the founder and was the longtime chair of Human Rights Watch, one of the most respected human rights organizations in the world.

. . .

For fifty years, the banner of Public Affairs Press was carried by its owner Morris B. Schnapper, who published Gandhi, Nasser, Toynbee, Truman, and about 1,500 other authors. In 1983 Schnapper was described by *The Washington Post* as "a redoubtable gadfly." His legacy will endure in the books to come.

Peter Osnos, *Publisher*